S0-DJW-763

Global Issues

99/00

Fifteenth Edition

EDITOR

Robert M. Jackson
California State University, Chico

Robert M. Jackson is a professor of political science and dean of the School of Graduate, International, and Sponsored Programs at California State University, Chico. In addition to teaching, he has published articles on the international political economy, international relations simulations, and political behavior. His special research interest is in the way northern California is becoming increasingly linked to the Pacific Basin. His travels include China, Japan, Hong Kong, Taiwan, Singapore, Malaysia, Portugal, Spain, Morocco, Costa Rica, El Salvador, Honduras, Guatemala, Mexico, Germany, Belgium, the Netherlands, Russia, and Czechoslovakia.

Dushkin/McGraw-Hill
Sluice Dock, Guilford, Connecticut 06437

Visit us on the Internet
http://www.dushkin.com/annualeditions/

World Map

This map has been developed to give you a graphic picture of where the countries of the world are located, the relationship they have with their region and neighbors, and their positions relative to the superpowers and power blocs. We have focused on certain areas to more clearly illustrate these crowded regions.

Scale: 1 to 125,000,000

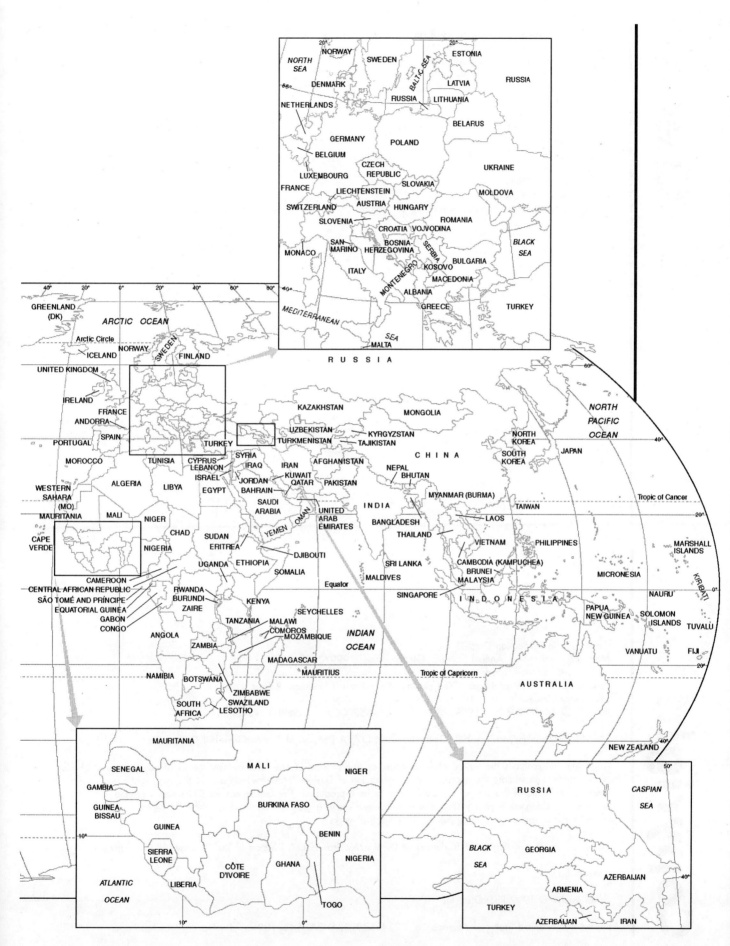

Credits

1. Global Issues in the Twenty-First Century: An Overview
Facing overview—Photo courtesy of NASA.
2. Population and Food Production
Facing overview—United Nations photo by Carolyn Redenius.
3. The Global Environment and Natural Resources Utilization
Facing overview—United Nations photo by Saw Lwin.
4. Political Economy
Facing overview—United Nations photo by M. Grant.
5. Conflict
Facing overview—Photo of B-2 bomber courtesy of Northrop Corporation.
6. Cooperation
Facing overview—United Nations photo.
7. Values and Visions
Facing overview—United Nations photo by Y. Nagata.

Copyright

Cataloging in Publication Data
Main entry under title: Annual Editions: Global issues. 1999/2000.
    1. Civilization, Modern—20th century—Periodicals. 2. Social prediction—
Periodicals. 3. Social problems—20th century—Periodicals. I. Jackson, Robert, *comp.* II.
Title: Global issues.
ISBN 0–07–039797–X   909.82'05   85–658006   ISSN 1093–278X

Fifteenth Edition

Cover image © 1999 PhotoDisc, Inc.

Printed in the United States of America   1234567890BAHBAH5432109   Printed on Recycled Paper

Members of the Advisory Board are instrumental in the final selection of articles for each edition of ANNUAL EDITIONS. Their review of articles for content, level, currentness, and appropriateness provides critical direction to the editor and staff. We think that you will find their careful consideration well reflected in this volume.

EDITOR

Robert M. Jackson
California State University, Chico

ADVISORY BOARD

Peter K. Angstadt
Wesley College

Thomas E. Arcaro
Elon College

Diane N. Barnes
University of Southern Maine

Eric N. Budd
Fitchburg State College

Leonard Cardenas
Southwest Texas State University

H. Thomas Collins
Project LINKS
George Washington University

E. Gene DeFelice
Purdue University
Calumet

Robert L. Delorme
California State University
Long Beach

Dennis R. Gordon
Santa Clara University

James E. Harf
Ohio State University

Hlib S. Hayuk
Towson University

Asad Husain
Northeastern Illinois University

Fayyaz Hussain
Michigan State University

D. Gregory Jeane
Samford University

Karl H. Kahrs
California State University
Fullerton

Sadat Kazi
Vanier College

Sondra King
Northern Illinois University

Steven L. Lamy
University of Southern California

T. David Mason
University of Memphis

Alexander Nadesan
Bemidji State University

Louis L. Ortmayer
Davidson College

Guy Poitras
Trinity University

Helen E. Purkitt
U.S. Naval Academy

Nicholas J. Smith-Sebasto
University of Illinois
Urbana-Champaign

Kenneth P. Thomas
University of Missouri
St. Louis

John H. P. Williams
East Carolina University

Kenneth L. Wise
Creighton University

Rodger Yeager
West Virginia University

EDITORIAL STAFF

Ian A. Nielsen, Publisher
Roberta Monaco, Senior Developmental Editor
Dorothy Fink, Associate Developmental Editor
Addie Raucci, Senior Administrative Editor
Cheryl Greenleaf, Permissions Editor
Joseph Offredi, Permissions/Editorial Assistant
Diane Barker, Proofreader
Lisa Holmes-Doebrick, Program Coordinator

PRODUCTION STAFF

Brenda S. Filley, Production Manager
Charles Vitelli, Designer
Lara M. Johnson, Design/
Advertising Coordinator
Laura Levine, Graphics
Mike Campbell, Graphics
Tom Goddard, Graphics
Juliana Arbo, Typesetting Supervisor
Jane Jaegersen, Typesetter
Marie Lazauskas, Word Processor
Kathleen D'Amico, Word Processor
Larry Killian, Copier Coordinator

In publishing ANNUAL EDITIONS we recognize the enormous role played by the magazines, newspapers, and journals of the public press in providing current, first-rate educational information in a broad spectrum of interest areas. Many of these articles are appropriate for students, researchers, and professionals seeking accurate, current material to help bridge the gap between principles and theories and the real world. These articles, however, become more useful for study when those of lasting value are carefully collected, organized, indexed, and reproduced in a low-cost format, which provides easy and permanent access when the material is needed. That is the role played by ANNUAL EDITIONS.

New to ANNUAL EDITIONS is the inclusion of related World Wide Web sites. These sites have been selected by our editorial staff to represent some of the best resources found on the World Wide Web today. Through our carefully developed topic guide, we have linked these Web resources to the articles covered in this ANNUAL EDITIONS reader. We think that you will find this volume useful, and we hope that you will take a moment to visit us on the Web at *http://www.dushkin.com* to tell us what you think.

As the twenty-first century begins, the issues confronting humanity are increasingly more complex and diverse.

While the mass media may focus on the latest crisis for a few days or weeks, the broad forces that are shaping the world of the twenty-first century are seldom given the in-depth analysis that they warrant. Scholarly research about these historic change factors can be found in a wide variety of publications, but these are not readily accessible. In addition, students just beginning to study global issues can be discouraged by the terminology and abstract concepts that characterize much of the scholarly literature. In selecting and organizing the materials for this book, we have been mindful of the needs of beginning students and have, thus, selected articles that invite the student into the subject matter.

Each unit begins with an introductory article providing a broad overview of the area to be explored. The remaining articles examine in more detail some of the issues presented. The unit then concludes with an article (or two) that not only identifies a problem but suggests positive steps that are being taken to improve the situation. The world faces many serious issues, the magnitude of which would discourage even the most stouthearted individual. Though identifying problems is easier than solving them, it is encouraging to know that many of the issues are being successfully addressed.

Perhaps the most striking feature of the study of contemporary global issues is the absence of any single, widely held theory that explains what is taking place. Therefore, we have made a conscious effort to present a wide variety of ideologies and theories. The most important consideration has been to present global issues from an international perspective, rather than from a purely American or Western point of view. By encompassing materials originally published in many different countries and written by authors of various nationalities, the anthology represents the great diversity of opinions that people hold on important global issues. Two writers examining the same phenomenon may reach very different conclusions. It is not a question of who is right and who is wrong. What is important to understand is that people from different vantage points have differing perceptions of issues.

Another major consideration when organizing these materials was to explore the complex interrelationship of factors that produce social problems such as poverty. Too often, dis-cussions of this problem (and others like it) are reduced to arguments about the fallacies of not following the correct economic policy or not having the correct form of government. As a result, many people overlook the interplay of historic, cultural, environmental, economic, and political factors that form complex webs bringing about many different problems. Every effort has been made to select materials that illustrate this complex interaction of factors, stimulating the beginning student to consider realistic rather than overly simplistic approaches to the pressing problems that threaten the existence of civilization.

Finally, we selected the materials in this book for both their intellectual insights and their readability. Timely and well-written materials should stimulate good classroom lectures and discussions. I hope that students and teachers will enjoy using this book. Readers can have input into the next edition by completing and returning the postage-paid *article rating form* in the back of the book.

Included in this edition of *Annual Editions: Global Issues* are *World Wide Web* sites that can be used to further explore topics addressed in the articles. These sites are cross-referenced in the *topic guide*.

I would like thank Tasha McCombs for her research assistance in selecting articles for this edition. Also, I want to acknowledge the help and support of Ian Nielsen. I am grateful for his encouragement and helpful suggestions in the selection of materials for *Annual Editions: Global Issues 99/00*. It is my continuing goal to encourage the readers of this book to have a greater appreciation of the world in which we live. I hope each of you will be motivated to further explore the complex issues faced by the world as we approach the twenty-first century.

Robert M. Jackson
Editor

Contents

UNIT 1

Global Issues in the Twenty-First Century: An Overview

Four articles in this section present distinct views on the present and future state of life on Earth.

UNIT 2

Population and Food Production

Five selections in this section discuss the contributing factors to the world's population growth and the challenge of providing food for this added strain on the world's capacity.

The concepts in bold italics are developed in the article. For further expansion please refer to the Topic Guide, the Glossary, and the Index.

UNIT 3

The Global Environment and Natural Resources Utilization

Five articles in this section discuss natural resources and their effects on the world's environment.

Overview   62

The concepts in bold italics are developed in the article. For further expansion please refer to the Topic Guide, the Glossary, and the Index.

Overview   **86**

A. *GLOBALIZATION DEBATE*

UNIT 4

Political Economy

Ten articles present various views on economic and social development in the nonindustrial and industrial nations.

The concepts in bold italics are developed in the article. For further expansion please refer to the Topic Guide, the Glossary, and the Index.

UNIT 5

Conflict

Eight articles in this section discuss the basis for world conflict
and the current state of peace
in the international community.

Cooperation

Five selections in this section
examine patterns of international
cooperation and the social structures that support this cooperation.

The concepts in bold italics are developed in the article. For further expansion please refer to the Topic Guide, the Glossary, and the Index.

UNIT 7

Values and Visions

Five articles discuss human rights, ethics, values, and new ideas.

Topic Guide

This topic guide suggests how the selections and World Wide Web sites found in the next section of this book relate to topics of traditional concern to students and professionals involved in the study of global issues. It is useful for locating interrelated articles and Web sites for reading and research. The guide is arranged alphabetically according to topic.

The relevant Web sites, which are numbered and annotated on pages 6 and 7, are easily identified by the Web icon (⊚) under the topic articles. By linking the articles and the Web sites by topic, this ANNUAL EDITIONS reader becomes a powerful learning and research tool.

TOPIC AREA	TREATED IN	TOPIC AREA	TREATED IN
Agriculture, Food, and Hunger	1. Special Moment in History 4. Redefining Security 8. How Much Food Will We Need in the 21st Century? 9. Angling for 'Aquaculture' 14. We *Can* Build a Sustainable Economy ⊚ *2, 7, 8, 9, 10, 19*		15. Complexities and Contradictions of Globalization 16. Prosper or Perish? 18. End of a "Miracle" 19. Fallen Idol 20. America and the Euro Gamble 21. Russia's Summer of Discontent 22. New Tiger 24. Asia's Drug Menace and the Poverty of Diplomacy 37. Child Labour 40. Future of Energy ⊚ *1, 2, 17, 18, 19, 20, 21, 29*
Communications	2. Many Faces of the Future 15. Complexities and Contradictions of Globalization 41. Telecommunications for the 21st Century ⊚ *1, 18, 20, 24, 25*	**Energy: Exploration, Production, Research, and Politics**	13. Rush for Caspian Oil 14. We *Can* Build a Sustainable Economy 40. Future of Energy ⊚ *11, 12, 13, 14, 15, 16, 18, 20*
Cultural Customs and Values	2. Many Faces of the Future 7. Refugees: The Rising Tide 14. We *Can* Build a Sustainable Economy 15. Complexities and Contradictions of Globalization 23. Africa Rising 33. First Fifty Years: The Main Achievements 35. Justice Goes Global 37. Child Labour: Rights, Risks, and Realities 38. Universal Human Values 40. Future of Energy 42. Women in Power ⊚ *1, 8, 12, 15, 20, 31, 32*	**Environment, Ecology, and Conservation**	1. Special Moment In History 6. Worldwide Development or Population Explosion 8. How Much Food Will We Need in the 21st Century? 9. Angling for 'Aquaculture' 10. Global Challenge 12. Stumped by Trees 14. We *Can* Build a Sustainable Economy 40. Future of Energy ⊚ *11, 12, 13, 14, 15, 16*
Development: Economic and Social	3. Life Is Unfair 4. Redefining Security 5. Before the Next Doubling 6. Worldwide Development or Population Explosion 10. Global Challenge 12. Stumped by Trees 14. We *Can* Build a Sustainable Economy 15. Complexities and Contradictions of Globalization 16. Proper or Perish? 17. Illusion for Our Time 22. New Tiger 37. Child Labour 38. Universal Human Values 39. Fourth Way? The Latin American Alternative to Neoliberalism 42. Women in Power ⊚ *2, 5, 6, 17, 18, 19, 20, 21, 29, 32*	**The Future**	1. Special Moment in History 2. Many Faces of the Future 3. Life Is Unfair 4. Redefining Security 5. Before the Next Doubling 6. Worldwide Development or Population Explosion 7. Refugees: The Rising Tide 8. How Much Food Will We Need in the 21st Century? 10. Global Challenge 11. Great Climate Flip-Flop 13. Rush for Caspian Oil 14. We *Can* Build a Sustainable Economy 15. Complexities and the Contradictions of Globalization 16. Prosper or Perish? 22. New Tiger 23. Africa Rising 29. Uncertainty, Insecurity, and China's Military Power 40. Future of Energy 41. Telecommunications for the 21st Century ⊚ *3, 4, 5, 6, 7, 8, 9, 10, 11, 13, 15, 16, 18, 19, 20, 29, 30, 31, 32*
Economics	1. Special Moment in History 3. Life Is Unfair 11. Great Climate Flip-Flop 12. Stumped by Trees 13. Rush for Caspian Oil 14. We *Can* Build a Sustainable Economy		

TOPIC AREA	TREATED IN	TOPIC AREA	TREATED IN
International Economics, Trade, Aid, and Dependencies	3. Life Is Unfair 12. Stumped by Trees 13. Rush for Caspian Oil 15. Complexities and Contradictions of Globalization 16. Prosper or Perish? 17. Illusion for Our Time 18. End of a "Miracle" 19. Fallen Idol 20. America and the Euro Gamble 21. Russia's Summer of Discontent 22. New Tiger 24. Asia's Drug Menace 39. Fourth Way? The Latin American Alternative to Neoliberalism ◎ **1, 2, 5, 6, 17, 18, 19, 20, 21, 29**	**Political and Legal Global Issues**	7. Refugees: The Rising Tide 10. Global Challenge 13. Rush for Caspian Oil 20. America and the Euro Gamble 33. First Fifty Years 34. Watchful Eye: Monitoring the Conventional Arms Trade 35. Justice Goes Global 36. Peace Prize Goes to Land-Mine Opponents 37. Child Labour: Rights, Risks, and Realities ◎ **18, 19, 20**
Military: Warfare and Terrorism	4. Redefining Security: The New Global Schisms 25. Post-Modern State and the World Order 26. New Arms Race 27. Ethnic Conflict 28. Nuclear Brinkmanship in South Asia 29. Uncertainty, Insecurity, and China's Military Power 30. Russian Foreign Policy in the Near Abroad and Beyond 31. Case for Nuclear Deterrence Today 32. Taking Nuclear Weapons Off Hair-Trigger Alert 34. Watchful Eye: Monitoring the Conventional Arms Trade 35. Justice Goes Global 36. Peace Prize Goes to Land-Mine Opponents ◎ **22, 23, 24, 25**	**Populations and Demographics (Quality of Life Indicators)**	1. Special Moment in History 4. Redefining Security 5. Before the Next Doubling 6. Worldwide Development or Population Explosion 7. Refugees: The Rising Tide ◎ **5, 6, 8, 10, 20**
		Science, Technology, and Research and Development	1. Special Moment In History 9. Angling for 'Aquaculture' 14. We *Can* Build a Sustainable Economy 40. Future of Energy 41. Telecommunications for the 21st Century ◎ **1, 2, 9, 11, 12, 13, 14, 17, 18**
Natural Resources	10. Global Challenge 12. Stumped by Trees 13. Rush for Caspian Oil 14. We *Can* Build a Sustainable Economy 40. Future of Energy ◎ **11, 12, 13, 14, 15, 16, 31**	**Undeveloped World**	3. Life Is Unfair 4. Redefining Security 5. Before the Next Doubling 6. Worldwide Development or Population Explosion 16. Prosper or Perish? 22. New Tiger 23. Africa Rising 36. Child Labour 39. Fourth Way? The Latin American Alternative to Neoliberalism ◎ **2, 5, 6, 7, 8, 9, 10, 12, 15, 16, 19, 20, 27, 31, 32**

AE: Global Issues

The following World Wide Web sites have been carefully researched and selected to support the articles found in this reader. If you are interested in learning more about specific topics found in this book, these Web sites are a good place to start. The sites are cross-referenced by number and appear in the topic guide on the previous two pages. Also, you can link to these Web sites through our DUSHKIN ONLINE support site at *http://www.dushkin.com/online/*.

The following sites were available at the time of publication. Visit our Web site—we update DUSHKIN ONLINE regularly to reflect any changes.

General Sources

1. U.S. Information Agency (USIA)
http://www.usia.gov/usis.html
USIA's home page provides definitions, related documentation, and discussions of topics of concern to students of global issues. The site addresses today's Hot Topics as well as ongoing issues that form the foundation of the field.

2. World Wide Web Virtual Library: International Affairs Resources
http://www.etown.edu/home/selchewa/international_studies/firstpag.htm
Surf this site and its extensive links to learn about specific countries and regions, to research various think tanks and international organizations, and to study such vital topics as international law, development, the international economy, human rights, and peacekeeping.

Global Issues in the Twenty-First Century: An Overview

3. The Henry L. Stimson Center
http://www.stimson.org
The Stimson Center, a nonpartisan organization, focuses on issues where policy, technology, and politics intersect. Use this site to find varying assessments of U.S. foreign policy in the post–cold war world and to research many other topics.

4. The Heritage Foundation
http://www.heritage.org
This page offers discussion about and links to many sites having to do with foreign policy and foreign affairs, including news and commentary, policy review, events, and a resource bank.

5. IISDnet
http://iisd1.iisd.ca
The International Institute for Sustainable Development presents information through links to business, sustainable development, and developing ideas. "Linkages" is its multimedia resource for policymakers.

6. The North-South Institute
http://www.nsi-ins.ca/info.html
Searching this site of the North-South Institute, which works to strengthen international development cooperation and enhance gender and social equity, will help you find information and debates on a variety of global issues.

Population and Food Production

7. The Hunger Project
http://www.thp.org
Browse through this nonprofit organization's site, whose goal is the sustainable end to global hunger through leadership at all levels of society. The Hunger Project contends that the persistence of hunger is at the heart of the major security issues threatening our planet.

8. Penn Library: Resources by Subject
http://www.library.upenn.edu/resources/websitest.html
This vast site is rich in links to information about subjects of interest to students of global issues. Its extensive population and demography resources address such concerns as migration, family planning, and health and nutrition in various world regions.

9. World Health Organization
http://www.who.ch/Welcome.html
This home page of the World Health Organization will provide you with links to a wealth of statistical and analytical information about health and the environment in the developing world.

10. WWW Virtual Library: Demography & Population Studies
http://coombs.anu.edu.au/ResFacilities/DemographyPage.html
A definitive guide to demography and population studies can be found at this site. It contains a multitude of important links to information about global poverty and hunger.

The Global Environment and Natural Resources Utilization

11. Friends of the Earth
http://www.foe.co.uk/index.html
This nonprofit organization pursues campaigns to protect Earth and its living creatures. This site has links to many important environmental sites, covering such broad topics as ozone depletion, soil erosion, and biodiversity.

12. National Geographic Society
http://www.nationalgeographic.com
This site provides links to a great deal of material related to the atmosphere, the oceans, and other environmental topics.

13. National Oceanic and Atmospheric Administration (NOAA)
http://www.noaa.gov
Through this home page of NOAA, part of the U.S. Department of Commerce, you can find information about coastal issues, fisheries, climate, and more. The site provides many links to research materials and to other Web resources.

14. Public Utilities Commission of Ohio (PUCO)
http://www.puc.state.oh.us/consumer/gcc/index.html
PUCO's site serves as a clearinghouse of information about global climate change. Its links explain the science and chronology of global climate change.

15. SocioSite: Sociological Subject Areas
http://www.pscw.uva.nl/sociosite/TOPICS/
This huge site provides many references of interest to those interested in global issues, such as links to information on ecology and the impact of consumerism.

16. United Nations Environment Programme (UNEP)
http://www.unep.ch
Consult this home page of UNEP for links to critical topics of concern to students of global issues, including desertification, migratory species, and the impact of trade on the environment.

Political Economy

17. Belfer Center for Science and International Affairs (BCSIA)
http://ksgwww.harvard.edu/csia/
BCSIA is the hub of Harvard University's John F. Kennedy School of Government's research, teaching, and training in international affairs related to security, environment, and technology.

18. Communications for a Sustainable Future
gopher://csf.colorado.edu
Information on topics in international environmental sustainability is available on this Gopher site. It pays particular attention to the political economics of protecting the environment.

19. U.S. Agency for International Development
http://www.info.usaid.gov
Broad and overlapping issues such as democracy, population and health, economic growth, and development are covered on this Web site. It provides specific information about different regions and countries.

20. Virtual Seminar in Global Political Economy/Global Cities & Social Movements
http://csf.colorado.edu/gpe/gpe95b/resources.html
This site of Internet resources is rich in links to subjects of interest in regional environmental studies, covering topics such as sustainable cities, megacities, and urban planning. Links to many international nongovernmental organizations are included.

21. World Bank
http://www.worldbank.org
News, press releases, summaries of new projects, speeches, publications, and coverage of numerous topics regarding development, countries, and regions are provided at this World Bank site. It also contains links to other important global financial organizations.

Conflict

22. DefenseLINK
http://www.defenselink.mil
Learn about security news and research-related publications at this U.S. Department of Defense site. Links to related sites of interest, among other things, are provided. The information systems BosniaLINK and GulfLINK can also be found here. Use the search function to investigate such issues as land mines.

23. Federation of American Scientists (FAS)
http://www.fas.org
FAS, a nonprofit policy organization, maintains this site to provide coverage of and links to such topics as global security, peace, and governance in the post–cold war world. It notes a variety of resources of value to students of global issues.

24. ISN International Relations and Security Network
http://www.isn.ethz.ch
This site, maintained by the Center for Security Studies and Conflict Research, is a clearinghouse for information on international relations and security policy. Topics are listed by category (Traditional Dimensions of Security, New Dimensions of Security, and Related Fields) and by major world region.

25. The NATO Integrated Data Service (NIDS)
http://www.nato.int/structur/nids/nids.htm
NIDS was created to bring information on security-related matters to within easy reach of the widest possible audience. Check out this Web site to review North Atlantic Treaty Organization documentation of all kinds, to read *NATO Review*, and to explore key issues in the field of European security and transatlantic cooperation.

Cooperation

26. Carnegie Endowment for International Peace
http://www.ceip.org
An important goals of this organization is to stimulate discussion and learning among both experts and the public at large on a wide range of international issues. The site provides links to *Foreign Policy*, to the Moscow Center, to descriptions of various programs, and much more.

27. Commission on Global Governance
http://www.cgg.ch
This site provides access to *The Report of the Commission on Global Governance*, produced by an international group of leaders who want to find ways in which the global community can better manage its affairs.

28. DiploNet
http://www.clark.net/pub/diplonet/DiploNet.html
DiploNet is concerned with the needs of diplomats in the post–cold war era. It provides avenues of research into negotiation and diplomacy. It also addresses conflict management and resolution, peacemaking, and multilateral diplomacy.

29. OECD/FDI Statistics
http://www.oecd.org/daf/cmis/fdi/statist.htm
Explore world trade and investment trends and statistics on this site from the Organization for Economic Cooperation and Development. It provides links to many related topics and addresses the issue on a country-by-country basis.

30. U.S. Institute of Peace
http://www.usip.org
USIP, which was created by the U.S. Congress to promote peaceful resolution of international conflicts, seeks to educate people and to disseminate information on how to achieve peace. Click on Highlights, Publications, Events, Research Areas, and Library and Links.

Values and Visions

31. Human Rights Web
http://www.hrweb.org
The history of the human rights movement, text on seminal figures, landmark legal and political documents, and ideas on how individuals can get involved in helping to protect human rights around the world can be found in this valuable site.

32. InterAction
http://www.interaction.org/advocacy/index.html
InterAction encourages grassroots action and engages government policymakers on advocacy issues. The organization's Advocacy Committee provides this site to inform people on its initiatives to expand international humanitarian relief, refugee, and development-assistance programs.

We highly recommend that you review our Web site for expanded information and our other product lines. We are continually updating and adding links to our Web site in order to offer you the most usable and useful information that will support and expand the value of your Annual Editions. You can reach us at: *http://www.dushkin.com/annualeditions/.*

www.dushkin.com/online/

Unit Selections

1. **A Special Moment in History,** Bill McKibben
2. **The Many Faces of the Future,** Samuel P. Huntington
3. **Life Is Unfair: Inequality in the World,** Nancy Birdsall
4. **Redefining Security: The New Global Schisms,** Michael T. Klare

Key Points to Consider

❖ Do the analyses of any of the authors in this section employ the assumptions implicit in the allegory of the balloon? If so, how? If not, how are the assumptions of the authors different?

❖ All the authors point to interactions among different factors. What are some of the relationships that they cite? How do the authors differ in terms of the relationships they emphasize?

❖ What assets that did not exist 100 years ago do people now have to solve problems?

❖ What events during the twentieth century have had the greatest impact on shaping the realities of contemporary international affairs?

❖ What do you consider to be the five most pressing global problems of today? How do your answers compare to those of your family, friends, and classmates?

 **Links** | **www.dushkin.com/online/**

3. **The Henry L. Stimson Center**
   http://www.stimson.org
4. **The Heritage Foundation**
   http://www.heritage.org
5. **IISDnet**
   http://iisd1.iisd.ca
6. **The North-South Institute**
   http://www.nsi-ins.ca/info.html

These sites are annotated on pages 6 and 7.

Imagine a clear, round, inflated balloon. Now imagine that a person begins to brush yellow paint onto this miniature globe; symbolically, the color yellow represents *people*. In many ways the study of global issues is ultimately the study of people. Today, there are more people occupying Earth than ever before. In addition, the world is in the midst of a period of unprecedented population growth. Not only are there many countries where the majority of people are under age 16, but because of improved health care, there are also more older people alive than ever before. The effect of a growing global population, however, goes beyond sheer numbers, for a growing population has unprecedented impacts on natural resources and social services. Population issues, then, are an appropriate place to begin the study of global issues.

Imagine that our fictional artist dips the brush into a container of blue paint to represent the world of *nature*. The natural world plays an important role in setting the international agenda. Shortages of raw materials, drought and crop failures, and pollution of waterways are just a few examples of how natural resources can have global implications.

Adding blue paint to the balloon also reveals one of the most important concepts found in this book of readings. Although the balloon originally was covered by yellow and blue paint (people and nature as separate conceptual entities), the two combined produce an entirely different color: green. Talking about nature as a separate entity or about people as though they were somehow removed from the forces of the natural world is a serious intel-lectual error. The people-nature relationship is one of the keys to understanding many of today's most important global issues.

The third color added to the balloon is red. It represents the *meta* component (i.e., those qualities that make human beings more than mere animals). These include new ideas and inventions, culture and values, religion and spirituality, and art and liter-ature. The addition of the red paint immediately changes the color green to brown, again empha-sizing the relationship among all three factors.

The fourth and final color added is white. This color represents *social structures*. Factors such as whether a society is urban or rural, industrial or agrarian, planned or decentralized, and consumer-oriented or dedicated to the needs of the state fall into this category. The relationship between this component and the others is extremely important. The impact of political decisions on the environment, for example, is one of the most unusual features of the contemporary world. Historically, the forces of nature determined which species survived or perished. Today, survival depends on political decisions—or indecision. Will the whales or bald eagles survive? The answer to this question will depend on governmental activities, not evolutionary forces.

Understanding this relationship between social structure and nature (known as "ecopolitics") is important to the study of global issues.

If the painter continues to ply the paintbrush over the miniature globe, a marbling effect will become evident. In some areas, the shading will vary because one element is greater than another. The miniature system appears dynamic. Nothing is static; relationships are continually changing. This leads to a number of theoretical insights: (1) there is no such thing as separate elements, only connections or relationships; (2) changes in one area (such as the weather) will result in changes in all other areas; and (3) complex relationships make it difficult to predict events accurately, so observers are often surprised by unexpected processes and outcomes.

This book is organized along the basic lines of the balloon allegory. The first unit explores a variety of perspectives on the forces that are shaping the world of the twenty-first century. Unit 2 focuses on population and food production. Unit 3 examines the environment and related issues. The next three units look at different aspects of the world's social structures. They explore issues of economics, national security, conflict, and international cooperation. In the final unit, a number of "meta" factors are discussed.

The reader should be aware that, just as it was impossible to keep the individual colors from blending into new colors on the balloon, it also is impossible to separate global issues into discrete chapters in a book. Any discussion of agriculture, for example, must take into account the impact of a growing population on soil and water resources, as well as new scientific breakthroughs in food production. Therefore, the organization of this book focuses attention on issue areas; it does not mean to imply that these factors are somehow separate.

With the collapse of the Soviet empire and the end of the cold war, the outlines of a new global agenda are beginning to emerge. Rather than being based on the ideology and interests of the two superpowers, new political, economic, and environ-mental factors are interacting in an unprecedented fashion. Rapid population growth, environmental decline, and uneven economic growth are all parts of a complex situation for which there is no historic parallel. As we begin the twenty-first century, signs abound that we are entering a new era. In the words of Abraham Lincoln, "As our case is new, so we must think anew." Compounding this situation, however, is a whole series of old problems such as ethnic and religious rivalries.

The authors in this first unit provide a variety of perspectives on the trends that they believe are the most important to understanding the historic changes at work at the global level. This discussion is then pursued in greater detail in the following units.

It is important for the reader to note that although the authors look at the same world, they often come to different conclusions. This raises an important issue of values and beliefs, for it can be argued that there really is no objective reality, only differing perspectives. In short, the study of global issues will challenge each thoughtful reader to examine her or his own values and beliefs.

A Special Moment in History

Bill McKibben

We may live in the strangest, most thoroughly different moment since human beings took up farming, 10,000 years ago, and time more or less commenced. Since then time has flowed in one direction—toward *more*, which we have taken to be progress. At first the momentum was gradual, almost imperceptible, checked by wars and the Dark Ages and plagues and taboos; but in recent centuries it has accelerated, the curve of every graph steepening like the Himalayas rising from the Asian steppe. . . .

But now—now may be the special time. So special that in the Western world we might each of us consider, among many other things, having only one child—that is, reproducing at a rate as low as that at which human beings have ever voluntarily reproduced. Is this really necessary? Are we finally running up against some limits?

To try to answer this question, we need to ask another: *How many of us will there be in the near future?* Here is a piece of news that may alter the way we see the planet— an indication that we live at a special moment. At least

Bill McKibben is the author of several books about the environment, including *The End of Nature* (1989) and *Hope, Human and Wild* (1995). His article in this issue will appear in somewhat different form in his book *Maybe One: A Personal and Environmental Argument for Single-Child Families*, published in 1998 by Simon & Schuster.

at first blush the news is hopeful. *New demographic evidence shows that it is at least possible that a child born today will live long enough to see the peak of human population.*

Around the world people are choosing to have fewer and fewer children—not just in China, where the government forces it on them, but in almost every nation outside the poorest parts of Africa. . . . If this keeps up, the population of the world will not quite double again; United Nations analysts offer as their mid-range projection that it will top out at 10 to 11 billion, up from just under six billion at the moment. . . .

The good news is that we won't grow forever. The bad news is that there are six billion of us already, a number the world strains to support. One more near-doubling—four or five billion more people—will nearly double that strain. Will these be the five billion straws that break the camel's back? . . .

LOOKING AT LIMITS

The case that the next doubling, the one we're now experiencing, might be the difficult one can begin as readily with the Stanford biologist Peter Vitousek as with anyone else. In 1986 Vitousek decided to calculate how much of the earth's "primary productivity" went to support human beings. He added together the grain we ate, the corn we fed our cows, and the forests we cut for timber and paper; he added the losses in food as we overgrazed grassland and turned it into desert. And when he was finished adding, the number he came up with was 38.8 percent. We use 38.8 percent of everything the world's plants don't need to keep themselves alive; directly or indirectly, we consume 38.8 percent of what it is possible to eat. "That's a relatively large number," Vitousek says. "It should give pause to people who think we are far from any limits." Though he never drops the measured tone of an academic, Vitousek speaks with considerable emphasis: "There's a sense among some economists that we're *so* far from any biophysical limits. I think that's not supported by the evidence."

For another antidote to the good cheer of someone like Julian Simon, sit down with the Cornell biologist David Pimentel. He believes that we're in big trouble. Odd facts stud his conversation—for example, a nice head of iceberg lettuce is 95 percent water and contains just fifty calories of energy, but it takes 400 calories of energy to grow that head of lettuce in California's Central Valley, and another 1,800 to ship it east. ("There's practically no nutrition in the damn stuff anyway," Pimentel says. "Cabbage is a lot better, and we can grow it in upstate New York.") Pimentel has devoted the past three decades to tracking the planet's capacity, and he believes that we're already too crowded—that the earth can support only two billion people over the long run at a middle-class standard of living, and that trying to support more is doing damage. He has spent considerable time studying soil erosion, for instance. Every raindrop that hits exposed ground is like a small explosion, launching soil particles into the air. On a slope, more than half of the soil contained in those splashes is carried downhill. If crop residue—cornstalks, say—is left in the field after harvest, it helps to shield the soil: the raindrop doesn't hit hard. But in the developing world, where firewood is scarce, peasants burn those cornstalks for cooking fuel. About 60 percent of crop residues in China and 90 percent in Bangladesh are removed and burned, Pimentel says. When planting season comes, dry soils simply blow away. "Our measuring stations pick up African soils in the wind when they start to plough."

The very things that made the Green Revolution so stunning—that made the last doubling possible—now cause trouble. Irrigation ditches, for instance, water 27 percent of all arable land and help to produce a third of all crops. But when flooded soils are baked by the sun, the water evaporates and the minerals in the irrigation water are deposited on the land. A hectare (2.47 acres) can accumulate two to five tons of salt annually, and eventually plants won't grow there. Maybe 10 percent of all irrigated land is affected.

... [F]ood production grew even faster than population after the Second World War. Year after year the yield of wheat and corn and rice rocketed up about three percent annually. It's a favorite statistic of the eternal optimists. In Julian Simon's book *The Ultimate Resource* (1981) charts show just how fast the growth was, and how it continually cut the cost of food. Simon wrote, "The ob-

vious implication of this historical trend toward cheaper food—a trend that probably extends back to the beginning of agriculture—is that real prices for food will continue to drop.... It is a fact that portends more drops in price and even less scarcity in the future."

A few years after Simon's book was published, however, the data curve began to change. That rocketing growth in grain production ceased; now the gains were coming in tiny increments, too small to keep pace with population growth. The world reaped its largest harvest of grain per capita in 1984; since then the amount of corn and wheat and rice per person has fallen by six percent. Grain stockpiles have shrunk to less than two months' supply.

No one knows quite why. The collapse of the Soviet Union contributed to the trend—cooperative farms suddenly found the fertilizer supply shut off and spare parts for the tractor hard to come by. But there were other causes, too, all around the world—the salinization of irrigated fields, the erosion of topsoil, and all the other things that environmentalists had been warning about for years. It's possible that we'll still turn production around and start it rocketing again. Charles C. Mann, writing in *Science*, quotes experts who believe that in the future a "gigantic, multi-year, multi-billion-dollar scientific effort, a kind of agricultural 'person-on the-moon project,'" might do the trick. The next great hope of the optimists is genetic engineering, and scientists have indeed managed to induce resistance to pests and disease in some plants. To get more yield, though, a cornstalk must be made to put out another ear, and conventional breeding may have exhausted the possibilities. There's a sense that we're running into walls.

... What we are running out of is what the scientists call "sinks"—places to put the by-products of our large appetites. Not garbage dumps (we could go on using Pampers till the end of time and still have empty space left to toss them away) but the atmospheric equivalent of garbage dumps.

It wasn't hard to figure out that there were limits on how much coal smoke we could pour into the air of a single city. It took a while longer to figure out that building ever higher smokestacks merely lofted the haze farther afield, raining down acid on whatever mountain range lay to the east. Even that, however, we are slowly fixing, with scrubbers and different mixtures of fuel. We can't so easily repair the new kinds of pollution. These do not come from something going wrong—some engine without a catalytic converter, some waste-water pipe without a filter, some smokestack without a scrubber. New kinds of pollution come instead from things going as they're supposed to go—but at such a high volume that they overwhelm the planet. They come from normal human life—but there are so many of us living those normal lives that something abnormal is happening. And that something is different from the old forms of pollution that it confuses the issue even to use the word.

Consider nitrogen, for instance. But before plants can absorb it, it must become "fixed"—bonded with carbon, hydrogen, or oxygen. Nature does this trick with certain kinds of algae and soil bacteria, and with lightning. Before human beings began to alter the nitrogen cycle, these mechanisms provided 90–150 million metric tons of nitrogen a year. Now human activity adds 130–150 million more tons. Nitrogen isn't pollution—it's essential. And we are using more of it all the time. Half the industrial nitrogen fertilizer used in human history has been applied since 1984. As a result, coastal waters and estuaries bloom with toxic algae while oxygen concentrations dwindle, killing fish; as a result, nitrous oxide traps solar heat. And once the gas is in the air, it stays there for a century or more.

Or consider methane, which comes out of the back of a cow or the top of a termite mound or the bottom of a rice paddy. As a result of our determination to raise more cattle, cut down more tropical forest (thereby causing termite populations to explode), and grow more rice, methane concentrations in the atmosphere are more than twice as high as they have been for most of the past 160,000 years. And methane traps heat—very efficiently.

Or consider carbon dioxide. In fact, concentrate on carbon dioxide. If we had to pick one problem to obsess about over the next fifty years, we'd do well to make it CO_2—which is not pollution either. Carbon *mon*oxide is pollution: it kills you if you breathe enough of it. But carbon *di*oxide, carbon with two oxygen atoms, can't do a blessed thing to you. If you're reading this indoors, you're breathing more CO_2 than you'll ever get outside. For generations, in fact, engineers said that an engine burned clean if it produced only water vapor and carbon dioxide.

Here's the catch: that engine produces a *lot* of CO_2. A gallon of gas weighs about eight pounds. When it's burned in a car, about five and a half pounds of carbon, in the form of carbon dioxide, come spewing out the back. It doesn't matter if the car is a 1958 Chevy or a 1998 Saab. And no filter can reduce that flow—it's an inevitable by-product of fossil-fuel combustion, which is why CO_2 has been piling up in the atmosphere ever since the Industrial Revolution. Before we started burning oil and coal and gas, the atmosphere contained about 280 parts CO_2 per million. Now the figure is about 360. Unless we do everything we can think of to eliminate fossil fuels from our diet, the air will test out at more than 500 parts per million fifty or sixty years from now, whether it's sampled in the South Bronx or at the South Pole.

This matters because, as we all know by now, the molecular structure of this clean, natural, common element that we are adding to every cubic foot of the atmosphere surrounding us traps heat that would otherwise radiate back out to space. Far more than even methane and nitrous oxide, CO_2 causes global warming—the greenhouse effect—and climate change. Far more than any other single factor, it is turning the earth we were born on into a new planet.

. . . For ten years, with heavy funding from governments around the world, scientists launched satellites, monitored weather balloons, studied clouds. Their work culminated in a long-awaited report from the UN's Intergovernmental Panel on Climate Change, released in the fall of 1995. The panel's 2,000 scientists, from every corner of the globe, summed up their findings in this dry but historic bit of understatement: "The balance of evidence suggests that there is a discernible human influence on global climate." That is to say, we are heating up the planet—substantially. If we don't reduce emissions of carbon dioxide and other gases, the panel warned, temperatures will probably rise 3.6° Fahrenheit by 2100, and perhaps as much as 6.3°.

You may think you've already heard a lot about global warming. But most of our sense of the problem is behind the curve. Here's the current news: the changes are already well under way. When politicians and businessmen talk about "future risks," their rhetoric is outdated. This is not a problem for the distant future, or even for the near future. The planet has already heated up by a degree or more. We are perhaps a quarter of the way into the greenhouse era, and the effects are already being felt. From a new heaven, filled with nitrogen, methane, and carbon, a new earth is being born. If some alien astronomer is watching us, she's doubtless puzzled. This is the most obvious effect of our numbers and our appetites, and the key to understanding why the size of our population suddenly poses such a risk.

STORMY AND WARM

What does this new world feel like? For one thing, it's stormier than the old one. Data analyzed last year by Thomas Karl, of the National Oceanic and Atmospheric Administration, showed that total winter precipitation in the United States has increased by 10 percent since 1900 and that "extreme precipitation events"—rainstorms that dumped more than two inches of water in twenty-four hours and blizzards—had increased by 20 percent. That's because warmer air holds more water vapor than the colder atmosphere of the old earth; more water evaporates from the ocean, meaning more clouds, more rain, more snow. Engineers designing storm sewers, bridges, and culverts used to plan for what they called the "hundred-year storm." That is, they built to withstand the worst flooding or wind that history led them to expect in the course of a century. Since that history no longer applies, Karl says, "there isn't really a hundred-year event anymore . . . we seem to be getting these storms of the century every couple of years." When Grand Forks, North Dakota, disappeared beneath the Red River in the spring of last year, some meteorologists referred to it as "a 500-year flood"—meaning, essentially, that all bets are off. Meaning that these aren't acts of God. "If you look out your window, part of what you see in terms of weather is produced by ourselves," Karl says. "If you look out the window fifty years from now, we're going to be responsible for more of it."

Twenty percent more bad storms, 10 percent more winter precipitation—these are enormous numbers. It's like opening the newspaper to read that the average American is smarter by 30 IQ points. And the same data showed increases in drought, too. With more water in the atmosphere, there's less in the soil, according to Kevin Trenberth, of the National Center for Atmospheric Research. Those parts of the continent that are normally dry—the eastern sides of mountains, the plains and deserts—are even drier, as the higher average temperatures evaporate more of what rain does fall. "You get wilting plants and eventually drought faster than you would otherwise," Trenberth says. And when the rain does come, it's often so intense that much of it runs off before it can soak into the soil.

So—wetter and drier. *Different.* . . .

The effects of . . . warming can be found in the largest phenomena. The oceans that cover most of the planet's surface are clearly rising, both because of melting glaciers and because water expands as it warms. As a result, low-lying Pacific islands already report surges of water washing across the atolls. "It's nice weather and all of a sudden water is pouring into your living room," one Marshall Islands resident told a newspaper reporter. "It's very clear that something is happening in the Pacific, and these islands are feeling it." Global warming will be like a much more powerful version of El Niño that covers the entire globe and lasts forever, or at least until the next big asteroid strikes.

If you want to scare yourself with guesses about what might happen in the near future, there's no shortage of possibilities. Scientists have already observed large-scale shifts in the duration of the El Niño ocean warming, for instance. The Arctic tundra has warmed so much that in some places it now gives off more carbon dioxide than it absorbs—a switch that could trigger a potent feedback loop, making warming ever worse. And researchers studying glacial cores from the Greenland Ice Sheet recently concluded that local climate shifts have occurred with incredible rapidity in the past—18° in one three-year stretch. Other scientists worry that such a shift might be enough to flood the oceans with fresh water and reroute or shut off currents like the Gulf Stream and the North Atlantic, which keep Europe far warmer than it would otherwise be. (See "The Great Climate Flip-flop," by William H. Calvin, January *Atlantic.*) In the words of Wallace Broecker, of Columbia University, a pioneer in the field, "Climate is an angry beast, and we are poking it with sticks."

But we don't need worst-case scenarios: best-case scenarios make the point. The population of the earth is going to nearly double one more time. That will bring it to a level that even the reliable old earth we were born on would be hard-pressed to support. Just at the moment when we need everything to be working as smoothly as possible, we find ourselves inhabiting a new planet, whose carrying capacity we cannot conceivably estimate. We have no idea how much wheat this planet can grow. We don't know what its politics will be like: not if there are going to be heat waves like the one that killed more than 700 Chicagoans in 1995; not if rising sea levels and other effects of climate change create tens of millions of environmental refugees; not if a 1.5° jump in India's temperature could reduce the country's wheat crop by 10 percent or divert its monsoons. . . .

We have gotten very large and very powerful, and for the foreseeable future we're stuck with the results. The glaciers won't grow back again anytime soon; the oceans won't drop. We've already done deep and systemic damage. To use a human analogy, we've already said the angry and unforgivable words that will haunt our marriage till its end. And yet we can't simply walk out the door. There's no place to go. We have to salvage what we can of our relationship with the earth, to keep things from getting any worse than they have to be.

If we can bring our various emissions quickly and sharply under control, we *can* limit the damage, reduce dramatically the chance of horrible surprises, preserve more of the biology we were born into. But do not underestimate the task. The UN's Intergovernmental Panel on Climate Change projects that an immediate 60 percent reduction in fossil-fuel use is necessary just to stabilize climate at the current level of disruption. Nature may still meet us halfway, but halfway is a long way from where we are now. What's more, we can't delay. If we wait a few decades to get started, we may as well not even begin. It's not like poverty, a concern that's always there for civilizations to address. This is a timed test, like the SAT: two or three decades, and we lay our pencils down. It's *the* test for our generations, and population is a part of the answer. . . .

The numbers are so daunting that they're almost unimaginable. Say, just for argument's sake, that we decided to cut world fossil-fuel use by 60 percent—the amount that the UN panel says would stabilize world climate. And then say that we shared the remaining fossil fuel equally. Each human being would get to produce 1.69 metric tons of carbon dioxide annually—which would allow you to drive an average American car nine miles a day. By the time the population increased to 8.5 billion, in about 2025, you'd be down to six miles a day. If you carpooled, you'd have about three pounds of CO_2 left in your daily ration—enough to run a highly efficient refrigerator. Forget your computer, your TV, your stereo, your stove, your dishwasher, your water heater, your microwave, your water pump, your clock. Forget your light bulbs, compact fluorescent or not.

I'm not trying to say that conservation, efficiency, and new technology won't help. They will—but the help will be slow and expensive. The tremendous momentum of growth will work against it. Say that someone invented a new furnace tomorrow that used half as much oil as old furnaces. How many years would it be before a substantial number of American homes had the new device? And what if it cost more? And if oil stays cheaper per gallon than bottled water? Changing basic fuels—to hydrogen, say—would be even more expensive. It's not like running out of white wine and switching to red. Yes, we'll get new technologies. One day last fall *The New York Times* ran a special section on energy, featuring many up-and-coming improvements: solar shingles, basement fuel cells. But the same day, on the front page, William K. Stevens reported that international negotiators had all but given up on preventing a doubling of the atmospheric concentration of CO_2. The momentum of growth was so great, the negotiators said, that making the changes required to slow global warming significantly would be like "trying to turn a supertanker in a sea of syrup."

There are no silver bullets to take care of a problem like this. Electric cars won't by themselves save us, though they would help. We simply won't live efficiently enough soon enough to solve the problem. Vegetarianism won't cure our ills, though it would help. We simply won't live simply enough soon enough to solve the problem.

Reducing the birth rate won't end all our troubles either. That, too, is no silver bullet. But it would help. There's no more practical decision than how many children to have. (And no more mystical decision, either.)

The bottom-line argument goes like this: The next fifty years are a special time. They will decide how strong and healthy the planet will be for centuries to come. Between now and 2050 we'll see the zenith, or very nearly, of human population. With luck we'll never see any greater production of carbon dioxide or toxic chemicals. We'll never see more species extinction or soil erosion. Greenpeace recently announced a campaign to phase out fossil fuels entirely by mid-century, which sounds utterly quixotic but could—if everything went just right—happen.

So it's the task of those of us alive right now to deal with this special phase, to squeeze us through these next fifty years. That's not fair—any more than it was fair that earlier generations had to deal with the Second World War or the Civil War or the Revolution or the Depression or slavery. It's just reality. We need in these fifty years to be working simultaneously on all parts of the equation—on our ways of life, on our technologies, and on our population.

As Gregg Easterbrook pointed out in his book *A Moment on the Earth* (1995), if the planet does manage to reduce its fertility, "the period in which human numbers threaten the biosphere on a general scale will turn out to have been much, much more brief" than periods of natural threats like the Ice Ages. True enough. But the period in question happens to be our time. That's what makes this moment special, and what makes this moment hard.

THE MANY FACES OF
the Future

Why we'll never have a universal civilization

By Samuel P. Huntington

Conventional Wisdom tells us that we are witnessing the emergence of what V.S. Naipaul called a "universal civilization," the cultural coming together of humanity and the increasing acceptance of common values, beliefs, and institutions by people throughout the world. Critics of this trend point to the global domination of Western-style capitalism and culture *(Baywatch,* many note with alarm, is the most popular television show in the world), and the gradual erosion of distinct cultures—especially in the developing world. But there's more to universal civilization than GATT and David Hasselhoff's pecs.

If what we mean by universal culture are the assumptions, values, and doctrines currently held by the many elites who travel in international circles, that's not a viable "one world" scenario. Consider the "Davos culture." Each year about a thousand business executives, government officials, intellectuals, and journalists from scores of countries meet at the World Economic Forum in Davos, Switzerland. Almost all of them hold degrees in the physical sciences, social sciences, business, or law; are reasonably fluent in English; are employed by governments, corporations, and academic institutions with extensive international connections; and travel frequently outside of their own countries. They also generally share beliefs in individualism, market economies, and political democracy,

From *Utne Reader,* May/June 1997, pp. 75–77, 102–103. Adapted from *The Clash of Civilizations and Remaking of World Order* by Samuel P. Huntington. © 1997 by Samuel P. Huntington. Reprinted by permission of Simon & Schuster.

which are also common among people in Western civilization. This core group of people controls virtually all international institutions, many of the world's governments, and the bulk of the world's economic and military organizations. As a result, the Davos culture is tremendously important, but it is far from a universal civilization. Outside the West, these values are shared by perhaps 1 percent of the world's population.

If a universal civilization is emerging, there should be signs of a universal language and religion. Nothing of the sort is occurring.

The argument that the spread of Western consumption patterns and popular culture around the world is creating a universal civilization is also not especially profound. Innovations have been transmitted from one civilization to another throughout history. But they are usually techniques lacking in significant cultural consequences or fads that come and go without altering the underlying culture of the recipient civilization. The essence of Western civilization is the Magna Carta, not the Magna Mac. The fact that non-Westerners may bite into the latter does not necessarily mean they are more likely to accept the former. During the '70s and '80s Americans bought millions of Japanese cars and electronic gadgets without being "Japanized," and, in fact, became considerably more antagonistic toward Japan. Only naive arrogance can lead Westerners to assume that non-Westerners will become "Westernized" by acquiring Western goods.

A slightly more sophisticated version of the universal popular culture argument focuses on the media rather than consumer goods in general. Eighty-eight of the world's hundred most popular films in 1993 were produced in the United States, and four organizations based in the United States and Europe—the Associated Press, CNN, Reuters, and the French Press Agency—

dominate the dissemination of news worldwide. This situation simply reflects the universality of human interest in love, sex, violence, mystery, heroism, and wealth, and the ability of profit-motivated companies, primarily American, to exploit those interests to their own advantage. Little or no evidence exists, however, to support the assumption that the emergence of pervasive global communications is producing significant convergence in attitudes and beliefs around the world. Indeed, this Western hegemony encourages populist politicians in non-Western societies to denounce Western cultural imperialism and to rally their constituents to preserve their indigenous cultures. The extent to which global communications are dominated by the West is, thus, a major source of the resentment non-Western peoples have toward the West. In addition, rapid economic development in non-Western societies is leading to the emergence of local and regional media industries catering to the distinctive tastes of those societies.

The central elements of any civilization are language and religion. If a universal civilization is emerging, there should be signs of a universal language and a universal religion developing. Nothing of the sort is occurring. Despite claims from Western business leaders that the world's language is English, no evidence exists to support this proposition, and the most reliable evidence that does exist shows just the opposite. English speakers dropped from 9.8 percent of the world's population in 1958 to 7.6 percent in 1992. Still, one can argue that English has become the world's lingua franca, or in linguistic terms, the principal language of wider communication. Diplomats, business executives, tourists, and the service professionals catering to them need some means of efficient communication, and right now that is largely in English. But this is a form of *intercultural* communication; it presupposes the existence of separate cultures. Adopting a lingua franca is a way of coping with linguistic and cultural differences, not a way of eliminating them. It is a tool for communication, not a source of identity and community.

The linguistic scholar Joshua Fishman has observed that a language is more likely to be accepted as a lingua franca if it is not identified with a particular ethnic group, religion, or ideology. In the past, English carried many of those associations. But more recently, Fishman says, it has been "de-ethnicized (or minimally ethnicized)," much like what happened to Akkadian, Aramaic, Greek, and Latin before it. As he puts it, "It is part of the relative good fortune of English as an additional language that neither its British nor its American fountainheads have been widely or deeply viewed in an ethnic or ideological context for the past quarter century or so." Resorting to English for intercultural communication helps maintain—

and, indeed, reinforce—separate cultural identities. Precisely because people want to preserve their own culture, they use English to communicate with people of other cultures.

A universal religion is only slightly more likely to emerge than a universal language. The late 20th century has seen a resurgence of religions around the world, including the rise of fundamentalist movements. This trend has reinforced the differences among religions, and has not necessarily resulted in significant shifts in the distribution of religions worldwide.

Of course, there have been increases during the past century in the percentage of people practicing the two major proselytizing religions, Islam and Christianity. Western Christians accounted for 26.9 percent of the world's population in 1900 and peaked at about 30 percent in 1980, while the Muslim population increased from 12.4 percent in 1900 to as much as 18 percent in 1980. The percentage of Christians in the world will probably decline to about 25 percent by 2025. Meanwhile, because of extremely high rates of population growth, the proportion of Muslims in the world will continue to increase dramatically and represent about 30 percent of the world's population by 2025. Neither, however, qualifies as a universal religion.

The argument that some sort of universal civilization is emerging rests on one or more of three assumptions: that the collapse of Soviet communism meant the end of history and the universal victory of liberal democracy; that increased interaction among peoples through trade, investment, tourism, media, and electronic communications is creating a common world culture; and that a universal civilization is the logical result of the process of global modernization that has been going on since the 18th century.

The first assumption is rooted in the Cold War perspective that the only alternative to communism is liberal democracy, and the demise of the first inevitably produces the second. But there are many alternatives to liberal democracy—including authoritarianism, nationalism, corporatism, and market communism (as in China)—that are alive and well in today's world. And, more significantly, there are all the religious alternatives that lie outside the world of secular ideologies. In the modern world, religion is a central, perhaps *the* central, force that motivates and mobilizes people. It is sheer hubris to think that because Soviet communism has collapsed, the West has conquered the world for all time and that non-Western peoples are going to rush to embrace Western liberalism as the only alternative. The Cold War division of humanity is over. The more fundamental divisions of ethnicity, religions, and civilizations remain and will spawn new conflicts.

2. Many Faces of the Future

The Real World

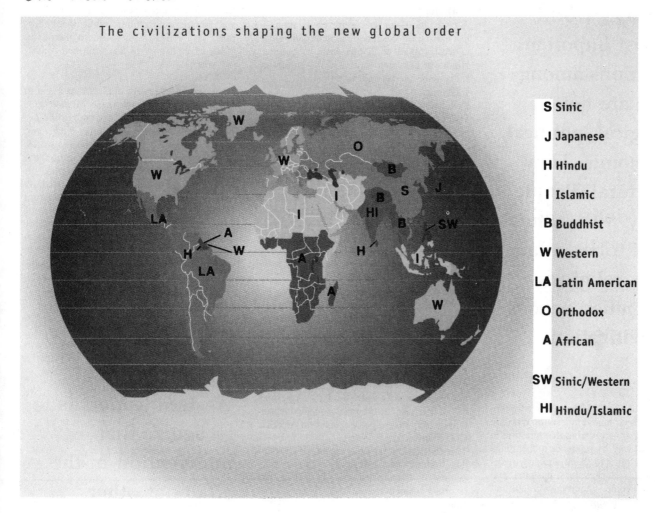

The civilizations shaping the new global order

S Sinic
J Japanese
H Hindu
I Islamic
B Buddhist
W Western
LA Latin American
O Orthodox
A African

SW Sinic/Western
HI Hindu/Islamic

The new global economy is a reality. Improvements in transportation and communications technology have indeed made it easier and cheaper to move money, goods, knowledge, ideas, and images around the world. But what will be the impact of this increased economic interaction? In social psychology, distinctiveness theory holds that people define themselves by what makes them different from others in a particular context: People define their identity by what they are not. As advanced communications, trade, and travel multiply the interactions among civilizations, people will increasingly accord greater relevance to identity based on their own civilization.

Those who argue that a universal civilization is an inevitable product of modernization assume that all modern societies must become Westernized. As the first civilization to modernize, the West leads in the acquisition of the culture of modernity. And as other societies acquire similar patterns of education, work, wealth, and class structure—the argument runs—this modern Western culture will become the universal culture of the world. That significant differences exist between modern and traditional cultures is beyond dispute. It doesn't necessarily follow, however, that societies with modern cultures resemble each other more than do societies with traditional cultures. As historian Fernand Braudel writes, "Ming China . . . was assuredly closer to the France of the Valois than the China of Mao Tse-tung is to the France of the Fifth Republic."

Yet modern societies could resemble each other more than do traditional societies for two reasons. First, the increased interaction among modern societies may not generate a common culture, but it does facilitate the transfer of techniques, inventions, and practices from one society to another with a speed and to a degree that were impossible in the traditional world. Second, traditional society was based on agriculture; modern society is based on industry. Patterns of agriculture and the social structure that goes with them are much more dependent on the natural environment than are patterns of industry. Differences in industrial organization are likely to derive from differences in culture and social structure rather than geography, and the former conceivably can converge while the latter cannot.

Modern societies thus have much in common. But do they necessarily merge into homogeneity? The argument that they do rests on the assumption that modern society must approximate a single type, the Western type. This is a totally false assumption. Western civilization emerged in the 8th and 9th centuries. It did not begin to modernize until the 17th and 18th centuries. The West was the West long before it was modern. The central characteristics of the West—the classical legacy, the mix of catholicism and protestantism, and the separation of spiritual and temporal authority—distinguish it from other civilizations and antedate the modernization of the West.

In the post–Cold War world, the most important distinctions among people are not ideological, political, or economic. They are

In today's world, the most important distinctions among people are not ideological, political, or economic. They are cultural. People identify with cultural groups: tribes, ethnic groups, religious communities, nations, and civilizations.

cultural. People and nations are attempting to answer a basic human question: Who are we? And they are answering that question in the traditional way, by reference to the things that mean the most to them: ancestry, religion, language, history, values, customs, and institutions. People identify with cultural groups: tribes, ethnic groups, religious communities, nations, and, at the broadest level, civilizations. They use politics not just to advance their interests but also to define their identity. We know who we are only when we know who we are not, and often only when we know who we are against.

Nation-states remain the principal actors in world affairs. Their behavior is shaped, as in the past, by the pursuit of power and wealth, but it is also shaped by cultural preferences and differences. The most important groupings are no longer the three blocs of the Cold War but rather the world's major civilizations (See map):

S Sinic

All scholars recognize the existence of either a single distinct Chinese civilization dating back at least to 1500 B.C., or of two civilizations—one succeeding the other—in the early centuries of the Christian epoch.

J Japanese

Some scholars combine Japanese and Chinese culture, but most recognize Japan as a distinct civilization, the offspring of Chinese civilization, that emerged between A.D. 100 and 400.

H Hindu

A civilization—or successive civilizations—has existed on the Indian subcontinent since at least 1500 B.C. In one form or another, Hinduism has been central to the culture of India since the second millennium B.C.

I Islamic

Originating on the Arabian peninsula in the 7th century A.D., Islam spread rapidly across North Africa and the Iberian Peninsula and also eastward into central Asia, the Indian subcontinent, and Southeast Asia. Many distinct cultures—including Arab, Turkic, Persian, and Malay—exist within Islam.

W Western

The emergence of Western civilization—what used to be called Western Christendom—is usually dated at about 700 A.D. It has two main components, in Europe and North America.

LA Latin American

Latin America, often considered part of the West, has a distinct identity. It has had a corporatist, authoritarian culture, which Europe had to a much lesser degree and North America did not have at all. Europe and North America both felt the effects of the Reformation and have combined Catholic and Protestant cultures, while Latin America has been primarily Catholic. Latin American civilization also incorporates indigenous cultures, which were wiped out in North America.

O Orthodox

This civilization, which combines the Orthodox tradition of Christianity with the Slav cultures of Eastern Europe and Russia, has resurfaced since the demise of the Soviet Union.

A African

There may be some argument about whether there is a distinct African civilization. North Africa and the east coast belong to Islamic civilization. (Historically, Ethiopia constituted a civilization of its own.) Elsewhere, imperialism brought elements of Western civilization. Tribal identities are pervasive throughout Africa, but Africans are also increasingly developing a sense of African identity. Sub-Saharan Africa conceivably could cohere into a distinct civilization, with South Africa as its core.

B Buddhist

Beginning in the first century A.D., Buddhism was exported from India to China, Korea, Vietnam, and Japan, where it was assimilated by the indigenous cultures and/or suppressed. What can legitimately be described as a Buddhist civilization, however, does exist in Sri Lanka, Burma, Thailand, Laos, Cambodia; and Tibet, Mongolia, and Bhutan. Overall, however, the virtual extinction of Buddhism in India and its incorporation into existing cultures in other major countries means that it has not been the basis of a major civilization.

(Modern India represents a mix of Hindu and Islamic civilizations, while the Philippines is a unique Sinic-Western hybrid by virtue of its history of Spanish, then American rule.)

As Asian and Muslim civilizations begin to assert the universal relevance of *their* cultures, Westerners will see the connection between universalism and imperialism and appreciate the virtues of a pluralistic world. In order to preserve Western civilization, the West needs greater unity of purpose. It should incorporate into the European Union and NATO the western states of central Europe; encourage the Westernization of Latin America; slow the drift of Japan away from the West and toward accommodation with China; and accept Russia as the core state of Orthodoxy and a power with legitimate interests.

The main responsibility of Western leaders is to recognize that intervention in the affairs of other civilizations is the single most dangerous source of instability in the world.

The main responsibility of Western leaders is to recognize that intervention in the affairs of other civilizations is the single most dangerous source of instability in the world. The West should attempt not to reshape other civilizations in its own image, but to preserve and renew the unique qualities of its own civilization.

Samuel P. Huntington is Albert J. Weatherhead III University Professor at Harvard University.

Life Is Unfair: Inequality in the World

by Nancy Birdsall

Exactly 150 years after publication of the *Communist Manifesto*, inequality looms large on the global agenda. In the United States, the income of the poorest 20 percent of households has declined steadily since the early 1970s. Meanwhile, the income of the richest 20 percent has increased by 15 percent and that of the top 1 percent by more than 100 percent. In Asia, the high concentrations of wealth and power produced by strong growth have been given a new label: crony capitalism. In Russia and Eastern Europe, the end of communism has brought huge income gaps. In Latin America, wealth and income gaps—already the highest in the world in the 1970s—widened dramatically in the 1980s, a decade of no growth and high inflation, and have continued to increase even with the resumption of growth in the 1990s.

At the global level, it seems that the old saw is still correct: The rich get richer and the poor get children. The ratio of average income of the richest country in the world to that of the poorest has risen from about 9 to 1 at the end of the nineteenth century to at least 60 to 1 today. That is, the average family in the United States is 60 times richer than the average family in Ethiopia. Since 1950, the portion of the world's population living in poor countries grew by about 250 percent, while in rich countries the population increased by less than 50 percent. Today, 80 percent of the world's population lives in countries that generate only 20 percent of the world's total income (see charts on next page).

Ironically, inequality is growing at a time when the triumph of democracy and open markets was supposed to usher in a new age of freedom and opportunity. In

NANCY BIRDSALL *is executive vice-president of the Inter-American Development Bank.*

fact, both developments seem to be having the opposite effect. At the end of the twentieth century, Karl Marx's screed against capitalism has metamorphosed into post-Marxist angst about an integrated global market that creates a new divide between well-educated élite workers and their vulnerable unskilled counterparts, gives capital an apparent whip hand over labor, and pushes governments to unravel social safety nets. Meanwhile, the spread of democracy has made more visible the problem of income gaps, which can no longer be blamed on poor politics—not on communism in Eastern Europe and the former Soviet Union nor on military authoritarianism in Latin America. Regularly invoked as the handmaiden of open markets, democracy looks more and more like their accomplice in a vicious circle of inequality and injustice.

Technology plays a central role in the drama of inequality, and it seems to be making the situation worse, not better. The television and the airplane made income gaps more visible, but at least the falling costs and increasing accessibility of communication and transportation reduced actual differences in living standards. The computer, however, represents a whole new production process and creates a world in which the scarce commodities commanding the highest economic returns are information and skills. As information technology spreads (see chart "Unplugged: The Rich and the Poor of the Information Age"), will some fundamental transformation take place that permanently favors an agile and educated minority? Or are we simply in the midst of a prolonged transition, analogous to the one that fooled Marx, to a postindustrial world with an expanded information age middle class?

In fact, postwar progress toward free trade and free politics has been dominated by the expectation of "convergence"—that those now lagging behind, whether nations or groups within nations, will inevitably catch up. But what happens if that expectation fails to materialize? How would the end of convergence affect conduct among nations? Can open and democratic societies endure the strains of high inequality? Will inequality become a lightning rod for dangerous populist rhetoric and self-defeating isolation? Even as we talk of disappearing national borders, is the worldwide phenomenon of inequality creating instead a new set of global rifts?

WHAT ARE THE FACTS?

In the United States, where the impact of global integration and the information revolution is probably the most widespread, the facts are sobering. Income inequality in the United States is increasing, not only because of gains at the top, but more disturbingly, because of losses at the bottom (see box on next page). The average wage of white male high-school graduates fell 15 percent from 1973 to 1993, and the number of men aged 25 to 54 years earning less than $10,000 a year grew. Possibly for the first time in the nation's history, educational gains may be reinforcing rather than offsetting income inequality: Higher education has become a prerequisite for economic success, but because access to it depends on family income, the poor are at a distinct disadvantage.

Elsewhere, the forces of change—whether the spread of capitalism and global integration, or simply the march of technological progress—have at best reinforced, or at worst exacerbated, high inequality. In Latin America, the ratio of income of the top 20 percent of earners to the bottom is about 16 to 1 (almost 25 to 1 in Brazil, probably the world's most unequal country, compared with about 10 to 1 in the United States and about 5 to 1 in Western Europe). The wage gap between the skilled and the unskilled increased in this decade by more than 30 percent in Peru, 20 percent in Colombia, and nearly 25 percent in Mexico. Ironically, these were the countries with the greatest wage increases.

The situation is less clear but no more heartening in other parts of the world. In China, the liberalization of agricultural and other markets has spurred growth, yet large segments of the population have been left behind. In the affluent countries of northern Europe, increases in poor immigrant populations, growing unemployment, and the stricter fiscal demands of the Maastricht Treaty are undermining the historic commitment of these nations to address inequality.

Economic growth (and for that matter lack of growth) in the postwar era has seemed everywhere to be accompanied by persistent, often high, and sometimes worsening, inequality within countries. The few exceptions include Hong Kong, Korea,

Malaysia, Singapore, Taiwan, and Thailand in East Asia—where several decades of extraordinarily high growth saw low and even declining levels of inequality. Even when income distribution does improve, it does so painfully slowly. A study that examined income distribution in 45 countries found that only eight, including Japan and three European nations, showed any improvement in income distribution over any time period, and this progress was minimal.

The idea of convergence of income across countries— that poor countries will ultimately catch up to the rich— has also gone by the wayside. China and India illustrate the difficulties of arguing for the eventual convergence in income of poor and rich countries. For the last 15 years, these two nations have experienced faster income growth than the rich countries, yet it would take them almost a century of constant growth at rates higher than those in today's industrialized countries just to reach current U.S. income levels.

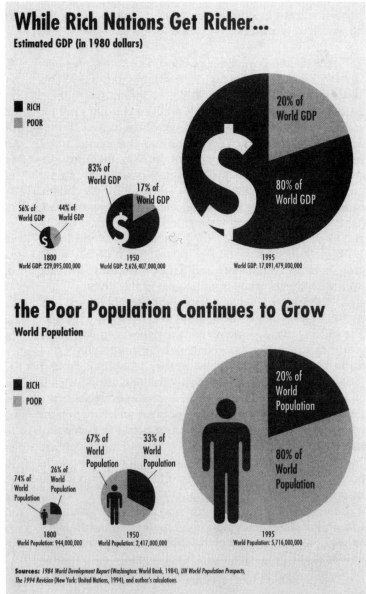

While Rich Nations Get Richer...

Estimated GDP (in 1980 dollars)

■ RICH
▨ POOR

56% of World GDP / 44% of World GDP
1800
World GDP: 229,095,000,000

83% of World GDP / 17% of World GDP
1950
World GDP: 2,626,407,000,000

20% of World GDP / 80% of World GDP
1995
World GDP: 17,091,479,000,000

the Poor Population Continues to Grow

World Population

■ RICH
▨ POOR

74% of World Population / 26% of World Population
1800
World Population: 944,000,000

67% of World Population / 33% of World Population
1950
World Population: 2,417,000,000

20% of World Population / 80% of World Population
1995
World Population: 5,716,000,000

Sources: *1984 World Development Report* (Washington: World Bank, 1984), *UN World Population Prospects, The 1994 Revision* (New York: United Nations, 1994), and author's calculations.

WHAT MAKES THE WORLD UNFAIR?

Inequality is nobody's fault and cannot be fixed in our lifetime. Understanding its causes helps us determine what can be done about it and what might actually make it worse. But what are the causes of inequality across and within countries?

History

Inequality begets inequality. Therefore, history matters. Consider Latin America. The combination of mineral wealth, soils and climate suitable for sugar production, and imported slave labor, or conquered indigenous labor, helped produce two castes: large landowners and politically unarmed workers. In 1950, just 1.5 percent of farm owners in Latin America accounted for 65 percent of all agricultural land; unequal land distribution, then the highest in the world, has risen since. Wealth in natural resources invited concentration of income. History and politics subsequently conspired to produce economic and institutional arrangements that have perpetuated that concentration.

The Poor's Rational Decisions

A source of some inequality lies in predictable human behavior. Because the rich and educated marry each other, as do the poor and uneducated, family income gaps widen. Rational differences in human behavior between the rich and the poor also add to inequality. In many countries, the poor are members of ethnic or racial groups. If they suffer discrimination in the labor market, their gains from schooling and job skills are small, prompting them to respond by investing little in these income-producing assets. But by handicapping their children economically, the sum of these parents' sensible decisions can lock society as a whole into another generation of inequality.

The same happens with fertility. For good reasons, the poor and the less educated tend to have more children. As is to be expected in these poor households, spending per child on nutrition, health, and education declines with the number of children. Less spending on the children of the poor creates a new generation in which the number of unskilled workers grows faster than skilled workers, bringing down wages for the former and thus perpetuating the cycle. In societies with high population growth (Africa, for example), the education levels of mothers are a major determinant of fertility rates. As poorly educated mothers have many more children than their well-educated sisters, the cycle of high fertility and poor opportunities for their children continues, helping perpetuate inequality in their societies.

East Asia provides an example of how fertility change can break this vicious cycle. A dramatic decline in infant mortality in the region after World War II was followed in the early 1960s by an equally dramatic, and very rapid, decline in fertility—which spread quickly to the poor and less educated. These changes had major demographic consequences: In Korea, for example, the percent of the population in the prime working ages of 25 to 59 rose from less than 35 percent to close to 50 percent between 1965 and 1990, while the percent of children between ages 0 and 14 fell. With this demographic growth in the work force came dramatic increases in

---

The Not-So-Great Leveler

Income inequality has been worsening in the United States since the early 1970s. Before 1973, all groups enjoyed healthy income gains, particularly the middle class. However, since 1979, the rich have gained far more than the middle class, while the income of the poor has fallen in absolute terms.

A recent study found that the richest 1 percent of families (average annual income: $800,000 for a family of four) captured 70 percent of the total rise in family income in the United States between 1977 and 1989.

America has always been considered a land of opportunity, where parents believe in the possibility of a "better life" for their children. Does upward mobility mean growing inequality is unimportant, since, with effort and a bit of luck, those at the bottom can still move toward the top?

Not exactly. First of all, we know that historically high rates of mobility in the United States resulted from fast economic growth that was shared across the board. Today, growth benefits the wealthy far more than the middle class, let alone the poor.

Second, although many families do move from one income category to another over time, individuals have suffered larger downward, and smaller upward, income changes since the 1970s—with the exception of the rich, whose earnings have jumped dramatically.

Third, though education has always been seen as the great leveler, it now reinforces initial advantages instead of compensating for initial handicaps. Because most elementary and secondary schools fail to provide students with basic skills, they no longer effectively make up for deep inequalities among children—in terms of their home environments, parents' help and expectations, preschool experiences, and out-of-school activities.

In addition, the high-school diploma—once a ticket to the job market for the working class—has lost its value. U.S. employers now insist on a college education as a measure of competence. And the children of the rich have always been more likely to go on to college. In 1995, 83 percent of high-school graduates from the wealthiest families (the top 20 percent of all households) enrolled in college, compared with 34 percent from the poorest (the bottom 20 percent).

So, if America is to remain the land of opportunity, elementary and secondary education must work for the poor. Otherwise, inequality of income will come to reflect not just differences in motivation, work effort, and sheer luck among players in a fair game, but different rules for rich and poor.

—*N.B.*

savings and investment (from about 15 to 35 percent in Korea and Indonesia) that helped fuel growth. Compared with those of other regions, East Asia's private and household savings and investment rates were especially high—including among poor households that invested heavily in the more affordable education of their fewer children.

Prosperity

Prosperity can produce inequality—an outcome that, within limits, may be economically justifiable. After all, some inequality may encourage innovation and hard work. Newfound inequality in China and in the economies of Eastern Europe may simply mean that new economic incentives are not only inducing growth but also creating opportunities for some individuals to excel and profit.

But the market reforms that bring prosperity also may not give all players an equal shot at the prize. In the short run, privatization and public-sector downsizing will penalize some workers; and open trade, because it hurts formerly protected industries and makes their inefficiencies unsustainable, can lead to wage reductions and higher unemployment. If corruption infects the privatization process, as in Russia, such reforms will provide windfalls to insiders. More insidious for the poor over the long run are the effects of reforms on the value of assets. During the Latin American debt crisis of the 1980s, many high-income citizens of indebted countries were able to store most of their financial assets abroad, even as their governments (and thus, their fellow taxpayers) assumed the bad debts incurred by enterprises either owned or controlled by the rich. Today's lower inflation and more realistic exchange rates mean dollar accounts held abroad can now buy more at home. Similarly, well-connected individuals in emerging markets who had previously profited from cheap credit, subsidized prices for hard foreign currency, or government regulatory exceptions (say, on the use of urban land) benefited again, as economic reforms raised the market value of assets that they had been able to acquire at low cost.

Bad Economic Policy

The most avoidable and thus most disappointing source of inequality are policies that hamper economic growth and fuel inflation—the most devastating outcome of all for the poor. Most populist programs designed to attract the political support of the working class hurt workers in the long run. When financed by unsustainable fiscal largesse, they bring the inflation or high interest rates that exacerbate inequality. Inflation worsens inequality because the poor are forced to hold money and cannot acquire the debts that inflation devalues. High interest rates, driven by unsustainable public debt, crowd out investments and jobs in small and medium enterprises, while encouraging easy gains in government bonds for those with plenty of money. Price controls, usually imposed on the products most consumed by the poor, often

lead to their disappearance from stores, as they are hoarded and resold at higher prices. The imposition of a minimum wage temporarily benefits those who have formal jobs but makes it harder for the unemployed to find work. Finally, regulatory privileges, trade protection, and special access to cheap credit and foreign exchange—all bad economic policies—will inevitably increase the profits of a wealthy minority. For all these reasons, IMF-style reforms, often attacked for hurting the poor majority, are key to ending corrupt practices that usually benefit only a few.

Bad policy also includes what governments fail to do. Failure to invest in the education and skills of the poor is a fundamental cause of inequality. When adequate education does not reach enough of any population, educated workers become scarce, and employers compete for them by offering higher wages. The widening wage gap between college graduates and others in the United States indicates that the demand for graduates still exceeds the supply, feeding inequality. In Brazil, during the 1970s, the salaries of scarce university graduates rose rapidly, worsening wage inequality. In contrast, wage differences in Korea between those with university education and their less-educated colleagues fell, as more and more students completed secondary school and attended universities. In fact, above-average spending on education characterizes each of the few countries that have managed high growth with low inequality in the postwar period.

TEMPTING AND DANGEROUS REMEDIES

Paradoxically, the rhetoric of fairness can encourage policies that worsen global and local inequalities. Some examples of these self-defeating policies include:

Protectionism

Protection from global competition is a dangerous nonremedy, whether it involves import barriers, high import tariffs, or currency controls. Developing countries that have been most open to trade have had the fastest growth, reducing global inequality; those least integrated into global markets, such as many African economies, have remained among the world's poorest. Historically, the same pattern holds. Those countries that aggressively sought commercial links to the outside world—Japan, beginning in the Meiji Era, and the East Asian countries after World War II—whether via technology licensing, openness to foreign investment or an export push, have had the fastest growth. Trade (along with mass migration) explains most of the convergence in income among the countries of Europe and between them and the United States in the late nineteenth century. Convergence of incomes in Europe stalled as economic links disintegrated from 1914 to 1950 and then resumed in force in the postwar period, when European economies became more integrated.

But does global integration create worsening inequality within countries, rich and poor alike? The growing wage gap in the United States coincides with increasing imports from developing countries that have large pools of unskilled labor. But most research shows that technology is more to blame than trade for most of the U.S. wage gap: Few U.S. workers (probably less than 5 percent) are in industries competing with low-wage goods from developing countries, and the wages of workers without a high-school diploma have fallen as much if not more in nontrade as in trade industries. True, more subtle forces are also at play—for example, the ability of firms to threaten to move jobs overseas may be undermining American unions. But a recourse to protectionism would almost surely hurt poor consumers more than it would help low-skilled workers.

Growing wage inequality is associated with increased trade and integration into global markets even in developing countries. One reason: Foreign capital inflows and higher domestic capital investment create new jobs for skilled workers, and skilled workers' wages then rise faster than average wages. But the bottom line is that international trade and open markets are less of a problem than worldwide changes in the technology of production that favor skilled workers everywhere.

Indeed, increases in trade and economic integration in poor countries, though associated with high wage inequality, may actually reduce inequality of income and consumption. There are two possible reasons: First, as obstacles to imports fall and price competition intensifies, prices drop—a boon for the poor, who use most of their income for consumption. Second, trade liberalization and open markets in general weaken the unfair advantages enjoyed by the rich and connected,

undermining the economic privileges and monopolies (reflected in wealth not wage gaps) that otherwise perpetuate high inequality.

Special Worker Entitlements

President Franklin Roosevelt's New Deal legislation set countrywide wage rates and labor standards for U.S. workers during the 1930s depression. Could a global minimum wage and global labor standards force up wages of the unskilled in poor countries, reducing in-country and worldwide wage gaps?

Advocates of a global New Deal have a point: Property rights remain elaborately protected in the complex codes of international trade agreements, while labor rights remain unacknowledged. Almost all countries can agree on some standards of behavior: the prohibition of slavery and debt bondage, assurance of a reasonable measure of safety in the workplace, a guarantee of rights to collective bargaining. The problem is that in developing countries, even standards that look noncontroversial (the prohibition of child labor, for example) may hurt those they are meant to protect. Most standards, including collective bargaining rights, which might increase wages in some firms, would affect only the usually small proportion of workers in the formal urban sector, thus increasing the gap between them and the majority of workers in rural and informal jobs. This result might do little harm if it helped a few without hurting others. But harm to many is likely because higher labor costs would then induce employers to invest in labor-saving technologies. The loss of new jobs would hurt mostly the poor and unskilled, whose main asset, after all, is their own labor.

Weaker infrastructure, unreliable judicial and regulatory regimes, and less education mean workers in developing countries produce less—even in well-equipped export firms. A global New Deal will only work when it is no longer needed: that is, when development progress in poor countries brings worker productivity—now as low as one-third the U.S. level—much closer to rich country levels. Only with convergence of worker productivity (and worker pay) across and within nations—as was the case across the United States in Roosevelt's time—could global rules on workers' rights help rather than hurt those now worse off.

Underpricing Public Services

For decades, governments have monopolized delivery of such public services as water, sanitation, electricity, and health care. They have also charged industries and households much less for these services than they actually cost—all in the name of helping the poor. Mountains of evidence demonstrate two virtually universal results:

First, in the face of any scarcity at all, prices that are too low reduce public supply of the underpriced

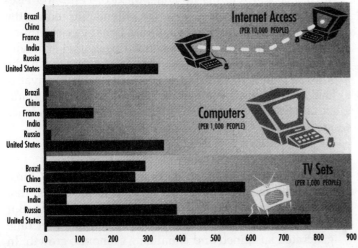

Unplugged: The Rich and Poor of the Information Age

Internet Access (PER 10,000 PEOPLE)

Brazil
China
France
India
Russia
United States

Computers (PER 1,000 PEOPLE)

Brazil
China
France
India
Russia
United States

TV Sets (PER 1,000 PEOPLE)

Brazil
China
France
India
Russia
United States

0 100 200 300 400 500 600 700 800 900

Source: 1997 World Development Indicators (Washington: World Bank, 1997).

service. India's public resources will never be sufficient to cover hospital care for its entire population. Short of privatization and adequate meter-based customer charges, electricity services in cities such as Lagos and Karachi will never catch up to demand, and "brownouts" (scheduled times without electricity) will continue.

Second, in the face of any kind of rationing, the poor will be last in line. The guarantee of free university education in Egypt and France, for example, is a false entitlement: Low-income families cannot afford the secondary schooling and tutoring needed to pass the university admissions test. In the Philippines, cheap electricity and water are available to powerful industrial interests, while the poor in the slums rely on jerrybuilt connections and buy bottled water at high prices from private trucks. In Mexico, for decades, general food subsidies benefited the urban middle class and created the incentives for food producers to bribe the politicians and government officials who controlled allocation of these subsidies. Meanwhile, the poor in rural areas and indigenous communities received little if any benefit.

Laissez-Faire Economics

Because trade protection, worker rights, and cheap public services can in fact hurt the poor does not mean the inequality problem can be left to the market. It is one mistake for government to restrict and distort market activity, reducing competition and perpetuating privileges; it is another to assume that market forces will automatically create opportunities for those at the margin.

Every society has some interest in avoiding the worst forms of inequality and injustice. That means in every society there is a role for government—not only to avoid the creation of unfair advantages for the rich and powerful, but to guarantee equal opportunities that market forces will naturally neglect, especially for those individuals who will otherwise be left on the sidelines. But this brings us to the question of what does work.

WHAT DOES WORK

The false remedies have short-run political appeal. Unfortunately, what does work takes time and patience.

Worker-Based Growth

Economic growth that is based on the intensive use of labor reduces income inequality—within as well as across countries. Oil-rich countries such as Venezuela and Nigeria have grown quickly at times, but the advantages of oil, bauxite, copper, and other mineral wealth can be short-lived. An abundance of natural resources invites concentration of income and discourages reliance on people, technology, and skills. Lack of natural resources, meanwhile, can be a hidden blessing, as the sustained and equitable growth of Switzerland and Hong Kong show. The labor-using growth of Taiwan and Singapore has reduced income gaps in those economies and propelled their convergence toward industrial-country income levels over the last three decades.

Worker-based growth is best encouraged by avoiding the wrong policies—those that directly or indirectly raise employers' cost of labor. In countries such as Costa Rica and Ghana, where agriculture is labor-using and generates exports, the correction of overvalued exchange rates (which make imports cheaper for urban consumers) has increased rural jobs and income. In England, and now in Venezuela, relaxation of onerous severance-pay rules has encouraged hiring, inducing employers to substitute people and skills for energy and environmentally costly production inputs. The United States could also encourage more hiring of unskilled workers by reducing payroll tax rates and raising the threshold at which these rates are applied.

Education: The People's Asset

In the increasingly service-oriented global economy, education and skills represent a kind of wealth. They are key assets—and once acquired cannot be taken away, even from those who are otherwise powerless. Moreover, as education is shared more broadly, other assets such as land, stocks, or money will become less important.

It should be no surprise that the best predictor of a child's education is her parents' education and income. The poor, especially in developing countries, are last in line for education, as well as other publicly financed services. (Among 13 industrialized countries studied, only in Sweden and the Netherlands have educational opportunities become less stratified by socioeconomic class during this century.) So without a jump-start from public policy, the rich will become educated and stay rich, and the poor will not, perpetuating the inequality of assets and income across generations. In the United States, Europe, and in today's poor developing countries, the single best weapon against income equality is educating the poor.

Other mechanisms to distribute and redistribute assets, including land reform and microcredit programs, can also improve the pattern by which income is distributed. Pension reforms in Chile, Mexico, Peru, and elsewhere in Latin America have the potential to reduce the disequalizing characteristics of traditional pay-as-you-go systems and to create stakeholders in a market economy among those once excluded from its benefits. In the United States, the current arguments against "privatizing" social security reflect in part the myth that traditional systems are highly redistributive. Much evidence suggests that this is not necessarily true.

Democracy

Relatively low levels of income inequality in China, Cuba, and the former Soviet Union seem to suggest that authoritarian politics can at least produce equality. But in fact, it is the Western democracies that have over time generated sustained and equalizing economic growth. In economically unequal societies, the one-person, one-vote system can offset the ability of the economically powerful to perpetuate their privileges by buying political power. Perhaps this is why the market today sees greater risk of social disorder fed by political privilege in Indonesia than in its more democratic neighbors, such as Thailand and Korea. In today's global market, good politics is good for equalizing growth.

Opportunities, Not Transfers

Although transfers and income subsidies to help the poor or reduce inequality make sense on paper, they are not long-run solutions. As declining spending on income-tied welfare programs in the United States shows, transfers and subsidies tied to low income are politically difficult to sustain. In fact, because the poor tend to be less organized and politically effective, redistributive programs often respond to more vocal entrenched interests, transforming these initiatives into a regressive tax rather than a safety net. For example, Senegal's program to cushion the effects of its economic reforms channeled state money to privileged groups within the system (civil servants and university graduates), while doing nothing to protect the urban and rural poor from rising consumer prices and unemployment. Often, even those subsidies originally meant for the poor are quickly captured by the middle class and the rich, as ample public spending on university education in California suggests. Finally, the taxes that pay for large transfer programs are increasingly regressive. Because global competition puts pressure on governments to reduce taxes on footloose capital and highly mobile skilled labor, workers and consumers must bear more of the tax burden associated with redistributive transfers, mainly in the form of growing payroll and sales taxes.

Public spending for the poor is more effective in the long run and politically more attractive when it enhances opportunities. But for such public spending to be effective, two rules must prevail: First, spending should concentrate on programs that reach everyone but benefit the poor most—in the United States, secondary education, child care, and immunizations. Second, the poor's access to opportunities should be improved not by directly providing services, but by giving them tax breaks and vouchers for school, health, and housing, which would help them become effective consumers. In Chile, public spending on universal services and on voucher-like programs ensures that more than 80 percent of all public health-care services and 60 percent of all education services go to the poorest 40 percent of household—raising the total income of the poorest one-fifth of households by nearly 50 percent.

Strengthen Domestic Policies for Global Integration

It bears repeating that the poorest countries of the world are those least integrated into global markets; the facts are so obvious that most poor developing countries have joined the bandwagon of unilateral trade opening. Since global markets reward skilled over unskilled labor, poor countries are adjusting to their growing wage inequality by increasing spending on education and training.

Then again, industrial countries are highly integrated among themselves but still relatively closed to poor country products and services. Rich countries could significantly ease global inequality by lifting their barriers to imports of agriculture and manufactured textiles. But progress against protection often implies visible short-run costs to communities and workers. Programs to retrain those workers hurt by opening markets in rich countries, and to top up their wages if they accept a lower-paying job, would reduce income inequality at home and indirectly around the world.

LEARNING TO LIVE WITH INEQUALITY

Any hopes for a quick fix to inequality are misplaced. Belying Marx, the biggest story of the last 150 years has been the emergence in the West of a prosperous and stable middle class. But it took time. During a long transition from agriculture to industry, changes in production and in the structure of employment caused wrenching inequality. Much inequality today may be the natural outcome of what is an analogous transition from an industrial to an information age.

Still, there is no reason to despair. Some inequality is healthy and will speed the transition. The rapidly growing wages of the educated and skilled are making education and training much more attractive personal investments. As more people get greater access to education, their relative income advantage over the unskilled will decline. Meanwhile, the high cost of skilled workers should eventually induce technological change that relies more on unskilled labor, increasing the demand for workers with less training.

More fundamentally, people may care less about their current ranking in a static picture of global income distribution than about just and fair access to a better future, especially for their children. In an unequal world, good opportunities represent fair rules and matter at least as much as current status. Greater opportunities—which can be delivered today—are a better guarantee of a socially coherent global community than improved distribution tomorrow.

The real danger is that growing inequality may become a lightning rod for populist rhetoric and self-defeating isolation. It would be unfortunate if such tempting but false remedies eclipsed the more promising policies—international and domestic—that can help the world manage the long transition to a less-divided postindustrial future.

WANT TO KNOW MORE?

For a thoughtful treatment of equity issues, consult Gosta Esping-Andersen's *The Three Worlds of Welfare*

Capitalism (Princeton: Princeton University Press, 1990). For a discussion of convergence—whether poor countries are catching up to their rich counterparts—see Jeffrey Williamson's **"Globalization, Convergence, and History"** (*Journal of Economic History,* June 1996) and Lant Pritchett's **"Forget Convergence: Divergence, Past, Present, and Future"** (*Finance and Development,* June 1996). Covering it all in a tour de force is David Landes' *The Wealth and Poverty of Nations* (New York: W.W. Norton & Company, 1998). Readers interested in more on inequality in the United States should see Daniel McMurrer and Isabel Sawhill's *Getting Ahead: Economic and Social Mobility in America* (Washington: Urban Institute Press, 1998) and Paul Krugman's **"The Right, the Rich, and the Facts: Deconstructing the Income Distribution Debate"** (*American Prospect,* Fall 1992). For more on income inequality in other parts of the world, refer to Michael Bruno, Martin Ravallion, and Lyn Squire's working paper, *Equity and Growth in Developing Countries: Old and New Perspectives on the Policy Issues* (Washington: World Bank, 1996) and Nancy Birdsall, David Ross, and Richard Sabot's **"Inequality and Growth Reconsidered: Lessons from East Asia"** (*World Bank Economic Review,* September 1995). For essays on reconciling growth and equity objectives, see Birdsall, Sabot, and Carol Graham, eds., *Beyond Trade-Offs: Market Reforms and Equitable Growth in Latin America* (Washington: Brookings Institution and Inter-American Development Bank, 1998, forthcoming). For views on the impact of trade on wage inequality and income distribution, consult William Cline's *Trade and Income Distribution* (Washington: Institute for International Economics, 1997); Dani Rodrik's *Has Globalization Gone Too Far?* (Washington: Institute for International Economics, 1997); Adrian Wood's *North-South Trade, Employment & Inequality* (Cambridge: Oxford University Press, 1995); and Ethan Kapstein's *"Workers and the World Economy"* (*Foreign Affairs,* May/June 1996). For perspectives on child labor, consult Christiaan Grootaert and Ravi Kanbur's *Child Labor, A Review* (Washington: World Bank, 1995). Finally, Estelle James offers the single best assessment of pension systems in *Averting the Old Age Crisis* (Washington: World Bank, 1994) and Martin Feldstein argues for individual accounts in **"The Pension Crisis: The Case for Privatization"** (*Foreign Affairs,* July/August 1997).

"The major international schisms of the twenty-first century will not always be definable in geographic terms. Many of the most severe and persistent threats to global peace and stability are arising not from conflicts between major political entities but from increased discord within states, societies, and civilizations along ethnic, racial, religious, linguistic, caste, or class lines. This is not to say the traditional geopolitical divisions no longer play a role in world security affairs. But it does suggest that such divisions may have been superseded in importance by the new global schisms."

Redefining Security:
The New Global Schisms

MICHAEL T. KLARE

Geopolitical boundaries—notably those separating rival powers and major military blocs—have constituted the principal "fault lines" of international politics during much of the twentieth century. Throughout the cold war, the world's greatest concentrations of military strength were to be found along such key dividing lines as the Iron Curtain between East and West in Europe and the demilitarized zone between North and South Korea.

When the cold war ended, many of these boundaries quickly lost their geopolitical significance. With the reunification of Germany and the breakup of the Soviet Union, the divide between East and West in Europe ceased to have any meaning. Other key boundaries—for example, the demilitarized zone in Korea—retained their strategic importance, but elsewhere thousands of miles of previously fortified frontier became open borders with a minimal military presence. The strategic alliances associated with these divisions also lost much of their prominence: the Warsaw Treaty Organization was eliminated altogether, while NATO was given new roles and missions in order to forestall a similar fate.

MICHAEL T. KLARE *is a professor of peace and world security studies at Hampshire College and director of the Five College Program in Peace and World Security Studies. He is the author of* Rogue States and Nuclear Outlaws: America's Search for a New Foreign Policy *(New York: Hill and Wang, 1995).*

BATTLE LINES OF THE FUTURE

The changes associated with the cold war's end have been so dramatic and profound that it is reasonable to question whether traditional assumptions regarding the nature of global conflict will continue to prove reliable in the new, post–cold war era. In particular, one could question whether conflicts between states (or groups of states) will remain the principal form of international strife, and whether the boundaries between them will continue to constitute the world's major fault lines. Certainly the outbreak of ethnonationalist conflict in the former Yugoslavia and several other former communist states has focused fresh attention on internal warfare, as has the persistence of tribal and religious strife in such countries as Afghanistan, Burundi, Liberia, Rwanda, Somalia, Sri Lanka, and Sudan.

Nevertheless, traditional concepts retain great currency among security analysts. Although the Iron Curtain has disappeared, it is argued, similar schisms of a geographic or territorial nature will arise to take its place. Indeed, several theories have been advanced positing the likely location of these schisms.

Some analysts contend that the territorial schisms of earlier periods—notably those produced by military competition among the major powers—will be revived in the years ahead. Professor Kenneth Waltz of the University of California at Berkeley suggests that such competition will eventually reappear, with Germany, Japan, or some other rising power such as China building its military strength in order to contest America's global paramounty. "Countries have always competed for wealth and security, and the competition has often led to conflict," he wrote in *International Security*'s summer 1993 issue. "Why should the future be different from the past?"

More novel, perhaps, is the suggestion that the principal schisms of the post–cold war era are to be found along the peripheries of the world's great civilizations: Western (including Europe and North America), Slavic-Orthodox (including Russia, Ukraine, and Serbia), Japanese, Islamic, Confucian (China), Latin American, and African. First propounded by Harvard's Samuel Huntington in the summer 1993 issue of *Foreign Affairs,* this argument holds that the economic and ideological antagonisms of the nineteenth and twentieth centuries will be superseded in the twenty-first by antagonisms over culture and cultural identity. "Nation-states will remain the most powerful actors in world affairs," Huntington wrote, "but the principal conflicts of global politics will occur between nations and groups of different civilizations." Although the boundaries between civilizations are not as precise as those between sovereign states, he noted, these loose frontiers will be the site of major conflict. "The clash of civilizations will dominate global politics. The fault lines between civilizations will be the battle lines of the future."

Others have argued that the world's future fault lines will fall not between the major states or civilizations, but between the growing nexus of democratic, market-oriented societies and those "holdout" states that have eschewed democracy or defied the world community in other ways. Such "pariah" states or "rogue" powers are said to harbor aggressive inclinations, to support terrorism, and to seek the production of nuclear or chemical weapons. "[We] must face the reality of recalcitrant and outlaw states that not only choose to remain outside the family [of nations] but also to assault its basic values," wrote President Clinton's national security adviser, Anthony Lake, in the March–April 1994 *Foreign Affairs.* Lake placed several nations in this category—Cuba, North Korea, Iran, Iraq, and Libya—and other writers have added Sudan and Syria. But while there is disagreement about which of these states might actually fall into the "outlaw" category, Lake and other proponents of this analysis hold that the United States and its allies must work together to "contain" the rogue states and frustrate their aggressive designs.

While these assessments of the world security environment differ in many of their particulars, they share a common belief that the "battle lines of the future" (to use Huntington's expression) will fall along geographically defined boundaries, with the contending powers (and their friends and allies) arrayed on opposite sides. This, in turn, leads to similar policy recommendations that generally entail the maintenance of sufficient military strength by the United States to defeat any potential adversary or combination of adversaries.

It is certainly understandable that many analysts have proceeded from traditional assumptions regarding the nature of conflict when constructing models of future international relations, but it is not at all apparent that such assessments will prove reliable. While a number of crises since the end of the cold war appear to have followed one of the three models described, many have not. Indeed, the most intense conflicts of the current period—including those in Algeria, Angola, Bosnia, Burma, Burundi, Haiti, Kashmir, Liberia, Rwanda, Somalia, Sri Lanka, and Sudan—cannot be fully explained using these models. Moreover, other forms of contemporary violence—terrorism, racial and religious strife, gang warfare, violence against women, and criminal violence—have shown no respect for geography or civilizational identity whatsoever, erupting in virtually every corner of the world.

THE THREAT FROM WITHIN

A fresh assessment of the world security environment suggests that the major international schisms of the twenty-first century will not always be definable in geographic terms. Many of the most severe and persistent threats to global peace and stability are arising not from conflicts between major political entities but from increased discord within states, societies, and civilizations along ethnic, racial, religious, linguistic, caste, or class lines.

The intensification and spread of internal discord is a product of powerful stresses on human communities everywhere. These stresses—economic, demographic, sociological, and environmental—are exacerbating the existing divisions within societies and creating entirely new ones. As a result, we are seeing the emergence of new or deepened fissures across international society, producing multiple outbreaks of intergroup hostility and violence. These cleavages cannot be plotted on a normal map, but can be correlated with other forms of data: economic performance, class stratification, population growth, ethnic and religious composition, environmental deterioration, and so on. Where certain conditions prevail—a widening gulf between rich and poor, severe economic competition between neighboring ethnic and religious communities, the declining habitability of marginal lands—internal conflict is likely to erupt.

This is not to say that traditional geopolitical divisions no longer play a role in world security affairs. But it does suggest that such divisions may have been superseded in importance by the new global schisms.

FOR RICHER
AND POORER: THE WIDENING GAP

The world has grown much richer over the past 25 years. According to the Worldwatch Institute, the world's total annual income rose from $10.1 trillion in 1970 to approximately $20 trillion in 1994 (in constant 1987 dollars). This increase has been accompanied by an improved standard of living for many of the world's peoples. But not all nations, and not all people in the richer nations, have benefited from the global increase in wealth: some countries, mostly concentrated in Africa and Latin America, have experienced a net decline in gross domestic product over the past few decades, while many of the countries that have achieved a higher GDP have experienced an increase in the number of people living in extreme poverty.

SOURCES OF HUMAN INSECURITY

Income	1.3 billion people in developing countries live in poverty; 200 million people live below the poverty line in industrial countries.
Clean Water	1.3 billion people in developing countries do not have access to safe water.
Literacy	900 million adults worldwide are illiterate.
Food	800 million people in developing countries have inadequate food supplies; 500 million of this number of chronically malnourished, and 175 million are under the age of five.
Housing	500 million urban dwellers worldwide are homeless or do not have adequate housing; 100 million young people are homeless.
Preventable Death	Between 15 million and 20 million people die annually because of starvation or disease aggravated by malnutrition; 10 million people die each year because of substandard housing, unsafe water, or poor sanitation in densely populated cities.

Source: Adapted from Michael Renner, *Fighting for Survival: Environmental Decline, Social Conflict, and the New Age of Insecurity.* (New York: Norton, 1996), p. 81.

Furthermore, the gap in national income between the richest and the poorest nations continues to increase, as does the gap between rich and poor people within most societies.

These differentials in economic growth rates, along with the widening gap between rich and poor, are producing dangerous fissures in many societies. As the masses of poor see their chances of escaping acute poverty diminish, they are likely to become increasingly resentful of those whose growing wealth is evident. This resentment is especially pronounced in the impoverished shantytowns that surround many of the seemingly prosperous cities of the third world. In these inhospitable surroundings, large numbers of people—especially among the growing legions of unemployed youth—are being attracted to extremist political movements like the Shining Path of Peru and the Islamic Salvation Front of Algeria, or to street gangs and drug-trafficking syndicates. The result is an increase in urban crime and violence.

Deep economic cleavages are also emerging in China and the postcommunist states of Eastern Europe and the former Soviet Union. Until the recent introduction of market reforms in these countries, the financial gap between rich and poor was kept relatively narrow by state policy, and such wealth as did exist among the bureaucratic elite was kept well hidden from public view. With the onset of capitalism the economic plight of the lowest strata of these societies has become considerably worse, while the newly formed entrepreneurial class has been able to accumulate considerable wealth—and to display it in highly conspicuous ways. This has generated new class tensions and provided ammunition for those who, like Gennadi Zyuganov of Russia's reorganized Communist Party, seek the restoration of the old, state-dominated system.

Equally worrisome is the impact of growing income differentials on intergroup relations in multiethnic societies. In most countries the divide between rich and poor is not the only schism that matters: of far greater significance are the divisions between various strata of the poor and lower middle class. When such divisions coincide with ethnic or religious differences—that is, when one group of poor people finds itself to be making less economic progress than a similar group of a different ethnic composition—the result is likely to be increased ethnic antagonisms and, at the extreme, increased intergroup violence. This is evident in Pakistan, where violent gang warfare in Karachi has been fueled by economic competition between the indigenous inhabitants of the surrounding region and several waves of Muslim immigrants from India and Bangladesh; it is also evident in Sri Lanka, where efforts by the Sinhalese to deny employment opportunities to the Tamils helped spark a deadly civil war.

KINDLING ETHNIC STRIFE

According to information assembled by the Stockholm International Peace Research Institute (SIPRI), ethnic and religious strife figured prominently in all but 3 of the 31 major armed conflicts under way in 1994. And while several long-running ethnic and sectarian conflicts have subsided in recent years, most analysts believe that such strife is likely to erupt repeatedly in the years ahead.

It is true that many recent ethnic and religious conflicts have their roots in clashes or invasions that occurred years ago. It is also true that the violent upheavals that broke out in the former Yugoslavia and the former Soviet Union drew upon deep-seated ethnic hostilities, even if these cleavages were not generally visible during much of the communist era (when overt displays of ethnic antagonism were prohibited by government decree). In this sense, the ethnic fissures that are now receiving close attention from international policymakers are not really new phenomena. Nevertheless, many of these schisms have become more pronounced since the end of the cold war, or have exhibited characteristics that are unique to the current era.

Greatly contributing to the intensity of recent ethnic and religious strife is the erosion or even disappearance of central state authority in poor third world countries experiencing extreme economic, political, and environmental stress. In such countries—especially Burundi, Liberia, Rwanda, Somalia, and Zaire—the flimsy state structures established after independence are simply unable to cope with the demands of housing and feeding their growing populations with the meager resources at hand. In such circumstances people lose all confidence in the state's ability to meet their basic needs and turn instead to more traditional, kinship-based forms of association for help in getting by—a process that often results in competition and conflict among groups over what remains of the nation's scarce resources. This shift in loyalty from the state to group identity is also evident in Bosnia and parts of the former Soviet Union, where various ethnic factions have attempted to seize or divide up the infrastructure (and in some cases the territory) left behind by the communist regime.

Also contributing to the intensity of intergroup conflict in the current era is the spread of mass communications and other instruments of popular mobilization. These advances have contributed to what Professor James Rosenau of George Washington University calls a "skill revolution" in which individual citizens "have become increasingly competent in assessing where they fit in international affairs and how their behavior can be aggregated into significant collective outcomes."[1] This competence can lead to calls for greater personal freedom and democracy. But it can also lead to increased popular mobilization along ethnic, religious, caste, and linguistic lines, often producing great friction and disorder within heterogeneous societies. An important case in point is India, where Hindu nationalists have proved adept at employing modern means of communication and political organization—while retaining traditional symbols and motifs—to encourage anti-Muslim sentiment and thereby erode the authority of India's largely secular government.

DEMOGRAPHIC SCHISMS

According to the most recent UN estimates, total world population is expected to soar from approximately 5.6 billion people in 1994 to somewhere between 8 billion and 12 billion by the year 2050—an increase that will undoubtedly place great strain on the earth's food production and environmental capacity. But the threat to the world's environment and food supply is not all that we have to worry about. Because population growth is occurring unevenly in different areas, with some of the highest rates of growth to be found in countries with the slowest rates of economic growth, future population increases could combine with other factors to exacerbate existing cleavages along ethnic, religious, and class lines.

Overall, the populations of the less-developed countries (LDCS) are growing at a much faster rate than those of the advanced industrial nations. As a result, the share of world

> *Greatly contributing to the intensity of recent ethnic and religious strife is the erosion or even disappearance of central state authority in poor third world countries*

population accounted for by the LDCS rose from 69 percent in 1960 to 74 percent in 1980, and is expected to jump to nearly 80 percent in the year 2000. Among third world countries, moreover, there have been marked variations in the rate of population growth: while the newly industrialized nations of East Asia have experienced a sharp decline in the rate of growth, Africa and parts of the Middle East have experienced an increase. If these trends persist, the global distribution of population will change dramatically over the next few decades, with some areas experiencing a substantial increase in total population and others moderate or even negligible growth.

This is where other factors enter the picture. If the largest increases in population were occurring in areas of rapid economic growth, the many young adults entering the job market each year would be able to find productive employment and would thus be able to feed and house their families. In many cases, however, large increases in population are coinciding with low or stagnant economic growth, meaning that future jobseekers are not likely to find adequate employment. This will have a considerable impact on the world security environment. At the very least, it is likely to produce increased human migration from rural areas (where population growth tends to be greatest) to urban centers (where most new jobs are to be found), and from poor and low-growth countries to more affluent ones. The former process is resulting in the rapid expansion of many third world cities, with an attendant increase in urban crime and intergroup friction (especially where the new urban dwellers are of a different ethnic or tribal group from the original settlers); the latter is producing huge numbers of new immigrants in the developed and high-growth countries, often sparking hostility and sometimes violence from the indigenous populations.

Rapid population growth in poor countries with slow or stagnant economic growth has other implications for world security. In many societies it is leading to the hyperutilization of natural resources, particularly arable soil, grazing lands, forests, and fisheries, a process that severely complicates future economic growth (as vital raw materials are depleted) and accelerates the pace of environmental decline. It can also overwhelm the capacity of weak or divided governments to satisfy their citizens' basic needs, leading eventually to the collapse of states and to the intergroup competition and conflict described earlier. Finally, it could generate fresh international conflicts when states with slow population growth employ stringent measures to exclude immigrants from nearby countries with high rates of growth. While some of this is speculative, early signs of many of these phenomena have been detected. The 1994 United States intervention in Haiti, for instance, was partly motivated by a desire on Washington's part to curb the flow of Haitian "boat people" to the United States.

---

[1]James N. Rosenau, "Security in a Turbulent World," *Current History,* May 1995, p. 194.

ENDANGERED BY ENVIRONMENT

As with massive population growth, the world has been bombarded in recent years with dire predictions about the consequences of further deterioration in the global environment. The continuing buildup of industrial gases in the earth's outer atmosphere, for example, is thought to be impeding the natural radiation of heat from the planet and thereby producing a gradual increase in global temperatures—a process known as "greenhouse warming." If such warming continues, global sea levels will rise, deserts will grow, and severe drought could afflict many important agricultural zones. Other forms of environmental degradation—the thinning of the earth's outer ozone layer, the depletion of arable soil through overcultivation, the persistence of acid rain caused by industrial emissions—could endanger human health and survival in other ways. As with population growth, these environmental effects will not be felt uniformly around the world but will threaten some states and groups more than others, producing new cleavages in human society.

The uneven impact of global environmental decline is being seen in many areas. The first to suffer are invariably those living in marginally habitable areas—arid grazing lands, coastal lowlands, tropical rainforests. As annual rainfall declines, sea levels rise, and forests are harvested, these lands become uninhabitable. The choice, for those living in such areas, is often grim: to migrate to the cities, with all of their attendant problems, or to move onto the lands of neighboring peoples (who may be of a different ethnicity or religion), producing new outbreaks of intergroup violence. This grim choice has fallen with particular severity on indigenous peoples, who in many cases were originally driven into these marginal habitats by more powerful groups. A conspicuous case in point is the Amazon region of Brazil, where systematic deforestation is destroying the habitat and lifestyle of the indigenous peoples and producing death, illness, and unwelcome migration to the cities.

States also vary in their capacity to cope with environmental crisis and the depletion of natural resources. While the wealthier countries can rebuild areas damaged by flooding or other disasters, relocate displaced citizens to safer regions, and import food and other commodities no longer produced locally, the poorer countries are much less capable of doing these things. As noted by Professor Thomas Homer-Dixon of the University of Toronto, "Environmental scarcity sharply raises financial and political demands on government by requiring huge spending on new infrastructure."[2] Because many third world countries cannot sustain such expenditures, he notes, "we have . . . the potential for a widening gap between demands on the state and its financial ability to meet these demands"—a gap that could lead to internal conflict between competing ethnic groups, or significant out-migration to countries better able to cope with environmental stresses.[3]

Finally, there is a danger that acute environmental scarcities will lead to armed interstate conflict over such vital resources as water, forests, and energy supplies. Some believe that the era of "resource wars" has already occurred in the form of recurring conflict over the Middle East's oil supplies and that similar conflicts will arise over control of major sources of water, such as the Nile, Euphrates, and Ganges Rivers.

THE NEW CARTOGRAPHY

These new and growing schisms are creating a map of international security that is based on economic, demographic, and environmental factors. If this map could be represented in graphic terms, it would show an elaborate network of fissures stretching across human society in all directions—producing large concentrations of rifts in some areas and smaller clusters in others, but leaving no area entirely untouched. Each line would represent a cleavage in the human community, dividing one group (however defined) from another; the deeper and wider clefts, and those composed of many fault lines, would indicate the site of current or potential conflict.

These schisms, and their continued growth, will force policymakers to rethink their approach to international security. It is no longer possible to rely on strategies of defense and diplomacy that assume a flat, two-dimensional world of contending geopolitical actors. While such units still play a significant role in world security affairs, they are not the only actors that matter; nor is their interaction the only significant threat to peace and stability. Other actors, and other modes of interaction, are equally important. Only by considering the full range of security threats will it be possible for policymakers to design effective strategies for peace.

When the principal fault lines of international security coincided with the boundaries between countries, it was always possible for individual states to attempt to solve their security problems by fortifying their borders or by joining with other nations in regional defense systems like NATO and the Warsaw Pact. When the fault lines fall *within* societies, however, there are no clear boundaries to be defended and no role for traditional alliance systems. Indeed, it is questionable whether there is a role for military power at all: any use of force by one side in these disputes, however successful, will inevitably cause damage to the body politic as a whole, eroding its capacity to overcome the problems involved and to provide for its long-term stability. Rather than fortifying and defending borders, a successful quest for peace must entail strategies for easing and erasing the rifts in society by eliminating the causes of dissension or finding ways to peacefully bridge the gap between mutually antagonistic groups.

The new map of international security will not replace older, traditional types. The relations between states will still matter in world affairs, and their interactions may lead, as they have in the past, to major armed conflicts. But it will not be possible to promote international peace and stability without using the new map as well, and dealing with the effects of the new global schisms. Should we fail to do so, the world of the next century could prove as violent as the present one.

[2]Thomas Homer-Dixon, "Environmental Scarcity and Intergroup Conflict," in Michael T. Klare and Daniel C. Thomas, eds., World Security: Challenges for a New Century (New York: St. Martin's Press, 1994), pp. 298–299.
[3]ibid.

Unit Selections

5. **Before the Next Doubling,** Jennifer D. Mitchell
6. **Worldwide Development or Population Explosion: Our Choice,** Gerard Piel
7. **Refugees: The Rising Tide,** Rony Brauman
8. **How Much Food Will We Need in the 21st Century?** William H. Bender
9. **Angling for 'Aquaculture,'** Gary Turbak

Key Points to Consider

❖ What are the basic characteristics of the global population situation? How many people are there?

❖ How fast is the world's population growing? What are the reasons for this growth? How do population dynamics vary from one region to the next?

❖ What regions of the world are attracting large numbers of international immigrants?

❖ How does rapid population growth affect the quality of the environment, social structures, and the ways in which humanity views itself?

❖ How does a rapidly growing population affect a poor country's ability to plan its economic development?

❖ How can economic and social policies be changed in order to reduce the impact of population growth on environmental quality?

❖ In an era of global interdependence, how much impact can individual governments have on demographic changes?

❖ How much food will we need in the twenty-first century and can current technologies meet this need?

❖ How is agricultural production a function of many different aspects of a society's economic and political structure?

 **Links** | **www.dushkin.com/online/**

7. **The Hunger Project**
   http://www.thp.org
8. **Penn Library: Resources by Subject**
   http://www.library.upenn.edu/resources/websitest.html
9. **World Health Organization**
   http://www.who.ch/Welcome.html
10. **WWW Virtual Library: Demography & Population Studies**
    http://coombs.anu.edu.au/ResFacilities/DemographyPage.html

These sites are annotated on pages 6 and 7.

After World War II, the world's population reached 2 billion people. It had taken 250 years to triple to that level. In the 55 years since the end of World War II, the population has tripled again to 6 billion. When the typical reader of this book reaches the age of 50, experts estimate that the global population will have reached 8 1/2 billion! By 2050, or about 100 years after the second world war ended, the world may be populated by 10 to 12 billion people. A person born in 1946 (a so-called baby boomer) who lives to be 100 could see a sixfold increase in population.

Nothing like this has ever occurred before. To state this in a different way, in the next 50 years, there will have to be twice as much food produced, twice as many schools and hospitals built, and twice as much of everything else provided just to maintain the current and rather uneven standard of living. We live in an unprecedented time in human history.

One of the most interesting aspects of this unprecedented population growth is that there is little agreement about whether this is good or bad. For example, the government of China has a policy that encourages couples to have only one child. In contrast, there are a few governments that use various financial incentives to promote large families.

The lead article in this section provides a historical overview of the demographic realities of the contemporary world. The unit continues with a discussion of conflicting perspectives on the implications of population growth. Some experts view population growth as the major problem facing the world, while others see it as secondary to social, economic, and political problems. The theme of conflicting views, in short, has been carried forward from the introductory unit of the book to the more specific discussion of population.

This broad discussion is followed by a series of articles that examine specific issues such as the movement of people from developing to industrial countries. This raises interesting questions about how a culture maintains its identity when it must absorb large numbers of new people, or how will a government obtain the resources necessary to integrate these new members into the mainstream of society.

As the world begins a new millennium, there are many population issues that transcend numerical and economic issues. The disappearance of indigenous people is a good example of the pressures of population growth on people who live on the margins of modern society. Finally, while demographers develop various scenarios forecasting population growth, it is important to remember that there are circumstances that could lead not to growth but to a significant decline in global population. The spread of AIDS and other infectious diseases reveals that confidence in modern medicine's ability to control these scourges may be premature. Nature has its own checks and balances to the population dynamic that are not policy instruments of some governmental organization. This factor is often overlooked.

No greater check on population growth is the ability to produce an adequate food supply. Some experts question whether current technologies are sustainable over the long run. How much food are we going to need in the decades to come, and how are farmers going to produce it? This fundamental question is the focus of the final articles in the unit.

Making predictions about the future of the world's population is a complicated task, for there are a variety of forces at work and considerable variation from region to region.

The danger of oversimplification must be overcome if governments and international organizations are going to respond with meaningful policies. Perhaps one could say there is not a global population problem, but many challenges that vary from country to country and region to region.

Population and Food Production

Before the Next Doubling

Nearly 6 billion people now inhabit the Earth—almost twice as many as in 1960. At some point over the course of the next century, the world's population could double again. But we don't have anything like a century to prevent that next doubling; we probably have less than a decade.

by Jennifer D. Mitchell

In 1971, when Bangladesh won independence from Pakistan, the two countries embarked on a kind of unintentional demographic experiment. The separation had produced two very similar populations: both contained some 66 million people and both were growing at about 3 percent a year. Both were overwhelmingly poor, rural, and Muslim. Both populations had similar views on the "ideal" family size (around four children); in both cases, that ideal was roughly two children smaller than the actual average family. And in keeping with the Islamic tendency to encourage large families, both generally disapproved of family planning.

But there was one critical difference. The Pakistani government, distracted by leadership crises and committed to conventional ideals of economic growth, wavered over the importance of family planning. The Bangladeshi government did not: as early as 1976, population growth had been declared the country's number one problem, and a national network was established to educate people about family planning and supply them with contraceptives. As a result, the proportion of couples using contraceptives rose from around 6 percent in 1976 to about 50 percent today, and fertility rates have dropped from well over six children per woman to just over three. Today, some 120 million people people live in Bangladesh, while 140 million live in Pakistan—a difference of 20 million.

Bangladesh still faces enormous population pressures—by 2050, its population will probably have increased by nearly 100 million. But even so, that 20 million person "savings" is a colossal achievement, especially given local conditions. Bangladeshi officials had no hope of producing the classic "demographic transition," in which improvements in education, health care, and general living standards tend to push down the birth rate. Bangladesh was—and is—one of the poorest and most densely populated countries on earth. About the size of England and Wales, Bangladesh has twice as many people. Its per capita GDP is barely over $200. It has one doctor for every 12,500 people and nearly three-quarters of its adult population are illiterate. The national diet would be considered inadequate in any industrial country, and even at current levels of population growth, Bangladesh may be forced to rely increasingly on food imports.

All of these burdens would be substantially heavier than they already are, had it not been for the family planning program. To appreciate the Bangladeshi achievement, it's only necessary to look at Pakistan: those "additional" 20 million Pakistanis require at least 2.5 million more houses, about 4 million more tons of grain each year, millions more jobs, and significantly greater investments in health care—or a significantly greater burden of disease. Of the two nations, Pakistan has the more robust economy—its

From *World Watch* magazine, January/February 1998, pp. 20-27. © 1998 by the Worldwatch Institute, Washington, DC. Reprinted by permission.

per capita GDP is twice that of Bangladesh. But the Pakistani economy is still primarily agricultural, and the size of the average farm is shrinking, in part because of the expanding population. Already, one fourth of the country's farms are under 1 hectare, the standard minimum size for economic viability, and Pakistan is looking increasingly towards the international grain markets to feed its people. In 1997, despite its third consecutive year of near-record harvests, Pakistan attempted to double its wheat imports but was not able to do so because it had exhausted its line of credit.

And Pakistan's extra burden will be compounded in the next generation. Pakistani women still bear an average of well over five children, so at the current birth rate, the 10 million or so extra couples would produce at least 50 million children. And these in turn could bear nearly 125 million children of their own. At its current fertility rate, Pakistan's population will double in just 24 years—that's more than twice as fast as Bangladesh's population is growing. H. E. Syeda Abida Hussain, Pakistan's Minister of Population Welfare, explains the problem bluntly: "If we achieve success in lowering our population growth substantially, Pakistan has a future. But if, God forbid, we should not—no future."

The Three Dimensions of the Population Explosion

Some version of Mrs. Abida's statement might apply to the world as a whole. About 5.9 billion people currently inhabit the Earth. By the middle of the next century, according to U.N. projections, the population will probably reach 9.4 billion—and all of the net increase is likely to occur in the developing world. (The total population of the industrial countries is expected to decline slightly over the next 50 years.) Nearly 60 percent of the increase will occur in Asia, which will grow from 3.4 billion people in 1995 to more than 5.4 billion in 2050. China's population will swell from 1.2 billion to 1.5 billion, while India's is projected to soar from 930 million to 1.53 billion. In the Middle East and North Africa, the population will probably more than double, and in sub-Saharan Africa, it will triple. By 2050, Nigeria alone is expected to have 339 million people—more than the entire continent of Africa had 35 years ago.

Despite the different demographic projections, no country will be immune to the effects of population growth. Of course, the countries with the highest growth rates are likely to feel the greatest immediate burdens—on their educational and public health systems, for instance, and on their forests, soils, and water as the struggle to grow more food intensifies. Already some 100 countries must rely on grain imports to some degree, and 1.3 billion of the world's people are living on the equivalent of $1 a day or less.

But the effects will ripple out from these "front-line" countries to encompass the world as a whole. Take the water predicament in the Middle East as an example. According to Tony Allan, a water expert at the University of London, the Middle East "ran out of water" in 1972, when its population stood at 122 million. At that point, Allan argues, the region had begun to draw more water out of its aquifers and rivers than the rains were replenishing. Yet today, the region's population is twice what it was in 1972 and still growing. To some degree, water management now determines political destiny. In Egypt, for example, President Hosni Mubarak has announced a $2 billion diversion project designed to pump water from the Nile River into an area that is now desert. The project—Mubarak calls it a "necessity imposed by population"—is designed to resettle some 3 million people outside the Nile flood plain, which is home to more than 90 percent of the country's population.

Elsewhere in the region, water demands are exacerbating international tensions; Jordan, Israel, and Syria, for instance, engage in uneasy competition for the waters of the Jordan River basin. Jordan's King Hussein once said that water was the only issue that could lead him to declare war on Israel. Of course, the United States and the western European countries are deeply involved in the region's antagonisms and have invested heavily in its fragile states. The western nations have no realistic hope of escaping involvement in future conflicts.

Yet the future need not be so grim. The experiences of countries like Bangladesh suggest that it is possible to build population policies that are a match for the threat. The first step is to understand the causes of population growth. John Bongaarts, vice president of the Population Council, a nonprofit research group in New York City, has identified three basic factors. (See figure on the next page.)

Unmet demand for family planning. In the developing world, at least 120 million married women—and a large but undefined number of unmarried women—want more control over their pregnancies, but cannot get family planning services. This unmet demand will cause about one-third of the projected population growth in developing countries over the next 50 years, or an increase of about 1.2 billion people.

Desire for the large families. Another 20 percent of the projected growth over the next 50 years, or an increase of about 660 million people, will be caused by couples who may have access to family planning services, but who choose to have more than two children. (Roughly two children per family is the "replacement rate," at which a population could be expected to stabilize over the long term.)

Population momentum. By far the largest component of population growth is the least commonly understood. Nearly one-half of the increase projected for the next 50 years will occur simply because the next reproductive generation—the group of people currently entering puberty or younger—is so much larger than the current reproductive generation. Over the next 25 years, some 3 billion people—a number equal to the entire world population in 1960—will enter their reproductive years, but only about 1.8 billion will leave that phase of life. Assuming that the couples in this reproductive bulge begin to have children at a fairly early age, which is the global norm, the global population would still expand by 1.7 billion, even if all of those couples had only two children—the longterm replacement rate.

Meeting the Demand

Over the past three decades, the global percentage of couples using some form of family planning has increased dramatically—from less than 10 to more than 50 percent. But due to the growing population, the absolute number of women not using family planning is greater today than it was 30 years ago. Many of these women fall into that first category above—they want the services but for one reason or another, they cannot get them.

Sometimes the obstacle is a matter of policy: many governments ban or restrict valuable methods of contraception. In Japan, for instance, regulations discourage the use of birth control pills in favor of condoms, as a public health measure against sexually transmitted diseases. A study conducted in 1989 found that some 60 countries required a husband's permission before a woman can be sterilized; several required a husband's consent for all forms of birth control.

Elsewhere, the problems may be more logistical than legal. Many developing countries lack clinics and pharmacies in rural areas. In some rural areas of sub-Saharan Africa, it takes an average of two hours to reach the nearest contraceptive provider. And often contraceptives are too expensive for most people. Sometimes the products or services are of such poor quality that they are not simply ineffective, but dangerous. A woman who has been injured by a badly made or poorly inserted IUD may well be put off by contraception entirely.

In many countries, the best methods are simply unavailable. Sterilization is often the only available nontraditional option, or the only one that has gained wide acceptance. Globally, the procedure accounts for about 40 percent of contraceptive use and in some countries the fraction is much higher: in the Dominican Republic and India, for example, it stands at 69 percent. But women don't generally resort to sterilization until well into their childbearing years, and in some countries, the procedure isn't permitted until a woman reaches a certain age or bears a certain number of children. Sterilization is therefore no substitute for effective temporary methods like condoms, the pill, or IUDs.

There are often obstacles in the home as well. Women may be prevented from seeking family planning services by disapproving husbands or in-laws. In Pakistan, for example, 43 percent of husbands object to family planning. Frequently,

Population of Developing Countries, 1950–95, with Projected Growth to 2050

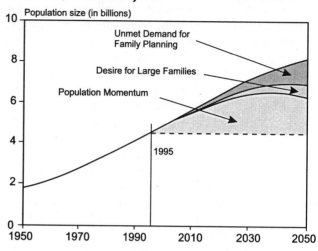

Source: U.N., *World Population Prospects: The 1996 Revision* (New York: October 1998); and John Bongaarts, "Population Policy Options in the Developing World," *Science,* 11 February 1994.

such objections reflect a general social disapproval inculcated by religious or other deeply-rooted cultural values. And in many places, there is a crippling burden of ignorance: women simply may not know what family planning services are available or how to obtain them.

Yet there are many proven opportunities for progress, even in conditions that would appear to offer little room for it. In Bangladesh, for instance, contraception was never explicitly illegal, but many households follow the Muslim custom of *purdah,* which largely secludes women in their communities.

Since it's very difficult for such women to get to family planning clinics, the government brought family planning to them: some 30,000 female field workers go door-to-door to explain contraceptive methods and distribute supplies. Several other countries have adopted Bangladesh's approach. Ghana, for instance, has a similar system, in which field workers fan out from community centers. And even Pakistan now deploys 12,000 village-based workers, in an attempt to reform its family planning program, which still reaches only a quarter of the population.

Reducing the price of contraceptives can also trigger a substantial increase in use. In poor countries, contraceptives can be an extremely price-sensitive commodity even when they are very cheap. Bangladesh found this out the hard way in 1990, when officials increased contraceptive prices an average of 60 percent. (Under the increases, for example, the cheapest condoms cost about 1.25 U.S. cents per dozen). Despite regular annual sales increases up to that point, the market slumped immediately: in 1991, condom sales fell by 29 percent and sales of the pill by 12 percent. The next year, prices were rolled back; sales rebounded and have grown steadily since then.

Additional research and development can help broaden the range of contraceptive options. Not all methods work for all couples, and the lack of a suitable method may block a substantial amount of demand. Some women, for instance, have side effects to the pill; others may not be able to use IUDs because of reproductive tract infections. The wider the range of available methods, the better the chance that a couple will use one of them.

Planning the Small Family

Simply providing family planning services to people who already want them won't be enough to arrest the population juggernaut. In many countries, large families are still the ideal. In Senegal, Cameroon, and Niger, for example, the average woman still wants six or seven children. A few countries have tried to legislate such desires away. In India, for example, the Ministry of Health and Family Welfare is interested in promoting a policy that would bar people who have more than two children from political careers, or deny them promotion if they work within the civil service bureaucracy. And China's well-known policy allows only one child per family.

But coercion is not only morally questionable—it's likely to be ineffective because of the backlash it invites. A better starting point for policy would be to try to understand why couples want large families in the first place. In many developing countries, having lots of children still seems perfectly rational: children are a source of security in old age and may be a vital part of the family economy. Even when they're very young, children's labor can make them an asset rather than a drain on family income. And in countries with high child mortality rates, many births may be viewed as necessary to compensate for the possible deaths (of course, the cumulative statistical effect of such a reaction is to *over*-compensate).

Religious or other cultural values may contribute to the big family ideal. In Pakistan, for instance, where 97 percent of the population is Muslim, a recent survey of married women found that almost 60 percent of them believed that the number of children they have is "up to God." Preference for sons is another widespread factor in the big

family psychology: many large families have come about from a perceived need to bear at least one son. In India, for instance, many Hindus believe that they need a son to perform their last rites, or their souls will not be released from the cycle of births and rebirths. Lack of a son can mean abandonment in this life too. Many husbands desert wives who do not bear sons. Or if a husband dies, a son is often the key to a woman's security: 60 percent of Indian women over 60 are widows, and widows tend to rely on their sons for support. In some castes, a widow has no other option since social mores forbid her from returning to her birth village or joining a daughter's family. Understandably, the fear of abandonment prompts many Indian women to continue having children until they have a son. It is estimated that if son preference were eliminated in India, the fertility rate would decline by 8 percent from its current level of 3.5 children per woman.

Yet even deeply rooted beliefs are subject to reinterpretation. In Iran, another Muslim society, fertility rates have dropped from seven children per family to just over four in less than three decades. The trend is due in some measure to a change of heart among the government's religious authorities, who had become increasingly concerned about the likely effects of a population that was growing at more than 3 percent per year. In 1994, at the International Conference on Population and Development (ICPD) held in Cairo, the Iranian delegation released a "National Report on Population" which argued that according to the "quotations from prophet Mohammad . . . and verses of [the] holy Quran, what is standing at the top priority for the Muslims' community is the social welfare of Muslims." Family planning, therefore, "not only is not prohibited but is emphasized by religion."

Promotional campaigns can also change people's assumptions and behavior, if the campaigns fit into the local social context. Perhaps the most successful effort of this kind is in Thailand, where Mechai Viravidaiya, the founder of the Thai Population and Community Development Association, started a program that uses witty songs, demonstrations, and ads to encourage the use of contraceptives. The program has helped foster widespread awareness of family planning throughout Thai society. Teachers use population-related examples in their math classes; cab drivers even pass out condoms. Such efforts have paid off: in less than three decades, contraceptive use among married couples has risen from 8 to 75 percent and population growth has slowed from over 3 percent to about 1 percent—the same rate as in the United States.

Better media coverage may be another option. In Bangladesh, a recent study found that while local journalists recognize the importance of family planning, they do not understand population issues well enough to cover them effectively and objectively. The study, a collaboration between the University Research Corporation of Bangladesh and Johns Hopkins University in the United States, recommended five ways to improve coverage: develop easy-to-use information for journalists (press releases, wall charts, research summaries), offer training and workshops, present awards for population journalism, create a forum for communication between journalists and family planning professionals, and establish a population resource center or data bank.

Often, however, the demand for large families is so tightly linked to social conditions that the conditions themselves must be viewed as part of the problem. Of course, those conditions vary greatly from one society to the next, but there are some common points of leverage:

Reducing child mortality helps give parents more confidence in the future of the children they already have. Among the most effective ways of reducing mortality are child immunization programs, and the promotion of "birth spacing"—lengthening the time between births. (Children born less than a year and a half apart are twice as likely to die as those born two or more years apart.)

Improving the economic situation of women provides them with alternatives to child-bearing. In some countries, officials could reconsider policies or customs that limit women's job opportunities or other economic rights, such as the right to inherit property. Encouraging "micro-leaders" such as Bangladesh's Grameen Bank can also be an effective tactic. In Bangladesh, the Bank has made loans to well over a million villagers—mostly impoverished women—to help them start or expand small businesses.

Improving education tends to delay the average age of marriage and to further the two goals just mentioned. Compulsory school attendance for children undercuts the economic incentive for larger families by reducing the opportunities for child labor. And in just about every society, higher levels of education correlate strongly with small families.

Momentum: The Biggest Threat of All

The most important factor in population growth is the hardest to counter—and to understand. Population momentum can be easy to overlook because it isn't directly captured by the statistics that attract the most attention. The global growth rate, after all, is dropping: in the mid-1960s, it amounted to about a 2.2 percent annual increase; today the figure is 1.4 percent. The fertility rate is dropping too: in 1950, women bore an average of five children each; now they bear roughly three. But despite these continued declines, the absolute number of births won't taper off any time soon. According to U.S. Census Bureau estimates, some 130 million births will still occur annually for the next 25 years, because of the sheer number of women coming into their child-bearing years.

The effects of momentum can be seen readily in a country like Bangladesh, where more than 42 percent of the population is under 15 years old—a typical proportion for many poor countries. Some 82 percent of the population growth projected for Bangladesh over the next half century will be caused by momentum. In other words, even if from now on, every Bangladeshi couple were to have only two children, the country's population would

still grow by 80 million by 2050 simply because the next reproductive generation is so enormous.

The key to reducing momentum is to delay as many births as possible. To understand why delay works, its helpful to think of momentum as a kind of human accounting problem in which a large number of births in the near term won't be balanced by a corresponding number of deaths over the same period of time. One side of the population ledger will contain those 130 million annual births (not all of which are due to momentum, of course), while the other side will contain only about 50 million annual deaths. So to put the matter in a morbid light, the longer a substantial number of those births can be delayed, the longer the death side of the balance sheet will be when the births eventually occur. In developing countries, according to the Population Council's Bongaarts, an average 2.5-year delay in the age when a woman bears her first child would reduce population growth by over 10 percent.

One way to delay childbearing is to postpone the age of marriage. In Bangladesh, for instance, the median age of first marriage among women rose from 14.4 in 1951 to 18 in 1989, and the age at first birth followed suit. Simply raising the legal age of marriage may be a useful tactic in countries that permit marriage among the very young. Educational improvements, as already mentioned, tend to do the same thing. A survey of 23 developing countries found that the median age of marriage for women with secondary education exceeded that of women with no formal education by four years.

Another fundamental strategy for encouraging later childbirth is to help women break out of the "sterilization syndrome" by providing and promoting high-quality, temporary contraceptives. Sterilization might appear to be the ideal form of contraception because it's permanent. But precisely because it is permanent, women considering sterilization tend to have their children early, and then resort to it. A family planning program that relies heavily on sterilization may therefore be working at cross purposes with itself: when offered as a primary form of contraception, sterilization tends to promote early childbirth.

What Happened to the Cairo Pledges?

At the 1994 Cairo Conference, some 180 nations agreed on a 20-year reproductive health package to slow population growth. The agreement called for a progressive rise in annual funding over the life of the package; according to U.N. estimates, the annual price tag would come to about $17 billion by 2000 and $21.7 billion by 2015. Developing countries agreed to pay for two thirds of the program, while the developed countries were to pay for the rest. On a global scale, the package was fairly modest: the annual funding amounts to less than two weeks' worth of global military expenditures.

Today, developing country spending is largely on track with the Cairo agreement, but the developed countries are not keeping their part of the bargain. According to a recent study by the U.N. Population Fund (UNFPA), all forms of developed country assistance (direct foreign aid, loans from multilateral agencies, foundation grants, and so on) amounted to only $2 billion in 1995. That was a 24 percent increase over the previous year, but preliminary estimates indicate that support declined some 18 percent in 1996 and last year's funding levels were probably even lower than that.

The United States, the largest international donor to population programs, is not only failing to meet its Cairo commitments, but is toying with a policy that would undermine international family planning efforts as a whole. Many members of the U.S. Congress are seeking reimposition of the "Mexico City Policy" first enunciated by President Ronald Reagan at the 1984 U.N. population conference in Mexico City, and repealed by the Clinton administration in 1993. Essentially, a resurrected Mexico City Policy would extend the current U.S. ban on funding abortion services to a ban on funding any organization that:

- funds abortions directly, or
- has a partnership arrangement with an organization that funds abortions, or
- provides legal services that may facilitate abortions, or
- engages in any advocacy for the provision of abortions, or
- participates in any policy discussions about abortion, either in a domestic or international forum.

The ban would be triggered even if the relevant activities were paid for entirely with non-U.S. funds. Because of its draconian limits even on speech, the policy has been dubbed the "Global Gag Rule" by its critics, who fear that it could stifle, not just abortion services, but many family planning operations involved only incidentally with abortion. Although Mexico City proponents have not managed to enlist enough support to reinstate the policy, they have succeeded in reducing U.S. family planning aid from $547 million in 1995 to $385 million in 1997. They have also imposed an unprecedented set of restrictions that meter out the money at the rate of 8 percent of the annual budget per month—a tactic that *Washington Post* reporter Judy Mann calls "administrative strangulation."

If the current underfunding of the Cairo program persists, according to the UNFPA study, 96 million fewer couples will use modern contraceptives in 2000 than if commitments had been met. One-third to one-half of these couples will resort to less effective traditional birth control methods; the rest will not use any contraceptives at all. The result will be an additional 122 million unintended pregnancies. Over half of those pregnancies will end in births, and about 40 percent will end in abortions. (The funding shortfall is expected to produce 16 million more abortions in 2000 alone.) The unwanted pregnancies will kill about 65,000 women by 2000, and injure another 844,000.

Population funding is always vulnerable to the illusion that the falling growth rate means the problem is going away. Worldwide, the annual population increase had dropped from a high of 87 million in 1988 to 80 million today. But dismissing the problem with that statistic is like comforting someone stuck on a railway crossing with the news that an oncoming train has slowed from 87 to 80 kilometers an hour, while its weight has increased. It will now take 12.5 years instead of 11.5 years to add the next billion people to the world. But that billion will surely arrive—and so will at least one more billion. Will still more billions follow? That, in large measure, depends on what policymakers do now. Funding alone will not ensure that population stabilizes, but lack of funding will ensure that it does not.

The Next Doubling

In the wake of the Cairo conference, most population programs are broadening their focus to include improvements in education, women's health, and women's social status among their many goals. These goals are worthy in their own right and they will ultimately be necessary for bringing population under control. But global population growth has gathered so much momentum that it could simply overwhelm a development agenda. Many countries now have little choice but to tackle their population problem in as direct a fashion as possible—even if that means temporarily ignoring other social problems. Population growth is now a global social emergency. Even as officials in both developed and developing countries open up their program agendas, it is critical that they not neglect their single most effective tool for dealing with that emergency: direct expenditures on family planning.

The funding that is likely to be the most useful will be constant, rather than sporadic. A fluctuating level of commitment, like sporadic condom use, can

end up missing its objective entirely. And wherever it's feasible, funding should be designed to develop self-sufficiency—as, for instance, with UNFPA's $1 million grant to Cuba, to build a factory for making birth control pills. The factory, which has the capacity to turn out 500 million tablets annually, might eventually even provide the country with a new export product. Self-sufficiency is likely to grow increasingly important as the fertility rate continues to decline. As Tom Merrick, senior population advisor at the World Bank explains, "while the need for contraceptives will not go away when the total fertility rate reaches two—the donors will."

Even in narrow, conventional economic terms, family planning offers one of the best development investments available. A study in Bangladesh showed that for each birth prevented, the government spends $62 and saves $615 on social services expenditures—nearly a tenfold return. The study estimated that the Bangladesh program prevents 890,000 births a year, for a net annual savings of $547 million. And that figure does not include savings resulting from lessened pressure on natural resources.

Over the past 40 years, the world's population has doubled. At some point in the latter half of the next century, today's population of 5.9 billion could double again. But because of the size of the next reproductive generation, we probably have only a relatively few years to stop that next doubling. To prevent all of the damage—ecological, economic, and social—that the next doubling is likely to cause, we must begin planning the global family with the same kind of urgency that we bring to matters of trade, say, or military security. Whether we realize it or not, our attempts to stabilize population—or our failure to act— will likely have consequences that far outweigh the implications of the military or commercial crisis of the moment. Slowing population growth is one of the greatest gifts we can offer future generations.

Jennifer D. Mitchell is a staff researcher at the Worldwatch Institute.

Worldwide Development or Population Explosion: Our Choice

The problem is not population; it is poverty. We can reach zero-growth population, if we expand the world economy fourfold and share the proceeds equitably. That would bring the poorest 20 percent out of poverty. The industrialized countries must climb out of their economic torpor and restart their economic engines.

Gerard Piel

No entry on the U.S. political agenda has fewer advocates than does "foreign aid." What little of it that remains in the budget carries forward subsidies to Cold War client states which are now relegated to holding the line against Muslim fundamentalism. The poor countries of the world had their last serious mention in U.S. policy in 1961, when John F. Kennedy made his only appearance at the U.N. General Assembly. There, he proposed that the industrial nations make the 1960s the "Decade of Development," and he pledged 1.0 percent of this country's GNP to the effort. Nothing came of that speech. Nothing like it has come from any president since.

But there was a time when U.S. citizens were in favor of giving economic and technical assistance to the poorer countries. That was at the end of World War II. For a few years, as they recoiled from the horror of that war, people all around the world embraced their sense of people as global family. Freedom from want had been declared an aim of the war by the Allies. They had spelled it out in the United Nations Declaration of 1942. In the "underdeveloped countries," which were then emerging from the disbanding colonial empires of the European industrial

From *Challenge*, July/August 1995, pp. 13–22. © 1995 by M. E. Sharpe, Inc., Armonk, NY 10504. Reprinted by permission.

powers, people were to be lifted out of poverty. With grants and soft loans under the Marshall Plan, U.S. taxpayers financed the economic recovery of the mother countries of those empires—allies (excepting only the USSR) and former enemies alike. In Point Four of his inaugural address to an approving electorate in 1949, Harry S Truman proposed making the Marshall Plan global.

> *The total capital requirement for the development of the pre-industrial nations is estimated at $19 billion per year. Some of that requirement would be filled by domestic savings within these countries themselves. Much the greater part of it would have to come from the industrial countries.*

In its interim headquarters at Lake Success, the United Nations began considering what it would take to develop the underdeveloped countries. The estimate was the work of a "Group of Experts"—respected economists from both the industrial and pre-industrial worlds. Two of the Experts—Theodore W. Schultz of the University of Chicago and W. Arthur Lewis of the University of Manchester—would share the Nobel prize in Economics in 1979. In effect, they reported, it was time to get on with the industrial revolution.

In the undeveloped nations, people were still living with the technology that began the agricultural revolution 10,000 years earlier. Given the extant population growth (1.5 percent per annum), it would be possible (and advisable) to move 1.0 percent of the population each year into nonagricultural employment. With a net increase of 1.0 percent in per capita income from industry, and another 2.0 percent increase from improved

(by industrial inputs) agricultural yield, incomes could be made to improve at twice the rate of population growth.

At $2,500 for each new industrial job, the Experts estimated the total capital requirement for this enterprise in development at $19 billion per year. Some of that requirement would be filled by domestic savings within the preindustrial countries themselves. Much the greater part of it would have to come from the industrial countries. The profit and interest-bearing part of that external investment would depend, however, upon antecedent investment. It would amount to $3 billion per year, and would be spent on the building of social capital and physical infrastructure. That kind of investment is customarily financed by taxes. That $3 billion would cost the industrial countries 0.5 percent of their combined GDP, and would be generated by outright grants from their governments—a classic example of priming the investment pump. Foreign aid at that level would see the underdeveloped countries through their industrialization to self-sustained economic development by the year 2000.

Business leadership in Europe and the United States was ready to entertain this proposition. The Experts' estimate was only round one, of course. But it was of the same dimension as the ongoing, successful undertaking of the Marshall Plan. The Great Depression was still fresh in their memories. The post-war generation of business managers was receptive to imaginative ideas for countercyclical outlays by the government. But the dispatch of troops to Korea in June 1950 extinguished the vision of an organized campaign of economic development. Foreign aid never reached the 0.5 percent goal—much less the Kennedy 1.0 percent.

A GLOBAL MARSHALL PLAN

Now, in 1995, the time has come to bring the vision of a global Marshall Plan into focus again. Getting on with the industrial revolution is the most urgent challenge civilization now faces. If foreign aid was being considered an act of common humanity at mid-century, it is now dictated by the exigiencies of common survival. The population of the world has more than doubled since 1950—from 2.5 billion to 5.3 billion. The number of people living in direst poverty has increased to 1.3 billion—close to the total population of the underdeveloped countries in 1950. The population is doubling now again. The number in direst poverty could equal the present world population. A doubling after that would bring the human species close to full occupation of the Earth.

In order to stabilize the world's population at some sustainable level, the industrial revolution must be carried out worldwide. Natural population increase has ceased in the

20 percent of the world population that is represented by the industrialized countries. Fertility is approaching the zero-growth rate in another 20 percent of the population currently living in the pre-industrial countries. That is happening in countries that have gotten on with their industrial revolutions since 1950. The population explosion that distresses so many well-off people in the industrialized countries is confined to the countries where the revolution has lagged and is now arrested. The sooner the industrial revolution reaches people everywhere, the smaller will be the world's population.

The lack of understanding of the connection between industrial revolution and population growth is due to the baleful legacy of Thomas R. Malthus. He wrote his famous *Essay on the Principle of Population* in 1798—just about when the industrial revolution and its attendant population explosion was getting under way. He was unaware of either development. His message is easily grasped: "Population, when unchecked, increases in a geometric ratio. Subsistence increases only in an arithmetic ratio. A slight acquaintance with numbers will shew the immensity of the first power in comparison with the second." Taking the two series out nine steps, Malthus nailed down his point: "In two centuries and a quarter, the population would be to the means of subsistence as 512 to 10."

Indeed, geometric and arithmetic series do diverge. But these series do not fit the trends of the last two centuries. World population increase (now in its third doubling since Malthus published his *Essay)* has been sustained by more than five doublings of the supply of the "means of subsistence." Since 1950, industrial technology (overriding any arithmetic constraint) has twice doubled the output of material goods—even as the population has doubled. But the doubling of average per capita production was accompanied by an unprecedented increase in the per capita consumption gap. It tripled. The difference between the best-off 20 percent of the world population and the worst-off 20 percent was 20 to 1 in 1960. It rose to 60 to 1 in 1990. Of course, some people have always been rich. And most people have always been poor. But with this latest increase in disparity, the industrial revolution has starkly divided the world into two camps—rich countries and poor.

THE ISSUE IS POVERTY

The problem is not population; it is poverty. We can reach zero-growth population, if we expand the world economy fourfold and share the proceeds equitably. That would bring the poorest 20 percent out of poverty. The industrialized countries must climb out of their economic torpor and restart their economic engines. Outlays for foreign aid could help to provide the necessary stimulus. In most industrialized countries (especially in the United States), governments appear to be unwilling or unable to take the initiative.

> *Outlays for foreign aid could help to provide the necessary stimulus for the revitalization of the developed countries' economies. In most industrialized countries (especially in the United States), governments appear to be unwilling or unable to take the initiative.*

The rich industrial country is an entirely new historical phenomenon. It is rich in the sense that none of its inhabitants need submit to toil and want. Poverty persists in the industrialized countries as a social institution. In the poor countries, rampant poverty is a familiar story. It exists as if by definition. Simply, there is not enough to go around. Even today, village people in the poor countries live very much as their forebears did when the agricultural revolution settled them in villages 10,000 years ago. They survive by the sweat of their brows. The biological energy of their bodies gets the means of subsistence to renew that energy, but not much more. With traditional tools and practice, they can increase the means of that subsistence only by bringing new land under cultivation.

Over the ten millennia of agricultural civilization, population increase proceeded at a near-zero rate. It doubled only seven times—from an estimated 5 million to 500 million around 1600. Malthus's principle of population approximately describes the equilibrium with the misery that bespoke the human condition. High birth rates offset high death rates. Through good times and bad, life expectancy hovered near twenty-five years of age. In most times and places, people could anticipate no improvement in their circumstances in the course of their life-

times. A person could improve his circumstances only at the expense of others. Status and force served this purpose and built high civilizations on the output of the traditional technology of the agricultural revolution.

INDUSTRIAL REVOLUTION

Now, the industrial revolution has brought rich countries abruptly into history. In Europe, around 1600 (where and when the industrial revolution had its earliest beginnings), life expectancy was no greater than twenty-five years of age. With the increase of production running ahead of population growth, death rates fell and life expectancies lengthened. The high birth rates that had barely offset the formerly high death rates began to deliver net additions to the population. In the 18th century, the curve of population increased steeply. Henry Adams dated his "acceleration of history" from that period. He found he could measure it because "it took the form of utilizing heat as force, through the steam engine, and this addition of power was measurable in the coal output." By the end of the 18th century, the growth of the European population had exploded. It doubled its 50-million census (extant in 1600) four times and over to nearly 1 billion by the middle of the 20th century. It constituted one-tenth of the world population in 1600, but it grew to a full one-third of it by 1950, having avalanched on to all the other continents.

During the 19th century, birth rates began to decline in the populations which were participating in the industrial revolution. At the outset, the birth control movement in Britain, on the continent, and in American found militant supporters. They recoiled from the other existing modes of population control—infanticide, abandonment, and abortion. The foundling hospitals and baby farms were evidence of their widespread practice. Too often,

these institutions had fewer alumni than matriculates. During the first half of the 20th century, declining birth rates began converging with the declining death rates in all the industrialized countries. The European population explosion was coming to an end.

THE DEMOGRAPHIC TRANSITION

By the middle of this century, demographers were recognizing an entirely new principle governing population growth—namely, that industrial revolution brings on a demographic revolution. In retrospect, it can now be seen that the population of the industrial world has made a transition since 1600 from near-zero growth at high death rates and high birth rates and life expectancy of less than thirty years to near-zero growth again at low birth rates and low death rates and life expectancy exceeding seventy years. Typically, this "demographic transition" has proceeded through two phases: (1) The population of an industrializing country sees its death rate fall first; its census then increases at rates measured by the difference between its death and birth rates; and (2) that difference narrows with the decline in the birth rate, and the rate of population growth approaches zero again.

Perfection of the technology of contraception around the middle of this century facilitated the final decline of the birth rate in the industrialized world. The total fertility rate fell everywhere to the replacement—zero-growth—rate of 2.1 infants per female reproductive lifetime. In some countries, it fell even lower. Natural population growth has all but ceased in the industrialized 20 percent of the world population. Immigration has brought most of its increase in numbers since 1950.

Figure 1 contrasts the age/sex structure of the U.S. population in 1900 and 1985. In passage through the demographic transition,

Figure 1   **Age/Sex Structure of U.S. Population, 1900–85** (millions)

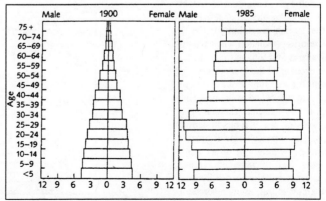

Source: Only One World, W.H. Freeman & Co., 1992.

> *When assured of survival of their first infant(s), people can plan their families. Making the inverse Malthusian calculation, they see that the fewer, the more—for each. The family in industrial civilization (and in any zero-growth population) is necessarily a small family.*

the population exploded from 75 to 240 million. The 1900 0–5 cohort is the largest, but the number of those surviving into older cohorts reflects an increase in life expectancy. The 1985 structure declares the near completion of the demographic transition. The 0–5 cohort is no longer the largest. Variation in sizes of cohorts reflects reproductive preferences of parent cohorts.

People, constrained to witnessing history in the short term, tend to make the simple cause-effect connection between contraceptive technology and that final decline in the fertility rate. On the other hand, as the demographer Paul Demeny has observed, "Effective methods of fertility control have always been known and available in all societies. Fertility transition implies social changes rather than merely a change in technology." The industrial revolution has surely brought such changes. It has transformed the human condition for the 25 percent of the world's population who have migrated from the farm and village to live in cities. They have exchanged the independence of self-employment for free time from wage employment. They are compelled to literacy. They get their living, not by muscular exertion in the field, but by stress on the nervous system in offices, shops, or service establishments. Women go to work (willingly or of necessity) outside the home. Sex roles de-differentiate. The mutual-aid extended-kinship family goes into decline, thereby setting its member families loose on their own. Liberated by freedom from want and toil, urban folk have been en-

larging their new freedom to make their individual existence relevant to wider communities.

The lengthening of life expectancy supplies the essential condition for restraint of fertility. People who can look forward to the full biologically permitted human lifetime permit themselves to be future dwellers. Assured of survival of their first infant(s), they can plan their families. Making the inverse Malthusian calculation, they see that the fewer, the more—for each. The family in industrial civilization (and in any zero-growth population) is necessarily a small family.

Demonstrating that the knack for industrial revolution is not somehow exclusively confined to Europeans, the Japanese proceeded to their own industrialization in the last decades of the 19th century. On a smaller scale, and in a much shorter time, they recapitulated the European demographic experience—population explosion included. They arrived at about the same time as the Europeans at the zero-growth fertility rate.

THE FIRST HUMAN POPULATION

The population of industrial civilization can be said to be the first human population. The populations of other species offer up their young in great number to the pruning process of natural selection. Survivors die away from the youngest in the largest number at each stage of development or metamorphosis—down to the minority that survives to reproduce the species. Closer to nature, such was the age-structure of populations in agricultural civilization. *Figure 2* shows that it persists in the populations of the developing countries today. Industrial civilization brings very nearly all its newborn to full human growth and capacity. The youngest may be the smallest age group. Variation in the size of age groups up to the mortal eldest reflects differences, not in survival, but in decisions

taken as to child-bearing in the parental age groups ahead. As mortality continues to yield to longevity, the eldest become the most rapidly growing age group.

THE BENIGN EXPLOSION

The population explosion that is rolling over the poor countries of the world may yet be recognized as a benign event. It declares the entrance of the rest of the human family into the first phase of the demographic transition.

Population growth began to rise above the near-zero rate in those countries early in their subjugation to the colonial empires of the European industrial powers. During the present half-century, as the leading edge of industrial revolution crossed the borders of these former colonies, their population growth entered the explosive phase. The modest flows of foreign aid that emanated from the United Nations were sufficient to carry out the most portable technologies of industrial revolution. Most potent were those delivered by multilateral funding through the U.N. technical agencies. The World Health Organization brought the rudiments of preventive medicine and sanitation. The Food and Agriculture Organization brought seed and scientific practice. The Educational, Scientific, and Cultural Organization brought mass literacy campaigns. These inputs, domestic economic growth, and bilateral foreign aid from those industrial countries most interested in the country's market and resources induced a surge of development in all of the now-developing countries during the first two decades after World War II and into the 1970s. Consequently, life expectancy had lengthened by a decade on all the continents by 1990. As birth rates fell away from death rates, population-growth rates reached more than 2 percent in almost all the countries and more than 3 percent in some of them. "Explosion" is the appropriate

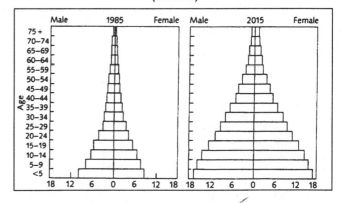

Figure 2   **Age/Sex Structure of Nigerian Population, 1985–2015** (millions)

Source: Only One World, W.H. Freeman & Co., 1992.

word for this development. Comparable declines in the death rates of the existing industrialized countries transpired over the course of a century or two.

Figure 2 charts the age/sex structure of the population of Nigeria as it was in 1985 (when it was a classical "natural selection" population) and as it is projected to be in 2015. The 1985 0–5 cohort is the largest, and the numbers rapidly diminish in older cohorts. The projection shows a "population explosion" that is caused by an increase in life expectancy. The number of 0–5-year-olds is projected to double by 2015. Though the fertility rate will drop by half, four times as many women will survive to child-bearing years.

From 1950 to 1970, the world's population-growth rate climbed to just over 2 percent. This was its all-time peak. The growth rate has been in decline ever since. That turning point declares the entrance of those developing countries which are proceeding most successfully with their development into the second phase of the demographic transition. The decline in their fertility rate (and now in their birth rates) is overtaking the decline in their death rates. When industrialization has brought the rest of the developing countries into the second phase, the world population growth rate will go below 1.0 percent again, and will be headed toward zero.

BIRTH RATES DECLINE

For the present time, this historic turning point is obscured from public understanding by its arithmetic. The declining growth rate is multiplying a larger population each year. Growth proceeds, accordingly, by the largest annual increments ever—in excess of 90 million people per year. If the decline in growth rate continues on its present slope, the annual increments will begin to shrink at the turn of the next century. That depends, of course, on the rate of development—especially in the poorest countries.

The neo-Malthusian alarm bells continue to ring. The cry is that "those people overpopulate their countries." In fact, the countries that have the highest population density —the seats of ancient civilizations in Asia— have moved most decisively into the industrial revolution and through the demographic transition. Africa, with the poorest and fastest-growing population, holds relatively the largest frontier open to human habitation.

In Latin America, disparity in income and wealth closes off another vast frontier to cultivation—the vast stretches of unused and underutilized latifundia. Meanwhile, the resources of these continents continue to fuel the economies of the industrial world. The underdeveloped countries await delivery of the less portable technologies of industrial revolution. Some day, these will permit them

> *The neo-Malthusian alarm bells continue to ring. The cry is that "those people overpopulate their countries." In fact, the countries that have the highest population density—the seats of ancient civilization Asia—have moved most decisively into the industrial revolution and through the demographic transition.*

to develop the value of their resources for their own uses.

NEO-COLONIAL ECONOMIES

The sanctimony and controversy that have surrounded foreign aid have grossly inflated its dimensions in the public understanding. Except in the national budgets of the Nordic countries and Canada, outright grants for development have rarely exceeded 0.3 percent of the output of the industrialized world. For more than a decade, that which is properly reckoned a foreign aid in the U.S. federal budget has never exceeded 0.2 percent of the country's GDP. The percentage was higher when foreign aid served Cold War ends. Most of the flow then went to a half-dozen countries in East and Southeast Asia and to those at the eastern end of the Mediterranean. In South Korea and Taiwan, the fallout from aid and the huge military expenditure was big enough to trigger genuine development. That and the regional boom that occurred as a result of the Korean and Vietnam wars metamorphosed those countries—along with the city states of Hong Kong and Singapore. They became the celebrated "Tigers" of East Asia.

As early as the 1960s, private direct investment from the industrialized countries in plantations, mines, and oil fields began to overtake governmental outlays to foreign aid. The underdeveloped countries became the developing countries. What development most of them have seen (with the notable exceptions of India and China) is due principally to private investment. The contribution to development was indirect. Private investment (and the bilateral foreign aid it often entrained) went primarily to expedite delivery of the country's agricultural commodities, metal ores and, especially, petroleum to the dockside.

This engagement in world commerce has divided many developing countries (especially the smaller ones) into dual economies. The "modern" sectors operate in closer cultural, as well as economic, identity with the industrial powers most interested in their resources than with the traditional sectors in their own hinterlands. These countries remain in colonial status as "hewers of wood and drawers of water." They serve as sources of the raw materials most required by the industrialized world and, above all, of the petroleum that sustains industrial civilization in Europe and North America. In many countries, domestic political leadership (in half of them, military dictatorship) is content with this state of affairs.

ENTER THE TRANSNATIONALS

Over time, an ever smaller number of progressively larger corporations have made the economic connection between the developing countries and the industrial world. The 350 largest nonfinancial transnational corporations now account for 30 percent of the output of the world economy. Their combined turnover is larger by several hundred billion dollars than the total product of all the developing countries. In trade between the two worlds, from three to not more than seven of these corporations make the market for the commodity at hand. In no small measure, they owe their enormous expansion in the past three decades to their advantage in negotiation of the terms under which the developing countries have supplied every commodity—from petroleum to labor. Under the supervision of the transnationals, the imperfections of the market have caused the flow of foreign aid to run uphill—from the poor to the rich countries. For four decades, the rising trade between the two worlds has proceeded on steadily worsening terms for the poor. OPEC could hold back the tide and control the price on petroleum for no more than a few years.

The 1980 OPEC price may serve, nonetheless, as an indicator of the dimensions of the reverse flow of foreign aid. It can be argued that it expressed the true scarcity value of petroleum and, therefore, charged a fair Ricardian rent. Discounted by inflation, the price has now returned to its pre-1973 level.

The difference between the two prices reflects the fact that petroleum alone carries an annual subsidy to the rich countries that approaches $200 billion. The most that OECD headquarters can claim for money flowing the other way is $50 billion.

In reaction to inflation set off by their momentary loss of control of the price of oil, the industrialized countries embraced deflation. They set aside the goal of full employment and shrank their welfare states. Even as the financial community has alternately celebrated and deplored signs of "recovery" and "recession" in the low-amplitude business cycle, the growth of the world economy has not exceeded population growth by much for two decades. Despite continued subsidy from the poor, persistent deflation in the rich countries has arrested development in the developing world. With the exceptions of China and the countries of East and Southeast Asia, economies have stopped growing and have gone into decline. The net result of four decades of trade with the industrialized world has been their combined debt of $1.4 trillion. To maintain their creditworthiness, they have been invited by the international financial institutions to "restructure" their economies in the deflated image of their creditors. In addition to their development having been aborted, restructuring has reduced their social expenditures. Progress through the demographic transition has halted in many developing countries. It has gone into reverse in the poorest countries.

One indicator of development (especially during the first two decades after World War II) was the increase in the reliability of the vital statistics kept by the developing countries. Based on these real data, the Population Division of the U.N. Secretariat has been perfecting a computer model of the world population. Confidence in the data encouraged the publication in 1980 of long-range projections, which would estimate the size of the ultimate stabilized world population. The medium-fertility projection found the population increasing to 6 billion in the year 2000 and stabilizing at 10 billion in the year 2100. The present doubling could be seen as the last. Significantly, the model showed that the present poorest billion people will contribute 4 billion descendants to that ultimate population. In the high projection, the population stabilizes at 15 billion in 2100, with still larger contributions from the poorest countries.

In 1990, with more confidence in the data and their model, the U.N. demographers ran a second long-range projection. This time, the median projection showed the population reaching 6.3 billion by the year 2000, passing 10 billion at 2100, and stabilizing at 11.5 billion in 2150. The high projection has the population growing past 28 billion in 2150. In that population, the present poorest billion will generate 14 billion descendants.

The difference between the two projections measures the ground and the time lost to persistent stagnation of the world economy. Another set of numbers suggests the reduction in the size of the ultimate population and the time that might have been gained, if an organized campaign of development had gone forward at the founding of the United Nations. The world's two most populous countries have achieved development on their own—with little or no foreign aid, and largely in isolation from the world economy. With the smaller populations of countries that have made similar progress added to their grand total, it can be reckoned that more than one-half of the population of the developing world has entered the second phase of the demographic transition. Birth rates in all these countries are falling. They reflect still steeper declines in their fertility rates.

Within this 2.2 billion population, a population of 100 million has actually completed the passage through the demographic transition. This includes the populations of the "Tigers" of East Asia—now classified as "newly industrializing countries"—and Thailand, which is on the verge of that classification. It also includes two countries—Sri Lanka and Cuba—that have shared the proceeds of what development they have achieved most widely in their populations. These countries have come through most of the first and all of the second phase of the demographic transition within the span of a human lifetime. That compares with the 300-year passage of the industrialized 20 percent of the world's population. The technologies which have been pioneered over the centuries by that 20 percent were, of course, there on the shelf—ready for installation in the countries that followed. With the sudden increase of life expectancy, the people of the developing countries were ready to reduce their fertility at a lower level of living than that which is enjoyed by the people of the industrial world. They are able to do so by employing the portable technology of contraception.

CHINA'S INDUSTRIAL REVOLUTION

Still more decisive for the prospect of zero population growth is the progress of China. The Chinese revolution has been no less industrial than political. In political isolation from the world economy, and from the next-door Soviet economy as well, China's industrial revolution built the world's ninth-largest economy. In the half-century since 1949, the first bridges crossed the Yangtze and the Yellow rivers, and the first dams impounded their waters for flood control, irrigation, and the generation of electrical power. Rail and highway networks tie together once-distant regions in a continental economy. China is the fifth-largest producer of steel and the

> *The "Tigers" of East Asia, Thailand, Sri Lanka, and Cuba have come through most of the first and all of the second phase of the demographic transition within the span of a human lifetime. That compares with the 300-year passage of the industrialized 20 percent of the world's population.*

largest producer of cement and nitrogen fertilizer. It had accomplished all of this before it opened its markets and labor force to the world economy. But with a population of 1.12 billion—equal to that of all of the industrial countries combined—China remains a country of the poor. Until recently, however, China divided its increasing product with equity that was enforced by revolutionary ardor. The average GDP per capita of $370 in 1990 hovered close to the modal share in GDP—the share of most of the population. It was double that of 1949, despite the concurrent doubling of the population since then.

Much of the GDP per capita reaches the people through public expenditures on education and health. Ninety percent of the people were illiterate in 1949. Now, 75 percent are literate. Nearly all the children—equal in number to the entire population of the United States—are in school. Life expectancy—less than 40 years in 1949—now exceeds 70 years. Under-five-year-old deaths had fallen to 35 per 1,000 live births in 1992—down from more than 200 in 1949. This is the setting in which the second 20 percent of the world's population approaches full passage through the second phase of the demographic transition. In 1992, China's total fertility rate approached the zero-growth fertility rate (2.1 infants per female reproductive lifetime). It fell to 2.3.

Popular discourse, especially in the United States, attributes this astonishing development to the aggressive promotion of contraception (lately the coercive promotion of the "one-child family") by the central government. Until recently, the press has had less to say about China's economic development. The aggressive measures undoubtedly secured wide distribution of contraceptives. It hastened the "contraceptive prevalence rate" to 70 percent of the reproductive population. It cannot be shown that the coercive policies have had any result other than revival of the practice of female infanticide and increase in the rate of abortion. Upon arrival at the zero-growth fertility rate, China will still experience huge population growth. The median age of the population is twenty-four years of age. With such a high percentage of the population in the reproductive years, the birth rate must remain high. China is bound to reach 1.5 billion population.

INDIA'S INDUSTRIALIZATION

The industrialization of India (with its 870 million population) lags behind that of China by about twenty-five years. With deference due to an already installed private industrial sector, the government of India has been constrained to a "socialist pattern of development." A succession of five-year plans, nonetheless, installed a considerable industrial infrastructure before the country lowered its barriers to foreign capital at the start of this decade. Industrial investment was dedicated, from the beginning, to increasing the productivity of agriculture. After an uncertain start, during which food aid from the United States fended off famine, India achieved self-sufficiency in food production that it maintains ahead of population growth. With an industrial plant about one-half the size of China's, and the largest railway system in Asia, India is the world's twelfth-largest economy. The average GDP per capita ($350) is close to China's, but that average is high above the modal share of about $100. Perhaps 20 percent of the population—nearly 200 million people—live comfortably in that economy—at home in an urban-industrial civilization. But the villages have had their place in the socialist pattern of development. It brought them the new technologies of agriculture, sanitation, and medicine. It enrolled the children in schools. It organized producer and marketing cooperatives. And it established the rudiments of democratic self-government against traditional landlord feudalism.

India's progress over the half-century is summed up in a total fertility rate of 4.0. That is more than halfway to the zero-growth rate from the country's fertility rate at its liberation in 1947. The combined fer-

tility rate of the eight largest countries that have arrived at comparable GDP per capita is 5.8. The U.N. population projections schedule India's arrival at the 2.1 fertility rate in the year 2015. The low median age of the population ensures that, even at zero-growth fertility, it must increase to an ultimate census of not less than 1.6 billion. But if India's development continues on course, the present doubling of its population will be the last.

> *After an uncertain start, during which food aid from the United States fended off famine, India has achieved self-sufficiency in food production.*

There is much more growth ahead in the rest of the world population. According to the 1990 U.N. long-range projection, Latin America will increase 2.5 times to 1.4 billion people, the rest of Asia 2.7 times to 2.8 billion, and Africa nearly five times to 3 billion. Half of the present world population will generate 7 billion of the 11.5 billion projected for the year 2150.

Today, the developing countries are being advised to develop by trade—not by aid. The international financial institutions have compelled the "restructuring" of their economies and now declare its success. The inflow of foreign private investment has increased to $40 billion from $14 billion in the early 1980s. Developing countries turn up as "players" in the financial pages. Their full incorporation in the world economy by the market process is said to be surely just a matter of time.

For two decades, however, two-thirds of private direct investment (principally by the 350 transnationals) has gone to ten countries with populations of less than 500 million. Among them are the six "newly industrializing" countries and two countries in the Japanese sphere on their way into that classification. All of them are far along on the road to industrialization under their own steam. For private investment in the ninth country now on that list—Egypt—Cold War outlays by the United States supplied the infrastructure. The combined fertility rate of these countries (3.2) puts them well on the

way through the second phase of the demographic transition.

The charmed circle of ten now includes China, which had nearly completed its demographic transition before it applied for admission to the world economy. With China aboard, the combined fertility rate of the countries favored by private investment comes down to 2.6. For the rest of the developing countries (with populations totaling nearly 3 billion and a combined fertility rate in excess of 5.0), the remaining one-third of the private investment flow can scarcely move the needle of development. Most of it goes, in any case, for the extraction of resources—with no more than indirect repercussion for development. None of it goes to the poorest countries—twenty-six of them in Africa, where the fertility rate exceeds 6.0.

Poverty, of course, presents obstacles to private investment. The Group of Experts declared: " . . . the amount which can be profitably invested at a 4 percent rate of interest depends on the amount which is being spent at the same time on improving social capital, and especially on public health, on education, and on roads and communications." Because incomes inadequate to sustain current consumption cannot generate it, the necessary capital must be supplied by way of "intergovernmental grants." Nothing that has happened since 1950 puts the wisdom of this counsel in doubt.

In the long-term transitional period, most developing countries have developed technically sophisticated indigenous intelligentsias. There has been time for these people to put flesh on the bare bones of the 1950 formulation of the essential role of foreign aid. On the floor of the U.N. General Assembly, and in bilateral negotiations between developing countries and prospective donors, their ongoing labors have lent tangible reality and specificity to the need for aid and the industrial technology it is supposed to transfer.

AGENDA 21

A comprehensive sampling of this now immense body of work is available in Agenda 21 and its underlying primary data bank. As the U.S. media failed to report, Agenda 21 is the principal work product of the U.N. Conference on Environment and Development that convened in Rio de Janeiro in June 1992. Agenda 21 spells out and prices out the program of "sustainable development" that will sustain the fourfold multiplication of the global GDP that will be required in the next century to eliminate poverty in a world population that has doubled to 10-to-12 billion. It is a program of development the Earth can sustain in bringing the human species through its demographic transition.

Agenda 21 is composed of 2,500 enterprises engineered and otherwise realized by indigenous experts in the developing countries and U.N. technical agencies. They specify work to be done in environmental repair and conservation, in resource (especially agricultural resource) development, in the building of urban infrastructure, and in the development of human capital. The 2,500 enterprises constitute, of course, no more than a start on the work that must engage hundreds of millions of men and women in every developing country over the next century.

Agenda 21 shows that the task is finite and within the bounds of the Earth's resources. The developing countries are to supply most of the approximately $600-billion annual investment. From "savings" which are latent in their underemployed work forces and underutilized resources, they are committed to invest $500 billion—about 10 percent of their GDP. The industrial countries are asked to invest $125 billion—0.7 percent of their combined GDP. It will be transferred principally in the form of technology necessary to catalyze the yield from people and resources. While the industrial countries signed the nonbinding document setting forth Agenda 21, they made no commitment to supply their 0.7 percent share.

For foreign aid there is "no money." The industrial countries were readier forty-five years ago to render economic assistance to the underdeveloped countries. Governments had retained war powers for the first tasks of peace. Now the globalized economy is in private hands. The 350 transnational corporations conduct their own foreign policies with the countries of the two worlds. Their 25 million employees and perhaps 100 million principal shareholders thrive in a financial hothouse that escapes the doldrums in which the industrial economies and populations are becalmed. The 24-hour world financial market, which conducts currency transactions at ten times the rate that facilitates the movement of goods and investment capital across national borders, disburses the credit to corporations and governments alike. A government that undertakes counter-cyclical fiscal measures, including outlays for foreign aid, invites trades against the value of its currency.

Agenda 21 asks, first of all, that the industrialized countries restart their economies. The electorates of those countries must soon assert their interest in the choice now being made by default. In the United States, apparently, the choice is to be deliberate. The "Contract with America" schedules the last best hope of Earth for zeroing-out to oblivion. For the survival of market economies and self-governing polities, the present doubling of the world's population must be the last. The logistics of sustaining a population of 28 billion would offer little slack for the market process and no tolerance for freedom of expression.

GERARD PIEL, President and Publisher of *Scientific American* from 1948 to 1986, is the author of *Only One World*, W.H. Freeman & Co., 1992.

P. Mountzis/UNHCR

Somali refugees arrive in Mombasa (Kenya), 1992.

REFUGEES: THE RISING TIDE

BY RONY BRAUMAN

There have never been so many
long-term refugees as there are today

There are over sixteen million refugees in the world today. The reality behind this stark figure is the multitude of human tragedies being played out in encampments, sometimes surrounded with barbed wire, where freedom is the price paid for survival and security is maintained not by the rule of law but by enclosure. To be a refugee is to exchange one injustice for another, one form of suffering for another.

But unless we are prepared to accept the refugee's condition as a permanent one, as is sometimes unfortunately the case, it is important to understand the origins of these mass movements and the course they take. Since 1990, for example, some 10 million exiles have managed to return home and pick up the threads of a way of life they had been forced to abandon. Another important fact is that half the total number of refugees, some 8.5 million people, originate from only four countries: Palestine, Afghanistan, Rwanda, and Bosnia and Herzegovina.

This does not mean that the refugee problem is confined to the Third World and that the refugee's plight has never been known in

Reprinted with permission from *The UNESCO Courier,* October 1996, pp. 25–28.

the countries which are today industrialized. The Huguenots, the French Protestants who fled from France after the revocation of the Edict of Nantes, the law which gave them a measure of religious liberty, in 1685 were the first group of refugees to be defined as such. To avoid *dragonnades,* the quartering of Louis XIV's soldiers in their households, forcible conversion, and exclusion from professional activities, 300,000 Protestants fled the kingdom and sought refuge in neighbouring Protestant countries. They were the first exiles for whom specific responsibility was acknowledged, in this instance a duty of religious solidarity.

Horror and humanitarianism

But the age of refugees that has outstripped all others has been the twentieth century, which seems to have been divided between humane sensitivity and political terror. Constant growth of concern for human rights—both in the minds of men and women and in international conventions and regulations—has been accompanied by the appearance of new forms of oppression, social control and destruction. Modern tyrants are probably no worse than those of the past, but the technical means at their disposal have enabled them to

envisage programmes of social surgery that their predecessors could never have imagined. Horror magnified by technology is a leitmotiv of the twentieth century, but it has been accompanied by a concomitant determination to react by taking humanitarian action. A year after it was founded in 1920, the League of Nations established the High Commission for Refugees under the leadership of Norway's Fridtjof Nansen, whose first task was to organize the repatriation of 1.5 million refugees and prisoners of war scattered all over Europe by the turmoil of the First World War.

In the Second World War, civilians were in the eye of the storm. At the end of the conflict there were a recorded 21 million refugees scattered across Europe. In 1951, the Office of the United Nations High Commissioner for Refugees (UNHCR) began its activities (see box "UNHCR: Facts and Figures"). According to the 1951 Geneva Convention relating to the Status of Refugees, which was drawn up in parallel with the creation of UNHCR, refugee status is accorded to any person who, "owing to well-founded fear of being persecuted for reasons of race, religion, nationality or political opinion, is outside the country of his nationality and is unable, or owing to such fear, is unwilling to avail himself to the protection of that country. . . ." One necessary (but not sufficient)

Liba Taylor/UNHCR

Refugees voluntarily leaving Mexico to return home to Guatemala.

THE OFFICE OF THE UNITED NATIONS HIGH COMMISSIONER FOR REFUGEES (UNHCR)

The Office of the United Nations High Commissioner for Refugees (UNHCR) was established in 1951 with responsibilities for "providing international protection... and ... seeking permanent solutions for the problems of refugees". Its work is humanitarian and entirely non-political. Initially, its mandate was limited to people outside their country of origin, but over the years it has increasingly been called on to protect or assist returnees in their home countries and particular groups of displaced people who have not crossed an international border but are in a refugee-like situation inside their country of origin.

The 1951 UN Convention relating to the Status of Refugees, which is the key to UNHCR's protection activities, is a legally binding treaty. It contains a general definition of the term "refugee" that no longer ties it to specific national groups, clearly establishes the principle of *non-refoulement*, whereby no person may be returned against his or her will to a territory where he or she may be exposed to persecution, and sets standards for the treatment of refugees, including their legal status, employment and welfare.

UNHCR endeavours:

☛ to encourage governments to ratify international and regional conventions concerning refugees, returnees and displaced people;

☛ to ensure that refugees are treated in accordance with recognized international standards and receive an appropriate legal status and the same economic and social rights as nationals of the country in which they have been given asylum;

☛ to promote the granting of asylum to refugees, i.e. to ensure that they are admitted to safety and protected against forcible return to a country where they have reason to fear persecution or other serious harm;

☛ to ensure that applications for asylum are examined fairly and that asylum-seekers are protected, while their requests are being examined, against forcible return to a country where their freedom or lives would be endangered;

☛ to help refugees to cease being refugees either through voluntary repatriation to their countries of origin, or through the eventual acquisition of the nationality of their country of residence;

☛ to help reintegrate refugees returning to their home country and to monitor amnesties, guarantees or assurances on the basis of which they have returned home;

☛ to promote the physical security of refugees, asylum-seekers and returnees.

UNHCR's material assistance activities include emergency relief, assisting efforts to promote voluntary repatriation or resettlement within new national communities, social welfare, education and legal aid.

condition of refugee status is the crossing of an international border. This differentiates refugees from people forced out of their usual place of residence, who are considered as "displaced persons" and are without legal status.

Changing status

This definition was hammered out by Europeans in the political context of the 1950s. Since then its practical application has broadened over the years in response to changing conditions. It was a straightforward matter when a Soviet or Hungarian dissident sought protection in a democratic country in the 1960s or 1970s. It was just as straightforward when it was a question of sav-

Munir Nasr/UNRWA

The United Nations Relief and Works Agency for Palestine Refugees in the Near East (UNRWA), established in 1949, runs 98 health units and 30 dental and special clinics. One third of the 2.39 million refugees registered with UNRWA live in crowded refugee camps. Shown here, a medical visit in Beqa'a camp.

M. Larsen/UNHCR

As persons displaced within their own national borders, these Chechen civilians fleeing the combat zone are of concern to UNHCR.

ing Iranians or Argentines from the claws of their gaolers in the 1970s. Serious complications began to appear in the second half of the 1970s when major upheavals occurred in several parts of the Third World. Changes of regime in Southeast Asia and in southern and eastern Africa, the invasion of Afghanistan and the rise of violence in Central America transformed the problem, although perception of it and the international instruments designed to

provide a response did not really change accordingly. The end of the Cold War saw the easing of a number of conflicts, enabling millions of exiles to return home. But other regions erupted into violence.

These political transformations have had profound consequences on the status of refugees. The problem was once solved by the integration of refugees in their host countries; today's solution is to provide aid in camps es-

UNHCR: FACTS AND FIGURES

UNHCR Public Information Section
Case postale 2500, CH-1211 Geneva 2 Dépôt
Switzerland
Tel: (41 22) 739 85 02
Fax: (41 22) 739 73 15
e-mail: hqpi∅∅@unhcr.ch

• UNHCR programmes are financed by voluntary contributions from governments and governmental and non-governmental organizations. UNHCR's budget has increased from some $550 million in 1990 to $1.3 billion in 1995. It also receives a subsidy from the regular budget of United Nations for administrative costs.
• In 1996 UNHCR employed 5,500 staff members working in 123 countries.
• In August 1996, 131 States were Parties to the 1951 Convention relating to the Status of Refugees and/or its 1967 protocol.
• Between 1981 and 1991, the number of refugees more than doubled, rising from 8 to 17 mil-

lion persons. 26 million refugees and persons of concern to UNHCR were recorded in 1996.
• In 1994, UNHCR confronted the largest and fastest exodus in its history when more than 2 million Rwandans fled to neighbouring countries between April and August.
• The conflict in the former Yugoslavia has given rise to more than 3.7 million refugees, displaced people and others of concern to UNHCR

M. Kobayashi/UNHCR

Above, voluntary Cambodian returnees head for a reception centre set up by UNHCR.

tablished along the borders of warring nations for people who hope eventually to return home. The last few years have shown that return can be possible and that exile is not inevitable.

Ethnic cleansing

A Third World phenomenon in the 1980s, refugee camps have since then reappeared in Europe for the first time for forty years. In conflicts of ethnic and political "cleansing" refugees are no longer a consequence of violence but its very purpose. Here, displacement is no longer a grim by-product of human passions but a strategic goal of total wars waged by armies, not against other armies, but against civilians.

Whatever the cause of the exodus may be, the international community's duty—its fundamental commitment—must be to protect these peoples, first of all by applying the principle of *non-refoulement* (see box "The Office of the United Nations..."). People do not choose to uproot themselves from their land voluntarily, for reasons of opportunism. They flee to escape oppression, and the international community has a collective duty to shelter and help those deprived by force of circumstances of the means to ensure their own survival. The defence of freedom and pluralism can only be based on recognition and defence of the right of asylum. In these uncertain times, the struggle is certainly a hard one, but it is more important than ever to wage it.

Rony Brauman is a French medical doctor.

How Much Food Will We Need in The 21st Century?

By William H. Bender

Seldom has the world faced an unfolding emergency whose dimensions are as clear as the growing imbalance between food and people.[1]

The world food situation has improved dramatically during the past 30 years and the prospects are very good that the 20-year period from 1990 to 2010 will see further gains. . . . If Malthus is ultimately to be correct in his warning that population will outstrip food production, then at least we can say: Malthus Must Wait.[2]

Ever since Malthus, society has worried periodically about whether it will be able to produce enough food to feed people in the future. Yet until recently, most of the debate surrounding the issue of food scarcity focused on the potential for increasing the food supply. The key questions were whether there would be enough land and water to produce the amount of food needed and whether technology could keep increasing the yields of food grains. Now, however, scientists are growing concerned that the intensive use of land, energy, fertilizer, and pesticides that modern agriculture seems to require jeopardizes the health of the environment. This anxiety has

been integrated into the general debate about food scarcity, but interestingly enough, the question of the demand for food—including the specific physiological needs and dietary desires of different peoples—has not. In fact, relatively little attention has been paid to the issue of demand despite the fact that like energy and water, food can be conserved and the demand for it adjusted to meet human needs and lessen the burden that modern agriculture places on the environment.

Unlike with many other forms of consumption, there are limits to the physical quantity of food that people can consume. In a number of high-income countries, that limit seems to have been reached already. If global population does double by 2050, as many have predicted, providing everyone with a rich and varied diet (equivalent to that enjoyed by today's wealthiest countries) would only require a tripling of food production. Alternatively, with sufficient improvements in efficiency and adoption of a healthier diet in high-income countries, it would be possible to provide such a diet for the entire global population with just a doubling of food production. But even a doubling of current production could strain Earth's ecosystems, as critics of modern agriculture's intensive use of resources will attest. Clearly, then, in-

creases in food demand will have to be slowed if we hope to achieve a sustainable agricultural system. Central to the issue of demand, however, is the question of how much food the world really needs.

From an analytical standpoint, the amount of food a given population (be it a country, a region, or the world) actually *needs* is the product of two factors: the number of people and the average (minimal) food requirement per person. The amount of food the population *consumes,* however, is determined not only by its basic needs but also by its income and dietary preferences. This difference is particularly important in high-income countries, where crops that could be consumed directly are instead fed to animals to produce eggs, meat, and milk. Finally, the amount of food a given population *requires* (i.e., has to produce or import) depends on how much is wasted in going from farm to mouth as well as on its level of consumption. In mathematical terms,

$$Req = Pop \cdot PFR \cdot Diet \cdot Eff,$$

where *Req* is the total number of food calories that has to be produced, *Pop* is population, *PFR* is the number of calories per person that is needed to sustain life and health, *Diet* is a factor reflecting

From *Environment,* March 1997, 7–11, 27–28. Reprinted with permission of the Helen Dwight Reid Educational Foundation. Published by Heldref Publications, 1319 Eighteenth St., N.W., Washington, D.C. 20036-1802. © 1997.

Table 1. World population supportable under different conditions

Conditions in	Population (billions)
United States	2.3
Europe	4.1
Japan	6.1
Balgladesh	10.9
Subsistence only	15.0
Addendum: Actual 1990 population	5.3

NOTE: This table shows the number of people that could be fed at the 1990 level of agricultural production if the dietary preferences and food system efficiencies in the countries (or area) shown prevailed throughout the world. Dietary preferences reflect both income and the extent to which cereal grains are fed to animals instead of being consumed directly. Food system efficiencies reflect the extent to which food is spoiled or wasted in going from farm to mouth.

SOURCE: Author's calculations.

the conversion of some plant calories to animal calories, and *Eff* is the ratio of calories available in the retail market to those consumed.

This article will address the neglected issue of food demand in terms of the four variables of this equation. In the process, it will question some of the assumptions previous analysts have made, particularly with regard to desirable diets and food system efficiency. Though not definitive, the analysis strongly suggests that the right policy choices can reduce the growth in the global demand for food. Indeed, the potential scope of such a reduction appears to be substantial: As Table 1 on this page shows, vastly different numbers of people can be supported by a given amount of agricultural production depending on dietary habits and degrees of efficiency.

Population

Global population will play an important role in determining how much food we will require in the future. For this reason, attempts to calculate future food requirements depend upon projections of population growth. Although demographers generally agree that the current global population will double by the middle of the next century, considerable uncertainty accompanies these projections.

The United Nations' estimates of the world's population in 2050, for example, vary from 7.9 billion to 11.9 billion. If global population reaches the higher value rather than the lower one, global food requirements will be 50 percent higher.

National and international policies that provide family planning services, maternal education, and social support systems can affect population growth, and these policies will undoubtedly have the single largest effect on food requirements in the 21st century. The availability of food will also play a role, however. Famine—the most dramatic example of lack of food—has fortunately been largely eliminated (except during wars) and no longer ranks as a major factor in global population growth. Even so, the relative abundance of food has a direct effect on the other key factors that influence population growth, and combined with the subtle influences exerted by the food and agriculture sector, it can have a significant impact. For example, in rural agricultural societies, the demand for agricultural labor affects fertility rates, while reductions in child mortality (which are influenced by food availability) usually precede reduction in fertility rates.

Physiological Requirements

Physiological food requirements, represented by PFR in the equation, are determined by several factors, including the population's age and gender distribution, its average height and weight, and its activity level. One may compute such requirements in two different ways, using either actual circumstances or normative ones (such as desired heights and weights or activity levels).[3]

Around the world, actual per capita caloric consumption varies from a low of 1,758 calories per day in Bangladesh to a high of 2,346 calories per day in the Netherlands. Caloric consumption is higher in the Netherlands for several reasons. First, the population is generally older, and adults require more food than children. Second, people in the Netherlands are on average taller and heavier than those in Bangladesh and therefore need more food. (Lower activity levels in the Netherlands partially offset these factors, however.) If the actual consumption levels in these two countries were to change, either the weights of individuals or their activity levels would have to change accordingly. Caloric consumption levels vary by no more than one-third on a national basis—far less than the variation in caloric availability.

When making future projections, normative considerations can also be very

important. A population's general health, for instance, affects the amount of food it needs. Parasites and disease can substantially increase an individual's energy requirements, with fever, for example, raising his or her basal metabolic rate (the number of calories he or she uses when at rest) approximately 10 percent for every one degree C increase in body temperature.[4] Disease can also impair the body's ability to absorb nutrients, while parasites siphon away food energy for their own use. Although not important globally, health factors are highly significant in certain low-income countries. In fact, in localized situations health interventions may be more effective than merely increasing the food supply in helping people to satisfy basic physiological food requirements.

Of course, to qualify as truly sustainable, the world's agricultural system has to produce enough calories to ensure food security around the globe. This is a normative concept, as is clear in the commonly accepted definition of food security: "access by all people at all times to enough food for an active, healthy life."[5] Thus, for future projections, we could consider a world with lower levels of undernutrition and stunting, leading to higher food requirements.

Table 2 shows estimates of physiological food requirements for the world as a whole, for high-income countries, and for low-income countries, all based on current circumstances. (The box on the next page discusses the way in which these estimates were prepared). High-income countries use much more than twice as much food per person. This variation is not due to differences in calories actually consumed but to differences in diet and the lower efficiency of food systems in those countries.

Dietary Patterns

Diets are largely determined by economic factors, particularly prices and incomes. In Africa, for example, people derive two-thirds of their calories from less expensive starchy staples (including cereals, roots, and tubers) and only 6 percent from animal products. In Europe, on the other hand, people derive 33 percent of their calories from animal products and less than one-third from starchy staples. The global diet falls somewhere in the mid-range between these two extremes.

As people's level of income increases, the share of starchy staples in their diet declines, and the shares of animal products, oils, sweeteners, fruits, and vegetables increase.[6] In fact, the absolute quantities of these products that people

Table 2. Numerical estimates for key food variables, 1991

Variable	World	High-income countries	Low-and middle-income countries	Best practice/ medically preferred
Calories per person per day				
Total food available[a]	3,939	6,964	3,007	n/a
Food available in retail markets	2,693	3,255	2,520	n/a
Physiological food requirements[b]	2,179	2,231	2,169	n/a
Ratio				
Dietary conversion factor[c]	1.46	2.14	1.19	1.5
End-use efficiency factor[d]	1.24	1.46	1.16	1.3

n/a Not applicable
[a]Includes animal feed
[b]1990 estimate
[c]Line 1 divided by line 2, except for last column, which is author's estimate
[d]Line 2 divided by line 3, except for last column, which is author's estimate

NOTE: Computational methods are described in the box on this page.

SOURCES: Line 1: Author's calculations; Line 2: United Nations Food and Agriculture Organization at http://www.foa.org; Line 3: Author's calculations.

eat increase even faster than the shares because caloric availability overall also increases as incomes increase. This growing dietary diversity provides a substantial health benefit for people at the low to medium income level.

The overall increase in food availability over the last several decades, while a welcome development, has created problems of its own. As people consume more animal products, they tend to consume more animal fats than recent medical research has shown to be healthy. Currently, the World Health Organization (WHO) recommends that people limit their dietary intake of fat to no more than 30 percent of calorie consumption, and some foresee a revision to no more than 25 to 20 percent in the future.[7]

At present, 16.8 percent of the global population lives in high-income countries, where, on average, fat consumption exceeds the 30 percent level. But health concerns have clearly begun to affect consumption patterns in those countries: Despite rising incomes and relatively stable prices, beef consumption has declined in a number of countries since the mid-1970s. In the United States, for instance, per capita beef consumption has dropped 25 percent.[8] (Overall meat consumption in the United States has remained approximately constant, however, because people merely shifted to eating poultry.)

Clearly, public policy that encourages people to reduce their consumption of animal fat has two benefits. It improves the health of the population while reducing the pressure that increased food production places on the global agricultural system. Table 3 on page 57 shows the conversion rates of grain to animal products in terms of two common measures: kilograms and calories. For the past 30 years, approximately 40 percent of all cereal grains produced globally have been used for feed, with 50 percent being used for food. (The remaining 10 percent have gone to seed, been used in processing, or ended up as waste.) As Table 2 shows, however, the use of grain for feed is much higher in high-income countries.

A NOTE ON COMPUTATIONS

Physiological food requirements. Estimating the number of calories that the average person in a given population actually consumes (as distinct from the number that is available in the retail market) entails a five-step procedure.[1] The first step is to determine the age-gender structure of the population, placing children in single-year age groups and adults in five-year age groups. The second step is to estimate the basal metabolic rates for each group based on group members' average heights and weights. The third step is to estimate the different groups' physical activity patterns and combine them with their basal metabolic rates to determine each group's energy requirements. The fourth step is to make allowances for such factors as pregnancy and infection rates and then multiply the average energy requirement for each group by the number of people in the group.

The final step is to sum the energy requirements for the different groups and divide by the total population. Normative food requirements (i.e., the number of calories needed to maintain desired heights, weights, and activity levels) can then be determined by adjusting appropriately for heights, weights, and activity levels.

Dietary conversion factor. This factor reflects the number of calories "lost" in using grain to produce animal products. It is computed as the ratio of the total number of calories produced to the number available (in final form) in the retail market. The denominator is usually per capita caloric availability as estimated by the United Nations Food and Agriculture Organization (FAO).[2] The numerator is more difficult to determine because some animals graze rather than being fed grain. The procedure used in this article was to sum three factors: the

number of plant calories available, excluding cereals, starchy roots, and tubers; the number of plant calories available from cereals, starchy roots, and tubers, whether used for feed or for human consumption; and the estimated number of animal calories derived from range feeding.

End-use efficiency factor. End-use efficiency—the proportion of calories produced that actually ends up in human mouths—is computed as the ratio of calories available in the retail market (from FAO) to calories consumed (as computed above).

1. See W. P. T. James and E. C. Schofield, Human Energy Requirements (Oxford, U.K.: Oxford University Press by arrangement with the United Nations Food and Agriculture Organization, 1990).
2. Available at http://www.fao.org.

Efficiency

The last factor affecting global food requirements is the efficiency with which food moves from farms to human mouths. Efficiency actually has two components, one pertaining to marketing and distribution and one pertaining to "end use." Losses in marketing and distribution, such as those due to rodents and mold, are important in low-income countries but decline steadily with increases in income.[9] Inefficiencies in end use, which include losses due to spoilage, processing and preparation waste, and plate waste, are most significant in high-income countries, however.

The United Nations Food and Agriculture Organization (FAO) estimates that per capita caloric availability (i.e., the amount of food that appears in the retail market) ranges from a low of 1,667 calories in Ethiopia to a high of 3,902 calories in Belgium-Luxembourg. These two figures differ by 234 percent—much more than the 33 percent difference in physiological consumption. Because it is physiologically impossible for the population of an entire country to consume an average of 3,902 calories, we know that a substantial amount of food in high-income countries is never consumed. According to estimates, losses from end-use inefficiencies equal 30 to 70 percent of the amount of food actually consumed.[10] With the exception of Belgium-Luxembourg, it is middle-income countries such as Greece, Ireland, Yugoslavia, Hungary, Bulgaria, Egypt, and Libya that have the highest levels of waste. But in every country where per capita income is more than $1,500 (U.S.), at least 20 percent more food is used than is consumed. The computed values for the end-use efficiency factor in Table 2 also reflect the discrepancy between high- and low-income countries.

It is unclear to what extent these losses are a necessary component of increased standards of living because little analysis has been done on the sources of this waste. Some intercountry comparisons provide useful insights, however. The Netherlands, Finland, Japan, and Sweden, which have comparable levels of income, waste only about 35 percent (on a per capita caloric basis), while the United States, Belgium-Luxembourg, Switzerland, and Italy waste nearly 60 percent.[11] This suggests that there is scope for reducing food requirements without lowering standards of living, much as high-income countries have done with energy use since the 1970s.

Given the current distribution of food consumption and food system efficiency, if every middle- and high-income country were to reduce its level of waste to 30 percent, global food requirements would decline 7.4 percent. (If consumption of animal products were to decrease in proportion, requirements would decline 12.5 percent owing to the lower demand for feed.) Clearly, as global incomes increase and the number of people living in countries with low food system efficiency continues to grow, the level of end-use waste will become an increasingly important part of overall food requirements.[12]

Final Thoughts

By its very nature, agricultural production has significant impacts upon natural ecosystems and the environment. There is little question that agricultural production must increase to meet population growth, but the magnitude of the increase necessary to improve human welfare is very much a question of policy tradeoffs between demand management and supply promotion.

Food is the only sector of the economy that has reached satiation for a large portion of the world's population. Tripling world food production would provide sufficient food for a doubled global population to have a varied, nutritious, and healthy diet comparable to today's European diet. The same goal could be reached by slightly more than doubling agricultural production if an effort were made to improve food system efficiencies and if diets low in fat became commonplace. This change will only take place if public policy creates explicit incentives for healthier diets and more efficient food systems, however.

It is environmentally and medically prudent to prevent the levels of waste and fat consumption in the wealthier developing economies from rising to those seen in North America today. It is also fiscally prudent: Grain imports tend to rise rapidly in maturing developing economies, so that decreased food system efficiency and increased fat consumption can lead directly to the loss of vital foreign exchange. Therefore, self-interest can be used to dramatically improve the long-term sustainability of the global agricultural system.

William H. Bender is an economist with extensive international experience in food and nutrition. He has consulted with the United Nations Children's Fund, the United Nations Food and Agriculture Organization, the World Bank, the United States Agency for International Development, the European Community, and many other organizations. His address is P.O. Box 66036, Auburndale, MA 02166 (telephone: (617) 647-9210; e-mail: bender@tiac.net).

NOTES

1. L. Brown et al., *State of the World, 1994* (New York: W. W. Norton & Company, 1994), 196.
2. D. O. Mitchell and M. D. Ingco, *The World Food Outlook* (Washington, D.C.: World Bank, 1993), 232.
3. Requirements are usually measured in terms of calories, both because food analysts tend to focus on producing sufficient calories and because even with a cereal-based diet, people can get adequate protein if they consume enough calories. (The exception to this rule lies in groups, such as infants, who have special nutritional needs.) Of course, consuming enough calories does not guarantee getting enough micronutrients such as iron, vitamin A, and iodine. To obtain those nutrients, people have to eat fruit, vegetables, and fat in addition to starchy staples. However, the inputs (e.g., land, water,

Table 3. Conversion rates of grain to animal products		
Animal product	**Kilograms of feed/ kilograms of output**	**Calories of feed/ calories of output**
Beef	7.0	9.8
Pork	6.5	7.1
Poultry	2.7	5.7
Milk	1.0	4.9

NOTE: These conversions are very approximate, as the caloric density of both feeds and animal products can vary greatly. Furthermore, data units are often not specified or precisely comparable.

SOURCE: Column 1: Office of Technology Assessment, *A New Technological Era for American Agriculture*, OTA-F-474 (Washington, D.C., 1992); Column 2: Author's estimates.

and fertilizer) needed to provide a diverse diet are minor compared with those needed to provide enough calories.

4. R. E. Behrman and V. C. Vaughn, *Nelson Textbook of Pediatrics,* 13th ed. (Philadelphia: W. B. Saunders Company, 1987).

5. World Bank, *Poverty and Hunger: Issues and Options for Food Security in Developing Countries* (Washington, D.C., 1986).

6. Calculations of income elasticities reflect how consumption patterns change as income increases. Income elasticity is the percentage change in the demand for a particular good that results from a 1 percent increase in income. Demand is considered elastic when the percentage change is greater than 1, inelastic when it is less than 1. Animal products, for instance, are income-elastic goods because their share in diets tends to increase more rapidly than income. Researchers at or-

ganizations like the World Bank, the International Food Policy Research Institute, and the International Institute for Applied Systems Analysis use such elasticities in global models that attempt to simulate future developments in the world agricultural system. Models like these can help provide insight into questions such as the effect increased demand for animal products is likely to have on grain production.

7. World Health Organization Study Group on Diet, Nutrition and Prevention of Noncommunicable Diseases, *Diet, Nutrition and the Prevention of Chronic Diseases: Report of a WHO Study Group,* World Health Organization Technical Report Series 797 (Geneva: World Health Organization, 1992), 109.

8. L. A. Duewer, K. R. Krause, and K. E. Nelson, *U.S. Poultry and Red Meat Con-*

sumption, Prices, Spreads, and Margins, Agriculture Information Bulletin Number 684 (Washington, D.C.: United States Department of Agriculture, Economic Research Service, 1993).

9. In low-income countries, such losses are as high as 15 percent for cereals and 25 percent for roots and tubers; in high-income countries they are less than 4 percent. See, for example, D. Norse, "A New Strategy for Feeding a Crowded Planet," *Environment,* June 1992, 6; and W. Bender, "An End Use Analysis of Global Food Requirements," *Food Policy* 19, no. 4 (1994): 381.

10. Bender, note 9 above, pages 388–90. In these countries, of course, data accuracy is also highest, giving us the most confidence in these estimates.

11. Ibid.

12. Ibid.

Angling for 'aquaculture'

Fish farms emerge as a viable alternative to dwindling sea harvests.

by Gary Turbak

For centuries, many viewed the seas as an inexhaustible source of food. High-tech breakthroughs increased the amount of fish harvested worldwide from 1959 to 1989 almost five-fold to nearly 100 million tons (90.7 million metric tons). Then suddenly, once abundant stocks of cod, bluefin tuna, salmon, and other species began disappearing from fish finder screens. The world's fishing fleets had accomplished the unthinkable—they had virtually depleted the oceans.

According to the Food and Agriculture Organizations (FAO) of the United Nations, 70 percent of the world's fish stocks are fully exploited, depleted, or in the process of rebuilding. It calls the situation "globally nonsustainable" and says that "major ecological and economic damage is already visible." Current shortages have resulted in fishing bans, antagonism among fishermen and nations for territorial rights, and the use of habitat-damaging harvesting methods like dynamite. But most worrisome is the potential loss of protein for a rising human population.

With oceans becoming increasingly barren, dinner plates are being filled by an industry almost as ancient as fishing itself—aquaculture, or fish farming. Since 1991, aquaculture's output has shot up from a million (907,000 metric) tons annually to more than 16 million (14.5

Examples of fish farming: salmon hatchery in Maine, U.S.A., salmon farm off Norway's coast.

million metric) tons in 1994. Globally, this $26 billion industry already accounts for 22 percent of all fish production, and by 2010, will account for four of every five fish consumed. Among freshwater species, farms already produce more fish than traditional harvesting methods.

Culturing fish is actually a centuries-old practice. The Egyptians raised tilapia 4,000 years ago, and Roman fish reservoirs predate the birth of Christ. In 460 B.C., a Chinese entrepreneur named Fen Li wrote "Fish Culture Classics" to describe his country's carp-raising endeavors. European noblemen often kept fish in the moats encircling their castles, and pools near the Washington Monument in the U.S. capital once harbored carp.

Modern aquaculture encompasses a variety of marine animal life. Carp and shrimp are common crops in many Asian countries, while salmon, crawfish, trout, bass, and the "king"—catfish—are popular in the U.S. Other underwater livestock include oysters, clams, redfish, tilapia, abalone, turbot, cod, and lobster. Virtually no aquatic creature is exempt—even eel ranching is big business in Japan and Taiwan. The Japanese annually eat 150 million pounds (68 million kilograms) of these snake-like creatures, and gastronomes in Europe and elsewhere are developing a taste for them.

Various species have been added to the roster as ocean stocks decline and technology improves. Salmon farming, for example, started in the 1960s in Norway, when researchers dammed some estuaries and turned loose a few million fingerlings. The practice later spread to other nations such as Chile, Canada, the United Kingdom, and the United States. Canada and Norway are now in the process of building efficient halibut-growing operations.

Fish farming booms in developing nations—especially those in Asia, home to more than 80 percent of the global total. China alone is responsible for half the worldwide production, followed by India and Japan. Europe produces about nine percent of the total, North America about four percent, and South America about three percent.

But even in regions with relatively low production, aquaculture boosts national economies. Chile has become the world's second leading producer of domestic salmon (after Norway), producing nearly 200 million pounds (90.8 million kilograms) annually. In Ecuador, exports of commercially raised shrimp now surpass even coffee, bananas, and cocoa. And for the last two decades, fish farming has been the fastest growing agricultural industry in the U.S.

Fish can be raised in various manmade habitats—flooded natural lowlands, inland ponds filled with well water, or coastal enclosures anchored near shore. Aquaculture even exists in the open sea (where it is referred to as "mariculture"). In the Gulf of Mexico, Sea Pride Industries plans a futuristic, sunken cage-like system capable of producing five million pounds (2.7 million kilograms) of red snapper, bass, and other species annually. Configured like spokes on a wheel, the tubular cages will be 40 feet (12.2 metres) in diameter and 172 feet (52.4 metres) long. Feeding pipes will run the length of each spoke, and air tanks at the hub will permit the entire apparatus to be raised and lowered. Gulf growers have even experimented with stretching tent-shaped net enclosures around the legs of offshore oil rigs.

Other methods feature high technology. In California, Solar Aquafarms raises tilapia in a sprawling operation covered by greenhouses and warmed by solar heaters. Computers control feeding, water temperatures, and levels of oxygen and nitrogen. The water is continually cleaned and reused with the resulting waste products turned into fertilizer.

Some growers breed fish using a hormone supplement that produces predominantly female offspring, which grow faster and produce better filets. Norwegian aquaculturists have even developed gene-altering techniques that make fish grow faster, help them better withstand disease, and produce a higher-quality taste. Another technique alters genes so that fish can survive in colder temperatures.

Retailers and restaurateurs like farm-raised fish for their standard reliable quality and year-round availability. Due to regulations or migratory behavior, some wild stocks—Alaskan salmon for example—can only be purchased during certain months.

Farm fish also stand head and fin above other livestock when it comes to efficiency. Chickens require five and a half pounds of feed to produce a single pound of meat. For pigs, the ratio is seven to one; for cattle, it's 15 to 1. Salmon, however, will produce a pound of filets from just two pounds of feed.

Although epicures argue about the taste of cultured versus wild fish, the former are generally thought to possess piscatorial palatability because they are raised in a controlled environment, fed a prescribed diet, and treated for diseases. Cultured fish can be processed in minutes, instantly

'King' Catfish

In the United States, catfish is the king of aquaculture. Today, this species accounts for more of the U.S. industry than all other fish combined—an annual production of nearly 500 million pounds (227 million kilograms). At one time a southern specialty, catfish is now available nationwide and per-capita consumption has doubled since 1985.

As with other livestock, catfish production begins with the mating of selected breeding animals. The resulting eggs are placed in environmentally controlled hatching tanks, where a week later they become infant catfish called fry. After two or three weeks, the fry have grown to an inch (2.5 centimetres) in length and become hardy enough to survive in outdoor maturing ponds.

Maturing ponds vary in size from a few to more than 20 acres (8.1 hectares), and a large farm operation may have several such reservoirs. A one-acre (.405 hectare) pond that is four to five feet (1.2 to 1.5 metres) deep can hold from 70,000 to 200,000 fry. In four states (Mississippi, Alabama, Arkansas, and Louisiana), there are an estimated 144,000 such ponds.

Catfish generally dine on commercially prepared pellets served via a computerized machine. This high-protein food consists of fish meal combined with ground soybeans or corn and a smattering of other nutrients. The pellets float, keeping the fish from feeding off the pond's bottom and allowing ranchers to see their herd.

After 18 months, catfish reach their ideal weight of one and a quarter to one and a half pounds (.56 to .68 kilograms). They are then scooped from the water into tank trucks for live shipment to processing plants. A few of the fish go into a frying pan immediately upon arriving. If they pass muster with taste testers, the entire load is processed; if not, they go back to the pond for a few days of "flavor improvement."

Renowned for their mild flavor, firm texture, and versatility as a cooking ingredient, catfish can be baked, grilled, stewed, broiled, poached —or batter-dipped and deep-fried, as nature intended.

—G.T.

---

frozen or shipped immediately to market. Many consumers, especially Americans, prefer their relatively mild flavor and "non-fishy" taste.

But not everything is rosy down on the old fish farm. "Much of the current expansion of aquaculture is creating an expensive product which only richer people and nations can afford," writes investigative journalist Alex Wilks in the British journal *The Ecologist*. One specific problem is that predatory fish such as salmon, trout, shrimp, bass, and others require a diet high in animal protein, which invariably comes from fish meal composed of herring and other less profitable species. Consequently, the raising of carnivorous fish may actually reduce the amount of fish protein available for human consumption.

Then there is the environmental issue. Fish farming requires large quantities of clean water, another endangered commodity. A 20-acre (8.1-hectare) salmon operation can produce as much organic waste as a city of 10,000 people. Disposal at sea can pollute surrounding waters and has in some cases made the area [un]inhabitable for native species.

Shrimp are typically raised in flooded coastal areas, but in some places this practice has destroyed thousands of acres of mangroves. "Half the world's mangrove forests have now been cut down, and in many cases, aquaculture is the lead cause," says Wilks. Such destruction is especially acute in Ecuador and Thailand.

Another problem occurs when farm fish escape and pollute the natural gene pool by breeding with their wild kin. And even in confinement, captive fish can spread diseases to their free-swimming cousins. Researchers in Ireland, for example, traced the demise of local trout fisheries to lice larvae coming from nearby salmon farms. When growers attacked the problem with a pesticide, it killed off much of the wild shellfish population.

Environmental questions notwithstanding, fish will continue to play an important role in human nutrition. Most seafood is low in cholesterol and high in calcium, phosphorous, potassium, and Vitamin A. "Worldwide, people eat more fish than beef and chicken combined," says Worldwatch Institute researcher Hal Kane, "and in many low-income countries fish provide most of the protein people get from animal sources." Advocates describe fish farming as a "blue revolution" that will do for aquatic food production what the green revolution did for terrestrial agriculture.

Currently, every man, woman, and child on the planet consumes an average of more than 30 pounds (13.6 kilograms) of seafood per year. With the human population expected to grow by more than eight billion over the next few decades, the demand will only increase. Thanks to aquaculture, much of that sustenance will come not from the ocean but from "down on the farm."

• *Frequent contributor Gary Turbak lives and fishes in Missoula, Montana, U.S.A.*

Unit 3

Unit Selections

10. **The Global Challenge,** Michael H. Glantz
11. **The Great Climate Flip-Flop,** William H. Calvin
12. **Stumped by Trees,** *The Economist*
13. **The Rush for Caspian Oil,** Bruce W. Nelan
14. **We *Can* Build a Sustainable Economy,** Lester R. Brown

Key Points to Consider

❖ How is the availability of natural resources affected by population growth?

❖ Do you think that the international community has adequately responded to problems of pollution and threats to our common natural heritage? Why or why not?

❖ What is the natural resource picture going to look like 30 years from now?

❖ How is society, in general, likely to respond to the conflicts between economic necessity and resource conservation?

❖ What is the likely future of energy supplies in both the industrial world and the developing world?

❖ What transformations will societies that are heavy users of fossil fuels have to undergo in order to meet future energy needs?

❖ Can a sustainable economy be organized and what changes in behavior and values are necessary to accomplish this?

 **Links** | **www.dushkin.com/online/**

11. **Friends of the Earth**
    http://www.foe.co.uk/index.html
12. **National Geographic Society**
    http://www.nationalgeographic.com
13. **National Oceanic and Atmospheric Administration (NOAA)**
    http://www.noaa.gov
14. **Public Utilities Commission of Ohio (PUCO)**
    http://www.puc.state.oh.us/consumer/gcc/index.html
15. **SocioSite: Sociological Subject Areas**
    http://www.pscw.uva.nl/sociosite/TOPICS/
16. **United Nations Environment Programme (UNEP)**
    http://www.unep.ch

These sites are annotated on pages 6 and 7.

In the eighteenth, nineteenth, and early twentieth centuries, the idea of the modern nation-state was conceived and developed. These legal entities were conceived of as separate, self-contained units that independently pursued their national interests. Scholars envisioned the world as an international political community of independent units, which "bounced off" each other (a concept that has often been described as a billiard ball model).

This concept of self-contained and self-directed units, however, has undergone major rethinking in the past 30 years, primarily because of the international dimensions of the demands being placed on natural resources. National boundaries are becoming less and less valid. The Middle East, for example, contains a majority of the world's known oil reserves; Western Europe and Japan are very dependent on this source of energy. Neither resource dependency nor problems such as air pollution recognize political boundaries on a map. Therefore, the concept that independent political units control their own destiny makes less sense than it may have 100 years ago. In order to understand why this is so, one must first look at how Earth's natural resources are being utilized and how this may be affecting the global environment.

The initial articles in the unit examine the international dimensions of the uses and abuses of natural resources. The central theme in these articles is whether or not human activity is in fact bringing about fundamental changes in the functioning of Earth's self-regulating ecological systems. In many cases a nonsustainable rate of usage is under way, and, as a consequence, an alarming decline in the quality of the natural resource base is taking place.

An important conclusion resulting from this analysis is that contemporary methods of resource utilization often create problems that transcend national boundaries. Global climate changes, for example, will affect everyone, and if these changes are to be successfully addressed, international collaboration will be required. The consequences of basic human activities such as growing and cooking food are profound when multiplied billions of times every day. A single country or even a few countries working together cannot have a significant impact on redressing these problems. Solutions will have to be conceived that are truly global in scope. Just as there are shortages of natural resources, there are also shortages of new ideas for solving many of these problems.

The unit continues with a series of articles that examine specific resource utilization. These case studies explore in greater detail new technologies, potential new economic incentives, and the impact that traditional power politics has on how natural resources are developed and for whose benefit.

The unit concludes with a discussion of the issues involved in moving from a perspective of the environment as simply an economic resource to be consumed to a perspective that has been defined as "sustainable development." This change is easily called for, but in fact it goes to the core of social values and basic economic activities. Implementing it, therefore, will be a challenge of unprecedented magnitude.

Nature is not some object "out there" to be visited at a national park. It is the food we eat and the energy we consume. Human beings are joined in the most intimate of relationships with the natural world in order to survive from one day to the next. It is ironic how little time is spent thinking about this relationship. The pressures that rapidly growing numbers of people are placing on Earth's carrying capacity suggest that this oversight will not continue much longer.

The Global Environment and Natural Resources Utilization

The Global Challenge

MICHAEL H. GLANTZ

Circulating freely around the planet, the atmosphere and oceans are shared resources whose resiliency is being tested by ever-growing human demands.

The atmosphere and the oceans are fluids that encircle the globe. Their movements can be described in physical and mathematical terms, or even by some popular adages: "what goes up, must come down" and "what goes around, comes around."

The atmosphere and oceans are two of Earth's truly global commons. In cycles that vary from days to centuries to millions of years, air and water circulate interactively around the globe irrespective of national boundaries and territorial claims.

With regard to the first adage, pollutants emitted into the atmosphere must come down somewhere on Earth's surface—unless, like the chlorofluorocarbons (CFCs), they can escape into the stratosphere until they are broken down by the Sun's rays. Depending on the form of the pollutant (gaseous or particulate), its size, or the height at which it has been ejected into the atmosphere, it can stay airborne for short or long periods. So, pollutants expelled into the air in one country and on one continent may make their way to other countries and continents. The same can be said of the various pollutants that are cast into the ocean. "What goes around, comes around" clearly applies to the global commons.

As human demands on the atmosphere and oceans escalate, the pressures on the commons are clearly increasing. Defining the boundaries between acceptable human impacts and crisis impacts is a demanding and rather subjective task.

The Atmosphere

The atmosphere is owned by no nation, but in a sense it belongs to all nations. Several types of human activity interact with geophysical processes to affect the atmosphere in ways that engender crisis situations. The most obvious example of local effects is urban air pollution resulting from automobile emissions, home heating and cooling, and industrial processes. The Denver "brown cloud" is a case in point, as is the extreme pollution in Mexico City. Such pollution can occur within one political jurisdiction or across state, provincial, or international borders. Air pollution is one of those problems to which almost everyone in the urban area contributes.

Acid rain is an example of pollution of a regional atmospheric commons. Industrial processes release pollutants, which can then interact with the atmosphere and be washed out by rainfall. Acid rain has caused the health of forest ecosystems to deteriorate in such locations as the northeastern part of North America, central Europe, and Scandinavia. The trajectories of airborne industrial pollutants moving from highly industrialized areas across these regions have been studied. The data tend to support the contention that while acid rain is a regional commons problem, it is also a problem of global interest.

A nation can put any chemical effluents it deems necessary for its well-being into its own airspace. But then the atmosphere's fluid motion can move those effluents across international borders. The purpose of the tall smokestack, for example, was to put effluents higher into the air, so they would be carried away and dispersed farther from their source. The tall stacks, in essence, turned local air pollution problems into regional ones. In many instances, they converted national pollution into an international problem.

Climate as a Global Commons

There is a difference between the atmosphere as a commons and the climate as a commons. Various societies have emitted a wide range of chemicals into the atmosphere, with little understanding of their potential effects on climate. For example, are industrial processes that produce large amounts of carbon dioxide

This article originally appeared in *The World & I,* April 1997, pp. 24-31. Reprinted by permission of *The World & I,* a publication of The Washington Times Corporation. © 1997.

(which contributes to atmospheric warming) or sulfur dioxide (which contributes to atmospheric cooling and acid rain) altering global climate? There seems to be a growing consensus among scientists that these alterations manifest themselves as regional changes in the frequencies, intensities, and even the location of extreme events such as droughts and floods.

Not all pollutants emitted in the air have an impact on the global climate system. But scientists have long known that some gases can affect global climate patterns by interacting with sunlight or the heat radiated from Earth's surface. Emission of such gases, especially CO_2, can result from human activities such as the burning of fossil fuels, tropical deforestation, and food production processes. The amount of CO_2 in the atmosphere has increased considerably since the mid 1700s and is likely to double the preindustrial level by the year 2050. Carbon dioxide is a highly effective greenhouse gas. Other greenhouse gases emitted to the atmosphere as a result of human activities include CFCs (used as refrigerants, foam-blowing agents, and cleansers for electronic components), nitrous oxide (used in fertilizers), and methane (emitted during rice production). Of these trace gases, the CFCs are produced by industrial processes alone; and others are produced by both industrial and natural processes.

The increase in greenhouse gases during the past two centuries has resulted primarily from industrial processes in which fossil fuels are burned. Thus, a large proportion of the greenhouse gases produced by human activity has resulted from economic development in the industrialized countries (a fact that developing countries are not reluctant to mention when discussing the global warming issue).

National leaders around the globe are concerned about the issue of climate change. Mandatory international limits on the emissions of greenhouse gases could substan-

tially affect their own energy policies. Today, there are scientific and diplomatic efforts to better understand and deal with the prospects of global atmospheric warming and its possible impacts on society. Many countries have, for a variety of motives, agreed that there are reasons to limit greenhouse gas emissions worldwide. National representatives of the Conference of Parties meet each year to address this concern. In the meantime, few countries, if any, want to forgo economic development to avoid a global environmental problem that is still surrounded by scientific uncertainty.

The Oceans

The oceans represent another truly global commons. Most governments have accepted this as fact by supporting the Law of the Sea Treaty, which notes that the seas, which cover almost 70 percent of Earth's surface, are "the common heritage of mankind." In the early 1940s, Athelstan Spilhaus made a projection map that clearly shows that the world's oceans are really subcomponents of one global ocean.

There are at least three commons-related issues concerning the oceans: pollution, fisheries, and sea level. Problems and possible crises have been identified in each area.

The oceans are the ultimate sink for pollutants. Whether they come from the land or the atmosphere, they are likely to end up in the oceans. But no one really owns the oceans, and coastal countries supervise only bits and pieces of the planet's coastal waters. This becomes a truly global commons problem, as currents carry pollutants from the waters of one country into the waters of others. While there are many rules and regulations governing

pollution of the oceans, enforcement is quite difficult. Outside a country's 200-mile exclusive economic zone are the high seas, which are under the jurisdiction of no single country.

In many parts of the world, fisheries represent a common property resource. The oceans provide many countries with protein for domestic food consumption or export. Obtaining the same amount of protein from the land would require that an enormous additional amount of the land's surface be put into agricultural production. Whether under the jurisdiction of one country, several countries, or no country at all, fish populations have often been exploited with incomplete understanding of the causes of variability in their numbers. As a result, most fish stocks that have been commercially sought after have collapsed under the combined pressures of natural variability in the physical environment, population dynamics, and fish catches. This is clearly a serious problem; many perceive it to be a crisis.

Bound Together by Air and Water

- "What goes up must come down" describes the fate of most pollutants ejected into the atmosphere. Taller smokestacks were used to assure that the pollutants did not come down "in my backyard."

- Fish stocks that naturally straddle the boundary between a country's protected zone and the open seas are a global resource requiring international protection measures.

- Sea level in all parts of the world would quickly rise some 8 meters (26 feet) if the vast West Antarctic ice sheet broke away and slid into the sea.

- Scientific controversy still surrounds the notion that human activities can produce enough greenhouse gases to warm the global atmosphere.

In many parts of the world, fisheries represent a common property resource.

For example, an area in the Bering Sea known as the "Donut Hole" had, until recently, also been suffering from overexploitation of pollack stocks. In the midst of the Bering Sea, outside the coastal zones and jurisdictions of the United States and Russia, there is an open-access area that is subject to laws related to the high seas, a truly global commons. Fishermen from Japan and other countries were overexploiting the pollack in this area. But these stocks were part of the same population that also lived in the protected coastal waters of the United States and Russia. In other words, the pollack population was a straddling stock—it straddled the border between the controlled coastal waters and the high seas.

To protect pollack throughout the sea by limiting its exploitation, the two coastal states took responsibility for protecting the commons (namely, the Donut Hole) without having to nationalize it. They did so by threatening to close the Bering Sea to "outsiders," if the outsiders were unable to control their own exploitation of the commonly shared pollack stock. There are several other examples of the overexploitation of straddling stocks, such as the recent collapse of the cod fishery along the Georges Bank in the North Atlantic.

Another commons-related issue is the sea level rise that could result from global warming of the atmosphere. Whereas global warming, if it were to occur, could change rainfall and temperature patterns in yet-unknown ways both locally and regionally, sea level rise will occur everywhere, endangering low-lying coastal areas worldwide. Compounding the problem is the fact that the sea is also an attractor of human populations. For example, about 60 percent of the U.S. population lives within a hundred miles of the coast.

This would truly be a global commons problem because *all* coastal areas and adjoining estuaries would suffer from the consequences of global warming. Concern about sea level rise is highest among the world's small island states, many of which (e.g., the Maldives) are at risk of becoming submerged even with a modest increase in sea level. In sum, there are no winners among coastal states if sea level rises.

Antarctica always appears on the list of global commons. Although it is outside the jurisdiction of any country, some people have questioned its classification as a global commons. It is a fixed piece of territory with no indigenous human population, aside from scientific visitors. It does have a clear link to the oceans as a global commons, however. One key concern about global warming is the possible disintegration of the West Antarctic ice sheet. Unlike Arctic sea ice, which sits in water, the West Antarctic ice sheet would cause sea level to rise an estimated eight meters if it broke away and fell into the Southern Ocean. Viewed from this perspective, the continent clearly belongs on the list of global commons. It is up to the global community to protect it from the adverse influences of human activities occurring elsewhere on the globe.

What's the Problem?

Are the changes in the atmosphere and oceans really problems? And if so, are they serious enough to be considered crises?

The consequences of the greenhouse effect are matters that scien-

ATHELSTAN SPILHAUS/COURTESY OF CELESTIAL PRODUCTS, PHILMONT, VA.

Our one-ocean world: The oceans are but one body of water, as highlighted by the World Ocean Map developed more than 50 years ago by oceanographer Athelstan Spilhaus.

In 5 or 10 years incremental changes can mount into a major environmental crisis.

tists speculate about. But changes in the environment are taking place *now*. These changes are mostly incremental: low-grade, slow-onset, long-term, but gradually accumulating. They can be referred to as "creeping environmental problems." Daily changes in the environment are not noticed, and today's environment is not much different from yesterday's. In 5 or 10 years, however, those incremental changes can mount into a major environmental crisis [see "Creeping Environmental Problems," THE WORLD & I, June 1994, p. 218].

Just about every environmental change featuring human involvement is of the creeping kind. Examples include air pollution, acid rain, global warming, ozone depletion, tropical deforestation, water pollution, and nuclear waste accumulation. For many such changes, the threshold of irreversible damage is difficult to identify until it has been crossed. It seems that we can recognize the threshold only by the consequences that become manifest after we have crossed it. With regard to increasing amounts of atmospheric carbon dioxide, what is the critical threshold beyond which major changes in the global climate system might be expected? Although scientists regularly refer to a doubling of CO_2 from preindustrial levels, the truth of the matter is that a doubling really has little scientific significance except that it has been selected as some sort of marker or milestone.

Policymakers in industrialized and developing countries alike lack a good process for dealing with creeping environmental changes. As a result, they often delay action on such changes in favor of dealing with issues that seem more pressing. Creeping environmental problems tend to be put on the back burner; that is, they are ignored until they have emerged as full-blown crises. The ways that individuals and societies deal with slow-onset, incremental adverse changes in the environment are at the root of coping effectively with deterioration and destruction of local to global commons.

Societal concerns about human impacts on commonly owned or commonly exploited resources have been recorded for at least 2,500 years. Aristotle, for example, observed "that which is common to the greatest number has the least care bestowed upon it." How to manage a common property resource, whether it is a piece of land, a fish population, a body of water, the atmosphere, or outer space, will likely confound decisionmakers well into the future.

Michael H. Glantz is program director of the Environmental and Societal Impacts Group at the National Center for Atmospheric Research (NCAR) in Boulder, Colorado. NCAR is sponsored by the National Science Foundation.

The Great Climate Flip-flop

by WILLIAM H. CALVIN

ONE of the most shocking scientific realizations of all time has slowly been dawning on us: the earth's climate does great flip-flops every few thousand years, and with breathtaking speed. We could go back to ice-age temperatures within a decade—and judging from recent discoveries, an abrupt cooling could be triggered by our current global-warming trend. Europe's climate could become more like Siberia's. Because such a cooling would occur too quickly for us to make readjustments in agricultural productivity and supply, it would be a potentially civilization-shattering affair, likely to cause an unprecedented population crash. What paleoclimate and oceanography researchers know of the mechanisms underlying such a climate flip suggests that global warming could start one in several different ways.

For a quarter century global-warming theorists have predicted that climate creep is going to occur and that we need to prevent greenhouse gases from warming things up, thereby raising the sea level, destroying habitats, intensifying storms, and forcing agricultural rearrangements. Now we know—and from an entirely different group of scientists exploring separate lines of reasoning

> "Climate change" is popularly understood to mean greenhouse warming, which, it is predicted, will cause flooding, severe windstorms, and killer heat waves. But warming could lead, paradoxically, to drastic cooling—a catastrophe that could threaten the survival of civilization

and data—that the most catastrophic result of global warming could be an abrupt cooling.

We are in a warm period now. Scientists have known for some time that the previous warm period started 130,000 years ago and ended 117,000 years ago, with the return of cold temperatures that led to an ice age. But the ice ages aren't what they used to be. They were formerly thought to be very gradual, with both air temperature and ice sheets changing in a slow, 100,000-year cycle tied to changes in the earth's orbit around the sun. But our current warm-up, which started about 15,000 years ago, began abruptly, with the temperature rising sharply while most of the ice was still present. We now know that there's nothing "glacially slow" about temperature change: superimposed on the gradual, long-term cycle have been dozens of abrupt warmings and coolings that lasted only centuries.

The back and forth of the ice started 2.5 million years ago, which is also when the ape-sized hominid brain began to develop into a fully human one, four times as large and reorganized for language, music, and chains of inference. Ours is now a brain able to anticipate outcomes well enough to practice ethical behavior, able to head off disasters in the making by extrapolating trends. Our civilizations began to emerge right after the continental ice sheets melted about 10,000 years ago. Civilizations accumulate knowledge, so we now know a lot about what has been going on, what has

---

William H. Calvin is a theoretical neurophysiologist at the University of Washington at Seattle.

 From *The Atlantic Monthly*, January 1998, pp. 47-50, 52-54. © 1998 by William H. Calvin. Reprinted by permission.

made us what we are. We puzzle over oddities, such as the climate of Europe.

Keeping Europe Warm

EUROPE is an anomaly. The populous parts of the United States and Canada are mostly between the latitudes of 30° and 45°, whereas the populous parts of Europe are ten to fifteen degrees farther north. "Southerly" Rome lies near the same latitude, 42°N, as "northerly" Chicago—and the most northerly major city in Asia is Beijing, near 40°N. London and Paris are close to the 49°N line that, west of the Great Lakes, separates the United States from Canada. Berlin is up at about 52°, Copenhagen and Moscow at about 56°. Oslo is nearly at 60°N, as are Stockholm, Helsinki, and St. Petersburg; continue due east and you'll encounter Anchorage.

Europe's climate, obviously, is not like that of North America or Asia at the same latitudes. For Europe to be as agriculturally productive as it is (it supports more than twice the population of the United States and Canada), all those cold, dry winds that blow eastward across the North Atlantic from Canada must somehow be warmed up. The job is done by warm water flowing north from the tropics, as the eastbound Gulf Stream merges into the North Atlantic Current. This warm water then flows up the Norwegian coast, with a westward branch warming Greenland's tip, 60°N. It keeps northern Europe about nine to eighteen degrees warmer in the winter than comparable latitudes elsewhere—except when it fails. Then not only Europe but also, to everyone's surprise, the rest of the world gets chilled. Tropical swamps decrease their production of methane at the same time that Europe cools, and the Gobi Desert whips much more dust into the air. When this happens, something big, with worldwide connections, must be switching into a new mode of operation.

The North Atlantic Current is certainly something big, with the flow of about a hundred Amazon Rivers. And it sometimes changes its route dramatically, much as a bus route can be truncated into a shorter loop. Its effects are clearly global too, inasmuch as it is part of a long "salt conveyor" current that extends through the southern oceans into the Pacific.

I hope never to see a failure of the northernmost loop of the North Atlantic Current, because the result would be a population crash that would take much of civilization with it, all within a decade. Ways to postpone such a climatic shift are conceivable, however—old-fashioned dam-and-ditch construction in critical locations might even work. Although we can't do much about everyday weather, we may nonetheless be able to stabilize the climate enough to prevent an abrupt cooling.

Abrupt Temperature Jumps

THE discovery of abrupt climate changes has been spread out over the past fifteen years, and is well known to readers of major scientific journals such as *Science* and *Nature*. The abruptness data are convincing. Within the ice sheets of Greenland are annual layers that provide a record of the gases present in the atmosphere and indicate the changes in air temperature over the past 250,000 years—the period of the last two major ice ages. By 250,000 years ago *Homo erectus* had died out, after a run of almost two million years. By 125,000 years ago *Homo sapiens* had evolved from our ancestor species—so the whiplash climate changes of the last ice age affected people much like us.

In Greenland a given year's snowfall is compacted into ice during the ensuing years, trapping air bubbles, and so paleoclimate researchers have been able to glimpse ancient climates in some detail. Water falling as snow on Greenland carries an isotopic "fingerprint" of what the temperature was like en route. Counting those tree-ring-like layers in the ice cores shows that cooling came on as quickly as droughts. Indeed, were another climate flip to begin next year, we'd probably complain first about the drought, along with unusually cold winters in Europe. In the first few years the climate could cool as much as it did during the misnamed Little Ice Age (a gradual cooling that lasted from the early Renaissance until the end of the nineteenth century), with tenfold greater changes over the next decade or two.

The most recent big cooling started about 12,700 years ago, right in the midst of our last global warming. This cold period, known as the Younger Dryas, is named for the pollen of a tundra flower that turned up in a lake bed in Denmark when it shouldn't have. Things had been warming up, and half the ice sheets covering Europe and Canada had already melted. The return to ice-age temperatures lasted 1,300 years. Then, about 11,400 years ago, things suddenly warmed up again, and the earliest agricultural villages were established in the Middle East. An abrupt cooling got started 8,200 years ago, but it aborted within a century, and the temperature changes since then have been gradual in comparison. Indeed, we've had an unprecedented period of climate stability.

Coring old lake beds and examining the types of pollen trapped in sediment layers led to the discovery, early in the twentieth century, of the Younger Dryas. Pollen cores are still a primary means of seeing what regional climates were doing, even though they suffer from poorer resolution than ice cores (worms churn the sediment, obscuring records of all but the longest-lasting temperature changes). When the ice cores demonstrated the abrupt onset of the Younger Dryas, researchers wanted to know how widespread this event was. The U.S. Geological Survey took old lake-bed cores out of storage and re-examined them.

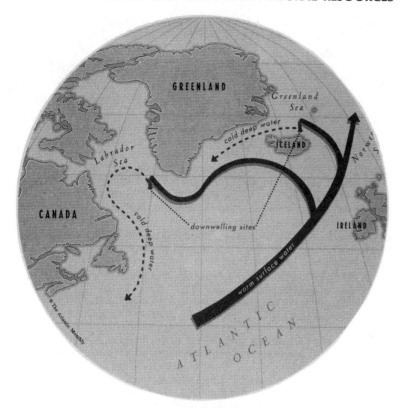

THE NORTHERN LOOP OF THE NORTH ATLANTIC CURRENT

Ancient lakes near the Pacific coast of the United States, it turned out, show a shift to cold-weather plant species at roughly the time when the Younger Dryas was changing German pine forests into scrublands like those of modern Siberia. Subarctic ocean currents were reaching the southern California coastline, and Santa Barbara must have been as cold as Juneau is now. (But the regional record is poorly understood, and I know at least one reason why. These days when one goes to hear a talk on ancient climates of North America, one is likely to learn that the speaker was forced into early retirement from the U.S. Geological Survey by budget cuts. Rather than a vigorous program of studying regional climatic change, we see the shortsighted preaching of cheaper government at any cost.)

In 1984, when I first heard about the startling news from the ice cores, the implications were unclear—there seemed to be other ways of interpreting the data from Greenland. It was initially hoped that the abrupt warmings and coolings were just an oddity of Greenland's weather—but they have now been detected on a worldwide scale, and at about the same time. Then it was hoped that the abrupt flips were somehow caused by continental ice sheets, and thus would be unlikely to recur, because we now lack huge ice sheets over Canada and Northern Europe. Though some abrupt coolings are likely to have been associated with events in the Canadian ice sheet, the abrupt cooling in the previous warm period, 122,000 years ago, which has now been detected even in the tropics, shows that flips are not restricted to

icy periods; they can also interrupt warm periods like the present one.

There seems to be no way of escaping the conclusion that global climate flips occur frequently and abruptly. An abrupt cooling could happen now, and the world might not warm up again for a long time: it looks as if the last warm period, having lasted 13,000 years, came to an end with an abrupt, prolonged cooling. That's how our warm period might end too.

Sudden onset, sudden recovery—this is why I use the word "flip-flop" to describe these climate changes. They are utterly unlike the changes that one would expect from accumulating carbon dioxide or the setting adrift of ice shelves from Antarctica. Change arising from some sources, such as volcanic eruptions, can be abrupt—but the climate doesn't flip back just as quickly centuries later.

Temperature records suggest that there is some grand mechanism underlying all of this, and that it has two major states. Again, the difference between them amounts to nine to eighteen degrees—a range that may depend on how much ice there is to slow the responses. I call the colder one the "low state." In discussing the ice ages there is a tendency to think of warm as good—and therefore of warming as better. Alas, further warming might well kick us out of the "high state." It's the high state that's good, and we may need to help prevent any sudden transition to the cold low state.

Although the sun's energy output does flicker slightly, the likeliest reason for these abrupt flips is an intermittent problem in the North Atlantic Ocean, one that seems to trigger a major rearrangement of atmospheric circulation. North-south ocean currents help to redistribute equatorial heat into the temperate zones, supplementing the heat transfer by winds. When the warm currents penetrate farther than usual into the northern seas, they help to melt the sea ice that is reflecting a lot of sunlight back into space, and so the earth becomes warmer. Eventually that helps to melt ice sheets elsewhere.

The high state of climate seems to involve ocean currents that deliver an extraordinary amount of heat to the vicinity of Iceland and Norway. Like bus routes or conveyor belts, ocean currents must have a return loop. Unlike most ocean currents, the North Atlantic Current has a return loop that runs deep beneath the ocean surface. Huge amounts of seawater sink at known downwelling sites every winter, with the water heading south when it reaches the bottom. When that annual flushing fails for some years, the conveyor belt stops moving and so heat stops flowing so far north—and apparently we're popped back into the low state.

Flushing Cold Surface Water

SURFACE waters are flushed regularly, even in lakes. Twice a year they sink, carrying their load of atmospheric gases downward. That's because water density changes with temperature. Water is densest at about 39°F (a typical refrigerator setting—anything that you take out of the refrigerator, whether you place it on the kitchen counter or move it to the freezer, is going to expand a little). A lake surface cooling down in the autumn will eventually sink into the less-dense-because-warmer waters below, mixing things up. Seawater is more complicated, because salt content also helps to determine whether water floats or sinks. Water that evaporates leaves its salt behind; the resulting saltier water is heavier and thus sinks.

The fact that excess salt is flushed from surface waters has global implications, some of them recognized two centuries ago. Salt circulates, because evaporation up north causes it to sink and be carried south by deep currents. This was posited in 1797 by the Anglo-American physicist Sir Benjamin Thompson (later known, after he moved to Bavaria, as Count Rumford of the Holy Roman Empire), who also posited that, if merely to compensate, there would have to be a warmer northbound current as well. By 1961 the oceanographer Henry Stommel, of the Woods Hole Oceanographic Institution, in Massachusetts, was beginning to worry that these warming currents might stop flowing if too much fresh water was added to the surface of the northern seas. By 1987 the geochemist Wallace Broecker, of Columbia University, was piecing together the paleoclimatic flip-flops with the salt-circulation story and warning that small nudges to our climate might produce "unpleasant surprises in the greenhouse."

Oceans are not well mixed at any time. Like a half-beaten cake mix, with strands of egg still visible, the ocean has a lot of blobs and streams within it. When there has been a lot of evaporation, surface waters are saltier than usual. Sometimes they sink to considerable depths without mixing. The Mediterranean waters flowing out of the bottom of the Strait of Gibraltar into the Atlantic Ocean are about 10 percent saltier than the ocean's average, and so they sink into the depths of the Atlantic. A nice little Amazon-sized waterfall flows over the ridge that connects Spain with Morocco, 800 feet below the surface of the strait.

Another underwater ridge line stretches from Greenland to Iceland and on to the Faeroe Islands and Scotland. It, too, has a salty waterfall, which pours the hypersaline bottom waters of the Nordic Seas (the Greenland Sea and the Norwegian Sea) south into the lower levels of the North Atlantic Ocean. This salty waterfall is more like thirty Amazon Rivers combined. Why does it exist? The cold, dry winds blowing eastward off Canada evaporate the surface waters of the North Atlantic Current, and leave behind all their salt. In late winter the heavy surface waters sink en masse. These blobs, pushed down by annual repetitions of these late-winter events, flow south, down near the bottom of the Atlantic. The same thing happens in the Labrador Sea between Canada and the southern tip of Greenland.

Salt sinking on such a grand scale in the Nordic Seas causes warm water to flow much farther north than it might otherwise do. This produces a heat bonus of perhaps 30 percent beyond the heat provided by direct sunlight to these seas, accounting for the mild winters downwind, in northern Europe. It has been called the Nordic Seas heat pump.

Nothing like this happens in the Pacific Ocean, but the Pacific is nonetheless affected, because the sink in the Nordic Seas is part of a vast worldwide salt-conveyor belt. Such a conveyor is needed because the Atlantic is saltier than the Pacific (the Pacific has twice as much water with which to dilute the salt carried in from rivers). The Atlantic would be even saltier if it didn't mix with the Pacific, in long, loopy currents. These carry the North Atlantic's excess salt southward from the bottom of the Atlantic, around the tip of Africa, through the Indian Ocean, and up around the Pacific Ocean.

There used to be a tropical shortcut, an express route from Atlantic to Pacific, but continental drift connected North America to South America about three million years ago, damming up the easy route for disposing of excess salt. The dam, known as the Isthmus of Panama, may have been what caused the ice ages to begin a short time later, simply because of the forced detour. This major change in ocean circulation, along with a climate that had already been slowly cooling for millions of years, led not only to ice accumulation most of the time but also to climatic instability, with flips every few thousand years or so.

Failures of Flushing

FLYING above the clouds often presents an interesting picture when there are mountains below. Out of the sea of undulating white clouds mountain peaks stick up like islands.

Greenland looks like that, even on a cloudless day—but the great white mass between the occasional punctuations is an ice sheet. In places this frozen fresh water descends from the highlands in a wavy staircase.

Twenty thousand years ago a similar ice sheet lay atop the Baltic Sea and the land surrounding it. Another sat on Hudson's Bay, and reached as far west as the foothills of the Rocky Mountains—where it pushed, head to head, against ice coming down from the Rockies. These northern ice sheets were as high as Greenland's mountains, obstacles sufficient to force the jet stream to make a detour.

Now only Greenland's ice remains, but the abrupt cooling in the last warm period shows that a flip can occur in situations much like the present one. What could possibly halt the salt-conveyor belt that brings tropical heat so much farther north and limits the formation of ice sheets? Oceanographers are busy studying present-day failures of annual flushing, which give some perspective on the catastrophic failures of the past.

In the Labrador Sea, flushing failed during the 1970s, was strong again by 1990, and is now declining. In the Greenland Sea over the 1980s salt sinking declined by 80 percent. Obviously, local failures can occur without catastrophe—it's a question of how often and how widespread the failures are—but the present state of decline is not very reassuring. Large-scale flushing at both those sites is certainly a highly variable process, and perhaps a somewhat fragile one as well. And in the absence of a flushing mechanism to sink cooled surface waters and send them southward in the Atlantic, additional warm waters do not flow as far north to replenish the supply.

There are a few obvious precursors to flushing failure. One is diminished wind chill, when winds aren't as strong as usual, or as cold, or as dry—as is the case in the Labrador Sea during the North Atlantic Oscillation. This El Niño-like shift in the atmospheric-circulation pattern over the North Atlantic, from the Azores to Greenland, often lasts a decade. At the same time that the Labrador Sea gets a lessening of the strong winds that aid salt sinking, Europe gets particularly cold winters. It's happening right now: a North Atlantic Oscillation started in 1996.

Another precursor is more floating ice than usual, which reduces the amount of ocean surface exposed to the winds, in turn reducing evaporation. Retained heat eventually melts the ice, in a cycle that recurs about every five years.

Yet another precursor, as Henry Stommel suggested in 1961, would be the addition of fresh water to the ocean surface, diluting the salt-heavy surface waters before they became unstable enough to start sinking. More rain falling in the northern oceans—exactly what is predicted as a result of global warming—could stop salt flushing. So could ice carried south out of the Arctic Ocean.

There is also a great deal of unsalted water in Greenland's glaciers, just uphill from the major salt sinks. The last time an abrupt cooling occurred was in the midst of global warming. Many ice sheets had already half melted, dumping a lot of fresh water into the ocean.

A brief, large flood of fresh water might nudge us toward an abrupt cooling even if the dilution were insignificant when averaged over time. The fjords of Greenland offer some dramatic examples of the possibilities for freshwater floods. Fjords are long, narrow canyons, little arms of the sea reaching many miles inland; they were carved by great glaciers when the sea level was lower. Greenland's east coast has a profusion of fjords between 70°N and 80°N, including one that is the world's biggest. If blocked by ice dams, fjords make perfect reservoirs for meltwater.

Glaciers pushing out into the ocean usually break off in chunks. Whole sections of a glacier, lifted up by the tides, may snap off at the "hinge" and become icebergs.

But sometimes a glacial surge will act like an avalanche that blocks a road, as happened when Alaska's Hubbard glacier surged into the Russell fjord in May of 1986. Its snout ran into the opposite side, blocking the fjord with an ice dam. Any meltwater coming in behind the dam stayed there. A lake formed, rising higher and higher—up to the height of an eight-story building.

Eventually such ice dams break, with spectacular results. Once the dam is breached, the rushing waters erode an ever wider and deeper path. Thus the entire lake can empty quickly. Five months after the ice dam at the Russell fjord formed, it broke, dumping a cubic mile of fresh water in only twenty-four hours.

The Great Salinity Anomaly, a pool of semi-salty water derived from about 500 times as much unsalted water as that released by Russell Lake, was tracked from 1968 to 1982 as it moved south from Greenland's east coast. In 1970 it arrived in the Labrador Sea, where it prevented the usual salt sinking. By 1971–1972 the semi-salty blob was off Newfoundland. It then crossed the Atlantic and passed near the Shetland Islands around 1976. From there it was carried northward by the warm Norwegian Current, whereupon some of it swung west again to arrive off Greenland's east coast—where it had started its inch-per-second journey. So freshwater blobs drift, sometimes causing major trouble, and Greenland floods thus have the potential to stop the enormous heat transfer that keeps the North Atlantic Current going strong.

The Greenhouse Connection

OF this much we're sure: global climate flip-flops have frequently happened in the past, and they're likely to happen again. It's also clear that sufficient global warming could trigger an abrupt cooling in at least two ways—by increasing high-latitude rainfall or by melting Greenland's ice, both of which could put enough fresh water into the ocean surface to suppress flushing.

Further investigation might lead to revisions in such mechanistic explanations, but the result of adding fresh water to the ocean surface is pretty standard physics. In almost four decades of subsequent research Henry Stommel's theory has only been enhanced, not seriously challenged.

Up to this point in the story none of the broad conclusions is particularly speculative. But to address how all these nonlinear mechanisms fit together—and what we might do to stabilize the climate—will require some speculation.

Even the tropics cool down by about nine degrees during an abrupt cooling, and it is hard to imagine what in the past could have disturbed the whole earth's climate on this scale. We must look at arriving sunlight and departing light and heat, not merely regional shifts on earth, to account for changes in the temperature balance. Increasing amounts of sea ice and clouds could reflect more sunlight back into space, but the geochemist Wallace Broecker suggests that a major greenhouse gas is disturbed by the failure of the salt conveyor, and that this affects the amount of heat retained.

In Broecker's view, failures of salt flushing cause a worldwide rearrangement of ocean currents, resulting in—and this is the speculative part—less evaporation from the tropics. That, in turn, makes the air drier. Because water vapor is the most powerful greenhouse gas, this decrease in average humidity would cool things globally. Broecker has written, "If you wanted to cool the planet by 5°C [9°F] and could magically alter the water-vapor content of the atmosphere, a 30 percent decrease would do the job."

Just as an El Niño produces a hotter Equator in the Pacific Ocean and generates more atmospheric convection, so there might be a subnormal mode that decreases heat, convection, and evaporation. For example, I can imagine that ocean currents carrying more warm surface waters north or south from the equatorial regions might, in consequence, cool the Equator somewhat. That might result in less evaporation, creating lower-than-normal levels of greenhouse gases and thus a global cooling.

To see how ocean circulation might affect greenhouse gases, we must try to account quantitatively for important nonlinearities, ones in which little nudges provoke great responses. The modern world is full of objects and systems that exhibit "bistable" modes, with thresholds for flipping. Light switches abruptly change mode when nudged hard enough. Door latches suddenly give way. A gentle pull on a trigger may be ineffective, but there comes a pressure that will suddenly fire the gun. Thermostats tend to activate heating or cooling mechanisms abruptly—also an example of a system that pushes back.

We must be careful not to think of an abrupt cooling in response to global warming as just another self-regulatory device, a control system for cooling things down when it gets too hot. The scale of the response will be far beyond the bounds of regulation—more like when excess warming triggers fire extinguishers in the ceiling, ruining the contents of the room while cooling them down.

Preventing Climate Flips

THOUGH combating global warming is obviously on the agenda for preventing a cold flip, we could easily be blindsided by stability problems if we allow global warming per se to remain the main focus of our climate-change efforts. To stabilize our flip-flopping climate we'll need to identify all the important feedbacks that control climate and ocean currents—evaporation, the reflection of sunlight back into space, and so on—and then estimate their relative strengths and interactions in computer models.

Feedbacks are what determine thresholds, where one mode flips into another. Near a threshold one can sometimes observe abortive responses, rather like the act of stepping back onto a curb several times before finally running across a busy street. Abortive responses and

rapid chattering between modes are common problems in nonlinear systems with not quite enough oomph—the reason that old fluorescent lights flicker. To keep a bistable system firmly in one state or the other, it should be kept away from the transition threshold.

We need to make sure that no business-as-usual climate variation, such as an El Niño or the North Atlantic Oscillation, can push our climate onto the slippery slope and into an abrupt cooling. Of particular importance are combinations of climate variations—this winter, for example, we are experiencing both an El Niño and a North Atlantic Oscillation—because such combinations can add up to much more than the sum of their parts.

We are near the end of a warm period in any event; ice ages return even without human influences on climate. The last warm period abruptly terminated 13,000 years after the abrupt warming that initiated it, and we've already gone 15,000 years from a similar starting point. But we may be able to do something to delay an abrupt cooling.

Do something? This tends to stagger the imagination, immediately conjuring up visions of terraforming on a science-fiction scale—and so we shake our heads and say, "Better to fight global warming by consuming less," and so forth.

Surprisingly, it may prove possible to prevent flip-flops in the climate—even by means of low-tech schemes. Keeping the present climate from falling back into the low state will in any case be a lot easier than trying to reverse such a change after it has occurred. Were fjord floods causing flushing to fail, because the downwelling sites were fairly close to the fjords, it is obvious that we could solve the problem. All we would need to do is open a channel through the ice dam with explosives before dangerous levels of water built up.

Timing could be everything, given the delayed effects from inch-per-second circulation patterns, but that, too, potentially has a low-tech solution: build dams across the major fjord systems and hold back the meltwater at critical times. Or divert eastern-Greenland meltwater to the less sensitive north and west coasts.

Fortunately, big parallel computers have proved useful for both global climate modeling and detailed modeling of ocean circulation. They even show the flips. Computer models might not yet be able to predict what will happen if we tamper with downwelling sites, but this problem doesn't seem insoluble. We need more well-trained people, bigger computers, more coring of the ocean floor and silted-up lakes, more ships to drag instrument packages through the depths, more instrumented buoys to study critical sites in detail, more satellites measuring regional variations in the sea surface, and perhaps some small-scale trial runs of interventions.

It would be especially nice to see another dozen major groups of scientists doing climate simulations, discovering the intervention mistakes as quickly as possible and learning from them. Medieval cathedral builders learned from their design mistakes over the centuries, and their undertakings were a far larger drain on the economic resources and people power of their day than anything yet discussed for stabilizing the climate in the twenty-first century. We may not have centuries to spare, but any economy in which two percent of the population produces all the food, as is the case in the United States today, has lots of resources and many options for reordering priorities.

Three Scenarios

FUTURISTS have learned to bracket the future with alternative scenarios, each of which captures important features that cluster together, each of which is compact enough to be seen as a narrative on a human scale. Three scenarios for the next climatic phase might be called population crash, cheap fix, and muddling through.

The population-crash scenario is surely the most appalling. Plummeting crop yields would cause some powerful countries to try to take over their neighbors or distant lands—if only because their armies, unpaid and lacking food, would go marauding, both at home and across the borders. The better-organized countries would attempt to use their armies, before they fell apart entirely, to take over countries with significant remaining resources, driving out or starving their inhabitants if not using modern weapons to accomplish the same end: eliminating competitors for the remaining food.

This would be a worldwide problem—and could lead to a Third World War—but Europe's vulnerability is particularly easy to analyze. The last abrupt cooling, the Younger Dryas, drastically altered Europe's climate as far east as Ukraine. Present-day Europe has more than 50 million people. It has excellent soils, and largely grows its own food. It could no longer do so if it lost the extra warming from the North Atlantic.

There is another part of the world with the same good soil, within the same latitudinal band, which we can use for a quick comparison. Canada lacks Europe's winter warmth and rainfall, because it has no equivalent of the North Atlantic Current to preheat its eastbound weather systems. Canada's agriculture supports about 28 million people. If Europe had weather like Canada's, it could feed only one out of twenty-three present-day Europeans.

Any abrupt switch in climate would also disrupt food supply routes. The only reason that two percent of our population can feed the other 98 percent is that we have a well-developed system of transportation and middlemen—but it is not very robust. The system allows for large urban populations in the best of times, but not in the case of widespread disruptions.

Natural disasters such as hurricanes and earthquakes are less troubling than abrupt coolings for two reasons: they're short (the recovery period starts the next day) and they're local or regional (unaffected citizens can help the overwhelmed). There is, increasingly, international cooperation in response to catastrophe—but no country is going to be able to rely on a stored agricultural surplus for even a year, and any country will be reluctant to give away part of its surplus.

In an abrupt cooling the problem would get worse for decades, and much of the earth would be affected. A meteor strike that killed most of the population in a month would not be as serious as an abrupt cooling that eventually killed just as many. With the population crash spread out over a decade, there would be ample opportunity for civilization's institutions to be torn apart and for hatreds to build, as armies tried to grab remaining resources simply to feed the people in their own countries. The effects of an abrupt cold last for centuries. They might not be the end of *Homo sapiens*—written knowledge and elementary education might well endure—but the world after such a population crash would certainly be full of despotic governments that hated their neighbors because of recent atrocities. Recovery would be very slow.

A slightly exaggerated version of our present know-something-do-nothing state of affairs is know-nothing-do-nothing: a reduction in science as usual, further limiting our chances of discovering a way out. History is full of withdrawals from knowledge-seeking, whether for reasons of fundamentalism, fatalism, or "government lite" economics. This scenario does not require that the shortsighted be in charge, only that they have enough influence to put the relevant science agencies on starvation budgets and to send recommendations back for yet another commission report due five years hence.

A cheap-fix scenario, such as building or bombing a dam, presumes that we know enough to prevent trouble, or to nip a developing problem in the bud. But just as vaccines and antibiotics presume much knowledge about diseases, their climatic equivalents presume much knowledge about oceans, atmospheres, and past climates. Suppose we had reports that winter salt flushing was confined to certain areas, that abrupt shifts in the past were associated with localized flushing failures, *and* that one computer model after another suggested a solution that was likely to work even under a wide range of weather extremes. A quick fix, such as bombing an ice dam, might then be possible. Although I don't consider this scenario to be the most likely one, it is possible that solutions could turn out to be cheap and easy, and that another abrupt cooling isn't inevitable. Fatalism, in other words, might well be foolish.

A muddle-through scenario assumes that we would mobilize our scientific and technological resources well in advance of any abrupt cooling problem, but that the solution wouldn't be simple. Instead we would try one thing after another, creating a patchwork of solutions that might hold for another few decades, allowing the search for a better stabilizing mechanism to continue.

We might, for example, anchor bargeloads of evaporation-enhancing surfactants (used in the southwest corner of the Dead Sea to speed potash production) upwind from critical downwelling sites, letting winds spread them over the ocean surface all winter, just to ensure later flushing. We might create a rain shadow, seeding clouds so that they dropped their unsalted water well upwind of a given year's critical flushing sites—a strategy that might be particularly important in view of the increased rainfall expected from global warming. We might undertake to regulate the Mediterranean's salty outflow, which is also thought to disrupt the North Atlantic Current.

Perhaps computer simulations will tell us that the only robust solutions are those that re-create the ocean currents of three million years ago, before the Isthmus of Panama closed off the express route for excess-salt disposal. Thus we might dig a wide sea-level Panama Canal in stages, carefully managing the changeover.

Staying in the "Comfort Zone"

STABILIZING our flip-flopping climate is not a simple matter. We need heat in the right places, such as the Greenland Sea, and not in others right next door, such as Greenland itself. Man-made global warming is likely to achieve exactly the opposite—warming Greenland and cooling the Greenland Sea.

A remarkable amount of specious reasoning is often encountered when we contemplate reducing carbon-dioxide emissions. That increased quantities of greenhouse gases will lead to global warming is as solid a scientific prediction as can be found, but other things influence climate too, and some people try to escape confronting the consequences of our pumping more and more greenhouse gases into the atmosphere by supposing that something will come along miraculously to counteract them. Volcanos spew sulfates, as do our own smokestacks, and these reflect some sunlight back into space, particularly over the North Atlantic and Europe. But we can't assume that anything like

this will counteract our longer-term flurry of carbon-dioxide emissions. Only the most naive gamblers bet against physics, and only the most irresponsible bet with their grandchildren's resources.

To the long list of predicted consequences of global warming—stronger storms, methane release, habitat changes, ice-sheet melting, rising seas, stronger El Niños, killer heat waves—we must now add an abrupt, catastrophic cooling. Whereas the familiar consequences of global warming will force expensive but gradual adjustments, the abrupt cooling promoted by man-made warming looks like a particularly efficient means of committing mass suicide.

We cannot avoid trouble by merely cutting down on our present warming trend, though that's an excellent place to start. Paleoclimatic records reveal that any notion we may once have had that the climate will remain the same unless pollution changes it is wishful thinking. Judging from the duration of the last warm period, we are probably near the end of the current one. Our goal must be to stabilize the climate in its favorable mode and ensure that enough equatorial heat continues to flow into the waters around Greenland and Norway. A stabilized climate must have a wide "comfort zone," and be able to survive the El Niños of the short term. We can design for that in computer models of climate, just as architects design earthquake-resistant skyscrapers. Implementing it might cost no more, in relative terms, than building a medieval cathedral. But we may not have centuries for acquiring wisdom, and it would be wise to compress our learning into the years immediately ahead. We have to discover what has made the climate of the past 8,000 years relatively stable, and then figure out how to prop it up.

> Those who will not reason
> Perish in the act:
> Those who will not act
> Perish for that reason.
>
> —W. H. Auden

Stumped by trees

*Even for poor countries, destroying forests
rarely makes economic sense*

PARAGOMINAS, a sweltering, mosquito-ridden town in the north of Brazil, is the stuff of an environmentalist's nightmares. The air is bitter with sawdust and smoke. Dozens of sawmills are slicing up prime rainforest tree-trunks, and each is surrounded by dozens of charcoal kilns spewing out black smoke. For hundreds of miles around, the landscape is bare of trees except for the odd stump. No one takes any notice of government regulations that restrict logging, explains a manager at one of the sawmills; and if officials try to enforce them, they can easily be bribed. "Everyone is out for a quick buck here," he says.

Yet Brazilians get annoyed when environmentalists from developed countries start moaning about the destruction of the rainforests. Most of the arguments for preserving the forests, they point out, are something of a rich man's luxury. They are about nebulous worries for the medium-term future, not about a developing country's crying need, here and now, to improve its people's living standards. Besides, satellite pictures show that despite decades of exploitation, over 85% of Brazil's Amazon jungle region is still covered in trees. So why, ask Brazilians, should they not be allowed to put some of their forests to commercial use?

The best answer is that rapid deforestation is rarely in the economic interest of the country concerned. More often it is due to a combination of bad policies, population growth and poverty. In some parts of the world, such as the highlands of Bolivia, Peru and Nepal, and in the countryside surrounding many fast-growing cities in Africa, trees are lost because the poor use wood for fuel. Elsewhere the culprit is war. During Cambodia's long civil war, both the government and the Khmers Rouges financed their military operations partly through logging. Since the 1970s, around half of Cambodia's forests have disappeared. Another reason for forest depletion is the slash-and-burn method of cultivation employed by the poorest farmers. In East Asia,

environmentalists think that the recent economic troubles will hurt the forests as poor families lose their city jobs and return to the countryside.

More intensive farming technology can help, by reducing the amount of land that poor families need to reclaim from forests to feed themselves. In parts of the Brazilian Amazon, where smallholders' farming techniques are still very basic, a local environmental group has helped reduce forest loss in one community by getting farmers to adopt a few simple improvements, such as planting their crops in rows rather than scattering seeds, and using hoes for weeding. The biggest potential gains from applying existing

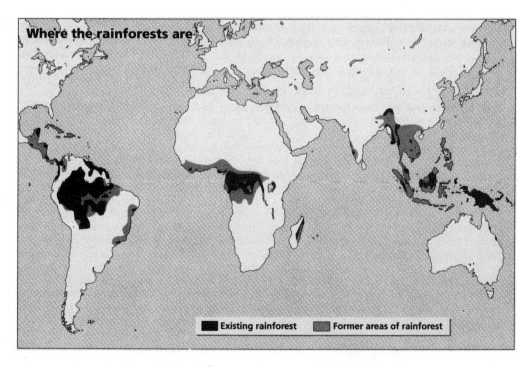

Where the rainforests are

■ Existing rainforest   ■ Former areas of rainforest

farming technology could be achieved in sub-Saharan Africa, where the use of fertiliser, for example, is running at only a quarter the level in India.

Perverse incentives

Commercial logging, too, is a big cause of deforestation. Demand for industrial timber is expected to increase from around 1.6 billion cubic metres a year in 1995 to 1.9 billion cubic metres in 2010, driven by rising standards of living. Developing countries with hot climates have a competitive advantage in this market, simply because trees grow much faster than in temperate climates. But plantation forestry can be as profitable as chopping trees from virgin forest, and has the obvious advantage that growers can choose which species to cultivate. The main reason why virgin forest is being cut down is not so much the simple pursuit of profit but a set of perverse economic incentives.

In the Brazilian Amazon, between the 1960s and the early 1990s the forest shrank largely because the government intended it to. Brazil's military rulers saw the region as a safety valve for the overpopulation, landlessness and poverty in the country's crowded coastal region; they also feared that a thinly inhabited Amazon was an invitation to foreign invaders.

In their attempt to give "the land without people to the people without land", the authorities colonised the region and built roads and schools. Newcomers qualified for ownership of a plot of land simply by clearing the trees on it. But usually the soil of cleared Amazon rainforest proved unsuitable for agriculture: after a few years crops would begin to fail, forcing farmers to deforest yet more land. The government also offered tax breaks to companies spending money on approved development schemes in the region. Firms poured in, many of them setting up giant cattle ranches.

In the early 1990s some of the more obvious incentives to wreak environmental havoc were dismantled. Partly to appease the green lobby abroad, the Brazilian government also passed a series of increasingly tough laws—first prohibiting landowners from logging more than 50% of their land, then lowering the limit to 20%. Yet satellite data released at the beginning of this year show that deforestation in the Brazilian Amazon in 1995 reached an all-time high of 29,000 square kilometres, an area about the size of Belgium. The figure for 1996 was down, but at 18,100 square kilometres still substantial. Why the continuing destruction?

On the face of it, the problem appears to be that existing rules are simply not enforced. Ibama, Brazil's environment agency, has a small number of officials to police a vast region. Last year it collected just 6% of the fines it levied. The Brazilian government has estimated that 80% of the timber in the region is harvested illegally. But a visit to a town such as Paragominas suggests that effective enforcement would take a lot more than hiring extra inspectors. The atmosphere is that of a frontier region where no one quite knows who owns the land and property disputes are often settled by violence. Everyone milks the forest for what they can get.

Because of confusion over land titles, conflicts often flare between Indians, squatters and loggers. Many owners deliberately do not register their property with the authorities because they fear it might restrict their logging. But they also burn trees as a sign of occcupation to discourage invasions from the country's militant landless.

Insecurity of land tenure explains the continuing popularity of cattle ranching in the region: if someone else takes the land, at least the cattle can be moved on. That same insecurity of tenure also means that plantation forestry, however sensible in theory, does not stand a chance in practice. Landowners would have to wait perhaps 20 years to harvest the trees, during which time squatters or accidental fires could easily wipe out their investment.

Deforestation in Indonesia—which last year caught the world's attention by producing a series of catastrophic smogs—has a similar tangle of causes. As in Brazil, the government had an official programme encouraging millions of people to move from the crowded islands of Java and Bali to less densely populated but heavily forested islands such as Kalimantan, Sumatra and Irian Jaya. And as in Brazil, property rights in the forests are often ill-defined, leading to violent conflicts between locals, migrants and forestry firms. Traditional *adat* law, which has governed the use of forest lands until the past few decades, clashes with more recent logging concessions handed out by the government in Jakarta, and fire is used as a weapon by both sides. Small farmers sometimes burn trees planted by big forestry companies, and large firms have in turn burnt land to drive out smallholders.

But whereas Brazil has abandoned government policies that explicitly encourage deforestation, Indonesia is further behind. The government levies high export taxes on unprocessed logs to help the domestic wood-processing industry. This has kept domestic timber prices below world levels, providing forestry firms with an implicit subsidy estimated at over $2 billion a year, but also encouraging them to use logs inefficiently. Government concessions to log a particular area have been handed out in what development bankers call "a non-transparent fashion" (ie, to friends of President Suharto's family), and for periods too short to give the firms an incentive to look after the forest. Only now, under pressure from the IMF, has the government promised to reform the timber trade.

In sum, the sort of policies that might help developing countries to reduce their rate of deforestation are also the sort of policies that are likely to promote economic growth: upholding the rule of law, securing property rights, weeding out corruption and reducing subsidies. That may seem obvious, but it challenges an assumption still widely held in rich and poor countries alike: that rapid development and rapid deforestation must go hand in hand.

As long as that belief persists, the pleas of the rich world's environmentalists will be seen as somewhat otherworldly. They want to preserve the forests for two main reasons: because burning them could eventually contribute to world climate change, and because they know that forest loss will reduce biodiversity. Both are worries for the longer term, although recent research suggests that burning trees is now beginning to affect the local climate of the Brazilian rainforest too, making it drier and more liable to accidental fires.

A loss of biodiversity will not start to show up until well into the next century, but it is an issue that gets environmentalists really excited. According to one estimate, tropical rainforests contain around half of all the world's species—far more than the temperate forests of Europe and America. (The Amazon forests also contain about 400 human tribes, which are gradually being squeezed out.) The depletion of rainforests is being blamed for the increasingly rapid rate at which the world is losing species. But scientific understanding of species loss, and its potential dangers, is riddled with uncertainties.

Life's rich pattern

Scientists have little idea how many species exist in the first place. Recent estimates range from 7m to 20m. According to the Global Biodiversity Assessment, a UN-sponsored report in which about 1,000 scientists have had a hand, a good working estimate is between 13m and 14m species. But of that number, says the report, only about 1.75m have been scientifically described.

If scientists have no clear idea how many species exist in the first place, rates of loss are necessarily even harder to divine. Since 1600, over 480 animal species and 650 plant species are recorded as having become extinct. But since the vast majority of all species are unknown, rates of loss of known species are not much of a guide to anything. Besides, species thought to be extinct occasionally pop up from nowhere. So scientists rely on a crude calculation. They have a very rough idea, from a number of detailed studies, how many species are likely to be lost if the size of a particular habitat—a tropical forest, say—is reduced by a certain amount. They then apply this number to the total area of tropical forest lost each year (another very approximate figure, often derived from incomplete satellite data). Using this method, scientists working on the Global Biodiversity Assessment have estimated that, if current rates of forest loss continue over the next 30 years, the number of species in tropical forests will fall by 5–10%.

Losing species, even bugs and spiders, might matter for a number of reasons. Ecosystems containing a broad diversity of species and genes are generally better able to adapt to changing conditions than those with just a handful of species, however abundant. Genetic variation is nature's insurance against all sort of eventualities. It might help cushion, for example, the impact of a sudden change in the world's climate. It also can help reduce the effect of disease. The Irish potato famine was so devastating because in the 19th century only a few varieties of potato were planted in Ireland, and these all happened to be vulnerable to the same disease. At present almost all the world's food crops are based on a mere nine species of plants, but in the future any of thousands of other species might prove invaluable. Today's apparently useless species may contain tomorrow's medicine.

To rich-world inhabitants, the best arguments for preserving the rainforests are spiritual: that the diversity of life is a wonder of nature, whether it has a practical application or not; and that it is good to hold on to some wildernesses in the world. But for developing countries trying to lift themselves out of poverty, such arguments seem utterly irrelevant.

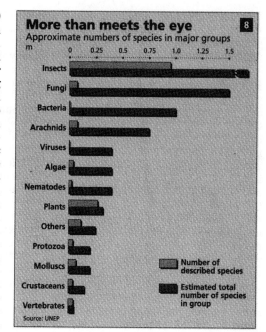

More than meets the eye   8
Approximate numbers of species in major groups

Insects, Fungi, Bacteria, Arachnids, Viruses, Algae, Nematodes, Plants, Others, Protozoa, Molluscs, Crustaceans, Vertebrates

Number of described species

Estimated total number of species in group

Source: UNEP

The Rush for Caspian Oil

Clinton started late, but the U.S. is gaining in the Great Game in central Asia

By BRUCE W. NELAN

WASHINGTON PUT ON QUITE A show last week for an improbable personage: Turkmenbashi, a plump, silver-haired strongman from an obscure country in central Asia who would normally rank far down the pomp-and-protocol chart.

But the title, which means "head of all Turkmen," belongs to one Saparmurat Niyazov, President of Turkmenistan, a parched former Soviet republic that happens to sit atop immense oil deposits and the fourth largest natural-gas reserves in the world. So last week Niyazov got the imperial treatment from the Clinton Administration and a host of U.S. businessmen eager to start exploiting those riches in earnest.

Niyazov was put up at Blair House, across the street from the White House, an honor reserved for true VIPs. He got 45 minutes with Clinton in the Oval Office and conferred with Cabinet officers and CIA Director George Tenet. More than two dozen oil and equipment companies kicked in to sponsor a dinner in Niyazov's honor at a downtown hotel, and 300 of America's top government decision makers, business executives and lobbyists thronged the ballroom.

Niyazov is one of the new kingpins of the Caspian Sea and the treasure it covers. The California-size Caspian, center of the last great oil rush of this century, laps across a huge mine of liquid gold. Some 200 billion bbl., or about 10% of the earth's potential oil reserves, are thought to lie under and around the sea. At today's prices that could add up to $4 trillion worth. The Caspian lies in a tough part of the world, studded with rugged mountains, Chechen guerrillas, dissident Kurds, crowded sea-lanes and unstable and corrupt governments in all directions. Laying hundreds of miles of pipe through such obstacles will carry a huge price tag and enormous risks.

The world's energy companies began scrambling for the prize as soon as the Soviet Union broke up, in 1991, and the biggest oil firms from the U.S., Europe, Russia, Japan, China and South America have bought into the action, forming consortiums and joint ventures with local companies to

generate the huge start-up costs. Some of the wells are already pumping, and in a few years oil will be flooding out of the Caspian reserves. But how will the precious stuff travel to energy-hungry consumers? Who will have a hand on the spigots as it flows to market?

The key to that decision probably lies in Baku, capital of Azerbaijan and headquarters of the biggest multinational oil consortium in the region. It's an old city but a new boomtown. The shoreline along the tree-shaded boardwalk is gray with oil, and the air is heavy with the dizzying stench of crude. The city sprouts new bars, cafés and nightclubs every week, and petro-barons fill the nights with the roar of their armored Mercedes-Benz.

So far this year, a 12-company consortium, led by British Petroleum and Amoco, has produced 160,000 tons of oil. This early production has traveled out through a 2-ft.-wide pipeline, heading north through Azerbaijan and west to the Russian port of Novorossisk on the Black Sea.

But soon, as production picks up, that line and a number of others already laid will be too small to handle the job. The consortiums want a new 3.5-ft.-wide line that will be able to carry up to 1 million bbl. a day in five years. At the bar of the Ragin' Cajun, a hot spot in Baku, a veteran of oil fields from Texas to Siberia explains, "The game's called pipeline poker. The Caspian is crazy. It's landlocked. We can drill all the oil you'd ever need. But can we get it out?"

It's a question that has ignited a tense struggle in the region and beyond. The coastal states of Azerbaijan, Kazakhstan and Turkmenistan gained their independence when the Soviet empire collapsed. All three want to exploit the riches under their sea without interference from Russia and Iran, the two other states that rim the Caspian. As major oil and gas producers, Russia and Iran are not overjoyed at their neighbors' good fortune.

In their day, the Soviets never worked seriously at developing Caspian wells, largely because they did not want to create competition for their already flowing Siberian oil. Moscow still feels the same but hasn't figured out how to head off the flow of Caspian oil or to grab a large chunk of the profit. Russia does insert an environmental argument: the oil industry could threaten the

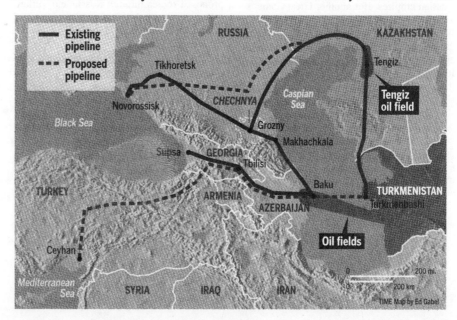

Caspian sturgeon and its oily treasure, caviar. For its part, Iran says it will cooperate in Caspian development only if it gets, say, a 20% share of the sea's resources. Both Russia and Iran prefer that pipelines carrying Caspian oil be built or expanded over their territory.

While American energy companies joined the Caspian rush early, the U.S. government was slow to get organized. Some of Washington's top power brokers and law firms went to work for Caspian governments or U.S. companies, selling, consulting, lobbying or opening doors. Among them were former Defense Secretary Dick Cheney, former Treasury Secretary Lloyd Bentsen, and John Sununu, who was George Bush's chief of staff. Perhaps the most active Washington name is former National Security Adviser Zbigniew Brzezinski, now a consultant for Amoco. He has long been a mentor to Secretary of State Madeleine Albright, and he has warned the White House for years that the U.S. was making a strategic mistake in paying so little attention to the new central Asian nations.

Albright and her senior State Department colleagues sat down for a full-dress CIA briefing on the Caspian last August. The agency had set up a secret task force to monitor the region's politics and gauge its wealth. Covert CIA officers, some well-trained petroleum engineers, had traveled through southern Russia, Azerbaijan, Kazakhstan and Turkmenistan to sniff out potential oil reserves. When the policymakers heard the agency's report, Albright concluded that working to mold the area's future was "one of the most exciting things that we can do."

American officials frown when outsiders call the battle over the Caspian another "Great Game," the term Rudyard Kipling used for the 19th century struggle for influence and control between the British and Russian empires. But another Great Game is what it is. Washington wants Caspian oil to flow through many pipelines so that no single country can bottle it up, and is adamantly against having a new pipeline pass through Iran. It is fine if some of the lines run through Russia, as they already do, but Russia should not be able to turn a valve and shut off all or most of the Caspian flow.

Specifically, the U.S. wants the big new carrier, the one the oilmen call the main export pipeline, to run westward from the Caspian to the Turkish port of Ceyhan, on the Mediterranean, because Turkey is a NATO

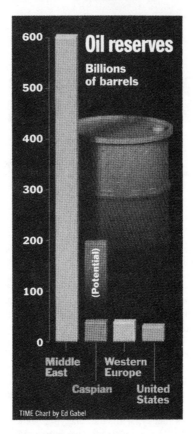

Oil reserves

Billions of barrels

600
500
400
300
200
100
0

(Potential)

Middle East
Western Europe
Caspian
United States

TIME Chart by Ed Gabel

ally. The U.S. does not entirely trust Russia, which resents the arrival of foreign influence in what were Soviet republics. To Washington, the Islamist regime in Iran looks even less friendly. "The last thing we need," says a White House aide, "is to rely on the Persian Gulf as the main access for more oil."

Officials in Tehran point out that a pipeline southward through Iran would be the shortest way to go. "This is all ridiculous," says Hossein Kazempour Ardebili, an adviser to the ministers of petroleum and foreign affairs in Tehran, as he draws a map of proposed routes through Russia and Turkey. "We have our hands in the Caspian Sea and our feet in the Persian Gulf, the simplest outlet for this energy."

The Iranians don't rely just on logic to press their case. They cite treaties with the Soviet Union dating back to 1921 and 1940 that declare the sea a common lake between the two countries. Tehran is willing to negotiate a new agreement but demands veto rights over any aspect it doesn't like. If Iran's interests are not taken into account, says Ardebili, it will deal with what it considers illegal activities in the Caspian by us-

ing "constructive—and possibly destructive" countermeasures.

By last fall the U.S. was pressing hard for the option it favors, a system of oil-and-gas lines starting through Kazakhstan and Turkmenistan, running under the Caspian Sea to Baku, then through Georgia and Turkey to the Mediterranean. This elaborate scheme is not an easy sell. The long pipeline would cost about $4 billion to build and add up to $4 to the cost of each barrel of oil it carried. To many company executives, it seems easier to use the southern route through Iran or the northern route through Russia to the Black Sea.

"If I had my way," says a senior Western oil executive, "we'd sign with the Iranians. In this part of the world, they are by far the most trustworthy partners for a pipeline deal. Terrorism? Who's going to blow up their own pipeline?" But the U.S. option, the east-west line, gathered support from some regional leaders—Azerbaijani President Heydar Aliyev, for example—who thought it would be more secure.

A breakthrough for the U.S. came at "the great pipeline shootout" on April 1 in Almaty, capital of Kazakhstan. More than 200 executives and experts from the region's oil consortiums gathered to present and compare their pet plans. To everyone's surprise, Total, the French oil giant, put forward revised numbers for its preferred option, a north-south pipeline through Iran to the gulf. By these new estimates, the Iran link would cost about $4 billion and would not be operational until 2004. This meant the line through Iran would cost as much and take as long to build as the east-west system through Turkey.

This is heartwarming news for the Clinton Administration. Despite the focus on strategic thinking, the final pipeline decision will depend heavily on costs. So U.S. officials were jubilant at Total's confession, and they got another boost last week. In a joint communiqué with Clinton, Niyazov affirmed that he was leaning toward an east-west gas-and-oil line under the Caspian as part of the larger system the U.S. is pushing. In October the huge consortium based in Baku is to decide which route it will support, and the Clinton Administration believes its side in this Great Game now has the momentum.

—Reported by Scott MacLeod/Tehran, Andrew Meier/Baku and Douglas Waller/Washington

We *Can* Build a Sustainable Economy

The keys to securing the planet's future lie in stabilizing both human population and climate. The challenges are great, but several trends look promising.

By Lester R. Brown

The world economy is growing faster than ever, but the benefits of this rapid growth have not been evenly distributed. As population has doubled since mid-century and the global economy has nearly quintupled, the demand for natural resources has grown at a phenomenal rate.

Since 1950, the need for grain has nearly tripled. Consumption of seafood has increased more than four times. Water use has tripled. Demand for beef and mutton has tripled. Firewood demand has tripled, lumber demand has more than doubled, and paper demand has gone up sixfold. The burning of fossil fuels has increased nearly fourfold, and carbon emissions have risen accordingly.

These spiraling human demands for resources are beginning to outgrow the earth's natural systems. As this happens, the global economy is damaging the foundation on which it rests.

To build an environmentally sustainable global economy, there are many obstacles, but there are also several promising trends and factors in our favor. One is that we know what an environmentally sustain-

able economy would look like. In a sustainable economy:

• Human births and deaths are in balance.

• Soil erosion does not exceed the natural rate of new soil formation.

• Tree cutting does not exceed tree planting.

• The fish catch does not exceed the sustainable yield of fisheries.

• The number of cattle on a range does not exceed the range's carrying capacity.

• Water pumping does not exceed aquifer recharge.

• Carbon emissions and carbon fixation are in balance.

• The number of plant and animal species lost does not exceed the rate at which new species evolve.

We know how to build an economic system that will meet our needs without jeopardizing prospects for future generations. And with some trends already headed in the right direction, we have the cornerstones on which to build such an economy.

Stabilizing Population

With population, the challenge is to complete the demographic transition, to reestablish the balance between births and deaths that characterizes a sustainable society. Since populations are rarely ever precisely stable, a stable population is defined here as one with a growth rate below 0.3%. Populations are effectively stable if they fluctuate narrowly around zero.

Thirty countries now have stable populations, including most of those in Europe plus Japan. They provide

From *The Futurist*, July/August 1996, pp. 8–12. © 1996 by The World Future Society, Bethesda, MD. http://www.wfs.org/wfs. Reprinted by permission.

the solid base for building a world population stabilization effort. Included in the 30 are all the larger industrialized countries of Europe—France, Germany, Italy, Russia, and the United Kingdom. Collectively, these 30 countries contain 819 million people or 14% of humanity. For this goal, one-seventh of humanity is already there.

The challenge is for the countries with the remaining 86% of the world's people to reach stability. The two large nations that could make the biggest difference in this effort are China and the United States. In both, population growth is now roughly 1% per year. If the global food situation becomes desperate, both could reach stability in a decade or two if they decided it were important to do so.

The world rate of population growth, which peaked around 2% in 1970, dropped below 1.6% in 1995. Although the rate is declining, the annual addition is still close to 90 million people per year. Unless populations can be stabilized with demand below the sustainable yield of local ecosystems, these systems will be destroyed. Slowing growth may delay the eventual collapse of ecosystems, but it will not save them.

The European Union, consisting of some 15 countries and containing 360 million people, provides a model for the rest of the world of an environmentally sustainable food/population balance. At the same time that the region has reached zero population growth, movement up the food chain has come to a halt as diets have become saturated with livestock products. The result is that Europe's grain consumption has been stable for close to two decades at just under 160 million tons—a level that is within the region's carrying capacity. Indeed, there is a potential for a small but sustainable export surplus of grain that can help countries where the demand for food has surpassed the carrying capacity of their croplands.

As other countries realize that continuing on their current population trajectory will prevent them from achieving a similar food/population balance, more and more may decide to do what China has done—launch an all-out campaign to stabilize population. Like China, other governments will have to carefully balance the reproductive rights of the current generation with the survival rights of the next generation.

Very few of the group of 30 countries with stable populations had stability as an explicit policy goal. In those that reached population stability first, such as Belgium, Germany, Sweden, and the United Kingdom, it came with rising living standards and expanding employment opportunities for women. In some of the countries where population has stabilized more recently, such as Russia and other former Soviet republics, the deep economic depression accompanying economic reform has substantially lowered birth rates, much as the Great Depression did in the United States. In addition, with the rising number of infants born with birth defects and deformities since Chernobyl, many women are simply afraid to bear children. The natural decrease of population (excluding migration) in Russia of 0.6% a year—leading to an annual population loss of 890,000—is the most rapid on record.

Not all countries are achieving population stability for the right reasons. This is true today and it may well be true in the future. As food deficits in densely populated countries expand, governments may find that there is not enough food available to import. Between fiscal year 1993 and 1996, food aid dropped from an all-time high of 15.2 million tons of grain to 7.6 million tons. This cut of exactly half in three years reflects primarily fiscal stringencies in donor countries, but also, to a lesser degree, higher grain prices in fiscal 1996. If governments fail to establish a humane balance between their people and food supplies, hunger and malnutrition may raise death rates, eventually slowing population growth.

Some developing countries are beginning to adopt social policies that will encourage smaller families. Iran, facing both land hunger and water scarcity, now limits public subsidies for housing, health care, and insurance to three children per family. In Peru, President Alberto Fujimori, who was elected overwhelmingly to his second five-year term in a predominantly Catholic country, said in his inaugural address in August 1995 that he wanted to provide better access

World Fertilizer and Grainland
(Per Person, 1950-94)

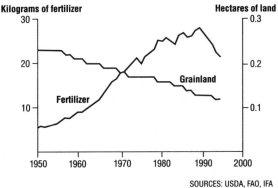

SOURCES: USDA, FAO, IFA

to family-planning services for poor women. "It is only fair," he said, "to disseminate thoroughly the methods of family planning to everyone."

Stabilizing Climate

With climate, as with population, there is disagreement on the need to stabilize. Evidence that atmospheric carbon-dioxide levels are rising is clear-cut. So, too, is the greenhouse effect that these gases produce in the atmosphere. That is a matter of basic physics. What is debatable is the rate at which global temperatures will rise and what the precise local effects will be. Nonetheless, the consensus of the mainstream scientific community is that there is no alternative to reducing carbon emissions.

How would we phase out fossil fuels? There is now a highly successful "phase out" model in the case of chlorofluorocarbons (CFCs). After two British scientists discovered the "hole" in the ozone layer over Antarctica and published their findings in *Nature* in May 1985, the international community convened a conference in Montreal to draft an agreement designed to reduce CFC production sharply. Subsequent meetings in London in 1990 and Copenhagen in 1992 further advanced the goals set in Montreal. After peaking

World Wind Energy
(Generating Capacity, 1980-94)

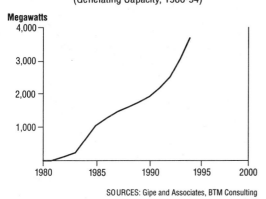

SOURCES: Gipe and Associates, BTM Consulting

in 1988 at 1.26 million tons, the manufacture of CFCs dropped to an estimated 295,000 tons in 1994—a decline of 77% in just six years.

As public understanding of the costs associated with global warming increases, and as evidence of the effects of higher temperatures accumulates, support for reducing dependence on fossil fuels is building. At the March 1995 U.N. Climate Convention in Berlin, environmental groups were joined in lobbying for a reduction in carbon emissions by a group of 36 island communities and insurance industry representatives.

The island nations are beginning to realize that rising sea levels would, at a minimum, reduce their land area and displace people. For some low-lying island countries, it could actually threaten their survival. And the insurance industry is beginning to realize that increasing storm intensity can threaten the survival of insurance companies as well. When Hurricane Andrew tore through Florida in 1992, it took down not only thousands of buildings, but also eight insurance firms.

In September 1995, the U.S. Department of Agriculture reported a sharp drop in the estimated world grain harvest because of crop-withering heat waves in the northern tier of industrial countries. Intense late-summer heat had damaged harvests in Canada and the United States, across Europe, and in Russia. If farmers begin to see that the productivity of their land is threatened by global warming, they, too, may begin to press for a shift to renewable sources of energy.

As with CFCs, there are alternatives to fossil fuels that do not alter climate. Several solar-based energy sources, including wind power, solar cells, and solar thermal power plants, are advancing rapidly in technological sophistication, resulting in steadily falling costs. The cost of photovoltaic cells has fallen precipitously over the last few decades. In some villages in developing countries where a central grid does not yet exist, it is now cheaper to install an array of photovoltaic cells than to build a centralized power plant plus the grid needed to deliver the power.

Wind power, using the new, highly efficient wind turbines to convert wind into electricity, is poised for explosive growth in the years ahead. In California, wind farms already supply enough electricity to meet the equivalent of San Francisco's residential needs.

The potential for wind energy is enormous, dwarfing that of hydropower, which provides a fifth of the world's electricity. In the United States, the harnessable wind potential in North Dakota, South Dakota, and Texas could easily meet national electricity needs. In Europe, wind power could theoretically satisfy all the continent's electricity needs. With scores of national governments planning to tap this vast resource, rapid growth in the years ahead appears inevitable.

A Bicycle Economy

Another trend to build on is the growing production of bicycles. Human mobility can be increased by investing in public transportation, bicycles, and automobiles. Of these, the first two are by far the most promising environmentally. Although China has announced plans to move toward an automobile-centered transportation system, and car production in India is expected to double by the end of the decade, there simply may not be enough land in these countries to support such a system and to meet the food needs of their expanding populations.

Against this backdrop, the creation of bicycle-friendly transportation systems, particularly in cities, shows great promise. Market forces alone have pushed bicycle production to an estimated 111 million in 1994, three times the level of automobile production. It is in the interest of societies everywhere to foster the use of bicycles and public transportation—to accelerate the growth in bicycle manufacturing while restricting that of automobiles. Not only will this help save cropland, but this technology can greatly increase human mobility without destabilizing climate. If food becomes increasingly scarce in the years ahead, as now seems likely, the land-saving, climate-stabilizing nature of bicycles will further tip the scales in their favor and away from automobiles.

The stabilization of population in some 30 countries, the stabilization of food/people balance in Europe, the reduction in CFC production, the dramatic growth in the world's wind power generating capacity, and the extraordinary growth in bicycle use are all trends for the world to build on. These cornerstones of an environmentally sustainable global economy provide glimpses of a sustainable future.

Regaining Control of Our Destiny

Avoiding catastrophe is going to take a far greater effort than is now being contemplated by the world's political leaders. We know what needs to be done, but politically we are unable to do it because of inertia and the investment of powerful interests in the status quo. Securing food supplies for the next generation depends on an all-out effort to stabilize population and climate, but we resist changing our reproductive behavior, and we refrain from converting our climate-destabilizing, fossil-fuel-based economy to a solar/ hydrogen-based one.

As we move to the end of this century and beyond, food security may well come to dominate international affairs, national economic policy making, and—for much of humanity —personal concerns about survival. There is now evidence from enough countries that the old formula of substituting fertilizer for land is no longer working, so we need to search urgently for alternative formulas for humanly balancing our numbers with available food supplies.

Unfortunately, most national political leaders do not even seem to be aware of the fundamental shifts occurring in the world food economy, largely because the official projections by the World Bank and the U.N. Food and Agriculture Organization are essentially extrapolations of past trends.

If we are to understand the challenges facing us, the teams of economists responsible for world food supply-and-demand projections at these two organizations need to be replaced with an interdisciplinary team of analysts, including, for example, an agronomist, hydrologist, biologist, and meteorologist, along with an economist. Such a team could assess and incorporate into projections such things as the effect of soil erosion on land productivity, the effects of aquifer depletion on future irrigation water supplies, and the effect of increasingly intense heat waves on future harvests.

The World Bank team of economists argues that, because the past is the only guide we have to the future, simple extrapolations of past trends are the only reasonable way to make projections. But the past is also filled with a body of scientific literature on growth in finite environments, and it shows that biological growth trends typically conform to an S-shaped curve over time.

The risk of relying on these extrapolative projections is that they are essentially "no problem" projections. For example, the most recent World Bank projections, which use 1990 as a base and which were published in late 1993, are departing further and further from reality with each passing year. They show the world grain harvest climbing from 1.78 billion tons in 1990 to 1.97 billion tons in the year 2000. But instead of the projected gain of nearly 100 million tons since 1990, world grain production has not grown at all. Indeed, the 1995 harvest, at 1.69 billion tons, is 90 million tons below the 1990 harvest.

One of the most obvious needs today is for a set of country-by-country carrying-capacity assessments. Assessments using an interdisciplinary team can help provide information needed to face the new realities and formulate policies to respond to them.

Setting Priorities

The world today is faced with an enormous need for change in a period of time that is all too short. Human behavior and values, and the national priorities that reflect them, change in response to either new information or new experiences. The effort now needed to reverse the environmental degradation of the planet and ensure a sustainable future for the next generation will require mobilization on a scale comparable to World War II.

Regaining control of our destiny depends on stabilizing population as well as climate. These are both key to the achievement of a wide array of social goals ranging from the restoration of a rise in food con-

sumption per person to protection of the diversity of plant and animal species. And neither will be easy. The first depends on a revolution in human reproductive behavior; the second, on a restructuring of the global energy system.

Serving as a catalyst for these gargantuan efforts is the knowledge that if we fail our future will spiral

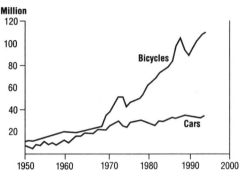

Bicycles vs. Cars
(Worldwide Production, 1950-94)

SOURCES: U.N., Interbike Directory

out of control as the acceleration of history overwhelms political institutions. It will almost guarantee a future of starvation, economic insecurity, and political instability. It will bring political conflict between societies and among ethnic and religious groups within societies. As these forces are unleashed, they will leave social disintegration in their wake.

Offsetting the dimensions of this challenge, including the opposition to change that is coming from vested interests and the momentum of trends now headed in the wrong direction, are some valuable assets. These include a well-developed global communications network, a growing body of scientific knowledge, and the possibility of using fiscal policy—a potentially powerful instrument for change—to build an environmentally sustainable economy.

Policies for Progress

Satisfying the conditions of sustainability—whether it be reversing the deforestation of the planet, converting a throwaway economy into a reuse-recycle one, or stabilizing climate—will require new investment. Probably the single most useful instrument for converting an unsustainable world economy into one that is sustainable is fiscal policy. Here are a few proposals:

• **Eliminate subsidies for unsustainable activities.** At present, governments subsidize many of the very activities that threaten the sustainability of the economy. They support fishing fleets to the extent of some $54 billion a year, for example, even though existing fishing capacity already greatly exceeds the sustainable yield of oceanic fisheries. In Germany, coal production is subsidized even though the country's scientific community has been outspoken in its calls for reducing carbon emissions.

• **Institute a carbon tax.** With alternative sources of energy such as wind power, photovoltaics, and solar thermal power plants becoming competitive or nearly so, a carbon tax that would reflect the cost to so-ciety of burning fossil fuels—the costs, that is, of air pollution, acid raid, and global warming—could quickly tip the scales away from further investment in fossil fuel production to investment in wind and solar energy. Today's fossil-fuel-based energy economy can be replaced with a solar/hydrogen economy that can meet all the energy needs of a modern industrial society without causing disruptive temperature rises.

• **Replace income taxes with environmental taxes.** Income taxes discourage work and savings, which are both positive activities that should be encouraged. Taxing environmentally destructive activities instead would help steer the global economy in an environmentally sustainable direction. Among the activities to be taxed are the use of pesticides, the generation of toxic wastes, the use of virgin raw materials, the conversion of cropland to nonfarm uses, and carbon emissions.

The time may have come also to limit tax deductions for children to two per couple: It may not make sense to subsidize childbearing beyond replacement level when the most pressing need facing humanity is to stabilize population.

The challenge for humanity is a profound one. We have the information, the technology, and the knowledge of what needs to be done. The question is, Can we do it? Can a species that is capable of formulating a theory that explains the birth of the universe now implement a strategy to build an environmentally sustainable economic system?

About the Author
Lester R. Brown is president of the Worldwatch Institute, 1776 Massachusetts Avenue, N.W., Washington, D.C. 20036. Telephone 202/452-1999; fax 202/296-7365.

Unit Selections

Key Points to Consider

❖ Are those who argue that there is in fact a process of globalization overly optimistic? Why or why not?

❖ What are some of the impediments to a truly global political economy?

❖ How are the political economies of traditional societies different from those of the consumer-oriented societies of the West?

❖ How are the developing countries dependent on the highly developed industrialized nations?

❖ Discuss some of the barriers that make it difficult for nonindustrial countries to develop.

❖ The international political economy is faced with unprecedented problems. What are some of these, and what are some of the proposals for addressing these problems?

❖ How are China, India, and other newly industrialized countries trying to alter their ways of doing business in order to meet the challenges of globalization? Are they likely to succeed?

 **Links** | **www.dushkin.com/online/**

17. **Belfer Center for Science and International Affairs (BCSIA)**
http://ksgwww.harvard.edu/csia/

18. **Communications for a Sustainable Future**
gopher://csf.colorado.edu

19. **U.S. Agency for International Development**
http://www.info.usaid.gov

20. **Virtual Seminar in Global Political Economy/Global Cities & Social Movements**
http://csf.colorado.edu/gpe/gpe95b/resources.html

21. **World Bank**
http://www.worldbank.org

These sites are annotated on pages 6 and 7.

An underlying debate that has shaped much of the twentieth century's social history focused on dramatically opposing views about how economic systems should be organized and what role government should play in the management of a country's economy. For some, the dominant capitalist economic system appeared to be organized for the benefit of the few, with the masses trapped in poverty, supplying cheap labor to further enrich the wealthy. This economic system, they argued, could be changed only by gaining control of the political system and radically changing the ownership of the means of production. In striking contrast to this perspective, others argued that the best way to create wealth and eliminate poverty was to encourage entrepreneurs with the motivation of profits and to allow a competitive marketplace to make decisions about production and distribution.

The debate between socialism/communism on the one hand and capitalism on the other (with variations in between) has been characterized by both abstract theorizing and very pragmatic and often violent political conflict. The Russian and Chinese revolutions overthrew the old social order and created radical changes in the political and economic systems in these two giant countries. The political structures created to support the new systems of agricultural production, along with the planning of all other aspects of economic activity, eliminated most private ownership of property; they were, in short, unparalleled experiments in social engineering.

The collapse of the Soviet Union and the dramatic reforms that have taken place in China have recast the debate about how to best structure contemporary economics. Some believe that with the end of communism and the resulting participation of hundreds of millions of new consumers in the global market economy, an unprecedented era has been entered. Proponents of this view argue that a new global economy is emerging, setting into motion a series of processes that will ultimately result in a single economic system characterized by interdependence and increased prosperity.

Many have noted that this process of "globalization" is being accelerated by the revolution in communication and computer technologies. Others are less optimistic about the prospects of globalization. They argue that the creation of a single economic system where there are no boundaries to impede the flow of capital does not mean a closing of the gap between the world's rich and poor.

The use of the term "political economy" for the title of this unit is a recognition that modern economic and political systems are not separable. All economic systems have some type of marketplace where goods and services are bought and sold. The government in most cases regulates these transactions, that is, it sets the rules that govern the marketplace. In addition, the government's power to tax in order to pay for defense and other public activities directly affects all economic activities (i.e., by determining how much money remains for other expenditures).

One of the most important concepts in thinking about the contemporary political economy is "development." If a group of experts were gathered to discuss this concept, it would soon be apparent that many define the word "development" in various ways. For some, development means becoming industrialized—like the United States or Japan. To others, development means having a growing economy, which is usually measured in terms of the expansion of the so-called gross domestic product (GDP). To still others, development is primarily a political phenomenon. They question how a society can change its economy if it cannot first establish collective goals and successfully administer their implementation. And to still others, development means attaining a certain quality of life, based on the establishment of adequate health care, leisure time, and a system of public education, among other things.

For purposes of this unit, the term "development" will be defined as an improvement in the basic aspects of life: lower infant mortality rates, greater life expectancy, lower disease rates, higher rates of literacy, healthier diets, and improved sanitation. Judged by these standards, some groups of people are more developed than others. A fundamental question that the thoughtful reader must consider is whether the apparent trend toward greater globalization is resulting in increased development, not only for a few people but for most of those participating in the global political economy.

The unit is organized into two subsections. The first is a general discussion of the concept of globalization. How do different people define the term, and what are their various perspectives on it? For example, is the idea of a global economy merely wishful thinking by those who sit on top of the power hierarchy, self-deluded into believing that globalization is an inexorable force that will evolve in its own way, following its own rules? Or will there always be traditional issues of power politics between the rich, those who are ascending in power, and the ever-present poor, which will result in clashes of interests just like those that have characterized history since the early years of civilization?

The second subsection focuses on case studies. These have been selected to help the reader draw his or her own conclusions about the validity of the globalization concept. What in fact is taking place in countries that have not participated directly in the industrial revolution? In addition, can countries like China and India find a significant economic role in the contemporary world? Does the contemporary political economy result in winners and losers, or can all benefit from its system of wealth creation and distribution?

Globalization, we are told, is what every business should be pursuing, and what every nation should welcome. But what, exactly, is it? James Rosenau offers a nuanced understanding of a process that is much more real, and transforming, than the language of the marketplace expresses.

The Complexities and Contradictions of Globalization

JAMES N. ROSENAU

The mall at Singapore's airport has a food court with 15 food outlets, all but one of which offering menus that cater to local tastes; the lone standout, McDonald's, is also the only one crowded with customers. In New York City, experts in *feng shui*, an ancient Chinese craft aimed at harmonizing the placement of man-made structures in nature, are sought after by real estate developers in order to attract a growing influx of Asian buyers who would not be interested in purchasing buildings unless their structures were properly harmonized.

Most people confronted with these examples would probably not be surprised by them. They might even view them as commonplace features of day-to-day life late in the twentieth century, instances in which local practices have spread to new and distant sites. In the first case the spread is from West to East and in the second it is from East to West, but both share

JAMES N. ROSENAU *is University Professor of International Affairs at George Washington University. His latest book is* Along the Domestic-Foreign Frontier: Exploring Governance in a Turbulent World *(Cambridge: Cambridge University Press, 1997). This article draws on the author's "New Dimensions of Security: The Interaction of Globalizing and Localizing Dynamics,"* Security Dialogue, *September 1994, and "The Dynamics of Globalization: Toward an Operational Formulation,"* Security Dialogue, *September 1996).*

a process in which practices spread and become established in profoundly different cultures. And what immediately comes to mind when contemplating this process? The answer can be summed up in on word: globalization, a label that is presently in vogue to account for peoples, activities, norms, ideas, goods, services, and currencies that are decreasingly confined to a particular geographic space and its local and established practices.

Indeed, some might contend that "globalization" is the latest buzzword to which observers resort when things seem different and they cannot otherwise readily account for them. That is why, it is reasoned, a great variety of activities are labeled as globalization, with the result that no widely accepted formulation of the concept has evolved. Different observers use it to describe different phenomena, and often there is little overlap among the various usages. Even worse, the elusiveness of the concept of globalization is seen as underlying the use of a variety of other, similar terms—world society, interdependence, centralizing tendencies, world system, globalism, universalism, internationalization, globality—that come into play when efforts are made to grasp why public affairs today seem significantly different from those of the past.

Such reasoning is misleading. The proliferation of diverse and loose definitions of globalization as well as the readiness to use a variety of seemingly comparable labels are not so much a reflection of evasive confusion as they are an early stage in a profound ontological shift, a restless search for new ways of understanding unfamiliar phenomena. The lack of precise formulations may suggest the presence of buzzwords for the inexplicable, but a more convincing interpretation is that such words are voiced in so many different contexts because of a shared sense that the human condition is presently undergoing profound transformations in all of its aspects.

WHAT IS GLOBALIZATION?

Let us first make clear where globalization fits among the many buzzwords that indicate something new in world affairs that is moving important activities and concerns beyond the national seats of power that have long served as the foundations of economic, political, and social life. While all the buzzwords seem to cluster around the same dimension of the present human condition, useful distinctions can be drawn among them. Most notably, if it is presumed that the prime characteristic of this dimension is change—a transformation of practices and norms—then the term "globalization" seems appropriate to denote the "something" that is changing humankind's preoccupation with territoriality and the traditional arrangements of the state system. It is a term that directly implies change, and thus differentiates the phenomenon as a process rather than as a prevailing condition or a desirable end state.

Conceived as an underlying process, in other words, globalization is not the same as globalism, which points to aspirations for a state of affairs where values are shared by or pertinent to all the world's more than 5 billion people, their environment, and their role as citizens, consumers, or producers with an interest in collective action to solve common problems. And it can also be distinguished from universalism, which refers to those values that embrace all of humanity (such as the values that science or religion draws on), at any time or place. Nor is it coterminous with complex interdependence, which signifies structures that link people and communities in various parts of the world.

Although related to these other concepts, the idea of globalization developed here is narrower in scope. It refers neither to values nor to structures, but to sequences that unfold either in the mind or in behavior, to processes that evolve as people and organizations go about their daily tasks and seek to realize their particular goals. What distinguishes globalizing processes is that they are not hindered or prevented by territorial or jurisdictional barriers. As indicated by the two examples presented at the outset, such processes can readily spread in many directions across national boundaries, and are capable of reaching into any community anywhere in the world. They consist of all those forces that impel individuals, groups, and institutions to engage in similar forms of behavior or to participate in more encompassing and coherent processes, organizations, or systems.

Contrariwise, localization derives from all those pressures that lead individuals, groups, and institutions to narrow their horizons, participate in dissimilar forms of behavior, and withdraw to less encompassing processes, organizations, or sys-

tems. In other words, any technological, psychological, social, economic, or political developments that foster the expansion of interests and practices beyond established boundaries are both sources and expressions of the processes of globalization, just as any developments in these realms that limit or reduce interests are both sources and expressions of localizing processes.

Note that the processes of globalization are conceived as only *capable* of being worldwide in scale. In fact, the activities of no group, government, society, or company have never been planetary in magnitude, and few cascading sequences actually encircle and encompass the entire globe. Televised events such as civil wars and famines in Africa or protests against governments in Eastern Europe may sustain a spread that is worldwide in scope, but such a scope is not viewed as a prerequisite of globalizing dynamics. As long as it has the potential of an unlimited spread that can readily transgress national jurisdictions, any interaction sequence is considered to reflect the operation of globalization.

Obviously, the differences between globalizing and localizing forces give rise to contrary conceptions of territoriality. Globalization is rendering boundaries and identity with the land less salient while localization, being driven by pressures to narrow and withdraw, is highlighting borders and intensifying the deep attachments to land that can dominate emotion and reasoning.

In short, globalization is boundary-broadening and localization is boundary-heightening. The former allows people, goods, information, norms, practices, and institutions to move about oblivious to despite boundaries. The boundary-heightening processes of localization are designed to inhibit or prevent the movement of people, goods, information, norms, practices, and institutions. Efforts along this line, however, can be only partially successful. Community and state boundaries can be heightened to a considerable extent, but they cannot be rendered impervious. Authoritarian governments try to make them so, but their policies are bound to be undermined in a shrinking world with increasingly interdependent economies and communications technologies that are not easily monitored. Thus it is hardly surprising that some of the world's most durable tensions flow from the fact that no geographic borders can be made so airtight to prevent the infiltration of ideas and goods. Stated more emphatically, some globalizing dynamics are bound, at least in the long run, to prevail.

The boundary-expanding dynamics of globalization have become highly salient precisely because recent decades have witnessed a mushrooming of the facilities, interests, and markets through which a potential for worldwide spread can be realized. Likewise, the boundary-contracting dynamics of localization have also become increasingly significant, not least because some people and cultures feel threatened by the incursions of globalization. Their jobs, their icons, their belief systems, and their communities seem at risk as the boundaries that have sealed them off from the outside world in the past no longer assure protection. And there is, of course, a basis of truth in these fears. Globalization does intrude; its processes do shift jobs elsewhere; its norms do undermine traditional mores. Responses to these threats can vary considerably. At one extreme are adaptations that accept the boundary-broadening processes and make the best of them by integrating them into local customs and practices. At the other extreme are responses intended to ward off the globalizing processes by resort to ideological purities, closed borders, and economic isolation.

THE DYNAMICS OF FRAGMEGRATION

The core of world affairs today thus consists of tensions between the dynamics of globalization and localization. Moreover, the two sets of dynamics are causally linked, almost as if every increment of globalization gives rise to an increment of localization, and vice versa. To account for these tensions I have long used the term "fragmegration," an awkward and perhaps even grating label that has the virtue of capturing the pervasive interactions between the fragmenting forces of localization and the integrative forces of globalization.[1] One can readily observe the unfolding of fragmegrative dynamics in the struggle of the European Union to cope with proposals for monetary unification or in the electoral campaigns and successes of Jean-Marie Le Pen in France, Patrick Buchanan in the United States, and Pauline Hanson in Australia—to mention only three examples.

It is important to keep in mind that fragmegration is not a single dynamic. Both globalization and localization are clusters of forces that, as they interact in different ways and through different channels, contribute to more encompassing processes in the case of globalization and to less encompassing processes in the case of localization. These various dynamics, moreover, operate in all realms of human activity, from the cultural and social to the economic and political.

In the political realm, globalizing dynamics underlie any developments that facilitate the expansion of authority, policies, and interests beyond existing socially constructed territorial boundaries, whereas the politics of localization involves any trends in which the scope of authority and policies undergoes contraction and reverts to concerns, issues, groups, and institutions that are less extensive than the prevailing socially constructed territorial boundaries. In the economic realm, globalization encompasses the expansion of production, trade, and investments beyond their prior locales, while localizing dynamics are at work when the activities of producers and consumers are constricted to narrower boundaries. In the social and cultural realms, globalization operates to extend ideas, norms, and practices beyond the settings in which they originated, while localization highlights or compresses the original settings and thereby inhibits the inroad of new ideas, norms, and practices.

It must be stressed that the dynamics unfolding in all these realms are long-term processes. They involve fundamental human needs and thus span all of human history. Globalizing dynamics derive from peoples' need to enlarge the scope of

There is no inherent contradiction between localizing and globalizing tendencies.

their self-created orders so as to increase the goods, services, and ideas available for their well-being. The agricultural revolution, followed by the industrial and postindustrial transformations, are among the major sources that have sustained globalization. Yet even as these forces have been operating, so have contrary tendencies toward contraction been continuously at work. Localizing dynamics derive from people's need for the psychic comforts of close-at-hand, reliable support—for the family and neighborhood, for local cultural practices, for a sense of "us" that is distinguished from "them." Put differently, globalizing dynamics have long fostered large-scale order, whereas localizing dynamics have long created pressure for small-scale order. Fragmegration, in short, has always been an integral part of the human condition.

GLOBALIZATION'S EVENTUAL PREDOMINANCE

Notwithstanding the complexities inherent in the emergent structures of world affairs, observers have not hesitated to anticipate what lies beyond fragmegration as global history unfolds. All agree that while the contest between globalizing and localizing dynamics is bound to be marked by fluctuating surges in both directions, the underlying tendency is for the former to prevail over the latter. Eventually, that is, the dynamics of globalization are expected to serve as the bases around which the course of events is organized.

Consensus along these lines breaks down, however, over whether the predominance of globalization is likely to have desirable or noxious consequences. Those who welcome globalizing processes stress the power of economic variables. In this view the globalization of national economies through the diffusion of technology and consumer products, the rapid transfer of financial resources, and the efforts of transnational companies to extend their market shares is seen as so forceful and durable as to withstand and eventually surmount any and all pressures toward fragmentation. This line acknowledges that the diffusion that sustains the processes of globalization is a centuries-old dynamic, but the difference is that the present era has achieved a level of economic development in which it is possible for innovations occurring in any sector of any country's economy to be instantaneously transferred to and adapted in any other country or sector. As a consequence,

when this process of diffusion collides with cultural or political protectionism, it is culture and protectionism that wind up in the shop for repairs. Innovation accelerates. Productivity increases. Standards of living improve. There are setbacks, of course. The newspaper headlines are full of them. But we be-

---

[1] For an extensive discussion of the dynamics of fragmegration, see James N. Rosenau, *Along the Domestic-Foreign Frontier: Exploring Governance in a Turbulent World* (Cambridge: Cambridge University Press, 1997), ch. 6.

lieve that the time required to override these setbacks has short-ened dramatically in the developed world. Indeed, recent ex-perience suggests that, in most cases, economic factors prevail in less than a generation. . . .

Thus understood, globalization—the spread of economic innovations around the world and the political and cultural adjustments that accompany this diffusion—cannot be stopped. . . . As history teaches, the political organizations and ideologies that yield superior economic performance survive, flourish, and replace those that are less productive.[2]

While it is surely the case that robust economic incentives sustain and quicken the processes of globalization, this line of theorizing nevertheless suffers from not allowing for its own negation. The theory offers no alternative interpretations as to how the interaction of economic, political, and social dynamics will play out. One cannot demonstrate the falsity—if falsity it is—of the theory because any contrary evidence is seen merely as "setbacks," as expectable but temporary deviations from the predicted course. The day may come, of course, when event so perfectly conform to the predicted patterns of globalization that one is inclined to conclude that the theory has been af-firmed. But in the absence of alternative scenarios, the theory offers little guidance as to how to interpret intervening events, especially those that highlight the tendencies toward fragmen-tation. Viewed in this way, it is less a theory and more an article of faith to which one can cling.

Other observers are much less sanguine about the future development of fragmegration. They highlight a litany of nox-ious consequences that they see as following from the eventual predominance of globalization: "its economism; its economic reductionism; its technological determinism; its political cyni-cism, defeatism, and immobilism; its de-socialization of the subject and resocialization of risk; its teleological subtext of inexorable global 'logic' driven exclusively by capital accu-mulation and the market; and its ritual exclusion of factors, causes, or goals other than capital accumulation and the market from the priority of values to be pursued by social action."[3]

Still another approach, allowing for either desirable or noxious outcomes, has been developed by Michael Zurn. He identifies a mismatch between the rapid extension of boundary-crossing ac-tivities and the scope of effective governance. Consequently, states are undergoing what is labeled "uneven denationalization," a pri-mary process in which "the rise of international governance is still remarkable, but not accompanied by mechanisms for . . . democratic control; people, in addition, become alienated from the remote political process. . . . The democratic state in the Western world is confronted with a situation in which it is undermined by the process of globalization and overarched by the rise of international institutions."[4]

While readily acknowledging the difficulties of anticipating where the process of uneven denationalization is driving the world, Zurn is able to derive two scenarios that may unfold: "Whereas the pessimistic scenario points to instances of frag-mentation and emphasizes the disruption caused by the tran-sition, the optimistic scenario predicts, at least in the long run, the triumph of centralization." The latter scenario rests on the presumption that the increased interdependence of societies will propel them to develop ever more effective democratic controls over the very complex arrangements on which inter-national institutions must be founded.

UNEVEN FRAGMEGRATION

My own approach to theorizing about the fragmegrative process builds on these other perspectives and a key presump-tion of my own—that there is no inherent contradiction be-tween localizing and globalizing tendencies—to develop an overall hypothesis that anticipates fragmegrative outcomes and that allows for its own negation: *the more pervasive globaliz-ing tendencies become, the less resistant localizing reactions will be to further globalization.* In other words, globalization and localization will coexist, but the former will continue to set the context for the latter. Since the degree of coexistence will vary from situation to situation (depending on the salience of the global economy and the extent to which ethnic and other noneconomic factors actively contribute to localization), I refer, borrowing from Zurn, to the processes depicted by the hypothesis as *uneven fragmegration.* The hypothesis allows for continuing pockets of antagonism between globalizing and lo-calizing tendencies even as increasingly (but unevenly) the two accommodate each other. It does not deny the pessimistic sce-nario wherein fragmentation disrupts globalizing tendencies; rather it treats fragmentation as more and more confined to particular situations that may eventually be led by the oppor-tunities and requirements of greater interdependence to con-form to globalization.

For globalizing and localizing tendencies to accommodate each other, individuals have to come to appreciate that they can achieve psychic comfort in collectivities through multiple memberships and multiple loyalties, that they can advance both local and global values without either detracting from the other. The hypothesis of uneven fragmegration anticipates a growing appreciation along these lines because the contrary premise, that psychic comfort can only be realized by having a highest loyalty, is becoming increasingly antiquated. To be sure, people have long been accustomed to presuming that, in order to derive the psychic comfort they need through collec-tive identities, they had to have a hierarchy of loyalties and that, consequently, they had to have a highest loyalty that could only be attached to a single collectivity. Such reasoning, how-ever, is a legacy of the state system, of centuries of crises that made people feel they had to place nation-state loyalties above all others. It is a logic that long served to reinforce the pre-dominance of the state as the "natural" unit of political or-

[2] William W. Lewis and Marvin Harris, "Why Globalization Must Prevail," *The McKinsey Quarterly,* no. 2 (1992), p. 115.
[3] Barry K. Gills, "Editorial: 'Globalization' and the 'Politics of Resistance,' " *New Political Economy,* vol. 2 (March 1997), p. 12.
[4] Michael Zurn, "What Has Changed in Europe? The Challenge of Globaliza-tion and Individualization," paper presented at a meeting on What Has Changed? Competing Perspectives on World Order (Copenhagen, May 14–16, 1993), p. 40.

ganization and that probably reached new heights during the intense years of the cold war.

But if it is the case, as the foregoing analysis stresses, that conceptions of territoriality are in flux and that the failure of states to solve pressing problems has led to a decline in their capabilities and a loss of legitimacy, it follows that the notion that people must have a "highest loyalty" will also decline and give way to the development of multiple loyalties and an understanding that local, national, and transnational affiliations need not be mutually exclusive. For the reality is that human affairs are organized at all these levels for good reasons; people have needs that can only be filled by close-at-hand organizations and other needs that are best served by distant entities at the national or transnational level.

In addition, not only is an appreciation of the reality that allows for multiple loyalties and memberships likely to grow as the effectiveness of states and the salience of national loyalties diminish, but it also seems likely to widen as the benefits of the global economy expand and people become increasingly aware of the extent to which their well-being is dependent on events and trends elsewhere in the world. At the same time, the distant economic processes serving their needs are impersonal and hardly capable of advancing the need to share with others in a collective affiliation. This need was long served by the nation-state, but with fragmegrative dynamics having undermined the national level as a source of psychic comfort and with transnational entities seeming too distant to provide the psychic benefits of affiliation, the satisfactions to be gained through more close-at-hand affiliations are likely to seem ever more attractive.

THE STAKES

It seems clear that fragmegration has become an enduring feature of global life; it is also evident that globalization is not merely a buzzword, that it encompasses pervasive complexities and contradictions that have the potential both to enlarge and to degrade our humanity. In order to ensure that the enlargement is more prevalent than the degradation, it is important that people and their institutions become accustomed to the multiple dimensions and nuances as our world undergoes profound and enduring transformations. To deny the complexities and contradictions in order to cling to a singular conception of what globalization involves is to risk the many dangers that accompany oversimplification.

> **"Globalization is not making the world less diverse and more equal . . . [True,] more and more people across the planet have become increasingly exposed to the amenities of the global marketplace, although mostly as permanent window-shoppers and silent spectators. The large majority of humankind, however, is rapidly being left outside and far behind."**

Prosper or Perish?
Development in the Age of
Global Capital

BLANCA HEREDIA

Dominant thinking about development today sees globalization as a matter of life or death for less developed countries. If embraced, it is argued, globalization will quickly propel developing nations into modernity and affluence; if resisted it will either crush them or throw them by the wayside. The matter, unfortunately, is not so clear and simple. The recent experience of much of sub-Saharan Africa shows that failure to catch the global train can prove deadly for underdeveloped countries. But a ride on that train does not provide a sure ticket to fast, stable, and equitable growth. Globalization may allow a few poor countries to leapfrog out of the backwater; but as the recent financial troubles in East Asia suggest, embracing global financial markets can also be treacherous, and costly.

The sharply unequal effects of globalized finance and production across and within developing countries stand in sharp contrast to the widely shared image of globalization as a formidable equalizer of tastes, incomes, outlooks, and lifestyles. Greater economic openness has made small parts of the developing world full-fledged members of the global village. But

in many developing nations, globalized islands of prosperity are thriving alongside vast and growing expanses of economic stagnation and human deprivation. Nothing is more common for an upper-middle-class professional in a large emerging market such as Brazil or Mexico than to switch off the Internet and, before stepping out the door, to switch on a heightened awareness of his or her surroundings in order to survive the dangers of the darker side of the global village.

Rather than allowing developing nations to quickly catch up, globalization has greatly exacerbated inequalities among and within them. Its mixed record at century's end has dampened the euphoric optimism of the 1980s and given rise to a more sober mood. Advocates of globalization continue to see it as essentially good news for lagging economies. While still calling for greater openness, they have also begun to recognize globalization's many costs and admit to the importance of effective state institutions in allowing developing nations to actually profit from it. Most illustrative of the new mood is the World Bank's tempered rehabilitation of the centrality of the state in its latest *World Development Report*.

The belated recognition by free marketeers of the importance of effective state institutions in mediating globalization's impact on economic development—a bit ironic given their committed efforts throughout the 1980s to dismantle state institutions—is a welcome sign. Heightened exposure to world

BLANCA HEREDIA *is a professor in the department of international studies and academic dean at the Center for Research and Teaching in Economics in Mexico City.*

markets will only become a true lever of economic development in the presence of institutions able to mitigate market failures and manage the competitive challenges and domestic dislocations produced by openness. Contrary to conventional wisdom, however, the absence of the requisite institutional conditions is not necessarily self-correcting.

In countries lacking the institutional capacity to regulate markets and compensate losers, openness does not necessarily lead to economic stagnation or social collapse. Exposure to global markets can promote exclusionary types of growth based on dynamic export enclaves and highly profitable—albeit volatile—domestic financial markets. Supported rather than punished by failure-prone global financial markets, and buttressed by political arrangements that limit losers' ability to organize, these disjointed and exclusionary varieties of outward-oriented growth may persist for long periods of time.

Liberalization and globalization are unlikely to promote stable and equitable development. The type of growth and the kind of society produced by economic openness hinge more on the number and the quality of a given nation's institutional resources. The problem for less developed countries is that exposure to unbridled international financial markets will not automatically generate the correct—let alone the best—institutions and may make efforts to assemble and pay for them increasingly costly and difficult.

GLOBALIZATION LAID BARE

Among the images associated with globalization, the most popular portrays it as a worldwide process of converging incomes and lifestyles driven by ever larger international flows of goods, images, capital, and people. In throwing hamburgers, money, and television shows into the same global hodgepodge, this conventional and immensely seductive view fails to single out what is truly distinctive about globalization.

The basic engine behind the emergence of a globalized world economy lies not in goods, people, money, and ideas becoming increasingly and similarly transportable across national frontiers. It lies, rather, in capital becoming historically more portable and more internationally mobile than anything else. Capital, moreover, is not only winning the international mobility race: it is also largely driving the globalization of all the rest.

Successive waves of financial deregulation in advanced economies along with new information and communication technologies helped power the dizzying growth experienced by international finance over the last 30 years. Initially fueled by the dramatic expansion of world trade and by growing competition among United States, European, and Japanese firms for one another's domestic markets, financial deregulation accelerated in the 1970s in the midst of the petrodollar boom, leading to a truly phenomenal resurrection of international finance. Cross-border transactions in equities and bonds in major advanced economies, for example, jumped from less than 10 percent of GDP in 1980 to well over 100 percent in 1995. Relative to world GDP, total foreign direct investment (FDI)

flows doubled between 1980 and 1994. The most explosive growth has occurred in the foreign exchange market, where the average *daily* turnover surged from about $200 billion in the mid-1980s to around $1.2 trillion in 1995—approximately 85 percent of total world reserves.

The growth of international finance has radically reshaped the structural and institutional makeup of the world economy. Few areas have been left untouched. Capital mobility and technological change have allowed production to become more transnationally integrated, which has introduced major changes in international trade. The share of world commerce channeled and managed by global corporations has spiraled upward. As a result, trade and investment have ceased to be substitutes for one another and have become mutually reinforcing. The mounting importance of intrafirm trade has contributed to the continued expansion of world commerce. Since intrafirm trade is less sensitive than arm's length trade to exchange rate movements as well as to a variety of trade policy instruments, the ability of governments to shape trade flows has declined.

Globalized financial markets have greatly heightened the structural power of capital holders and have drastically reduced the policy options open to governments. Room for sustaining, let alone building, the kinds of extensive welfare systems that allowed small open economies in Europe to reconcile high trade openness with domestic social stability during the postwar period has dramatically narrowed. The same holds for the activist industrial and financial policy strategies employed by the miracle economies of East Asia from the 1960s through the 1980s. Thus, with untrammeled capital mobility the highly interventionist credit allocation schemes deployed by the South Korean government during the era of super-high growth have become unworkable and unthinkable.

The newest developmental orthodoxy of free markets and sound money has yet to prove its merits. Ever more fierce competition for financial resources and export markets can help limit monetary and fiscal folly and may well generate important efficiency and productivity gains. But the kind of growth promoted by the disciplining embrace of global markets is not necessarily high, stable, balanced, and equitable; unfortunately, not all good things go together. A country—such as Mexico during the first half of the 1990s—may open up but then experience slow, polarizing, and unstable growth. Or take Thailand, furiously embracing free and open finance in the early 1990s only to find itself saddled in 1997 with a banking system on the brink of collapse, the prospect of slower growth, and no option but to cut back on investment as well as on attempts to reduce poverty or upgrade human capital.

As United States Treasury Secretary Robert Rubin kindly reminded us during his appearance this September in Hong Kong at the IMF-World Bank joint annual meeting, the root of the recent financial malaise in East Asia—and the root of all the troubles spurred by globalization across the developing world, for that matter—may well lie in poor nations not opening up deep and fast enough. The problem with the "more openness, less government intervention" solution is that it pushes the issue, once again, into the unknown future. Judging from the record so far, what more of the same is likely to mean for developing nations is less and less room for building or sustaining the kinds of institutions that are necessary to ensure that the developmental benefits of globalization materialize.

INEQUALITIES WITHOUT . . .

Developing countries today are a much more heterogeneous group than at the beginning of the postwar period. Globalization is not helping them become more equal; the poorest are not catching up the fastest. Instead, globalization is making the differences between developing countries increasingly deep and wide.

Contrary to the predictions of neoclassical economic theory, the freeing up of international capital flows is not benefiting countries where capital is most scarce. The lion's share of private international financial flows has continued to go to capital-abundant nations. In 1995, for example, 65 percent of FDI inflows went to the developed world. The bulk of the recent growth of capital inflows into developing countries, moreover, has been concentrated in a handful of relatively rich emerging markets.

Still, international financial flows to developing countries have grown significantly in recent years; their composition has also changed. Throughout most of the postwar period, private foreign financing for developing nations was relatively small and tended to be heavily dominated by FDI. In the 1970s, international bank lending to less advanced countries resumed on a grand scale, but after the global debt crisis fell sharply. Starting in the late 1980s, and fueled by deregulation in the North as well as by major episodes of financial liberalization and privatization in many developing countries, FDI and especially portfolio investment flows underwent a formidable expansion. The share of world FDI going to developing countries jumped from an average of 24 percent between 1983 and 1987 to 32 percent in 1995. Equity and bond flows grew even faster, rising from 0.5 percent of GDP in 1983 to 1989 to between 2 and 4 percent from 1994 to 1996.

The lion's share of private international financial flows has continued to go to capital-abundant nations.

The developing countries' expanded access to international private financing has been unevenly distributed. Between 1989 and 1992, for example, 72 percent of total FDI flows to developing countries went to only 10 countries (China, Mexico, Malaysia, Argentina, Thailand, Indonesia, Brazil, Nigeria, Venezuela, and South Korea). The distribution of portfolio investment flows has been even more heavily skewed. Between 1989 and 1993, only 10 countries received 90 percent of the total gross portfolio investments flowing to the developing world (Mexico, Brazil, Argentina, Hungary, South Korea, Greece, Turkey, China, Venezuela, and Thailand).

The poorest countries have seen little profit from the recent boom in international financial flows, while suffering a great deal from major cuts and reorientations in aid flows from advanced nations. Net official development assistance over the past decade has stagnated in terms of value and has declined as a share of donors' GDP, reaching in 1994 its lowest level since 1973. Given the strong reorientation in favor of disaster relief and peacekeeping operations, aid flows for supporting economic development have actually contracted. Meanwhile, and largely due to deteriorating terms of trade since the early 1980s, aid dependence among least developed nations has risen sharply in the past few years.

The gains for those developing countries that have benefited from greater access to international financial resources have come at a significant price. International financial integration has entailed an important loss of policy autonomy and has increased host countries' vulnerabilities to external financial shocks. The rapidly growing importance of highly mobile and liquid portfolio investment flows has proved, in this sense, especially challenging.

Heightened dependence on larger volumes of short-term external capital flows has vastly complicated monetary and exchange rate management and has severely limited governments' ability to use exchange rate and monetary policy in ways conducive to growth in the real economy. Globalized finance has also contributed to the increasing fragility of domestic financial systems in developing countries. Since 1980, more than 100 developing nations have experienced serious banking crises. The public cost of these crises has been extremely high. In Mexico, for example, the 1995 collapse of the banking system—which came in the wake of fast financial liberalization—has cost the Mexican public around 12 percent of GDP.

Much of the cost of heightened exposure to global financial markets has resulted from the lack of appropriate regulatory capacities as well as domestic institutions able to ensure the sound use and the proper management of larger volumes of external financial flows. Much of it, though, has stemmed from the tendency of global financial markets to wait until the crisis hits to impose their discipline stringently—and then to impose it with a vengeance. In short, domestic government failures have certainly magnified the costs of financial openness. Global market failures—such as the propensity of global investors to engage in euphoric rides followed by equally intense panic attacks—have also been a major contributor.

. . . AND INEQUALITIES WITHIN

Globalization has exacerbated differences not only among developing nations, but also within them. Heightened exposure to global markets has magnified and multiplied domestic inequalities. It is true that in a handful of countries, liberalization and expanded access to global finance have resulted in significant advances in poverty reduction. The most notable among this select group is China, where over the past 15 years poor people as a share of total population fell from 33 percent to 10 percent. The bulk of the developing world has not been as fortunate.

Since the 1980s, poverty has grown in absolute terms throughout developing countries and has increased in both absolute and relative terms in much of Africa and Latin America. In the latter, after a sharp rise in the 1980s, the proportion of poor people started to slowly decrease from the early 1990s onward, but in only two countries: Chile and Colombia. In the rest of the region poverty has continued to grow and, if current trends persist, will continue to do so in the next 10 years at the rate of two more poor people per minute.

The rush to free markets and openness has also coincided with increasing inequality throughout the developing world. Even in Southeast Asia's fastest-growing economies, income differentials have been widening slowly since the early 1990s. It is, again, in Latin America where inequalities have recently become larger and most glaring. Income inequality has grown significantly in the region as a whole over the past few decades. In 1995, 15 of the region's 17 countries had levels of income inequality exceeding those normally associated with their level of development.

High levels of poverty and extreme income inequality are not new to Latin America. Economic theory would predict, though, that greater openness should have helped alleviate both: trade openness by promoting labor-intensive export growth and financial openness by expanding the pool of capital available for productive investment, especially in those sectors and regions where capital is scarce. But extremely fast-paced trade and financial liberalization in Latin America has not helped reduce poverty or inequality.

Latin America's faster and deeper economic liberalization has thus coincided with a significant widening of income differentials as well as increasing poverty. As a result, initially large social deformities in many Latin American countries have become, over the past decade, larger still. In much of the region, the globalizing 1980s and 1990s have brought more Mercedes and more homeless children to the streets; they have also brought more Norwegian salmon, more youngsters involved in crime, more Nike sneakers to dream about, and more violence in and outside the home. In the midst of growing poverty and inequality, life, even for those fully wired into the global mall, has become much more harsh.

Other aspects of Latin America's recent economic performance have also left much to be desired. Despite more radical liberalization than in other developing regions, between 1990 and 1995 Latin America's average annual GDP grew 3.2 percent; in South Asia and East Asia the corresponding figures were 4.6 percent and 10.3 percent, respectively. More important, average total factor productivity between 1989 and 1994

> *The bulk of the developing world has not been as fortunate [as China].*

has, with the exception of Chile and Argentina, fallen in all major Latin American economies compared to the period between 1950 and 1980, and has remained lower than in East Asia.

In most Latin American countries, the resumed growth of recent years has been based in a very small number of sectors, regions, and firms. The two most dynamic sectors have been exports and finance, but even here the number of winners has been small. Though with important cross-national variations, export growth has tended to be highly concentrated and heavily dominated by transnational firms. In 1995, for example, the share in total exports of the top 25 exporting firms—many of them transnationals—was 44 percent in Argentina, 26 percent in Brazil, and 56 percent in Mexico.

Foreign financial inflows and domestic financial sectors, on the other hand, have experienced impressive, if unstable, growth. Latin American stock markets have grown rapidly in the past few years. Between 1990 and 1995, market capitalization as a percentage of GDP jumped from 2.3 to 13.5 in Argentina, from 3.4 to 21.8 in Brazil, and from 13.2 to 36.3 in Mexico. In contrast to Southeast Asia, where stock exchange growth has been accompanied by a significant increase in the number of participating firms, the number of listed domestic companies has remained remarkably small in most Latin American countries. Particularly noteworthy is the contrast between Indonesia, with almost 8,000 listed firms in 1995, and Brazil, with only 543. The benefits of greater access to foreign financial funds have also been unevenly shared. In Mexico, 10 firms received over 50 percent of total foreign investment in equities in 1993.

The most important exception to these regional economic trends is Chile. After the 1982 economic collapse associated with the dogmatic monetarism employed during the initial years of General Augusto Pinochet's dictatorship, the Chilean government adopted a more pragmatic economic policy approach. Most of the structural reforms pushed through in the 1970s—trade liberalization and privatization—were left in place, but a series of important adjustments was introduced. These included controls on short-term financial inflows, fiscal policies oriented to raising domestic savings, pension systems reform, large poverty alleviation programs, and a flexible exchange rate regime that was used to maintain a high real exchange rate.

Through this mix of openness, moderately interventionist financial and exchange rate policies, and compensatory schemes for the most vulnerable, Chile has managed to combine over the last 10 years relatively high and stable growth rates that have averaged 6 percent annually, along with important advances in poverty reduction. While Chile's recent performance has been less spectacular than that of East Asia's superachievers, its record remains significantly brighter than that of its more financially liberal, more overvaluation-prone, and less welfare proactive regional neighbors.

INSTITUTIONS AND TYPE OF GROWTH

Globalization is not making the world less diverse and more equal. A growing but still small part of the world's population is becoming more similar in what it eats, buys, wears, and thinks. And more and more people across the planet have become increasingly exposed to the amenities of the global marketplace, although mostly as permanent window-shoppers and silent spectators. The large majority of humankind, however, is rapidly being left outside and far behind.

The drastic unevenness of globalization's effects among less developed countries can be traced to major cross-national differences in preexisting social and economic conditions as well as to the depth and breadth of recent market-oriented reforms. Crucial in accounting for the widely diverse kinds of growth spurred by globalization are the differing state capacities and institutional resources through which these countries have dealt with the manifold challenges and opportunities posed by globalized capital.

The strongest message coming from international financial institutions, development agencies, and professional economists over the past 15 years is that state intervention is bad for economic growth. Though views on the issue have become more tempered and balanced in recent years, the central idea remains firmly in place: reducing state intervention is the most effective and efficient way to kindle growth. Sophisticated modeling and endless repetition of this dictum notwithstanding, recent experience suggests that matters are much more complicated.

Differences in the size of state intervention (as measured by central government spending as a percentage of GDP) are not very good at explaining variations in rates of economic growth or levels of domestic welfare. Between 1980 and 1994, extensive state intervention in the Middle East and North Africa was associated with poor growth, while lower—though still very high—state intervention produced an even worse growth record in sub-Saharan Africa. During this same period, government intervention in Latin America—which was smaller than its counterpart in East Asia—did not lead to higher growth rates or higher levels of welfare. The reverse turned out to be the case.

It is not the size of the government that appears to determine the different cross-national growth trajectories of developing nations in the recent past; more important than size in mediating the growth and welfare effects of globalization have been the large variations in the type and quality of government intervention. In accounting for why liberalization and globalization have led to unstable, slow, and exclusionary growth in some poor countries, high and inequitable growth in others, and extremely rapid, stable, and widely shared growth in a small number of developing nations, one must move beyond the quantity of state intervention and focus on its quality instead.

Classifications of state institutional capacities and resources can easily get complicated, as can typologies of different kinds and qualities of economic growth. The typology of state functions provided by the 1997 *World Development Report* offers a useful first attempt at addressing the issue. The report singles out three basic types of state functions: minimal (the provision of pure public goods, such as law and order, property rights, and macroeconomic stability); intermediate (interventions to address market failures such as externalities and monopolies); and activist (coordination of market activity and redistribution of assets).

What does this typology tell us about recent economic performance in developing countries? We can make the following preliminary observations. Countries where the state was able to fulfill all three functions—notably the star performers in East Asia—did best. For them, and only for them, the winds of global openness have delivered the full bundle of goodies: very high, very stable, and widely shared growth. In those countries where the state managed to fulfill only minimal and intermediate functions—Chile, for example—growth has been high and stable and has been accompanied, if not by a lessening of inequality, at least by a significant reduction in poverty. In those developing nations, such as most of Latin America, where greater openness has been managed by states that fulfill only minimal functions—and unevenly so at that—growth has been slower, less stable, and much more inequitable.

THE CHALLENGES

The good news coming out of the admittedly sketchy picture that has been presented is that focusing on sustaining or enhancing state institutional capacities can make a huge difference in allowing developing countries to profit from closer international economic integration. The bad news?

First, following the World Bank's advice to states—namely, restricting state intervention to those areas in which state capabilities exist—is unlikely to make developing nations richer and nicer places to live in. Given the limited state capabilities in most developing countries, and based on the record so far, following the bank's recommendations will tend to promote only the least desirable kinds of growth (as in Bolivia, where profound market reform during the 1980s led to 1.7 percent annual average growth between 1985 and 1994).

Second, continued fast-paced liberalization and globalization are likely to make it more difficult for states to maintain or acquire the capacity to translate openness into an effective springboard into greater prosperity for most of a country's people. Further financial deregulation in the absence of effective international discipline and domestic regulation could be especially costly. An ever more frantic competition among nations to retain and attract private investors would not necessarily benefit anybody except private globalized investors themselves. Rather than promoting a race to the top, more unbridled competition for mobile funds may well fuel a race to the bottom in regulatory standards and fiscal burdens on capital. If unchecked, such a race is likely to severely erode the fiscal and institutional capacities required to allow developing countries not only to grow, but to grow in ways that allow them to become more livable places.

The false promise of globalization.

AN ILLUSION FOR OUR TIME

By Peter Beinart

International finance has become so interdependent and so interwoven with trade and industry that ... political and military power can in reality do nothing. ... These little recognized facts, mainly the outcome of purely modern conditions (rapidity of communication creating a greater complexity and delicacy of the credit system), have rendered the problems of modern international politics profoundly and essentially different from the ancient." These words come from perhaps the best-selling book on international relations ever written. That book, *The Great Illusion*, sold more than a million copies in seventeen languages. Its author, Norman Angell, was knighted, and won the Nobel Peace Prize. In the years following the book's publication, close to 100 organizations arose to spread its message: that the world had entered a new era in which economic interdependence made war unthinkable. *The Great Illusion* was published in 1910.

On March 20, 1997, *New York Times* columnist Thomas Friedman wrote that we have entered a "new world of globalization—a world in which the integration of financial networks, information and trade is binding the globe together and shifting power from governments to markets." In his December 8, 1996, column, Friedman wondered whether "a country, by integrating with the global economy, opening itself up to foreign investment and empowering its consumers, permanently restricts its capacity for troublemaking and promotes gradual democratization and widening peace." And on February 14, 1996, in a column on the impending Russian elections, he wrote: "Sure, a Communist or radical populist in the Kremlin would be worrying. But their room for maneuver would be constricted—much more than we realize and much, much more than they realize. Russia today is connected with the global economy."

The conventional wisdom about post-cold war American foreign policy is that there is no conventional wisdom—no unifying theory that traces disparate phenomena to a single source. But one candidate for conceptual preeminence may be breaking from the pack, and it is Friedman's candidate, globalization. The idea is that technology has led to unprecedented and irreversible economic integration among countries. The only way

governments can survive is to do what global business demands: observe the rule of law at home, and act peacefully abroad. For the United States that means abiding by the imperatives of the global economy and informing others that they must do the same. It is a foreign policy vision for a world where politics barely matters.

And it is a vision that the Clinton administration has embraced. On June 19, in a speech prior to the summit of the eight industrial powers in Denver, President Clinton said, "Protectionism is simply not an option because globalization is irreversible." On June 6, in a speech arguing that trading with China would make it less dangerous, National Security Adviser Samuel Berger explained that "the fellow travelers of the new global economy—computers and modems, faxes and photocopiers, increased contacts and binding contracts—carry with them the seeds of change." A couple of years ago an unnamed State Department official told *The Washington Post*: "People who trade don't fight. They have shared interests in a way that autarchic economies do not."

The globalization doctrine builds on an idea popular in the early years of the Clinton administration: that American foreign policy should seek to widen the international community of democracies because democracies don't go to war with one another. But it goes a crucial step further. The earlier idea implied American pressure on democratization's behalf. For that reason, as the Clintonites discovered when they tried to apply it to China, it provoked real conflicts. The new doctrine, by contrast, does not require the United States to levy sanctions and create diplomatic rows. Globalization—powered by the inexorable march of technology and trade—will do democratization's work more effectively than State Department pressure ever could. America need simply warn renegades that if they menace neighbors or torture dissidents, they will be disciplined by the all-powerful global market. Foreign policy becomes an exercise not in coercion but in education.

This is globalization's appeal to a country both obligated to keep the world safe and increasingly reluctant to do so. It allows American elites to imagine that the security won for this country in struggle is now protected by a force both unstoppable and benign. And it allows them to imagine that rising and aggrieved powers will embrace a world governed by free trade as well, even though it locks them into a position of political and military subservience. Globalization is the narcissism of a superpower in a one superpower world. It allows America to look at the world and see its own contentment and its own fatigue. And it has provided the same false comfort to lone superpowers in the past. That's where Norman Angell comes in.

It is obvious to any casual observer of international affairs that today's world is far more interdependent than ever before. But it is not true. International trade and investment have indeed been increasing since the 1950s. Yet after four decades of growing interdependence, the world is just now becoming as economically integrated as it was when Norman Angell wrote *The Great Illusion*. According to Paul Bairoch of the Center for International Economic History at the University of Geneva, merchandise exports by the industrial countries were 13 percent of their Gross Domestic Product in 1913. In 1992, they were 14 percent.

As for financial integration, Bairoch estimates that by 1993 Foreign Direct Investment as a percentage of gross product had risen to roughly the level of 1914: around 11 percent for the industrial countries. A more elaborate study by the U.S. Trust Company's Robert Zevin, which examines financial integration by measuring "cross-market correlations between asset price movements" concludes that "every available descriptor of financial markets in the late nineteenth and early twentieth centuries suggests that they were more fully integrated than they were before or have been since."

So Norman Angell was right that he lived in a highly interdependent world. He considered this the result of technology, of "the incredible progress of rapidity in communication." All around him he saw technology forging a global economy that forced states to fit a single, fiscally responsible mold. "Just note what is taking place in South America," he wrote. "States in which [debt] repudiation was a commonplace of everyday politics have of recent years become as stable and as respectable as the City of London." "[C]ircumstances stronger than ourselves are pushing us," he insisted, and for those countries that resisted, "punishment is generally swift and sure."

But Angell's interest in the global economy was not merely descriptive. He sought to convince his fellow Britons, some of whom feared the outbreak of war with Germany, that the German threat was an illusion. After all, Britain and Germany were probably the two most economically interdependent nations on earth. Germany was Britain's second largest trading partner, and Germany sold more goods to the United Kingdom than to any other country. And even trade doesn't reveal the true depth of Anglo-German economic ties, since the City of London largely financed German industry. A Committee of Imperial Defence study noted that, since Lloyds insured the German merchant marine, it would have to pay the Kaiser for any lost ships, even if they were sunk by the British navy.

Under such circumstances, Angell argued, the key to preventing war was awakening people to their self-interest. He rejected suggestions that Britain contain Germany through military preparation and balance-of-power diplomacy. Any German penchant for aggression, he insisted, was "founded upon illusions which she would be bound sooner or later to shed." To speed up this inevitable process, Britons should forge ever deeper economic links with Germany while teaching people in both countries that war was self-defeating.

In Britain, a country ideologically committed to free trade, Angell's educational campaign struck a chord within the ruling elite. Of the 100 societies which sprang up to do the job, the most prominent included former Conservative Party Prime Minister Arthur Balfour, and Lord Esher, chairman of the Committee of Imperial Defence. If Germany was challenging Britain's industrial supremacy, Britain remained the world's undisputed financial capital, and London's powerful financiers more than counterbalanced the few farmers and manufacturers who wanted tariffs against German imports. Even Benjamin Disraeli, whose Conservative Party had fought for the Corn Laws in the mid-nineteenth century, announced that the Tories were now free traders. "Musty phrases of mine forty years ago," he said, were no longer relevant.

The British elite's enthusiasm for globalization implicitly rested on their country's privileged international position. Britain had been the world's leading military and economic power for close to a century. The relatively open trading system of the late nineteenth century, of which Britain was the chief beneficiary, was sustained by the protective power of the British navy. But Britain's military primacy had gone unchallenged for so long that many in Britain had lost sight of its importance. So Norman Angell, and others in the British establishment, saw globalization not as a fact of politics based on a security system, but as a fact of technology, independent of politics.

In Germany, however, which had been recently weak, divided, and at war, security concerns didn't seem so irrelevant. From Berlin, globalization did not look like a panacea; it looked like British hegemony. Britain's navy controlled the waterways on which German ships traveled, and Britain, through its empire, controlled many of the raw materials Germany's burgeoning industries needed. Britain saw the continent's division as evidence of a stable international order. Germany, which believed it deserved a central European sphere of influence, saw that division as a sign of British domination.

Quite aware that Britain had industrialized before the era of free trade, many Germans regarded London's continual preaching about the immorality of protectionism as rank hypocrisy. Starting in the 1870s, German governments began protecting their industries behind a tariff wall. As Paul Kennedy shows in *The Rise of the Anglo-German Antagonism*, Germany's reigning ideology was mercantilism. Its leaders knew that trade could be a means to wealth and power. But they also believed that, for a rising power beset by deep social conflicts, unregulated free trade could be a threat to political stability and governmental control. While Norman Angell followed in the tradition of Adam Smith and Richard Cobden, Germany in the late nineteenth century saw a revival of interest in the works of Friedrich List, who wrote in his 1841 classic *The National System of Political Economy* that the ideology of free trade was a "clever device that when anyone has attained the summit of greatness, he kicks away the ladder by which he has climbed up, in order to deprive others of the means of climbing up after him."

For Germany to climb up, it would have to be strong enough to integrate with the world economy on its terms. So while many Britons argued that globalization was rendering military power irrelevant, the German elite believed globalization made it all the more crucial. Concerned that its trade routes were at the mercy of the British navy, Germany embarked in 1897 on a massive ship-building program. This naval challenge pushed Britain gradually closer to France and Russia, and set in place the alliance system that would turn a local squabble into World War I.

The United States in 1997 differs from Britain in 1897 in obvious ways. Its empire is informal, not formal; its democracy is mature, not embryonic. But its elite shares turn-of-the-century Britain's fascination with economic interdependence. Today, as then, globalization suggests a world in which the imperatives of economic integration overwhelm those of politics. And in today's America, as in Norman Angell's Britain, there is a strong, intuitive sense that globalization is connected to wondrous new developments in communications technology: satellites, faxes, the Internet.

But if technological progress by itself produced integration, globalization would have risen steadily during the twentieth century. It has not. The period between 1914 and 1950 saw a revolution in both transportation and communication. The automobile assembly line was introduced in 1913; the first transatlantic flight took place in 1919; and the first commercial radio broadcast was in 1920. But during that time interdependence decreased dramatically. The reasons, of course, were World War I, World War II, and the economic depression in between. The era's technological breakthroughs did not prevent the rise of aggressive, expansionist ideologies in Germany and Japan. And those forces swamped the supposedly inevitable trend toward a more peaceful, globalized world.

Similarly, the rise in global integration since World War II stems more from politics than from technology. In particular, it stems from two institutional shifts, both made

possible by American political and military power. The first was the establishment of a liberal trading and monetary regime in the 1940s. America built the regime—whose key components were the International Monetary Fund, the General Agreement on Tariffs and Trade, the Marshall Plan, and the American nuclear umbrella—both because free trade was in the U.S.'s self-interest, and because the U.S. wanted to help Western Europe and Japan recover so they would not fall prey to communism. Economic integration grew because the GATT reduced tariffs, the International Monetary Fund stabilized world currencies, and the Marshall Plan rebuilt European industry. From 1950 to 1975, trade among the industrial countries grew twice as fast as their economies.

In 1974, the United States made the second key decision: it abolished its controls on the movement of foreign capital. This decision, like the first, can be traced to American self-interest. Declining U.S. productivity had spawned a trade deficit, which was pushing the dollar down and threatening the fixed exchange rate system. Abandoning both the fixed exchange rate and capital controls allowed the dollar to drop to its natural level, and let in the foreign capital America needed to finance its trade deficit. The decision was possible because Western Europe and Japan had grown strong enough that they no longer needed fixed exchange rates to stabilize their economies and fend off communism. Deregulating its capital market cemented the United States' position as the world's financial center, and it eventually forced America's competitors to end their capital control as well.

To be sure, by the time America scrapped capital controls, advances in telecommunications technology had already rendered them less effective. But as Eric Helleiner of York University in Toronto argues in *States and the Reemergence of Global Finance*, the United States could have restored their efficacy had it wanted to. It did not, and the result was an explosion of globalized finance that dwarfs even the rise in trade. In the late 1970s, the industrial nations invested $34 billion a year overseas. By 1990, that figure had reached $214 billion.

So we too live in a highly interdependent world. The problem is the widespread American belief that economic integration, because it stems from technology, is both all-powerful and politically neutral—that is, not identified with the interests of any one country. This leads to soothing assumptions about the restraints the global market imposes on potential aggressors, restraints that only exist if the potential aggressors also see globalization as both inevitable and benign.

Consider the way globalization looks from Beijing. Americans often see East Asia as the vanguard of the new economics-dominated world. But Japan, South Korea, and Taiwan all emerged as major world traders and investors under the protection of the American military. The U.S. Navy guarantees the South and East China Sea trade routes on which all three rely. Each has profited from access to U.S. markets, access granted in part to foster prosperity, and thereby to ensure they remained on the American side during the cold war. The United States has promoted growth and economic integration in East Asia, but as part of a broader American strategy to prevent any Asian power from gaining regional hegemony.

If Americans sometimes forget this, the leadership in Beijing—which seeks exactly that regional sphere of influence—does not. What Washington calls globalization, Beijing calls American hegemony, and this difference of perspective helps explain why China is violating globalization's core imperative. Like Imperial Germany before World War I, China's links to the world economy are making its leaders more interested in the accumulation and projection of military power, not less.

As Princeton's Kent E. Calder wrote last year in *Foreign Affairs*, China's growing international trade has led to a tremendous boom in manufacturing, and in air and car travel. This in turn has made China a net importer of energy. Shell China Petroleum Development estimates that by 2015 Beijing will need to import as much oil as the United States does today. This is one reason China has in recent years tried hard to establish a sphere of influence in the South and East China Seas. In January 1995, the Chinese navy forced a group of Filipino fishermen off Mischief Reef, part of the disputed Spratly Islands. The Spratlys contain considerable oil reserves, and sit astride the South China Sea, through which Middle Eastern oil travels on its way to China (as well as to Japan, South Korea, and Taiwan). In December 1995, Chinese ships were spotted encroaching on the Senkaku Islands (the Chinese call them the Diauyutai) in the East China Sea. The Senkakus, claimed by both China and Japan, are also oil-rich and near key international shipping routes.

Just as China's growing economic interdependence may foster, rather than restrain, military aggression, many of Beijing's economic reformers are also its biggest hawks. The People's Liberation Army, which has grown more powerful within the political hierarchy since the Tiananmen Square massacre, strongly favors economic reform. In his book *China After Deng Xiaoping*, Hong Kong journalist Willy Wo-Lap Lam estimates that there are perhaps 50,000 PLA-owned businesses, in which foreigners have invested over $1 billion. But Lam also shows that the army is one of the most expansionist elements within the Chinese leadership. The PLA pushed the government to be aggressive in the Spratlys, and in November 1992, a group of retired generals reportedly wrote Jiang Zemin and Li Peng a letter demanding a "stern reaction" to American and French sales of fighter jets to Taiwan. In early twentieth-century Germany, many industrialists encouraged their government's challenge to British naval dominance. In China, the industrialists and the admirals are often one and the same.

According to the theory of globalization, it is irrational for China to keep demanding that the U.S. Navy vacate the South China Sea. After all, it is there protecting free trade, which benefits everyone. But to China today, as to Germany in 1900, free trade looks less like a universal good, and more like the expression of a hegemon's self-interest. From Beijing's perspective, it is dangerous to have the U.S. military patrolling its trade routes—not necessarily because China fears the U.S. will cut off access to its key imports, but because it fears America might use the threat to force China to acquiesce in the total opening of its market (something China was forced to do in the nineteenth century).

To see how "American" free trade can look, consider Beijing's relations with multinational corporations. In America it has become fashionable to say that today's multinationals have no national identity. On this view, it is self-defeating for the Chinese to insist, as they do, that, as a condition of selling in China, multinationals transfer technology to Chinese companies. After all, this raises the cost of imports for the Chinese consumer.

But the men who run Beijing don't think multinational corporations lack a national identity. They see them as the agents of the United States and its allies, which is not altogether unreasonable. In 1991, only 2 percent of the corporate directors of American multinationals were non-American. As Louis W. Pauly of the University of Toronto and Simon Reich of the University of Pittsburgh have shown, multinationals are deeply tied to their home countries in corporate style, ownership, and the production of their highest value components. Beijing knows this, and it fears Western multinationals will not give it the knowledge it needs to move from making toys to making microchips unless China insists on technology transfer as the price of increased trade.

China's rulers are mercantilists. They believe economic engagement can help make their country powerful, but they also believe unregulated commerce can sow instability. They know tariffs played a key role in the industrialization of the United States and Japan, and they suspect that American insistence on free trade today is a clever attempt to prevent China from adopting the same tested formula for national greatness. That's what Beijing hears when American officials say that free trade will undermine Beijing's current authoritarian regime and foment a democratic revolution.

This raises a question that Thomas Friedman and other globalization enthusiasts seldom bother to ask: Why is globalization such an attractive theory in this country at this time? The answer is that the U.S. is in a position only one other country has known in the last two centuries. Like Victorian Great Britain, the U.S. today is the world's lone superpower. Its old rivals are dead, and its new ones are not yet born. Its security is so assured that it suspects military power has become irrelevant. And so America can afford to dream of a world without conflict, of an end to History.

But globalization reflects not only America's success. It also bespeaks its quiet fears. It is possible to be the world's only superpower and also be in decline. That decline has been impressively obscured in the past decade, by the Soviet Union's collapse and by economic troubles in competitors like Germany, France, and Japan. Most of all, it has been obscured by American industry's return to international preeminence over the past decade. But from a long-term perspective, America's economic decline relative to other nations is indisputable. In 1950, the United States represented 39 percent of world GNP. In 1995, it represented 26 percent. In 1953, the United States accounted for 45 percent of the world's manufacturing output. In 1990, it accounted for 22 percent.

This decline in global economic dominance is making it harder for the United States to sustain its apparatus of political and military power, even though the challenges to that apparatus are currently quite minor. America has recently closed a number of embassies and consulates. According to a recent study by UNICEF, it now ranks lowest among twenty-one industrial countries in the percentage of GNP it devotes to foreign aid. The percentage of World Bank lending underwritten by the U.S. has fallen by half since the institution was founded. Between 1989 and 1995, America's troop strength in the Pacific fell 15 percent.

To the superpower's worry that it cannot maintain its security system with declining resources, globalization offers a reassuring answer: it isn't the security system that keeps the peace, but rather the global market. And while military power waxes and wanes, the expansion of the global market—as Thomas Friedman and Bill Clinton never tire of saying—is unstoppable. American foreign policy can content itself with helping globalization along, and with reminding other countries of the restraints it imposes.

This is the story of the Clinton administration's policy toward China. In 1993, Bill Clinton took office threatening sanctions to force China to be less repressive at home and less aggressive abroad. In 1994, Warren Christopher took this message with him on a trip to Beijing, and was publicly humiliated. America's allies and American business rejected any effort to isolate China, and the United States backed down. The Clintonites realized that they lacked the power to change China's behavior, at least its domestic behavior. From this realization came "engagement"—globalization in policy form. The policy assumes that China's growing integration with the world economy will tame it, even without U.S. pressure. This is what Friedman means when he writes that, "Hong Kong will be a largely self-sanctioning diplomatic problem." When Christopher returned to China in November 1996, he told his hosts that, "history shows that nations with accountable governments and open societies make for . . . better places for foreign investment and economic growth." In other words, China's desire for wealth will improve its behavior, and keep it from becoming a threat.

These are dangerous assumptions. The better response to America's relative decline would be to get our increasingly wealthy allies to accept a greater share of maintaining the security system from which they benefit. In East Asia, that means putting trade conflicts with countries like Japan, South Korea, and Indonesia on the back burner, and giving them more say in how the U.S. deals with China. Since those countries have no interest in China's internal affairs, America would have to downplay human rights considerations. But it has done so anyway. This is a price worth paying in order to convince China's neighbors to assume more of the burden of thwarting China's hegemonic push. America would base its policy not on the imperatives of the global market, but on a renewed balance of power. And this would mean accepting, though we would rather not, that neither the march of technology nor the spread of wealth can keep us safe absent the mobilization of national resources and national will.

In 1939, with one world war past and another looming, the renowned British historian E.H. Carr reflected on why events had proved Norman Angell wrong. He wrote in *The Twenty Years' Crisis*: "To make the harmonisation of interests the goal of political action is not the same thing as to postulate that a natural harmony of interests exists; and it is this latter postulate which has caused so much confusion in international thinking." The theorists of globalization, then and now, are not wrong because they believe peace is possible. They are wrong because they believe peace is possible without politics.

The End of a "Miracle"

Speculation, Foreign Capital Dependence and the Collapse of the Southeast Asian Economies

by Walden Bello

BANGKOK—Environmentalists received an early Christmas gift when the Malaysian government announced in early December that it was suspending plans to build the controversial Bakun Dam in Sarawak. Constructing the dam would have resulted in the clearcutting of 70,000 hectares of forestland in an area that is already experiencing one of the world's highest rates of deforestation and in the displacement of approximately 9,500 indigenous people.

What years of international and local pressure on and lobbying of the Malaysian government could not do was achieved by the one message that the country's strong-willed leader Mohammed Mahathir could understand: no more dollars. Expected to cost $5 billion, the Bakun Dam—like Mahathir's other vision of building a two kilometer-long "Linear City" that would have been the world's longest building—fell victim to the financial crisis that is presently wracking Southeast Asia.

In the several months, the Philippines and Southeast Asia have been gripped by an economic downturn that has yet to hit bottom. The Philippine peso, the Thai baht, the Malaysian ringgit and the Indonesian rupiah have collapsed, falling in value by as much as 80 percent in the case of the rupiah. Stock markets from Jakarta to Manila have hit record lows, dragging down via a curious "contagion effect" Hong Kong and even Wall Street, at least momentarily.

Governments throughout the region were paralyzed by the crisis. In Thailand, the ruling coalition has lost its last ounce of credibility as people look toward the curious combination of the King and the International Monetary Fund (IMF) for salvation in these frightening times. In the Philippines, the administration of President Fidel Ramos is reduced to telling people to count their blessings because the crisis is worse in

Walden Bello is professor of sociology and public administration at the University of the Philippines and co-director of Focus on the Global South, a research program at Chulalongkorn University in Bangkok, Thailand. He is author of A Siamese Tragedy: Development and Disintegration in Modern Thailand. *(Food First Book, 1998).*

Thailand, Malaysia and Indonesia. In Kuala Lumpur, Mahathir rails angrily against what he sees as a conspiracy to debauch Southeast Asia's currencies led by speculator George Soros, also hinting darkly at a Jewish plot against Islamic Malaysia.

Once proud of their freedom from IMF stabilization and structural adjustment programs, the Thai and Indonesian governments have run to the Fund, which has assembled multi-billion dollar bailout funds in return for draconian programs that pull the plug from banks and finance companies, mandate deep spending cuts and accelerate liberalization and deregulation in economies marked by significant state intervention. The Philippines never left IMF management, and it is now likely to postpone its "exit." True to form, Malaysia's Mahathir refused to go to an institution that he sees as part of the problem rather than the solution.

CRISIS OF A MODEL

Many informed analysts, while dismissing Mahathir's conspiracy theories, have pinned part of the blame for the crisis on the uncontrolled flow of trillions of dollars across borders owing to the globalization of financial markets over the last few years. Increasingly, some assert, capital movements have become irrational and motivated by no more than a herdlike mentality, where one follows the movement of "lead" fund managers like Soros, without really knowing about the "economic fundamentals" of regions they are coming to or withdrawing from.

Surprisingly, Stanley Fischer, the deputy managing director of the IMF, lent support to this interpretation about irrational markets, telling the recent World Bank annual meeting in Hong Kong that "markets are not always right. Sometimes inflows are excessive, and sometimes they may be sustained too long. Markets tend to react late, but then they tend to react fast, sometimes excessively."

The merits of this analysis notwithstanding, it fails to grapple with a more fundamental issue: the pattern of development that has rendered the region so vulnerable to such variations in foreign capital inflows and outflows. To a considerable ex-

From *Multinational Monitor,* January/February 1998, pp. 10-16. © 1998 by Multinational Monitor, P.O. Box 19405, Washington, DC 20036. Reprinted by permission.

tent, the current downspin of the region's economies should be seen as the inevitable result of the region's closer integration into the global economy and heavy reliance on foreign capital.

More than in the case of the original newly industrializing countries (NICs) of Northeast Asia, the Southeast Asian NICs have been dependent for their economic growth on foreign capital inflows. The first phase of this process of foreign capital-dependent growth occurred between the mid-eighties and the early 1990s, when a massive inflow of capital from Japan occurred, lifting the region out of recession and triggering a decade of high 7 to 10 percent growth rates that were the envy of the rest of the world.

Central to this development was the Plaza Accord of 1985, which drastically revalued the yen relative to the dollar, leading Japanese corporations to seek out low-cost production sites outside of Japan so they could remain globally competitive. Some $15 billion in Japanese direct investment flowed into the region between 1986 and 1990. This infusion brought with it not only billions more in Japanese aid and bank capital but also an ancillary flow of capital from the first generation NICs of Taiwan, Korea and Hong Kong.

By providing an alternative access to tremendous sums of capital, Japanese investment had another important result: it enabled Southeast Asian countries to slow down the efforts of the IMF and World Bank to carry out the wide-ranging "structural adjustment" of their economies in the direction of greater trade liberalization, deregulation and privatization—something the Fund and Bank were successfully imposing on Latin America and Africa at the time.

By the early 1990s, however, Japanese direct investment inflows were leveling off or, as in the case of Thailand, falling. By that time, the Southeast Asian countries had become addicted to foreign capital. The challenge confronting the political and economic elite of Southeast Asia was how to bridge the massive gap between the limited saving and investments of the Southeast Asian countries and the massive investments they needed for their strategy of "fast track capitalism."

But happily for them, a second source of foreign capital opened up in the early 1990s: the vast amounts of personal savings, pension funds, corporate savings and other funds—largely from the United States—that were deposited in mutual funds and other investment institutions that sought the highest returns available anywhere in the world.

These funds were not, however, going to come in automatically, without a congenial investment climate. To attract the funds, government financial officials throughout Southeast Asia devised come-hither strategies that had three central elements:

- Financial liberalization or the elimination of foreign exchange and other restrictions on the inflow and outflow of capital, fully opening up stock exchanges to the participation of foreign portfolio investors, allowing foreign banks to participate more fully in domestic banking operations and opening up other financial sectors, like the insurance industry, to foreign players.
- Maintaining high domestic interest rates relative to interest rates in the United States and other world financial

centers in order to suck in speculative capital that would seek to capture the enormous difference from the spread between, say, interest rates of 5 to 6 percent in New York and 12 or 15 percent in Manila or Bangkok.
- Fixing the exchange rate between the local currency and the dollar to eliminate or reduce risks for foreign investors stemming from fluctuations in the value of the region's currencies. This guarantee was needed if investors were going to come in, change their dollars into pesos, baht or rupiah, play the stock market or buy high-yielding government or corporate bonds, and then transform their capital and their profits back into dollars and move on to other markets where more attractive opportunities awaited them.

This formula had the blessing of the IMF and the World Bank, where one of the key elements of reigning economic doctrine was capital account liberalization.

The policy was wildly successful in achieving its objective of attracting foreign portfolio investment and bank capital. U.S. mutual funds led the way, supplying new capital to the region on the order of $4 billion to $5 billion a year for the past few years.

THAILAND'S RECORD RISE AND FALL

A close look at two countries—Thailand and the Philippines—reveals the dynamic of the rise and unravelling of foreign capital-driven "fast track capitalism."

In the case of Thailand, net portfolio investment or speculative capital inflow came to around $24 billion in the last three to four years, while another $50 billion came in the form of loans via the innovative Bangkok International Banking Facility (BIBF), which allowed foreign and local banks to make dollar loans to local enterprises at much lower rates of interest than those in baht terms. With the wide spread—6 or 7 percent—between U.S. interest rates and interest rates on baht loans, local commercial banks could borrow abroad and still make a mean profit relending the dollars to local customers at lower rates than those charged for baht loans.

Thai banks and finance companies had no trouble borrowing abroad. With the ultimate collateral being an economy that was growing at an average rate of 10 percent a year—the fastest in the world in the decade from 1985 to 1995—Bangkok became a debtors' market.

Contrary to the current IMF and World Bank attempts to rewrite history, the massive inflow of foreign capital did not alarm the Fund or the Bank, even as short-term debt came to $41 billion of Thailand's $83 billion foreign debt by 1995. In fact, the Bank and the IMF were not greatly bothered by a conjunction of a skyrocketing foreign debt and a burgeoning current account deficit (a deficit in the country's trade in goods and services) which came to 6 to 8 percent of gross domestic product in the mid 1990s. At the height of the borrowing spree in 1994, the official line of the World Bank on Thailand was: "Thailand provides an excellent example of the dividends to be obtained through outward orientation, receptivity to foreign investment and a market-friendly philosophy backed by conservative macro-economic management and cautious external borrowing policies."

Indeed, as late as 1996, while expressing some concern with the huge capital flows, the IMF was still praising Thai authorities for their "consistent record of sound macroeconomic management policies." While the Fund recommended "a greater degree of exchange rate flexibility," there was certainly no advice to let the baht float freely.

The complacency of the IMF and World Bank when it came to Thailand—and their failure to fully appreciate the danger signals—is traced by some analysts to the fact that the debt was not incurred and financed by the government but by the private actors. Indeed, the high current account deficits of the early 1990s coincided with government budget surpluses. In the Fund/Bank view, since the financial flows were conducted by private sectors, there was no need to worry, as they would be subject to the self-correcting mechanisms of the market. That, at least, was the theory.

SIAM'S TWIN

Turning to the Philippines, Manila's technocrats were in the early 1990s very hungry for foreign capital since the country had been, for reasons of political instability, skirted by the massive inflow of Japanese investment into the Southeast Asian region in the late 1980s. Eager to join the front ranks of the Asian tigers, the Philippine technocrats saw Thailand as a worthy example to follow and in the next few years, in matters of macroeconomic strategy, the Philippines became Siam's twin.

Cloned by Manila, the formula of financial liberalization, high interest rates and a virtually fixed exchange rate attracted some $19.4 billion of net portfolio investment to the Philippines between 1993 and 1997. And dollar loans via the Foreign Currency Deposit Units—Manila's equivalent of the Bangkok International Banking Facility—rose from $2 billion at the end of 1993 to $11.6 billion in March 1997. As one investment house put it, with the peso "padlocked" at 26.2 to 26.3 to the dollar since September 1995, "they [Filipino banks] are not fools in Manila. They were offered U.S. dollars at 600 basis points cheaper than the peso rates along with currency protection from the BSP [the central bank]. They took it."

REAL EVENTS VERSUS THE REAL ECONOMY

Had these foreign capital inflows gone into the truly productive sectors of the economy, like manufacturing and agriculture, the story might have been different. But they went instead principally to fuel asset-inflation in the stock market and real estate, which were seen as the most attractive in terms of providing high yield with a quick turnaround time. Indeed, the promise of easy profits via speculation subverted the real economy as manufacturers in Thailand and the Philippines, instead of plowing their profits into upgrading their technology or skills of their workforce, gambled much of them in real estate and the stock market.

The inflow of foreign portfolio investment and foreign loans into real estate led to a construction frenzy that has resulted in a situation of massive oversupply of residential and com-mercial properties from Bangkok to Jakarta. By the end of 1996, an estimated $20 billion worth of the residential and commercial property in Bangkok remained unsold. Monuments of the property folly were everywhere evident, such as Bangkok Land Company's massive but virtually deserted residential complex near the Don Muang International Airport and the sleek but near empty 30-story towers in the Bangna-Trat area. Yet developers were still rushing new highrises to completion as late as mid-1997.

In Manila, the question by the beginning of 1997 was no longer if there would be a glut in real estate. The question was how big it would ultimately be, with one investment analyst projecting that by the year 2000, the supply of highrise residential units would exceed demand by 211 percent while the supply of commercial units would outpace demand by 142 percent. In their efforts to cut their losses in the developing glut, real estate developers refrained from major new investments in office space and condos, pouring billions of pesos instead into tourist resorts and golf courses.

Oversupply also overtook property development in Kuala Lumpur and Jakarta.

This all spelled bad news for commercial banks and finance companies in all four countries, since their real estate loan exposure was heavy. As a percentage of commercial banks' total exposure, real estate or real estate-related loans came to 15 to 25 percent in the case of the Philippines and 20 to 25 percent in the case of Malaysia and Indonesia. In Thailand, where the exposure in real estate was grossly underestimated by official figures and calculated by some to come to as high as 40 percent of total bank loans, half of the loans made to property developers were said to be "non-performing" by early 1997.

Unchecked by any significant controls by governments that had internalized the IMF and World Bank theory about the self-correcting mechanisms of the financial market, the frenzied flow of capital had led to the creation of a giant speculative bubble over the real economy that would explode in a highly destabilizing fashion.

STAMPEDE AND SPECULATION

It was the massive oversupply in the real estate sector that underlined to foreign investors and creditors that, despite creative accounting techniques, many of the country's finance companies that had borrowed heavily, floated bonds or sold equities to them were saddled with billions of dollars worth of bad loans. This led them to reassess their position in Thailand in the beginning of 1997. They began to panic when they saw the real estate glut in the context of the country's deteriorating macroeconomic indicators, like a large current account deficit, an export growth rate of near zero in 1996 and a burgeoning foreign debt of $89 billion, half of which was due in a few months time.

Of these figures, the current account deficit loomed largest in foreign investors' consciousness, because it was thought to indicate that Thailand would not be able to earn enough foreign exchange in order to service its foreign debt. Nevertheless, during the boom years, investment analysts shrugged off deficits that came to 8 to 11 percent of gross domestic product (GDP) and continued to give Thailand A to AA+ credit ratings on the strength of its high growth rate. However, the combination of the massive buildup of private debt and the real estate glut put the country's "macroeconomic fundamentals," to borrow investors' jargon, in a new, and to many, scary light in 1997. Thailand's deficit in 1996 came to 8.2 percent of GDP, and this was now emphasized as roughly the same figure as that of Mexico when that economy suffered its financial meltdown in December 1994.

It was time to get out, first, and with over $20 billion jostling around in Bangkok, parked in speculative investment in Thai companies or nestled in nonresident bank accounts, the stampede was potentially catastrophic. It meant the unloading of hundreds of billions of baht for dollars. The result was tremendous downward pressure on the value of the baht, making it difficult to maintain the now-sacrosanct one-dollar-to-25-baht rate.

The scent of panic attracted speculators who sought to make profits from the well-timed purchases and unloading of baht and dollars by gambling on the baht's eventual devaluation. The Bank of Thailand, the country's central monetary authority, tried to defend the baht at around 25 baht to one dollar by dumping its dollar reserves on the market. But the foreign investors' stampede that speculators rode on was simply too strong, with the result that the central bank lost $9 billion of its $39 billion reserves before it threw in the towel and let the baht float "to seek its own value" in July.

Speculators spotted the same skittish foreign investor behavior in Manila, Kuala Lumpur and Jakarta, where the same conjunction of overexposure in the property sector, weak export growth and widening current account deficits was stoking fears of a devaluation of the currency. Speculators rode on the exit of foreign investors, which accelerated tremendously after the effective devaluation of the baht on July 2. Central bank authorities attempted the same strategy of dumping their dollar reserves to defend the value of their currencies, with the only result being the massive rundown of their reserves. By the end of August, the "fixing" of the dollar value of the Malaysian ringgit, Indonesian rupiah and the Philippine peso that had been one of the ingredients of the Southeast Asian "miracle" had been abandoned by all the region's central banks, as the currencies were let go to seek their own value in the brave new world of the free float.

THE FUTURE

Seldom in economic history has a region fallen so fast from economic grace. From being one of the world's hottest economic zones, Southeast Asia now faces a bleak future marked by the following likely developments:

First, despite statements made by some Southeast Asian governments (as well as by professional Asian miracle boosters like Harvard's Jeffrey Sachs) that the crisis is a short-term one—a phase in the normal ebb and flow of capital—there is a strategic withdrawal of finance capital from the Southeast Asian region. Capital movements may indeed be dedicated by a mixture of rationality and irrationality. But one thing is certain: foreign capital is not so irrational as to return to Southeast Asia anytime soon. For in most investors' minds, the most likely scenario is one of prolonged crisis. The current instability will last from seven to 12 months, if the earlier experiences of Mexico, Finland and Sweden were any indication, says the chair of Salomon Brothers Asia Pacific, during which there will be weak domestic demand and "severe contraction in GDP in some of them."

A second likely development is that foreign investors will follow the lead of the banks and portfolio investors and significantly decrease their commitments to the region.

General Motors is now said to be regretting its 1996 decision to set up a major assembly plant in Thailand to churn out cars for what was then seen as the infinitely growing Southeast Asian market.

How Japanese direct investors who dominate the region will react is, however, the decisive question. Some analysts say that new investment flows from Japan are not likely to be reduced much since the Japanese are continuing to pursue a strategic plan of making Southeast Asia an integrated production base. More than 1,100 Japanese companies are ensconced in Thailand alone, they point out.

However, there are now wrinkles that make the situation different than the early 1990s. Japanese investment strategies in the last few years have targeted Southeast Asia not just as an export platform but increasingly as prosperous middle-class markets to be exploited themselves—and these markets are expected to contract severely. Diverting production from Southeast Asian markets to Japan will be difficult since Japan's recession, instead of giving way to recovery, is becoming even deeper. And redirecting production to the United States is going to be very difficult, unless the Japanese want to provoke the wrath of Washington.

The upshot of all this is that Japan is likely to be burdened with significant overcapacity in its Southeast Asian manufacturing network, and this will trigger a significant plunge in the level of fresh commitments of capital to the region. Already, nearly all of the Japanese vehicle manufacturers—Toyota, Mitsubishi and Isuzu—have either shut down or reduced operations in Thailand.

A third likely development that will lengthen the shadow of gloom in the region is that the United States and the IMF are likely to take advantage of the crisis to press for further liberalization of the ASEAN economies. While many Asian economic managers are now coming around to the position that the weak controls on the flow of international capital ha[ve] been a major cause of the currency crisis, U.S. officials and economists are taking exactly the opposite position: that it was incomplete liberalization that was one of the key causes of the crisis. The fixing of the exchange rate has been identified as the major culprit by Northern analysts, conveniently forgetting that it was the Northern fund managers who had emphasized the stability that fixed rates brought to the local investment scene and not even the IMF had advocated a truly free float for Third World currencies owing to its fears of the inflationary pressures and other forms of economic instability this might generate.

But the agenda of U.S. economic authorities goes beyond the currency question to include the accelerated deregulation, privatization and liberalization of trade in goods and services.

Formerly, the economic clout of the Southeast Asian countries enabled them to successfully resist Washington's demands for faster trade liberalization. Indeed, they were able to derail Washington's rush to transform the Asia-Pacific Economic Cooperation (APEC) into a free trade area. But with the changed situation, the capacity to resist has been drastically reduced and there is virtually no way to prevent Washington and the IMF from completing the liberalization or structural adjustment of the economies where the process was aborted (with the significant exception of financial liberalization) in the late eighties owing to the cornucopia of Japanese investment.

Indeed, as part of the package of reforms agreed with the IMF, Thai authorities have removed all limitations on foreign ownership of Thai financial firms and are pushing ahead with even more liberal foreign investment legislation to allow foreigners to own land. Even before it sought the help of the IMF, Jakarta abolished a 49 percent limit for foreign investors to buy the initial public offering (IPO) shares in publicly listed companies.

Because of depressive effects of severe spending cuts, currency depreciation and the channeling of national financial resources to service the foreign debt, structural adjustment programs in Latin America and Africa brought a decade of zero or minimal growth in the 1980s. It is likely that with the resumption of structural adjustment that was aborted in the mid-eighties by the cornucopia of Japanese investment, Southeast Asia's economies will see the recession induced by the current crisis turn into a longer period of economic stagnation, possibly leading to political instability.

FLOTSAM AND JETSAM

All this has translated into a pervasive feeling throughout the region that an era has passed, that the so-called "Southeast Asian miracle" has come to an end. Increasingly, some say that the miracle was a mirage, that high growth rates for a long time put a lid on what was actually a stripmine type of growth that saw the development of the financial and services sector at the expense of agriculture and industry, intensified inequalities and disrupted the environment, probably irretrievably.

In Thailand, where the crisis in the real economy is spreading most quickly, with unemployment rates fast approaching double digits, the balance of costs and benefits of the last decade of fast-track growth is painfully evident. The legacy of this process is an industry whose technology is antiquated, a countryside marked by continuing deep poverty and a distribution of income worse than it was more than two decades ago. Indeed, inequality has reached Latin American (or U.S.) levels, with the income going to the top 20 percent of households rising from 50 percent in 1975 to 53 percent in 1994, while the income of the bottom 40 percent declined from 15 to 14 percent.

As the World Bank admitted in a recent study, this pattern of growing inequality has marked most of the other "tiger" economies.

But it is probably the rapid rundown of natural capital and the massive environmental destabilization that will serve as an enduring legacy of the miracle that has vanished.

In Indonesia, deforestation has accelerated to 2.4 million hectares a year, one of the highest levels in the world. Industrial pollution is pervasive in urban centers like Jakarta and Surabaya, with about 73 percent of water samples taken in Jakarta discovered to be highly contaminated by chemical pollutants. In the East Malaysian state of Sarawak, 30 percent of the forest disappeared in 23 years, while in peninsular Malaysia, only 27 percent of 116 rivers surveyed by authorities were said to be pollution free, the rest being ranked either "biologically dead" or "dying."

In this dimension, too, Thailand is the paradigm. According to government statistics, only 17 percent of the country's land area remains covered by forest, and this is probably an overestimate. The great Chao Phraya River that runs through Bangkok is biologically dead to its lower reaches. Only 50,000 of the 3.5 million metric tons of hazardous waste produced in the country each year are treated, the rest being disposed of in ways that gravely threaten public health, like being dumped in shallow underground pits where seepage can contaminate aquifers. So unhealthy is Bangkok's air that, a few years ago, a University of Hawaii team measuring air pollution reportedly refused to return to the city.

"I ask myself constantly what we have been left with that is positive," Professor Nikhom Chandravithun, one of the country's most respected civic leaders, recently told a public meeting. "And, honestly, I can't think of anything."

Fallen idol

Japan was once feared for its economic might. Today it is feared for its economic weakness—and the harm its ailing system might do to the rest of Asia and the world. Just how sick is Japan?

SOON, and for the first time, Japan will have a higher jobless rate than America—a telling moment in the shifting fortunes of the two economies. While America continues to enjoy rapid growth, Japan is in recession. The country's GDP fell by an annualised 5.3% in the three months to March—much more than expected and the second consecutive quarterly fall. Its banks are creaking under their burden of bad loans; this week the yen hit an eight-year low of ¥147 against the dollar, before joint intervention by America and Japan pulled it back; the unemployment rate, with further to rise, already stands at a post-war high of 4.1%.

Things will probably get worse before they get better. Consumer and business confidence is severely depressed. Worries about jobs and the fragility of financial institutions is likely to cause families to save more and spend less in coming months, adding to fears of a self-reinforcing deflationary spiral. Firms, struggling under a mountain of debt and excess capacity, are slashing investment, and exports to the rest of Asia are falling. Over the next year or so more firms will go bust, unemployment will climb, and the scale of the banks' problems

may well turn out to be even worse than has been admitted so far. If the recession in the rest of Asia deepens or if America's economy—tripped by a sharp fall on Wall Street, say—falls suddenly into recession, then Japan's economic prospects will look grimmer still.

What a transformation. Ten years ago, anybody predicting that America would grow faster than Japan and have lower unemployment would have been called a fool. Then, Japan's economic superiority was seen not as a momentary or cyclical thing but as something inseparable from its "model". In particular, the blueprint for Japan Inc was based on close links between firms, banks and government officials. These arrangements sheltered managers from impatient shareholders and foreign competition, allowing them to take a long view. Anglo-Saxon capitalism, obsessed with the short term, didn't stand a chance.

Now, many trace Japans' failure back to that same financial root. Under ministry guidance, banks kept weak firms in business, they say, in the end undermining the entire economy. Echoing the earlier logic, the country's current condition is again seen not as a temporary thing but as something that is so deeply embedded as to be almost inevitable. Unless Japan abandons its distinctive model, it will stagnate (or worse) indefinitely.

Economists love to extrapolate. America's current phase of strong non-inflationary growth is expected to continue indefinitely—just as its previous underperformance, relative to Japan, was regarded as permanent. In the same way, many commentators see no way out of Japan's difficulties. Bad as these are, however, they are not as bad as they are often made out to be. The mood of much of today's commentary, which sees a grim future for Japan however far into the future you look, is too bleak.

Japan's recession is likely to grow worse in the short term—but maybe not much worse. Beyond the short term, Japan's prospects are brighter than many currently expect. In the midst of financial crisis, the short term can seem like an age, and people determined to panic will find no consolation in looking further ahead. But the open-minded may indeed find some consolation there—not to mention a better basis for their economic forecasts.

Demand or supply?

A first question is whether Japan's downturn is due to deep structural defects or merely to inadequate demand. Many claim that Japan's weak growth of 1.3% a year, on average, over the past six years is largely the fault of stifling regulation and weak industrial management, which in turn have bred widespread inefficiency and a dwindling return on capital. Some conclude that Japan's potential output (what the economy could produce if its capacity were fully employed) has been growing at no more than 1% a year of late, compared with 3–4% a year in the 1980s. If this were true, stimulating demand in the economy would be to little purpose. The only way to spur growth would be to embark on wide-ranging deregulation and structural reform—a process that would take years, however determinedly it was followed. In this case, the medium-term outlook would indeed be bleak.

Undeniably, Japan's structural defects (especially excessive borrowing by firms to invest in projects with low returns) have worsened its problems. But most of the blame for the country's stagnation lies with the government's failure to boost demand. The authorities made a series of errors in monetary and fiscal policy. They were too

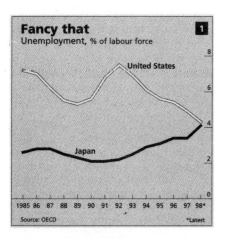

Fancy that
Unemployment, % of labour force

United States

Japan

1985 86 87 88 89 90 91 92 93 94 95 96 97 98*
Source: OECD   *Latest

reluctant to raise public borrowing and cut interest rates in the early 1990s, after Japan's financial bubble burst, and then much too quick to tighten fiscal policy again last year.

Viewed from the supply-side, the answer is the same. In any economy, growth in potential output depends on the growth in the labour force and rising productivity. Japan's labour-force growth has slowed from just over 1% a year in the 1980s to around 0.5% in the 1990s, and the workforce is expected to decline in the next century. On the other hand, economic rigidities have not worsened over the past decade (if anything, they may have eased, thanks to some deregulation), so there is no reason to suppose that underlying growth in productivity has fallen sharply. Indeed, productivity growth in manufacturing has averaged 3% during the past five years, exactly the same as in the 1980s.

On this basis, Japan's potential output is probably still growing by around 2% a year. Since actual growth has been less than this over the past six years, the economy now has a sizeable "output gap"—meaning that it could grow faster for several years without encountering bottlenecks. This is another way of saying that the problem is (lack of) demand, not supply.

Fiscal follies

At this point one faction of the pessimists makes a different argument: supposing that demand is indeed part of the problem, they say, the government is powerless, for one reason or another, to use fiscal and monetary policy to address it. The government did in fact announce a fiscal stimulus of about 2% of GDP in April; and interest rates are currently set at a historic low of 0.5%. But it makes no difference, according to this view: neither easy money nor public spending can prevent Japan being sucked into a deflationary spiral.

As it happens, Japan is not yet in fact suffering from a full-scale deflation. True, producer prices fell 1.7% in the year to May and the prices of equities and land are falling. But a one-off drop in prices due to cheaper imports from Asia, lower oil prices or deregulation in telecommunications is not the same as "deflation". Producer prices are falling in lots of other rich economies, thanks to lower commodity prices. Japanese consumer prices in the aggregate are not yet declining, nor are wages.

There is a danger that Japan may indeed drift towards deflation—but macroeconomic policy ("demand man-

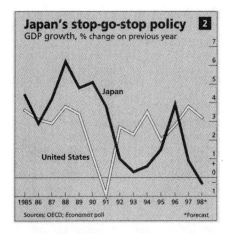

Japan's stop-go-stop policy 2
GDP growth, % change on previous year

Japan

United States

1985 86 87 88 89 90 91 92 93 94 95 96 97 98*

Sources: OECD; *Economist* poll   *Forecast

agement") can prevent this. It is true that interest rates cannot go much lower, but monetary policy can stimulate the economy in other ways. One is through the exchange rate. The 20% drop in the yen against the dollar over the past year will help not only to boost exports but, more important, to raise import prices and prevent deflation. It will also make Japanese assets look cheaper by international standards and therefore more attractive to foreign buyers.

The argument that fiscal policy is impotent is also flawed. Umpteen packages over the past five years have, it is claimed, failed to boost the economy. But if the impact appeared modest, so was the stimulus. Ministers overstated the scale of their packages by including measures without a direct impact on growth (such as lending by government agencies and the frontloading of previously planned public works). The actual amount injected into the economy over the past five years—through increased public works or tax cuts—was only one-third of all the measures announced by the government[*]. Much of the deterioration in Japan's budget—from a general-government surplus of 1.5% of GDP in 1992 to a deficit of 3% last year—reflected the automatic fall in tax revenues due to the downturn.

Also, to measure the effects of any stimulus you need to look not just at actual growth rates, but at what growth would otherwise have been. Given the plunge in equity and property prices, the 85% rise in the yen between 1990 and 1995 and the troubles in East Asia, Japan's output would have been expected to fall sharply. A large stimulus in 1995–96 did deliver GDP growth of 3.9% in 1996 (see chart

[*]For details see "How Much is Enough for Japan?", by Adam Posen, published by the Institute for International Economics (July 1998).

2). But then the government was too eager to contain borrowing: it tightened policy prematurely in 1997 and the economy slowed.

Might fiscal policy be failing now for new reasons? One common argument is that public-sector debt (at almost 100% of GDP) has climbed too high, especially if you take account of increasing future pension liabilities as the population ages. This implies that taxes will have to rise sharply in future—and, in turn, that far-sighted households will therefore save any tax cut rather than spend it. However, long-term government bond yields of only 1.2% hardly suggest that investors are worried about the scale of government borrowing.

In any case, Japan's future pensions bill needs to be put in context. According to the OECD, the ratio of retired people to the labour force will not rise as much in Japan as in Germany or France (see chart 3). Japan also has more room to raise taxes: its tax burden is only 32% of GDP, compared with 45–50% in continental Europe.

Debtors' prison

A more plausible reason to think that Japan's recession might get much worse is the sorry state of its banking system. This will not neutralise the effects of a fiscal stimulus entirely (as the experience of 1995–96 showed), but it may be enough to dampen them. The banks' overhang of bad loans—estimated at ¥80 trillion, or 12% of GDP—serves as a brake on new lending, and thus on demand. Also, the bad debts raise anxieties about the security of the banking system, further undermining consumer confidence. The debts need to be acknowledged in all their awfulness, and written off.

The government has persistently shied away from that—although it is wrong to

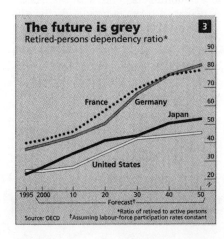

The future is grey 3
Retired-persons dependency ratio*

France   Germany   Japan

United States

1995 2000 10 20 30 40 50
Forecast†
*Ratio of retired to active persons
Source: OECD   †Assuming labour-force participation rates constant

accuse it of doing nothing at all. In a policy U-turn in February it announced a ¥30 trillion plan to strengthen deposit insurance and to help banks write off bad loans. As yet, little of this has been used, and rumours about banks or life insurers in trouble continue to rattle the markets. Doubts remain over how the money will be used—foolishly, to bail out insolvent banks, or wisely, to support sound ones? But at least money is now available both to prevent a severe interruption of credit and, should the need arise, to reduce the risk of system-wide failure if more banks go under.

On balance, if—and it is a big if—the immediate storm in global markets can be weathered, Japan's current recession is likely to prove short-lived. The government's latest fiscal stimulus, its biggest yet, combined with the weaker yen, will boost growth strongly in the second half of this year. Calculations by Dresdner Kleinwort Benson suggest that a 10% fall in the yen will boost GDP by 1.7% by 1999—roughly the same amount as the fiscal package itself.

Unfortunately, this has to fill a deepening hole left by the slump in exports to the rest of Asia. Two-fifths of Japan's exports go to the region, equivalent to 4.2% of its GDP, compared with only 2.4% of GDP bound for America and Germany. It seems likely that the slump in East Asia will knock up to 2% off Japan's GDP this year. Taking all this into account, the Japanese economy is likely at best to see output broadly unchanged, year on year, in 1998.

If demand merely stabilises in emerging East Asia next year, then Japan's exports will not fall much further. Some of Japan's current fiscal stimulus will also make itself felt in 1999, so the economy could enjoy a reasonable recovery. But further fiscal measures will still be required. It is essential to avoid repeating last year's mistake of tightening policy too soon.

Policy will need to be kept loose, ideally combining tax cuts with tax reform. A review of taxes is promised after the Upper House elections in July. Cuts in marginal income-tax rates combined with a broadening of the tax base would both boost spending and make the economy more efficient. Japan's top rate of income tax, 65%, is currently the highest among the rich economies. This is likely to be cut to 50%.

The reform agenda

Given sufficient resolve, the government has the means to close the out-put gap. But it should take steps, in addition, to speed the growth of the economy's productive capacity: demand-side measures and supply-side measures do not exclude each other. Again, the government has made more of a start in regulatory reform, for instance, than it is given credit for. Much more remains to be done, but telecommunications, retailing, transport and energy have all seen deregulation of various kinds. And in April Japan's "Big Bang" began to set its financial sector free.

Relaxing the laws controlling large stores has already increased competition by encouraging rapid growth in the number of big supermarkets and foreign retailers. Deregulation in the oil industry—allowing more oil imports and self-service stations—has sharply reduced petrol prices. The cost of telephone calls has fallen thanks to liberalisation. Since the mobile-phone market was set free in 1994, rates have plummeted and the number of phones has jumped from 2m in 1994 to nearly 40m.

In other ways too, the platform for faster productivity growth is already in place. Japan's labour market is not as rigid as Germany's, say. Wages are more flexible—thanks to the larger part played by bonuses—and trade unions are weaker. In some industries, lifetime employment can make it hard for firms to cut costs—but only about one-fifth of all workers in their 40s are actually in lifetime employment.

Indeed, by international standards, Japan does not measure up that badly. Its rate of return on capital may be a lot less than America's—a fact that has attracted attention lately—but it is no worse than in many European economies. The World Economic Forum's latest ranking of competitiveness puts Japan in 12th place, well above France and Germany (22nd and 24th, respectively). To be sure, continental Europe is hardly a model to aspire to—but then again nobody is condemning continental Europe to perpetual stagnation. Indeed, France and Germany are now enjoying relatively brisk growth.

The biggest supply-side obstacle to future growth may no longer be (if it ever was) excessive regulation or inflexible labour markets, but a corporate culture that finds it easy to tolerate low returns and difficult to tolerate outright failure. If the economy's return on capital is to improve, it will be necessary to close ailing companies more promptly. This is the aspect of the Japanese model which now matters most—and may be the most difficult to change. But recession, financial liberalisation and the squeeze on banks are all playing their part.

Traditionally, managers have faced little pressure to improve their return on assets. Most of their capital came from banks which also held equity in the firm. Troubled firms could stay in business by borrowing more. But as bad loans erode their capital, banks are starting to say "no" to companies, or to charge higher risk premiums. Firms are being forced to turn to the bond market and—thanks to this year's financial deregulation—compete with foreign firms to attract capital.

As markets tumble and commentators tear their hair, it is difficult to accept that Japan's recession may have useful side-effects of this kind—but that makes it no less true. Kevin Hebner, an analyst at SBC Warburg, points to several promising signs. For instance, companies are starting to offer stock-option schemes to managers, giving them an incentive to pursue shareholders' interests. More firms are setting explicit targets for return on equity. And some companies have announced plans to buy back shares, as a way to improve that return.

In the new climate, the threat of takeover may also start to play its part in spurring efficiency. Firms have traditionally been protected by their relationship with their bank and by cross-shareholdings held by friendly companies. But as friendly firms themselves face financial pressure, some are demanding a better return, or, desperate for cash, are selling some of their shareholdings to financial institutions. Recent cross-border M&A activity such as the deal between Travelers and Nikko and current talks between Daimler Benz and Nissan Diesel is just the start. Opaque company accounts remain an obstacle to a vigorous market for corporate control—but next year the country is moving to international accounting standards which will improve disclosure.

If all this works, mind you, it will hurt. These new pressures will encourage firms to cut costs, shed labour and use assets more efficiently. In the short term that means plant closures, rising unemployment, and hence more gloomy headlines about Japan's economic prospects. But creative destruction will help Japan to raise its return on capital. Redundancies and bankruptcies are evidence that the economic adjustment mechanism is working at last. Capitalism, you might say, is finally coming to Japan. Pity it had to be the hard way.

America and the Euro Gamble

—Owen Harries

A S THE AMERICAN foreign policy establishment has been preoccupied in recent months with such things as the fall of Suharto, the Indian bomb, and Kosovo—all serious issues—an event of much greater long-term significance has received scant attention.

This is the adoption of a common currency—the euro—by the members of the European Union. This has the potential of changing the basic structure of world politics by bringing the brief era of the single super-power world to an abrupt end. For a common currency implies political unity. While Americans worry about the emergence of China as a rival that will challenge the supremacy of the United States, a United Europe will be a much better equipped and more convincing candidate for that role.

That is the geopolitical significance of the creation of European Monetary Union (EMU). Despite that significance, however, the event has received very modest attention in the American media. In so far as they have paid attention to EMU, the main theme has been that of uncertainty. Until a few months ago, there were serious doubts as to whether the thing would get off the ground at all; then, once it became clear that it would, uncertainty shifted to prospects of its success. In the first half of May, for example, the *New York Times* published two articles on the subject under the titles "Europe's Colossal Coin Toss" and "Rolling Some Big Dice in the Euro Casino"; and when the Washington-based magazine *International Economy* ran a symposium on the subject, it put on its cover two huge dice. Newt Gingrich characterizes the common currency as "an extraordinary experiment—and an extraordinary gamble." James Glassman, in a generally favorable analysis of the move toward the euro in *U.S. News and World Report*, acknowledges that it is "the greatest financial experiment in the past quarter century, and no one can foresee its consequences." The emphasis on the element of risk and uncertainty, then, is pronounced.

There are exceptions, of course, and some influential figures come down unambiguously on one side or the other. The distinguished Harvard economist, Martin

Feldstein, writing in *Foreign Affairs* and the *New York Times*, insists that the EMU venture is a serious mistake, pregnant with political and economic trouble. So does the *New York Times* columnist William Satire. On the other hand, Jeffrey Garten, dean of the Yale School of Management, writing in *Business Week*, asserts firmly that EMU will succeed, and that the United States should be bracing itself to meet the challenge it will pose.

Garten at least acknowledges that EMU will represent a serious problem for the United States. The Clinton administration's position is that it will do nothing of the kind. If uncertainty has characterized the media, serene confidence apparently prevails in official circles. The assumptions there are that, as a major step toward European integration, EMU is, without qualification, a good thing, and that there will be a complete harmony of interests between the anticipated United Europe and the United States of America. Thus President Clinton: "I have never felt the United States should feel threatened by the prospect of a European Currency nor by the prospect of European integration in general" (*Euro* magazine, September 1997); and again, "An integrated Europe is America's natural best partner for the 21st century" (*Financial Times*, May 5, 1998).

Officials express themselves a bit more guardedly, but convey essentially the same message. In the same issue of the *Financial Times*, for example, Lawrence Summers, deputy secretary of the Treasury, puts it in conditional terms: "If EMU is good for Europe, it will be good for us." But the qualification here—the "If" word—refers only to the euro's prospects of success and does not challenge the assumption of a harmony of interests across the Atlantic. It is still taken for granted that European and American interests coincide on this issue, that it is a plus, not a zero, sum game. The prevailing line is that the only thing that would cause problems for the United States is the failure of EMU, not its success.

All this is very questionable. American conventional wisdom about Europe reflects the mental habits of half a century, rather than serious thought about the particular issue of EMU (or, for that matter, about that other contentious issue, the expansion of NATO). For nearly fifty years it has been an article of faith for Americans that European division is a bad thing, the cause of wars; that

Owen Harries is editor of *The National Interest*.

Reprinted with permission from *The National Interest*, Fall 1998, pp. 88-91. © 1997 by National Affairs, Inc., Washington, DC.   **111**

Europe should therefore be urged to integrate; and that a federal United States of Europe, created in emulation of the United States of America, would be the best outcome of such a process of integration. All very comfortable and reassuring, but are these assumptions likely to hold as things proceed? I think not.

Henry Kissinger has identified a paradox concerning the future of EMU: "It is difficult to see how the European Monetary Union can succeed. It is even more difficult to imagine that it will be permitted to fail" (*Washington Post*, May 12, 1998). The fact is, however, that it is almost certainly going to do one or the other over the next few years, and it is worth considering now what would be the consequences for the United States of either outcome.

THE REASONS WHY EMU might fail have been well rehearsed by its critics. It is, allegedly, putting the economic cart before the political horse. It is imposing a single currency on what is not a single economy. It will deprive individual countries and economies of the shock absorbers and safety valves necessary to cope with local and regional economic problems—the "asymmetrical shocks" that will occur inevitably to economies in different stages of development and different phases of the trade cycle. It will require the peoples of Europe to endure stern measures, imposed not by their own government but by an external body in which foreigners will always constitute a majority—conditions that, as former European Commissioner Christopher Tugendhat suggests, will "become a gift to every xenophobic and chauvinistic politician in Europe." There will be serious differences—there are already—concerning the priorities and policies of the European Central Bank. Before it has proceeded very far, the whole project will demand a degree of political unity going far beyond the Europe of nations envisaged by De Gaulle, a condition that will prove unsustainable in a highly differentiated continent lacking a common language and culture. And so on and on.

The political and economic strains are clearly going to be very formidable. Given the enormous political capital vested in it, should these cause EMU to end up as a dismal failure the consequences will be dire. These consequences will include the discrediting of whole political establishments, the collapse of the momentum of what has been the central driving idea in the continent over the last decade, a resulting conceptual void and a general demoralization, and bitter mutual recrimination and scape-goating (both within individual countries and among them)—in short, political turmoil on a serious scale. Kissinger anticipates that the Europe that would result would be "either extremely left wing or extremely right wing, or a combination of both."

All this would be a matter of extreme concern for the United States. It would mean that a major part of the world's "zone of peace" would have become a zone of turbulence. Anti-Americanism would certainly be a prominent feature of the scape-goating process. At the same time, Washington would be required to take a leading part in sorting out the mess. All pretty bad—and especially bad because there would be no mechanisms in place to reverse the process; that is, to allow easy and peaceful withdrawal from the union by those who had become thoroughly disenchanted with it (as some Americans will recall, a state of affairs roughly analogous to that existing in their own country in the period leading up to the Civil War).

FROM ALL THIS it might seem self-evident that, indeed, for America the success of EMU must be far preferable to its failure. But success would also have its serious downside. A very successful EMU, with the political unification it would necessarily involve, would amount to the creation of a second, and rival, superstate. It would have a larger economy and a larger population than the United States, as well as comparable intellectual, scientific, and technological capital—a combination of features that the Soviet Union never had and that China will not have for a long, long time. As to what kind of policies this new superstate would pursue, one cannot be certain. But if one believes, as I do, that there is a lot of accumulated but suppressed resentment in Europe of its subordination to and dependence on the United States over the last half a century, then one would expect the expression of that pent-up resentment to be a cardinal feature of the new superpower's behavior—certainly in the form of an assertion of independence and difference; probably in the form of competition, obstruction, and rivalry; possibly in the form of outright hostility.

That resentment is today most evident in the case of France, but it should not be assumed that it is restricted to France. Even as things stand today, most European states disagree with the United States over a host of issues, among them extraterritorial sanctions, the power of international criminal courts, Arab-Israeli relations, and the policy of dual containment in the Persian Gulf. If, as happened earlier this year, France can stymie U.S. policy toward Iraq even with a weak partner like Russia, how much more will it be capable of thwarting Washington's will if and when it has the weight of "Europe" behind it?

In his discussion of this issue, Kissinger poses it in terms of a prospective competition between Britain and France as to whether an attitude of Atlantic cooperation or Atlantic challenge should come to characterize a European foreign policy. But put in those terms it is surely no contest. Britain is at best going to be a late arriving, reluctant, and somewhat marginalized member of Europe; France is at its heart and dominates its powerful bureaucracy. But what about Germany—might it not restrain, and prevail over, the French in foreign policy? That seems very doubtful. The Germans are largely passive in foreign policy, self-distrusting and full of self-doubt; indeed, it is precisely a distrust of his own people that has seemed to motivate Helmut Kohl most strongly in his insistence on a rapid move toward a united Europe. The French, on the other hand, have strong views and are expert at playing games of diplomatic chicken to get those views accepted. In the shaping of a new Europe, it is not unlikely that an implicit bargain will be struck: the Germans will substantially have their way on economic policy and expansion to the east, in return for which the French will be allowed to make the running on foreign policy, especially in its Atlantic and global dimensions.

If indeed this happens, the consequences for the United States will not be pleasant, and there will be a strong feeling of resentment on this side of the Atlantic at what many Americans will regard as base ingratitude. For just as Europeans have resented their dependence on the United States over the last half century, Americans will surely and bitterly resent any effort to displace them (first regionally and then globally) as the dominant power, especially should it look capable of succeeding.

THERE WAS AN interesting foretaste of this recently at a meeting at the American Enterprise Institute, a Washington think tank. In the discussion following a talk by former British Defense Minister Michael Portillo, one senior fellow, a specialist in foreign policy, characterized an anticipated attempt by a European superpower to compete with the United States for the position of dominance as "malign." He did so with the air of someone making an obvious point. To his credit Portillo immediately disassociated himself from that view, but it may be a sign of things to come. Certainly those Americans now fond of describing their country as "the sole remaining superpower", "the benign hegemon", and "the indispensable nation"—and their ranks include not only ardent conservatives but the current secretary of state—would fiercely resent being seriously challenged, let alone displaced, by a more populous and prosperous Europe.

If all this is right, then a smashingly successful EMU would mean not a strengthening of that entity known as "the West" but its sundering. A few years ago I wrote an article for Foreign Affairs arguing that, in its political sense, "the West" was a construct essentially born of a shared sense of danger and fear, not of natural affinity, and that it tends to break up into its constituent—and rival—parts in more placid periods. I believe a successful EMU process leading to European political unity would prove this true.

If both dismal failure and smashing success hold out unattractive prospects for the United States, what is the best outcome that could be hoped for from an American point of view? When I put this question to Portillo at the AEI meeting, he first answered that he considered failure preferable to success. But after further thought he said, "What I really aspire to is untidiness." I suppose that I mean something similar when I say that moderate and inconclusive success or failure, spun out over an extended period, would be a better outcome than a sudden and spectacular conclusion in either direction. But whether such moderation is going to be possible is a moot point. It is in the nature of big gambles that they tend to be a matter of double or quits, all or nothing at all.

This analysis will no doubt strike some as unduly alarmist. But after half a century without serious conflict in the West, and in the wake of the triumphant end of the Cold War, the main cause for concern today stems not from the exaggeration of danger but from complacency and a facile optimism. Someone once said—was it Henry James?—that those who lack the imagination of disaster are doomed to be surprised by the world. At the beginning of this century, after decades of peace had dulled its sense of danger, a prosperous and self-satisfied Europe experienced such a disastrous surprise. Today, action based on a set of mutually reinforcing assumptions—that liberal democracy has triumphed decisively and permanently; that democracies do not fight each other; that the market economy will indefinitely produce the goods; that interdependence naturally creates harmony; that nationalism is an artificial, invented phenomenon; that being "whole" is Europe's proper and natural condition—risks producing more very nasty surprises, unless it is balanced and restrained by an awareness of the possibility of disaster.

> *"For the first time in several years, politicians across the spectrum—liberals, communists, and nationalists alike—have begun to speak about the specter of Russian fascism should the current economic and political crises continue. Others, including even President Yeltsin, have warned of coup plots aimed at toppling Russia's fragile democracy. What went wrong, so quickly?"*

Russia's Summer of Discontent

Michael McFaul

Nineteen ninety-eight was supposed to be the year that Russia turned the corner. The 1996 presidential election had marked the end of a transitional period for Russia's political system and had seen Boris Yeltsin receive a renewed mandate to pursue his reform agenda. Equally important, all major political actors participated in the election and accepted the results as legitimate. The street protests, mass social action, and violent conflict that had constituted Russian politics in the country's first years of independence had given way to the electoral process. Gubernatorial elections in the fall of 1996 and spring of 1997 reconfirmed the primacy of elections in determining who rules Russia. Because elections rather than revolution were the focus of attention for most politicians, 1997 was politically the quietest year in Russia since independence in 1991.

This relative calm provided the perfect context for finally tackling Russia's economic woes. When Yeltsin introduced his reform plan in January 1992 to transform Russia's command economic system into a market economy, he warned citizens of tough times ahead, but promised that the transitional economic downturn would last just 10 or 11 months. Six years later, only a handful of people had realized any benefit from this "reform"; Russia recorded negative growth rates from 1992 to 1997, while the

Michael McFaul, *an assistant professor of political science and a Hoover fellow at Stanford University, is also a senior associate at the Carnegie Endowment for International Peace. His books include* Russia's 1996 Presidential Election: The End of Polarized Politics (*Stanford, Calif.: Hoover Institution Press, 1997) and* Privatization, Conversion, and Enterprise Reform in Russia (*Boulder, Colo.: Westview, 1995).*

majority of citizens reported in opinion polls that they were worse off in 1997 than they had been in 1991.

But 1998 was going to be different. At the end of 1997, Russian government officials as well as several Western financial institutions predicted positive growth rates, increased foreign investment, and a continuing bullish stock market for 1998. Yeltsin had reorganized his government in the spring of 1997 to empower a group of young reformers. He made an even bolder reconfiguration in the spring of 1998 when he dismissed Prime Minister Viktor Chernomyrdin and appointed a more reformist government headed by a young banker, Sergei Kiriyenko. Labeled a reformer's "dream team" by many Russian and Western commentators, the new government came into office with the expressed desire to reform Russia's robber baron capitalism. As First Deputy Prime Minister Boris Nemtsov reflected, "A transition is now taking place from unlimited semibandit capitalism, where the rules are dictated by those who are trying to take control of state property, to a situation where the rules are dictated by the state."

The plans for radical economic reform were never realized. Instead, throughout the summer and fall of 1998, Russia has been mired in its most serious financial crisis since independence. The financial crisis, in turn, has threatened to undermine the political stability achieved in the previous two years. For the first time in several years, politicians across the spectrum—liberals, communists, and nationalists alike—have begun to speak about the specter of Russian fascism should the current economic and political crisis continue. Others, including even President Yeltsin, have warned of coup plots aimed at toppling Russia's fragile democracy. What went wrong, so quickly?

INTO THE PRECIPICE

The immediate causes of Russia's financial crisis in 1998 were straightforward. Early in the year, falling international oil prices greatly reduced revenues anticipated for the Russian budget. More important, however, were the unrealistic projections underlying the 1998 budget. Projected tax revenues were more than double the actual amount. Moreover, 40 percent of taxes paid to the federal government in 1997 were paid in kind, not in cash, a practice that continued in 1998. In addition, the Asian financial crisis created a further international strain on Russia's economy as projected inflows of foreign capital into the country's emerging market also decreased.

Given these revenue shortages, the Russian government was compelled to borrow heavily through the international bond market and by issuing short-term domestic treasury bills known as GKOS (state short-term bonds). Over the course of the summer, holders (both foreign and domestic investors) of GKOS became increasingly nervous about the government's ability to honor its debts. Reflecting this lack of confidence, interest rates for GKOS soared, climbing to over 120 percent in the second week of July. Even at this rate, buyers for the government debt were still scarce. At the same time, the stock market continued to fall throughout the year and had lost 50 percent of its January value by July, giving Russia the distinction of having, along with Indonesia, the worse performing stock market in the world.

This situation was not sustainable over the long run, since the amount the government owed to holders of GKOS would soon exceed the foreign reserves held by the Russian central bank. Western analysts predicted that by August the government would be bankrupt and would face the difficult choice of devaluing the ruble or defaulting on outstanding debts.

Before the central bank depleted its reserves, however, the International Monetary Fund intervened. In cooperation with the World Bank and the Japanese government, the IMF offered Russia new loans amounting to $17.1 billion. In negotiations over this bailout package, IMF officials attempted to secure commitments from the Russian government to undertake several reform policies. This package of reforms was to include over 20 new draft laws that would streamline and rationalize the tax code, decrease the profit tax, raise individual income taxes, create a national sales tax and land tax, raise taxes on imported goods as well as on alcohol sales and precious metals exports, and cut government expenditures even further to bring the deficit under 2.8 percent of GDP in 1999.

The bailout package failed. The first transfer of IMF funds under the new agreement—totaling nearly $5 billion—disappeared almost immediately as investors converted their rubles into dollars to get their money out of Russia. This put extreme pressure on the value of the ruble. In a desperate response, the Kiriyenko government surprised the world in August by pursuing a policy of both default and devaluation. On August 17, the government announced a compulsory conversion of short-term GKOS into longer-term debt instruments. The Russian debt market immediately collapsed as investors became convinced that the government would never pay back the borrowed money. On this same day, the government also imposed a 90-day moratorium on payments of all hard currency loans owed to Western commercial banks. Simultaneously, it announced a new trading price for the ruble 30 percent lower than the day before. In a single day, the two major economic achievements of the Yeltsin era—control of inflation and a stable, transferable currency—were eliminated.

These emergency measures did little to halt the economic crisis. The stock market all but disappeared, the ruble continued to fall, and banks began to close. Responding desperately to a desperate situation, Yeltsin fired Kiriyenko and his government the next week and nominated Viktor Chernomyrdin as his candidate for prime minister. After Chernomyrdin was rejected twice by the Russian parliament, Yeltsin nominated Foreign Minister Yevgeni Primakov as a compromise candidate, and he was quickly approved. In the meantime, the economy continued to collapse. The ruble plummeted, banks refused to allow withdrawals, prices soared, and stores emptied as people started to stockpile goods such as cigarettes, sugar, and flour.

THE CRISIS BEHIND THE CRISIS

No matter who emerges from the current crisis to rule the country, there are no immediate solutions to the economic problems. Russia's latest crisis was not caused by failed macroeconomic policy undertaken by the Kiriyenko government or the IMF. Rather, the roots are microeconomic: ill-defined property rights and a lack of institutions capable of clarifying and enforcing these rights. Failure to appreciate the importance of this problem will lead to further misdirected "reforms" and continued economic depression in Russia.

In 1992, the Russian government launched an ambitious and comprehensive program to privatize most of the economy. Two years later, the Russian government (as well as the United States Agency for International Development and its Western contractors who assisted the privatization effort) trumpeted the success of its program by noting that more than 100,000 enterprises had been privatized.

While speedy, this privatization program did not produce effective owners. At two-thirds of all large enterprises, insiders—the directors in cooperation with the trade union officials loyal to them—gained a controlling share. At the time of privatization, the vast majority of these enterprises subtracted rather than added value to the economy. Amazingly, with the exception of a handful of energy exporters and a few other companies, most have continued to operate as net subtractors of value since privatization. Directors are not accountable to outside shareholders interested in profit maximization, so they can avoid restructuring, downsizing, product improvement, and efficiency enhancements. Through complex arbitrage schemes, the withholding of wages, and the use of parasitic "offshore" companies, these directors can amass individual wealth while their companies continue to operate in the red. More recently, several of Russia's financial-industrial groups have begun to acquire control of the potentially profitable enterprises still operating at a loss, but these new outside owners have yet to pursue restructuring (let alone new investment) vigorously.

Under market conditions, these companies would be forced into bankruptcy, their assets would be reorganized and auctioned, and either owners interested in profit making would assume control or the enterprises would be shut down. In Russia, however, bankruptcies rarely occur. Instead, the state has continued to subsidize ailing companies, initially through direct transfers and now by allowing these companies not to pay taxes. In the wake of the latest financial crisis, many predict that the new Russian government will resort to printing money and issuing credits again, further delaying the reorganization of these enterprises into value-producing assets.

Given these conditions at the micro level, anti-crisis plans for raising revenues will not have an immediate positive effect. No matter what the tax code, most companies do not have the means to pay since they are bankrupt. There are some exceptions and the government must insist that profit generators like Gazprom, the energy monopoly, and oil companies pay their taxes. But this is only a short-term solution. After all, Gazprom responds to government requests for tax payments with its own unpaid invoices for gas supplied to government enterprises. At some point the government must break this vicious circle by enforcing bankruptcy procedures as the first step toward restructuring enterprises, clarifying property rights, and ultimately finding owners for these enterprises who are interested in profit maximization. And these new owners, it must be remembered, will invest only under the right conditions—conditions that include lower interest rates, a rational tax code, and state protection (rather than mafia protection) of their property.

The financial meltdown during the summer of 1998 will further delay fundamental reform at the firm level. Because the government defaulted on its loans, there will be little foreign capital flowing into the country in the immediate future. Strapped for cash, the government will be forced to print money, which will fuel inflation. Faced with the prospect of hyperinflation again, the new government will be tempted to introduce wage and price controls; some provincial governors already have begun to do so. Price controls will spawn a black market and the reintroduction of the dollar as the currency of choice. In the very near future, the Russian economy may come to resemble the Soviet economy in the year leading up to the collapse of the Soviet Union. The road to recovery from this bleak situation will be long and difficult, especially because the very concept of "market reform" has now been discredited.

THE POLITICAL CONSEQUENCES

Soon after the announcement of the ruble's devaluation, Russia's economic crisis became a political crisis. Even before the devaluation, social tensions and workers' strikes had escalated throughout the summer, culminating in hundreds of unpaid miners camping outside the White House (the building that houses the government), demanding their back wages and Yeltsin's resignation. Given this highly charged political environment, not only liberal supporters of the government but

Russian citizens have begun to lose faith in the democratic process because it has produced few tangible benefits to the average person.

even communist and nationalist opponents of Yeltsin made dire predictions about the disastrous political consequences of a devaluation. Analysts speculated that a sudden rise in prices resulting from devaluation would trigger mass social unrest. Trade union officials and Communist Party leaders feared that they might lose the support of their constituencies, who would turn to more radical political groups in times of crisis. Yeltsin also appeared to be worried about these extremists when he issued a warning in early July to potential non-democratic challengers that his regime retained enough military force to defeat any coup attempt.

To date, Russia's patient citizens have not rebelled in response to devaluation. And in contrast to Weimar Germany, Russia does not have a nationally organized fascist party ready to take advantage of the situation. The Russian National Union, Russia's closest equivalent to Hitler's Nazi Party, still does not enjoy a mass following. The one nationalist group that has organized throughout the country, Vladimir Zhirinovsky's Liberal Democratic Party of Russia, has shunned radical solutions and has cooperated with Yeltsin (for a price) in finding a solution to the political crisis. On the left, some radical communist organizations have advocated revolutionary tactics, but the leadership of the Russian Communist Party has remained committed to following the democratic process. Most important, all major political actors adhered to the democratic rules of the game in appointing a prime minister, demonstrating the resilience of Russia's new democratic institutions.

As with any revolutionary situation, this social calm could evaporate quickly. If one trigger-happy soldier fires into a peaceful demonstration, calls for a violent overthrow of the regime will escalate. Likewise, if Yeltsin and his team violate the constitution by attempting to delay elections or rule by decree, their enemies also will no longer feel compelled to respect the democratic rules of the game.

DEMOCRACY'S FRAGILITY

These scenarios of coups, state collapse, and revolution seem more compelling when one remembers how weak and fragile the current Russian political system has become. The administrative apparatus of the Russian state lacks the capacity to execute even the most basic of state policies. The Soviet state, like the Soviet economy, collapsed in the fall of 1991. After this collapse, Russian reformers rightly devoted energy and resources to transforming the economy from a command system to a market, but they failed to undertake a commensurate reform program to create a market-friendly, democratic, and effective state. Consequently, the Russian state cannot collect taxes, and fails to provide basic public goods such as security, welfare, and education. This is not a government that has the capacity to withstand even spontaneous and disorganized social challenges.

Russia's democratic institutions are also fragile and unconsolidated. As affirmed through successful parliamentary, presidential, and gubernatorial elections over the last several years, Russia is an electoral democracy. But the system still lacks many of the qualities of a liberal democracy. The constitution gives too many powers to the president, the judiciary does not act as a third and independent branch of government, political parties are weak, mass-based interest groups are marginal, the rule of law has only begun to take hold, and the media are becoming less independent. More generally, Russian citizens have begun to lose faith in the democratic process because it has produced few tangible benefits to the average person.

In addition to a weak state and fragile democratic institutions, Russia also has a president who lacks popular support and legitimacy. Yeltsin's approval rating has fallen back into single digits and even many of his longtime allies have begun to call for his resignation. Yeltsin is not the kind of leader who has the authority to carry out radical economic reforms. Nor could his regime mobilize a popular defense if challenged by a coup or other nondemocratic acts.

As pressures mount for Yeltsin's removal, many predict that Russia's next presidential election will be held sooner rather than later, and well before the end of Yeltsin's term in the summer of 2000. Opinion polls suggest that anyone affiliated with Yeltsin or the current government has little chance of winning the next election. Even in 1996, Yeltsin won not because voters approved of his record in office (his approval rating peaked on the day of the election at 29 percent), but because they feared a return to communism. Yeltsin was the lesser of two evils. However, in the next presidential election the anticommunist card will not work, since no one now believes in the threat of Soviet-style communist restoration. Given the economic and political uncertainties that erupted after his dismissal, former Prime Minister Viktor Chernomyrdin might be able to run as the candidate of stability. However, even with the generous backing of Gazprom and financial industrialists Boris Berezovsky and Vladimir Gusinsky, Chernomyrdin is still a long-shot candidate, since he presided as the head of government during years of economic stagnation.

A communist victory in a presidential election is also unlikely. Communist Party leader Gennadi Zyuganov has worked hard since his electoral defeat in 1996 to transform his party into a nationalist movement in an attempt to attract new supporters. To date, the strategy has not succeeded. If he runs again, Zyuganov will enjoy solid enough support from his party loyalists to ensure that he will make it into the runoff—which he is almost equally assured of losing. If given the choice between Zyuganov and any other leading presidential contender, the majority of voters in opinion polls say they would support the noncommunist on the ballot.

The absence of viable candidates from either the current government or the communist opposition opens the door for new challengers. Today, two dominate the pack: Moscow

American foreign policymakers must make renewed efforts to promote liberal democracy and a liberal market economy in Russia.

Mayor Yuri Luzhkov and Krasnoyarsk Governor Aleksandr Lebed. Luzhkov's program of state-led capitalism laced with ethnic nationalism offers a potentially attractive alternative to the more liberal economic reforms pursued by Yeltsin's government. Although his critics charge that Luzhkov is corrupt, authoritarian, and chauvinistic toward minorities, the city he governs has produced positive growth rates. His supporters hope that he can do for Russia what he has done for Moscow.

At a time of growing popular dissatisfaction, Lebed is the consummate protest candidate. A former general with a reputation for getting things done, Lebed appeals to those who long for law and order. His views regarding market reform and democracy are still ill-defined. But if Russia continues to record negative growth rates the next two years, Russian voters may be ready to reject markets and democracy altogether in favor of a new "third" way.

THE UNITED STATES AND RUSSIA

Russia's latest crisis will deliver another blow to United States–Russian relations. Over the last several years, the Start II arms reduction treaty, NATO expansion, trade with Iran and Iraq, and Russia's new draconian law sanctioning only certain religions have dominated relations between the two countries. To historians of Soviet-American relations, this agenda should sound familiar: arms control, European security, regional conflicts, and human rights were the main components of most summit talks between the two superpowers during the cold war. This old agenda suggests that the promise of a new post-communist strategic partnership between the United States and Russia has yet to emerge. Some now argue that, given the balance of power in the international system, the United States and Russia are simply destined to be adversaries. This camp believes that Russia's latest economic crisis will propel to power Russian leaders hostile to the West, compelling the Western world to contain the Russian threat to markets and democracy once again.

This is a premature conclusion. The Soviet communist system—not Russia as a country or Russians as a people—threatened America's national interests during the cold war. As long as Russia continues on the path of democratization and marketization, Russian-American relations hold the promise of moving beyond these old issues of division and confrontation. It was the collapse of communism, not skilled diplomacy, that brought the greatest progress on all these issues earlier this decade. Consequently, United States strategic interests in the post–cold war era are tied intimately to the fate of Russia's new political and economic system.

The heightened domestic turmoil Russia has suffered during the last several months suggests that American foreign policy-makers must make renewed efforts to promote liberal democracy and a liberal market economy in Russia. If democracy and capitalism collapse there, then the issues of contention between Russia and the United States will multiply and new threats to American security will emerge.

President Bill Clinton's administration demonstrated leadership in responding aggressively to Russia's latest financial crisis by urging the IMF to negotiate a new set of loans to Russia, but the rescue mission failed. Until Russia forms a government and outlines a genuine anticrisis program, it is premature for the IMF, the Group of Seven, or the United States to provide additional funds to the Russian state (although assistance to nongovernmental actors and institutions can and should continue). Once the new Russian government devises a plan to end the crisis, however, it will need Western help to succeed.

In addition to assistance for achieving macroeconomic stabilization provided through the IMF, the United States should focus on facilitating the development of important market institutions such as laws governing property rights, financial disclosure, bankruptcy, pension funds, taxes, and securities markets to promote enterprise restructuring. Especially as American funds for assistance to Russia continue to decrease, a focus on institutions rather than individual projects or technical assistance for specific economic actors should remain a top priority.

The West must rethink basic assumptions about political reform in Russia. Russian reformers wrongly believed that economic reform had to precede political reform. American assistance programs also adopted this logic and channeled the lion's share of American aid to Russia into economic reform while only a fraction went to promoting democratic institutions. The record of reform in the postcommunist world, however, has demonstrated that the fastest democratizers also have conducted the most successful economic reforms.

Programs that provide expertise on the development of the basic institutions that constitute a liberal democracy—that is, programs that promote parties, federalism, the rule of law, independent media, and civil society—should be expanded, not curtailed. The United States also can do more to foster basic democratic values in Russia by providing civics textbooks, funding public policy programs, developing higher education courses on democracy, and continuing student exchanges. While the market creates incentives for Russians to learn how to become entrepreneurs, Russians today have few incentives to learn how to be good democrats.

Finally, at the highest levels, American officials must send clear signals to Russian elites about the negative consequences of circumventing the democratic process. For instance, Clinton should urge Yeltsin to establish a precedent for the peaceful transfer of political power through the electoral process. Because such a transfer would be a first in Russian history, no single event is more important for the consolidation of Russia's democracy than the upcoming presidential election. The Clinton administration also must send an unequivocal message to the Russian government that the West will not condone any extraconstitutional seizures of power, be they radical plots to overthrow the current regime or plans by the Yeltsin group to institute martial law.

Many Americans have grown weary of Russia; achievements have been few and headaches many. Now is not the time to give up on it. Only seven years since the Soviet collapse, Russia's revolution has by no means ended. The country's current leaders remain committed to developing a market economy and a democratic polity, and to joining rather than threatening the community of democratic states; it is in the vital national interest of the United States to ensure that this trajectory remains in place. Continued engagement with Russia's reformers, sustained promotion of Russian liberal market and democratic institutions, and gradual integration of Russia into the world capitalist system and the international community of democratic states: these are the policies that will prevent Russia's transition from turning belligerent. Containment, isolation, and neglect of institutional development in Russia are policies that will help transform Russia's revolution into a security threat, both to democratic states in the West and to democratizing states closer to Russia.

A NEW TIGER

India used to pride itself on poverty-stricken self-sufficiency. Now it seeks growth, exports and foreign investment, and the economy is booming.

BY STEVEN STRASSER AND SUDIP MAZUMDAR

TRAVEL INTO THE DEPTHS OF Bihar, India's poorest state, along the dirt paths that connect its stagnant pools of humanity, past government signs touting chimerical health and education programs, into the hopeless heart of a subcontinent where the squalid villages might remind you of sub-Saharan Africa—except that the poorest Africans fare better than the destitute of Bihar. Eventually you will stumble onto the village of Kalipahari, blessed with electricity thanks to a nearby hydroelectric dam. Here you will see, in practically every hovel, an incongruous sight: a television set, pulling down American soap operas and Scotch whisky ads from Hong Kong. This is the Indian dream at ground level. As the vision of "Baywatch" filters through Bihar, so even the poorest of the poor finally begin to rise from the depths of rotted isolation.

And so does poor old India. For 50 years the national identity has depended on isolation from perceived enemies—from plotting neocolonialists in the West, from greedy multinational companies, even from those intrepid Indians who resisted the official creed of self-sufficiency. But now satellite TV has come to Bihar, and Coca-Cola, too. Health and education will one day follow. The leaders in New Delhi have a new national ideal—rapid growth—and, at least in spirit, they have thrown open the doors to multinationals everywhere. More important, they are forging a national identity more suited to modern times. India, at last, has begun to see itself as another Asian nation dedicated to the accumulation of wealth and the spread of prosperity. In the next century that vision will hold infinitely more power than the old asceticism. "Perhaps our industrialization is not complete," says Srini Rajam, head of the Texas Instruments branch in booming Bangalore, "but we can leapfrog into the Information Age."

India has always had pride. Now it has ambition. In the early years of independence, Jawaharlal Nehru's government rejoiced in standing apart, the epitome of the "nonaligned" nation. As a conglomeration of peoples with seven major religions and 18 official languages, India made its own rules: a democracy on a continent ruled by despots, a planned economy whose bureaucratic stewards were satisfied to creep along at a 3 or 4 percent "Hindu rate of growth." Only when the New Delhi elite squarely acknowledged that its hubris had put the nation on the sidelines of the global economy—while India's great rival China was getting rich—did real reforms begin. Now, six years into India's opening to the world, the economy is growing by nearly 7 percent a year, a rate that by 2020 will transform its economy into the world's fourth largest (after China, the United States and Japan). "There is a lot of political cacophony," says Finance Minister P. Chidambaram, who has served under two coalition governments in the last 14 months. "But we are on course."

There is no lilt to his optimism. A visitor to urban China (which is churning along at a growth rate of 9.5 percent a year) can almost hear the hum of enterprise in a nation that is fairly bursting to build a better life. The reformers of India, by contrast, tend to bow under the weight of their nation's great poverty. Even now, 52 percent of their people still live on incomes of less than $1 a day, according to World Bank figures. Nearly two thirds of Indian children younger than 5 are malnourished, and those who reach school age can count on an average of only 3.5 years of education if they are boys, 1.5 if they are girls. By the time they reach adulthood, half are still illiterate. Think of it: India is trying to accelerate onto the Information Superhighway with nearly 300 million adults who cannot read road signs.

Comparisons between India and the economic tigers of East Asia are equally dismal. Pacific Rim economies that once ranked far below India and its South Asian neighbors now enjoy per capita incomes 27 times greater, according to the Human Development Centre, a Pakistani think tank that studies regional economic trends. The blunt reality of India's failures is now driving its reforms, and most Indians agree on what must be done. From the Marxists running Calcutta to the Hindu nationals running Bombay (they call it Mumbai), the bywords of the new India are growth, foreign investment and, most hallowed of all, exports.

The strategy, formed in 1991 by the then prime minister P. V. Narasimha Rao and his finance minister, Manmohan Singh, was ruthlessly simple: to dismantle the stifling bureaucracy that once ruled India as intrusively as Moscow's planners once ran the Soviet Union. Rao and Singh cut much of the bureaucracy's "license raj" of red tape, then went on to simplify taxes, reduce the scope of the state sector (which provided everything from power to motor scooters), liberalize foreign investment and cut tariffs. From the earliest days, says Singh, "our goal has been to show the world that India can compete with any country in Southeast Asia in our hospitality to investment and our spirit of enterprise."

India's culture has also been a force for reaching out to the world. The film industry turns out both masterpieces and tawdry B movies in astonishing profusion. Using the imported English language in their own unique way, novelists like Arundhati Roy, 37, a former actress and screenwriter, have become international best sellers. The literary tradition has deep roots; Hindu poet and philosopher Rabindranath Tagore won the Nobel Prize in Literature as long ago as 1913.

From *Newsweek*, August 4, 1997, pp. 42-4,46. © 1997 by Newsweek, Inc. All rights reserved. Reprinted by permission.

Neither culture nor industry has done anything yet for the dregs of Indian society, the 200 million or so people at the very bottom of the ladder. But for the first time in history, economic growth and the spread of communications are working a revolution among many millions of India's other poor. New Delhi's program of teaming with foreign investors to string out copper wire for telephones is proceeding in fits and starts. Even in the capital, the wait for a new phone can still stretch to three years. Nonetheless, the government's decision to let in foreign satellite television has led to an explosion of more than 20 million cable-TV connections within the last two years. That alone had helped to spur demand among low-income consumers to unprecedented levels. A manufacturer of $1.20 bottles of shampoo for middle-class Indians found a huge new market for two-cent packets of the brand in poor areas. The race is on to produce cheap television sets and appliances. One entrepreneur found a way to convert devices for making *lassi* (a yogurt drink) into cheap washing machines. And the first developer of a good $50 refrigerator, suggests economist S. L. Rao, would now find a huge new market in rural India.

More important, India's poor are beginning to find their political voice. Indian democracy has always been hobbled by the primitive state of its grass-roots politics. Too many local leaders bubbled up to national power on their ability to buy votes and deliver favors—and subsequently used their national platforms mainly to enrich themselves. But the rural awakening that came with reform also has revived state and local politics. State competition for the spoils of reform is now common. Tamil Nadu attracted a Ford plant by waiving state sales taxes and offering land at a concessionary price. Uttar Pradesh won the battle to lure an electronics project set up by the Korean giant Daewoo.

The southern city of Bangalore, India's Silicon Valley, stands as the glittering tiara of the new India. Indians themselves own only 1.8 million installed personal computers—about a third the number in New York City. But what the info-tech companies stand for is vitally important. The homegrown firms and those allied with all the big names, from IBM to Intel, have exuberantly cut through red tape and protectionism, welcoming competition while becoming successful software exporters themselves. "If we can't compete with international brands in our own country, we can't hope to ever compete in other countries," says software-industry spokesman Dewang Mehta.

As India streamlines its bureaucracy and unclogs its courts, New Delhi and Mumbai may become more attractive to multinational corporations than the regulatory wilds of Beijing and Shanghai. If India can mobilize its hundreds of millions of young, cheap workers at a time when the work force of the developed world is aging, a boom of Chinese magnitude might not be out of the question. "Just think of the economic output we can generate from this population when our per capita income of $330 doubles early in the next century," says Mukesh Ambani, vice chairman of Mumbai's Reliance Indus-

tries. "That will clearly boost us into range of becoming an economic superpower."

Somehow the mantle of "superpower" does not quite fit the personality of a huge, poor country that will continue to regard itself, culturally and politically, as the world's great exception. Nor will India likely become a classic Asian tiger. As a vibrant democracy that must always tend to its own first, the nation will never produce a Deng Xiaoping to dictate its strategy from on high. The new Indian dynamo will muddle along, sure of its direction but never of its strategy, obsessed always with the myriad demands from within. "We will take one sector at a time, show that it works and build confidence," says Manmohan Singh. "There can be no big-bang theory of growth."

An outsider can gauge India's progress by measuring the market's success at shifting resources to the government's neediest constituents—something the centralized bureaucracy never could accomplish. How will life change in the most desolate regions of Bihar? At the absolute end of the line, in the village of Devnagra, a foreign donor recently gave $7,000 for a new well, the kind of gesture that short-circuits India's inefficiencies (to put it politely) rather than validating reform. Nonetheless, once fresh water comes to the village, it will be less hard to imagine a school, a clinic, even a road—and along that road, a thin copper wire connecting the darkest corner of India to the riches of the world.

With RON MOREAU *in Mumbai,* TONY CLIFTON *in New Delhi and* JOSHUA KWAN *in Hong Kong*

AFRICA RISING

A new spirit of self-reliance is taking root among many Africans as they seize control of their destiny. What are they doing right?

By JOHANNA MC GEARY and MARGUERITE MICHAELS

HOPE IS AFRICA'S RAREST COMmodity. Yet buried though it is amid the despair that haunts the continent, there is more optimism today than in decades. Francisco Mucavele found hope last September when an armored steel Casspir rolled over the hill and began to blow up the land mines contaminating Mozambique's rich soil. Olga Haptemariam acquired it in Eritrea's warscarred port city of Massawa when she laid down 2,000 birr for a license to open a building-supply store. The villagers of N'Tjinina are finding it as they prepare for the solemn experience of voting in Mali's first local elections. Sarah Galloway Hage-Ali is spreading hope in Ghana, where she purchased the country's sole manufacturer of sanitary napkins in 1994 and launched a feminine-hygiene crusade.

This story is not about the Africa you think you know. The usual images are painted in the darkest colors. At the end of the 20th century, we are repeatedly reminded, Africa is a nightmarish world where chaos reigns. Nothing works. Poverty and corruption rule. War, famine and pestilence pay repeated calls. The land, air, water are raped, fouled,

polluted. Chronic instability gives way to lifelong dictatorship. Every nation's hand is out, begging aid from distrustful donors. Endlessly disappointed, 740 million people sink into hopelessness.

That portrait is real, all right, in places like Nigeria, Somalia, Burundi, Sudan, Kenya. But it is no longer the whole picture. Academics, diplomats and bankers who do business there talk seriously these days about an African renaissance. A grand word, it turns out, for the slow, fragile, difficult changes that are giving the continent a second chance. But the description fits. Out of sight of our narrow focus on disaster, another Africa is rising, an Africa that works: the Africa of Mozambique and Mali and Eritrea and Ghana, of South Africa and Uganda, Benin and Botswana, Ethiopia, Ivory Coast, Tanzania.

What's new is how some nations are figuring out ways to harness their natural and human resources into working models of development, even while others cannot. What's new is the astonishing extent to which ordinary Africans are searching out their own paths to progress. What's new is how much of the still limited prosperity and security they have managed to acquire is homegrown—political

and economic advances rooted in the soil of local culture. What's new is that the enduring example of Nelson Mandela has heartened all Africans with a fresh vision of leadership, how men of their own kind can be admired, respected, even emulated.

For so long the victim of historical circumstance, Africa is finally a beneficiary. The end of the cold war freed countries from 30-odd years of disastrous involvement in the superpowers' proxy conflicts. Old ideologies crumbled, taking with them the failed socialist methods of Marx and opening the way to capitalist reforms. The demise of apartheid gave the continent a huge psychological—and economic and political—boost. A generation of African leaders who grew up to despise the exploitation of postcolonial dictators and kleptocrats has begun to supplant them.

In recognition of all that, Bill Clinton set off last Sunday on the first extensive tour of Africa by a sitting U.S. President. His aim is to cast a high-wattage spotlight on the continent's emerging democracies, economic growth and social progress and to promote a new relationship with the U.S. Of course, the Administration also sees a largely un-

From *Time*, March 30, 1998, pp. 34-46. © 1998 by Time Inc. Magazine Company. Reprinted by permission.

tapped market and wants to encourage American businessmen to get there first. Africans hope Clinton will show them that the U.S. is ready to be a partner instead of patron.

The good news in Africa is less in such momentary gestures than in the small stories of steady progress made, the handiwork of hundreds and thousands of individuals laying foundations for a better future. Two TIME correspondents recently spent a month traveling in four countries to look at the many ways in which Africa actually works.

Let's first stipulate some common truths. By any Western standard, Mozambique, Eritrea, Mali and Ghana are countries in awful straits. Their statistics still show an abysmal record of poverty, illiteracy, early mortality. While all four have achieved a dose of national economic success, with higher growth rates, lower inflation and more stable currencies that flow from obedience to stringent International Monetary Fund reform programs, they have yet to see their growing wealth trickle down very far. For ordinary citizens, daily hardships are intense: few jobs, few schools, few hospitals, poor diets, rising prices, no money. For the majorities of these populations that are ill fed, ill clothed, illiterate and just plain ill, what Mozambicans dubbed the "years of cabbage" are not over.

Let us also acknowledge that for every optimistic tale we tell, even these countries can tell 10 times as many despairing ones. Nevertheless, each of these countries is moving ahead, and what we discovered was the reasons—some unique, some replicable—they are doing so.

MOZAMBIQUE

WHAT ARE THE EYES OF A child soldier supposed to look like? Felfiel Manhica's are downcast and blank in a face that rarely smiles. He is 22 now, still undersize and boyish, but he was just 13 when rebel Renamo soldiers crept into the hamlet of Taninga before dawn in 1988 to steal food and took him too. They threatened to execute him, armed him with an AK-47 assault rifle and turned him into a pitiless killing machine aimed at his family, friends and neighbors on the government side of Mozambique's civil war. "They told me

I must fight in order to eat," he stutters, loath to recall those years. "I killed people. I saw their faces when I hurt them." He cannot look a questioner in the eyes. "Now," says this boy-man who subsists by cutting bamboo, "life is good, because I don't have the heavy heart of a fighter."

Not long before the ruling Frelimo government signed a peace accord with Renamo in October 1992, Felfiel escaped and walked for three days back to Taninga. The village allowed him to undergo the forgiving rites of traditional cleansing. Felfiel's mother went to the spiritual guardian for a muti, a physical and psychological purgative. It took three days for Felfiel to vomit up the "bad things" he had done and earn atonement. After the cleansing, Felfiel stopped having nightmares, and his neighbors embraced him once again.

Call it witchcraft if you like, but such rural healing is a major reason that nearly 95,000 demobilized soldiers and 5 million refugees have been absorbed back into society. In less than five years, Mozambique (pop. 18 million) has forged cohesion out of the animosities that tore it apart. The revered practices of communal tradition have succeeded, better than any modern forms of psychotherapy, in restoring a sense of unity to Mozambique's deeply riven clans. "National reconciliation started in the communities themselves," says Roberto Chavez, the World Bank director in Mozambique. "They were the main factor in bringing the country back together."

The Frelimo government was smart enough to help too. Anxious about the potential for trouble from 90,000 unemployed guys with guns, it contracted with the United Nations to develop a plan that would rapidly resettle soldiers and refugees in their home villages. In 1994 the government and donor countries scraped together $20 million to pay all demobbed soldiers a minimum salary for two years to help them rebuild their shambas (farms) and restock their corrals. "We wanted to get them out of the military and make them civilians right away," explains Sam Barnes, a program administrator. "We wanted the soldiers to be part of rebuilding the country from the ground up."

Recovery from the ravages of war is the baseline against which Mozambique's progress must be measured. Almost from the day the former Portuguese colony won independence in 1975, it was

dragged into a vicious struggle between its new rulers, the Marxist Mozambique Liberation Front, known as Frelimo, and a rebel movement called Renamo that was trained, armed and supplied mostly from sources in South Africa. Sixteen years of guerrilla warfare devastated the country. A million men, women and children died. Two million people fled across the borders; 3 million more moved off their farms into safer urban enclaves. When hostilities ceased, some 2 million unmapped mines laid waste the nation's arable lands.

That is where more rural magic comes into play. The newest local healer lumbers into the countryside on 17 tons of armor plate and giant steel wheels. The Frelimo government has invested its scarce cash to bring in a fleet of Casspir demining vehicles, operated by a private subsidiary of the South African army, to get rid of the mines that keep farmers and herders off the country's lush lands.

As fast as the vehicles roll over the acres around Sabié, west of the capital of Maputo, destroying the mines, the farmers stream in behind, planting corn and squash, grazing goats and cows. Francisco Mucavele is one of them. For 10 years he was confined within the perimeter of the little settlement of Chavane, bounded by fear of the minefields. "We felt like prisoners in the village," he says. "Now I can go anywhere I want."

Standing among corn shoots already knee high, Francisco waves toward other fields where the telltale puffs of black smoke show mines detonating beneath the Casspir's wheels and talks of planting there too. Then he can not only feed his family of seven children but also sell for a profit. "As we get our land back, we can cultivate more and graze more cows. Then maybe we can get roads, and trucks will come to take our food to market. And then the stores and clinics will come back," he says. Already his younger children can go to school again, and a midwife has moved into the village.

The essential first step for African nations is the step back from the edge of famine. The Mozambicans are doing other things right too. Theirs is a people's peace, driven by popular refusal to continue the conflict and a fierce determination to live a normal life. Today political stability—though not much democracy—has been achieved through the government's policy of "no victor, no vanquished." Four years ago, Renamo elected impressive numbers to the national assembly; now it has a stake in running the country, and hostilities find voice mainly as parliamentary debate. Frelimo jettisoned its socialist economic credo by 1989 and decided not only to adopt market-based capitalism but to take the bitter IMF-ordered medicine required for international investment.

What really fuels Mozambique's climb, though, is the energy of individuals tackling problems from the bottom up. Take the "Italian roads." Instead of paying foreign companies for expensive foreign-built, high-maintenance asphalt roads, local authorities are copying a cheap labor-intensive, low-tech alternative pioneered in Italy: roads constructed of small, handmade stone or concrete pavers that can be laid directly on the sandy soil and individually replaced when rains wash them out.

Or take the little restaurant on the beach at Xia Xia, a great sweep of sand running for miles north of Maputo. Nuno Fonseca and his second wife Paola spent the war years in Maputo but came back to her largely destroyed hometown in early 1994. Once there were swank hotels along the strand for tourists. "When we got here there was nothing, nothing," says Nuno.

He "saw opportunity in abundance" and told the government he wanted to set up a campground on the beach, maybe a little restaurant. He brought in water and electric lines, put up a concrete toilet-shower building, then opened for business. Now he owns a caravan park, 12 rental bungalows and the restaurant, and he has plans for more. "I'm very confident about the future," says Nuno. "No one is interested in war ever again." As he sips a coffee, he muses, "You know, a lot of people here are trying to do things just like me. Sure, the government can help, but we've got to start taking care of ourselves."

ERITREA

BY LOGIC, THE NATION OF Eritrea (Pop. 3 million) should not exist. The secessionist province's independence fighters ought never to have defeated Ethiopia in their 30-year-long struggle. They were outmanned, outgunned, abandoned or betrayed by every ally; their cause was hopeless. They won

by force of character, a unity and determination so steely not all the modern armaments, superpower support or economic superiority of Ethiopia could withstand it. The spirit that saw the Eritreans through 10 years in the trenches of their mountain redoubt at Nakfa has built them a nation from scratch, since independence was finally consummated in 1993.

The emergence of Eritrea as a working state in so short a time is a remarkable testament to self-reliance. "We learned the hard way," says President Issaias Afewerki, the rebel leader turned chief executive, "that our own sense of purpose, our own unity, our own organized capabilities were the only things that we could count on to succeed." Alone in Africa, Eritrea carries little debt and accepts virtually no foreign assistance. Over the past four years, it has asked all but six aid providers to leave, including Oxfam and every religious organization. "It's not that we don't need the money," says Issaias, "but we don't want the dependence." Aid, he says, subsidizes but corrupts the government, blocks innovative solutions to problems, so that people do not seek out and use their own resources.

Just the physical improvements are impressive. All the rusted metal detritus of battle has been swept up into neat piles waiting to be recycled into rail lines, girders and tools. Men and women break rock by hand to repave the highway that spirals down 7,000 ft. from the capital of Asmara to the seaport of Massawa. Workers trained by the grandfathers who built the railroad in the '30s lay reforged rails back toward Asmara; they have completed 26 miles in two years and cunningly restored the country's two 1938 Italian steam engines.

What sets Eritrea apart is the self-sacrificing character of its people, the thousands like Olga Haptemariam who rely solely on their own gumption. We meet her behind the counter of the building-supply shop she has opened in Massawa, striving to capitalize on the construction boom resuscitating this shattered equatorial port. "It's my own business," she says, pointing to the stacked cans of paint and tools lining the shelves. "It is doing very well, very nice." She can't wait to expand. "When I get more money, I want to get more materials from Italy, China. If I can bring them in, I can improve this business fast."

Olga is a self-made woman. While her brother went to university, she was married off at 16, already pregnant. Two years ago, she sought a divorce and demanded 30,000 birr as alimony. Out of that she paid the 2,000 birr for a business license and 18,000 birr for the shop. She earns 3,000 or 4,000 birr a month, occasionally as much as 7,500. She can afford to send her daughter to a private school, preparing her to study abroad and become a "doctor for women." Olga vows never to remarry. "I think of business only," she says. "I want to make this business very big, and I can do that best myself."

Nothing symbolizes this nation's true grit better than the mountain retreat of Nakfa. There the near defeated rebel troops hewed out miles of rock trenches with bayonets and survived for 10 years beneath the shelling of the Ethiopian army. It still takes 10 hours in a four-wheel to drive the 137 miles from the capital over rugged mountain tracks. But Nakfa is a place of veneration akin to Valley Forge. "It reminds us forever of our resistance," says Zacharias, a teacher at the new technical school. The national emblem is the camel that carried supplies to Nakfa; the country's new currency, introduced in November to replace the Ethiopian birr, is called the nakfa. Despite Nakfa's 9,000-ft.-high chill and barren soil, the government is determined to turn this inhospitable locale into a regional magnet.

Many of the 10,000 current residents moved into their first concrete buildings just this year. Helping replace the city's tin huts are young people doing their national service. Every Eritrean male is required to spend six months in the army and 12 more working on rehabilitation projects. Up here, some are also planting trees to revive the blighted landscape. "I like doing it," says 24-year-old Daniel. "I teach people how to do things, and that is a way to develop our country fast."

In his blacksmith shop in the busy market town of Keren, Fikad Ghoitom explains the national attitude: show me, don't tell me; ingenuity applied to example; homegrown know-how. Fikad's brother saw a wood-cutting machine in an English magazine and forged one out of scrap metal. Down in the artisans' suq in Asmara, men in blue overalls don masks cut from cardboard to weld new pots from old oil tins and cooking braziers from rusted rods. The clang, hammer, sizzle of makeshift industry are everywhere as boys flatten old iron bars for their brothers to beat into new shovels.

Eritreans are extraordinarily dedicated to the public welfare. Doctors living abroad came back during the war as volunteer medics and still visit for six-month stints. Former fighters who went into the civil service took no pay for three years.

This is not Africa, people will tell you in Eritrea. What they mean is that the country is astonishingly free of the social plagues that taint much of the continent. There is no tribalism or sectarian division here. National pride supersedes loyalties to nine main ethnic groups, at least 10 languages, Islam and Christianity, in part the consequence of the rebels' insistence on mixing everyone together in its army units and now in national-service teams.

Egalitarianism is ingrained, reinforced in the days when army officers wore no insignia of their rank on their shoulders.

There is no begging, no corruption, virtually no crime. "We would not be so dishonorable," says Russon, an Asmara taxi driver. However poor they are, families share with the truly destitute. A fierce sense of personal rectitude makes thievery unthinkable. "It is not the police who prevent crime but the honor inside us," insists Fikad, the blacksmith. "The corruption is the lowest of any government I've ever worked for, including in Santa Rosa, Calif.," says Michael O'Neill, an American adviser to the Commercial Bank of Eritrea. "They will not tolerate it in any way, shape or form." During the war, the fighters were too desperate for money to put any into people's pockets, and that scrupulous use of every precious resource carries over into the government today.

What also sets Eritrea apart is the dedication to national purpose of its leader. President Issaias is one of Africa's new men, hammered into leadership by the rigors of long war. Though soft-spoken, he is stern, almost paternalistic in his confidence that he knows best. His government is firmly controlled, even secretive, yet people seem to admire him. He is sharp and decisive, says what is on his mind, accepts diplomatic criticism when he considers it right and rejects it when he doesn't. "What you hear is what you get," says O'Neill. "He doesn't dicker or pussyfoot."

The President has few doubts about his methods, even if they differ from those practiced in the rest of Africa. "We learned from the bad experiences of others," he says, "what is bad governance." He and his countrymen are determined to do better, on their own. "We are not rich; we do not have many resources; we are affected by things we cannot control. But we prefer to face our problems ourselves. If you teach someone to fish, instead of giving him fish, then he has a sustainable future." He turns his nearly impassive face toward the reporter. "This is difficult for people; it takes a long time," he says. "But in the long term, success can only come from inside us."

MALI

THE STORY OF MALI'S AScent out of poverty begins at 6 a.m. on March 26, 1991. Then Lieut. Colonel Amadou Toumani Touré—called A.T.T. by everyone—went on the radio to announce that he had just arrested his commanding general, the nation's President, and taken control. "I said that as soon as minimum security was established we would organize elections," recalls Touré. "And as soon as the elections were held, we would go back to our barracks."

On April 26, 1992, after two rounds of voting widely judged to have been free and fair, civilian Alpha Oumar Konaré was elected President, and A.T.T., now an immensely powerful and popular general, stepped down. Instead of returning to the barracks, he took on the job of fighting Guinea worm disease and now also mediates regional disputes.

In the 14th century Mali (pop. 11 million) was the biggest, richest empire in West Africa, encompassing all or part of Senegal, Gambia, Guinea and Mauritania, the legendary land of gold and learning, grower of cotton, source of salt, trader across the Sahara to all the countries of Europe. Almost 700 years later, the Republic of Mali found itself the fourth poorest country in the world, destroyed by tribal and religious wars, colonialism, crashing commodity prices, soaring fuel prices, bad weather, bad governments.

The dictatorial President Moussa Traoré had run the country dismally for 23 years. "I made a coup," says Touré, "but sometimes you have to give a quick kick to democracy." Rare among Africa's military bosses, A.T.T. had the courage to return his country to civilian control. "I watched officers my age in other countries take over," he says.

"These men came in to save their countries, then stayed 20 years. But when a country is well managed, the constitution is respected, no captain can come out of his barracks. The vaccination against a coup is good government."

Mali seems to have that under the guiding hand of Konaré, its first ever popularly elected President. The 52-year-old former teacher and history Ph.D. once taught A.T.T. and served in the regime A.T.T. ousted, resigning in 1980 to join a clandestine democracy movement. "He understands human capital," says Tore Rose, head of the U.N. Development Program in Mali. "It's not the people themselves, but how they work with one another, and with groups and institutions."

The history of Mali is marked by the trust people have in these dealings, institutionalized in the traditional "palaver tree" approach to decision making, where village elders consult under a tree until a consensus is reached. Since its creation in 1993, Mali's Decentralization Mission has been educating the public about a modern democratic version of such local control. The country is divided into eight regions, 50 districts, 701 communes and thousands of villages. District chiefs are no longer appointed from the capital of Bamako but elected locally. Later this year, the communes will hold elections. "Reinforcing democracy," says President Konaré, "means devolution of power to the communities."

Although CMDT, the Malian Company for the Development of Textiles, which monopolizes the country's cotton production, is state owned, it is decentralizing, transforming a money-losing dinosaur into an engine for local development. Putting cotton plants into rotation with cereal crops, CMDT not only grows higher-quality cotton but also keeps farmers producing less pricey but essential maize, millet, sorghum and rice. Says Chaka Berte, a CMDT management director: "The farmers are taking their cotton money and diversifying. Good for them. Good for Mali."

The profits have helped transform N'Tjinina, a hamlet of 49 families, 1,263 people, deep in the countryside southeast of Bamako. There are still no paved roads, no electricity, no running water anywhere in the district. But with help from its CMDT-sponsored village association, which bought insecticides, oxen and a weighing machine, the families regularly harvest bumper crops. Mali's Producers' Union, a rarity in Africa, negotiates with CMDT to set prices for the farmer, and the village association receives block earnings. Extra profits are pooled, and so far N'Tjinina has bought two water pumps and built three primary schools, paying the three teachers' salaries too. "Before, our children left the village," says N'Tjikoua Sangare. "Now they are staying."

Women have always labored twice as hard as men in Africa, tending house, raising children, harvesting their husbands' fields. When we met Awa Koné, she was watering, bucketful by bucketful, young banana and mango trees and small plots of onions, tomatoes and eggplants. This garden in the tiny 10-family settlement of Tenemakana is a cooperative moneymaker for the village wives. The women pool the profits and then loan out the money to each other at 9% interest. No woman has ever defaulted. When they have earned enough, Koné and her friends plan to build a clinic.

These credit schemes are giving village women their first independent source of cash. That is changing the societies they live in, turning tiny profits into wells, protective fences and, most important, schools. Since 1992, villagers have built and staffed 128 primary schools; with U.S. grants, an additional 447 local schools were opened. Today 46.5% of Mali's children attend primary school, and the literacy rate, 19% seven years ago, is now 32%. "I've never seen such effective community systems," says the U.S. Agency for International Development's Timm Harris.

Awa Koné is not surprised. "If you are educated," she says, "you can solve problems." For the first time in her life, such ideas are shared by the nation's leaders. A.T.T. has started a private foundation dedicated to the education and health of Mali's children. "Here in this country," he says, "everyone works for the community."

GHANA

THE RISE AND SLUMP AND rise again of Ashanti Goldfields, the only black-African-operated mining company on the New York and London stock exchanges, mimics the fortunes of Ghana itself. The British outpost in French-dominated West Africa lived well on its gold and cocoa exports until the production of both plummeted during the first two decades

after Ghana's independence in 1957, under Kwame Nkrumah, one of the founding fathers of modern Africa. As Ashanti's output tumbled, the first sub-Saharan colony liberated from colonialism never did live up to Nkrumah's promise that "all else" would follow the act of *uhuru,* freedom.

The junior air-force flight lieutenant named Jerry Rawlings who seized power firmly in 1981 spouting Marxist rhetoric hardly seemed the man to turn things around. Yet within two years of his coup, Rawlings pirouetted to the right and embraced Adam Smith capitalism. It was the practical move of a military man wise to who had the money to help dig Ghana (pop. 18 million) out of its sinkhole. For the sake of foreign investment and IMF loans, he swallowed one of Africa's harshest doses of free-market medicine. The result: one of the most diversified economies in Africa and a more than embryonic middle class.

Rawlings also brought Sam Jonah into the boardroom. Jonah was the seventh child of 10; he grew up in Obuasi, site of Ashanti's richest gold mine. Jonah went down into the mine while awaiting a promised scholarship from Ashanti. "It was character forging," he says. "I know about teamwork, and I can still speak the mining slang." After study at University of Exeter's Camborne School of Mines, he returned to Obuasi, starting as a shift boss deep in the pits and working his way up—and out—the first black man to climb the ranks.

Rawlings chose Jonah in 1982 as deputy managing director of Ashanti, then owned 55% by the government and 45% by London's Lonrho Corp. "I didn't know him," says Jonah. "He just reached out for the highest-ranking Ghanaian." In 1986 Jonah rose to the top job, becoming, according to him, the only black African CEO of a multinational company. "The obstacle to there being more like me on this continent relates to one thing," says Jonah. "Ownership. If Rawlings had not taken a personal interest in the mining sector, the level of prejudice would have kept me underground forever. I still tell my Ghanaians," he adds, " 'Don't accept no!' "

Under Jonah, Ghana has learned the art, rare in Africa, of managing its natural resources effectively. Ashanti has led the country's gold production to record highs. Floating public shares on the New York Stock Exchange in 1994, the government sold off 30% of its interest. Then Jonah went shopping, acquiring

mining interests and prospecting rights in 15 other African states. Instead of confirming that any multinational company involving foreign owners will only exploit African labor and steal Africa's natural resources for the benefit of shareholders overseas, Rawlings and Jonah have turned Ashanti into a model for made-in-Africa industrialization.

Modernization is also the byword of Nat Nii Amar Nuno-Amarteifio, the mayor of Accra, a sprawling port city that in 20 years will be home to 50% of Ghana's population. Rawlings has just launched an ambitious plan known as Vision 2020, aimed at making Ghana a middle-income country by then. Part of that is spinning off responsibility for local governance to district assemblies, shifting the jobs of housing, feeding, educating and picking up the garbage of Ghana's population to trained technocrats like Nuno-Amarteifio. Local government was career exile before decentralization; now, says the mayor with gusto, "it is where reality catches up with even the best politicians. If we don't make things work here, then we become Liberia."

Nii Quaynor saw what modernization can do when he went to study computer science in the U.S. But when he returned home in 1969 to spread the technology gospel, "I was too advanced. Computer science was too new." Twenty-four years later, Quaynor finally hooked his country into the Web. In 1993 his company brought the Internet to West Africa, and in 1995 Ghana became the second sub-Saharan nation to have full connectivity. "We're sharing the same information as everyone else in the world," says Quaynor. His most prized client: President Rawlings, an avid Web surfer. Soon, Quaynor hopes, wireless technology will let the phone-short country leap straight into airborne access.

Farsighted enterprise is also the business of women in Ghana, and the prospect of making money brought Sarah Galloway Hage-Ali back from a comfortable life in England. In 1994 Hage-Ali bought Accra-based Sapad Manufacturing Co., Ghana's only maker of sanitary napkins. Changing the company's name to Fay International, she revamped its marketing philosophy into an ambitious campaign to teach Ghana's often infected women to use her hygienic product. Only 15% to 20% of Ghanaian women use sanitary towels; genital ailments are among the most prevalent problems of women patients. In the past two years, the company has conducted more than 30 workshops, bringing its message to secondary schools, village associations, market traders.

Lucia Quachey, president of the Ghana Association of Women Entrepreneurs, is proud that Hage-Ali is showing the world the other side of the African woman. "Not just the woman with the child on her back, pregnant, wood on her head," she explains, "but the African women who operate computers, who employ people, who generate resources to help in the growth of the national economy." Those are the women Nana Konadu Agyemang Rawlings, Ghana's First Lady, has drawn into the biggest and best-organized women's association in Ghana, the 31st December Women's Movement, named after the day her husband took over the country. Before, she says, "we did not ask for our due; we were not politicized."

Five-year-old Fridous Abu Tofic is learning simple arithmetic along with 295 other preschoolers because the movement opened a day-care center in Nima, a Muslim enclave in one of Accra's poorest and most neglected neighborhoods. 31st December runs tree-planting programs, immunizes children, offers family-planning services and initiates rural-development projects. Once funded by foreign donors, it now gets 95% of its operating funds from income-generating programs, one of which provides the army with bread and a local staple called *kenkey*. The movement, claiming some 1.5 million members, even produces a children's television program. "We have changed the face of Ghanaian women," says Mrs. Rawlings.

YOU MIGHT CALL IT A SECOND-CHANCE African revolution. What every country striding forward shows is that progress comes first to those who adopt the principles and practices of capitalist democracy. There are some common lessons here that any African nation can learn: free-market economics works, including privatization, entrepreneurship and often the stern measures of wholesale reform to jump-start failed economies. So does agricultural self-sufficiency, starting from the bottom up. And decentralization, spreading development outside urban capitals to the vast rural majority. And women's empowerment.

Other elements may be harder to acquire but are no less essential: Good governance,

---

DIVIDING LINE

Jack E. White

My Dungeon Shook

And so will Clinton's, at slavery's Door of No Return

I BROKE DOWN AND CRIED WHEN I STOOD IN THE DOOR OF No Return for the first time, nearly 20 years ago. Bill Clinton will too, when Joseph Ndiaye, the 74-year-old curator, holds up a rusty set of chains and begins his matter-of-fact recital of the mundane facts about the slave trade that flourished on Goree Island for more than 200 hundred years.

That little speck of rock in the harbor of Dakar, Senegal, is the black-American equivalent of Auschwitz or Treblinka, a blood-drenched monument to a genocidal past that all too often is ignored. On it stands the House of Slaves, where tens of thousands of Africans were herded into cramped holding pens to be fattened up for the Middle Passage to a life of slavery in the New World. Their last contact with the African motherland came at the Door of No Return, where they were whipped across a narrow gangplank to the slave ships.

When I stood in that doorway, looking out at the rolling Atlantic, and realized that some despairing, shackled ancestor of mine might have passed that way . . . well, in the words of a great Negro spiritual, "my dungeon shook" and I was moved beyond my power to describe it. After Hillary and Chelsea Clinton visited Goree Island last year, the First Lady declared it "one of the most heartbreaking monuments anywhere in the world." The Door of No Return, she said, "represents nothing less than the depths of human depravity."

Hillary insisted that Goree Island be included on the President's African tour, according to White House sources, because she felt it would be the emotional high point of his trip. Of course, she knows her man. This is a President who connects with blacks so strongly that some of us jokingly maintain that he's only passing for white. No President has forged such abiding personal relationships with African Americans, or put so many in positions of real authority. That helps to explain why blacks, more than any other group, have remained loyal to Clinton through his current ordeal: we've been treating him like one of our own. Just as black voters re-elected Marion Barry to a fourth term as mayor of Washington after his drug conviction, and black parishioners refused to oust the Rev. Henry Lyons from the leadership of the National Baptist Convention after he allegedly embezzled hundreds of thousands of dollars, we're sticking with the President come hell, high water, or a new plague of bimbos. As Jesse Jackson, who has become Clinton's Billy Graham, puts it, blacks tend to reject the sin but not the sinner. We believe in forgiveness—when transgressors ask for it.

Clinton should keep that in mind when he considers his response to the clamor from the Congressional Black Caucus for an official apology for slavery. White House spokesman Mike McCurry has already declared that the President will not make such a gesture on this trip because "that is not an issue that is central in the minds of many Americans." But surely Clinton knows that it is on the minds of many African Americans, who are convinced that the great rift between the races cannot be healed until America seeks forgiveness for one of the most monstrous eras in history. What better place to ask forgiveness than Goree Island, the scene of the crime?

caring for the welfare of the people, not the potentates. New leaders, pragmatic and progressive, honest and efficient in their exercise of power. Eritrea's President Issaias is but one of them, along with South Africa's Nelson Mandela, Uganda's Yoweri Museveni, Rwanda's Paul Kagame, Botswana's Quett Ketumile Masire. National reconciliation where necessary, national cohesion everywhere, the sublimation of narrow loyalties to a larger good.

You will note that there is not yet much stable democracy. Mali is still struggling to institutionalize democratic practices, and Rawlings still runs Ghana after two questionable elections. Neither of these countries—along with Eritrea and Mozambique—qualifies as anything other than a one-party state, despite token oppositions. Many African leaders, good and bad, share Museveni's belief that real multiparty elections are a luxury these fragile states cannot afford until they have the education, the middle class, the rule of law and the firm economic base on which American-style democracy rests.

But it's easy to see only the Africa that's broken. While many of these countries cannot quite stand on their own, what they want from the West is no longer just a benefactor but a partner. Although the U.S. trade-liberalization bill passed two weeks ago by the House of Representatives is mostly symbolic in easing the terms for America's minuscule trade with Africa, it moves in the right direction of shifting aid from handouts to the development of sustainable economies.

There is a word we heard over and over in Africa: *ubuntu.* It's different in every dialect, but the meaning is always roughly the same: a complex, highly nuanced precept governing the way individuals relate to the community. *Ubuntu* is the organizing principle of the African mind, defining the pre-eminence of the interests of the community over the individual, the duties and responsibilities the individual owes the community, the obligation of the individual to share what he has with the community. It is both blessing and curse, the root of Africa's strong families and social customs and the root cause of its debilitating corruption and crime. Yet as the continent embraces Western ways, its people do not want to lose everything African. What we need to encourage—what Africa needs to make for itself—is lives and systems that mesh modernization with an African way of doing things. That's what works.

> The United States and the countries of Asia "have been curiously slow in adding narcotics to the diplomatic agenda, unable to move beyond pious expressions of concern to tackle the problem together. What happened to the anticipated Golden Age of multilateral cooperation that was to have unfolded in Asia in the post–cold war era?"

Asia's Drug Menace and the Poverty of Diplomacy

JAMES SHINN

Optimists on both sides of the Pacific hoped that the end of the cold war would also hasten the end of Asia's undeclared drug war. Rapid economic development would ease the grinding poverty that fostered both poppy cultivation and narcotics addiction, political liberalization would root out corrupt officials and impose the rule of law on criminal dealers, and multilateral cooperation by Pacific Rim governments would crush Asia's *narcotrafficantes*.

The optimists were wrong.

Rising incomes have stimulated demand for narcotics throughout the region, creating a booming market for opium cultivators in the rural backwaters left untouched by Asia's economic miracle. Politicians and police in Asian democracies have shown themselves no more immune to "donations" from drug syndicates than their counterparts in South or North America. Meanwhile, lingering suspicion, bureaucratic distaste, and multilateral sloth impede regional efforts to suppress the drug trade; the Association of Southeast Asian Nations (ASEAN), the Asia Pacific Economic Cooperation (APEC) forum, and the UN have been equally impotent in addressing the foreign policy problem of narcotics.

THE MIRACLE'S OTHER SIDE

Asia's rising economic tide has made the drug problem worse, since the demand for narcotics increases with higher income levels. Higher incomes also lead to more variety in drug consumption. Hmong tribesmen in the Vietnamese highlands may still smoke raw opium, but urban Asians can choose from a wide assortment of refined narcotics that range from heroin, cocaine, and crystal methamphetamine (known as "ice") to so-called designer drugs—synthetic narcotics or hallucinogens—such as Ecstasy. The narcotics problem in Asia is not primarily an issue of drug smuggling from the Golden Triangle to the United States but of new consumption patterns on both sides of the Pacific (the Golden Triangle is the traditional opium-growing region that incorporates parts of northern Thailand, eastern Burma, and western Laos).

Laos is a classic example of this change in consumption habits: Laotian addicts now consume almost half the estimated 200 metric tons of opium produced in Laos each year, most of which used to be exported. Overall, at least 50 percent of the 3,000 metric tons of opium grown in Asia is consumed within the region.[1] Ominously, Asia has become the largest and fastest-growing narcotics market in the world, accounting for 40 percent of world consumption. The number of drug addicts in the region is huge: 1.2 million heroin addicts in Thailand and 400,000 in Burma, and 500,000 ice addicts in Japan. China has 500,000 registered heroin addicts, but estimates of the actual number range from 1 million to 2 million.

Along with higher incomes, rapid urbanization and internal migration are fueling this explosion in demand. Asian megacities such as Jakarta, Bangkok, and Guangdong are ringed with teeming slums where young men and women are cut off from their rural roots and community support networks. China has at least 100 million people drifting around the country in search of work. The onslaught of "modernity" corrodes traditional values quickly, and drug consumption is a tempting form of relief and recreation.

Soaring drug demand has been accompanied by supply-side improvements in price, quality, and delivery. For example, heroin street prices in the United States have fallen by two-thirds over the past 15 years, from $3,400 per gram in 1981 to $1,200 per gram in 1995, and purity has soared from 15 percent to 50 percent because of better production technology in Asia and more sophisticated smuggling around the Pacific.

JAMES SHINN *was a senior fellow at the Council on Foreign Relations from 1993 to 1997. He is the editor of the forthcoming book* Fires across the Water: Transnational Problems and Asian Politics *(New York: Council on Foreign Relations Press).*

---

[1] These production and consumption figures are based on Stephen Flynn's chapter, "Asian Narcotics: Rethinking the War," in James Shinn, ed., *Fires across the Water: Transnational Problems and Asian Politics* (New York: Council on Foreign Relations Press, forthcoming).

PUTTING GLOBALIZATION TO WORK

The Chinese criminal gangs that traffic most of Asia's narcotics have moved drug production labs into the jungles of Southeast Asia, near the opium harvest, taking advantage of better equipment and more easily obtainable precursor chemicals used in the refining process. These smaller portable labs can also be used to "cook" methamphetamines (a smelly and potentially dangerous process) and synthesize designer drugs. Taiwanese criminal syndicates have moved their ice production sites to China's coastal provinces such as Fujian, just as many legitimate Taiwanese chemical companies have moved their bulk production to the mainland while supplying complex precursor ingredients from Taiwan.

The entrepreneurs behind this production innovation, Chinese criminal "triads" such as the Sun Yee On, Wo Hop To, United Bamboo, and the 14K gang, are equally skilled in delivering the finished product throughout Asia and to the United States and Europe. Narcotics are produced locally but sold globally.

Two-thirds of the world's opium is grown in Southeast Asia, most of it in Burma, whose annual output is estimated at 2,500 metric tons (which equals 250 metric tons of heroin), grown under the protection of local drug warlords such as Khun Sa and his Mong Tai "Army." Once refined, the heroin is transported south to Bangkok where it is shipped to the wider world, or northeast across the border into China's Yunnan province and then overland to Guangdong and Hong Kong, where the triads can tap into the global shipping network. Chinese authorities were shocked in April 1996 when they stumbled across 600 kilograms of heroin in Guangdong on its way to Hong Kong.

The triads have formed strategic alliances with other criminal organizations to distribute the entire pharmacopoeia of narcotics and to launder the resulting cash flow. The triads, for example, supply ice to Japanese *yakuza* or criminal gangs, such as the Inagawa-gai and the Yamaguchi-gumi, who import rather than produce most of Japan's methamphetamine supply. They also assist the yakuza in recycling their revenues offshore, frequently through real estate investments in Asian cities or in Hawaii. The triads also work closely with Nigerian smuggling rings that supply Europe with Asian heroin, and with Latin American gangs, such as the infamous Cali syndicate, trading Burmese heroin for Colombian cocaine to satisfy Asia's burgeoning crack market.

One of the engines of Asia's economic dynamism—free trade in goods and liberalized financial transactions—also makes it easy for the triads to smuggle narcotics and launder the revenues. In Taiwan, 3.8 million marine shipping containers arrive each year at the major ports of Keelung and Kaohsiung. Of these, 1.8 million are labeled transit containers; Taiwan Customs ignores these and merely samples the other 2 million containers on a random basis, resulting in an inspection—often cursory—of only about 300,000 containers.[2]

It is clear that even with the best of intentions, Taiwan's Customs authorities are overwhelmed by the scale of their country's trade—it would require an army of agents just to inspect the marine container traffic (United States Customs estimates that it takes 5 agents 3 hours to fully inspect a standard marine container). In the region's many free-trade zones, such as the ports of Hong Kong and Macau, Masan and Iri in South Korea, Batam in Indonesia, and China's special economic zones of Shenzhen, Zhuhai, Xiamen, and Shantou, there is no customs revenue to be gained from inspecting freight traffic, so the authorities do not even try to inspect for drugs. Asia's stream of narcotics simply vanishes in the vast river of Asian commerce.

Laundered drug money is even more difficult to trace. By "chaining" money transfers between multiple institutions (that is, making multiple transfers back-to-back), triads can effectively delete a paper trail. Even if law enforcement authorities successfully trace a transactions needle through a funds-transfer haystack, they often end up stymied by bank confidentiality. No longer an exclusive feature of the Channel or Cayman Islands banks, such confidentiality is now offered to Asian customers at new offshore banking facilities on the Pacific Islands of Vanuatu, Samoa, and Nauru.

But the triads do not need to travel so far. With its unregulated and sophisticated financial markets, Hong Kong—the city built on the nineteenth-century opium trade—remains the Mecca of money laundering in Asia. The city's authorities have long turned a blind eye to this activity. A senior Chinese official bitterly observed to the author in June 1996 that "Soon we will recover Hong Kong from the British, who are already complaining that we will wreck the colony's rule of law. What rule of law? [This is] the transshipment point for most of Asia's narcotics, the place where most of the drug money is laundered, and where the triad criminals hide their investments in bank accounts or flats on Victoria Peak. If we move into Hong Kong in 1997 and clean up this nest of thieves, the Western press will pillory us for trampling on the colony's civil rights."

MONEY'S CORROSIVE POLITICAL INFLUENCE

Not only have economic growth, free trade, and unfettered financial flows compounded Asia's narcotics problem, but political liberalization and democratization throughout the region have failed to deliver on the promise of imposing "law and order" on the drug trade.

It is ironic that criminal triads have been among the first beneficiaries of the transition from "hard" to "soft" authoritarianism in Vietnam and China. When an authoritarian state begins to liberalize, it creates more space free of government—space where criminals can thrive as easily as other citizens under the protection of law and due process. Law enforcement becomes essentially reactive: the police cannot simply swoop down on triads or yakuza and arrest their members. Once jailed, due process makes it harder to hold criminals; it also imposes rules governing evidence and property seizure, and forces the state to at least go through the motions of a trial.

The political transition of states such as China and Vietnam has also compounded the pervasive corruption among police and customs officials and in the justice system and the armed forces.

---

[2] See Flynn, op. cit.

Why fight the police when you can buy political protection?

It is a mark of China's openness to the world trade system that customs officials no longer strictly regulate what crosses its borders. This has been a boon to the triads which, with modest gratuities to poorly paid Chinese officials, can now transit China with ease en route to Hong Kong. Vietnam is increasingly permeable for the same reason; the 1997 United States State Department's *International Narcotics Control Strategy Report* concludes that "corruption is endemic at all levels of the Socialist Republic of Vietnam's police and military authorities."

Authoritarian states in Asia do not have a monopoly on corruption: politicians in Asia's democracies are as cash hungry as their counterparts in Latin America and the United States. Money is the mother's milk of electoral politics in Japan, South Korea, Taiwan, Thailand, and Malaysia, and criminal syndicates are eager contributors to campaign coffers.

Why fight the police when you can buy political protection? The triads and the yakuza closely studied Colombia's narcotraficantes. They saw that the Medellín cartel, which virtually declared war on the government, killing 250 judges and even the minister of justice, provoked a campaign by the government that ultimately crushed their syndicate. The Cali cartel eschewed such violence. Instead, it quietly injected cash into the electoral process, including contributions to the campaign of President Ernesto Samper, and remained in business.

In Asia, the triads sometimes cross the line between smuggling and participating directly in politics, as in the case of Thanong Siriprechapong, a member of the Thai Parliament who was extradited to the United States in January 1996 on narcotrafficking charges. The influence of drug money on Thai politics is pervasive: parliament has refused to pass a bill that would make it more difficult to disguise drug money, despite numerous entreaties from the United States. This has led the State Department to complain that "Thailand's sophisticated banking system and an active quasi-legal non-bank financial system provide a hospitable climate for money launderers."

GEOPOLITICAL ROADBLOCKS...

Public opinion polls in Asia and North America regularly put narcotics near the top of the list of international problems. It is the most salient of all "global government" concerns, such as illegal migration or pollution, and easily the most intrusive in the daily life and personal security of the average citizen. Narcotics busts, tales of addiction, and violent, drug-related crimes grab headlines on a regular basis. But governments on both sides of the Pacific have been curiously slow in adding narcotics to the diplomatic agenda, unable to move beyond pious expressions of concern to tackle these problems together. What happened to the anticipated Golden Age of multilateral cooperation that was supposed to unfold in Asia in the post–cold war era?

The passing of the cold war superpower standoff did not change Asian politics as dramatically as it transformed the political landscape of Europe. Two unresolved national unity problems—between China and Taiwan, and between the two Koreas—fuel a high level of suspicion in the region. And two failed states—Burma and Cambodia—are locked in violent internal struggles for power even as they provide a haven for narcotics production and organized crime.

The Burmese junta known as the State Peace and Development Council (formerly SLORC) remains locked in a civil war that has been waged in the country's northeastern provinces for decades, opposed by the Mong Tai Army, the Eastern Shan State Army, the Kachin Defense Army, and the so-called Myanmar National Democratic Alliance—which field tens of thousands of irregulars, heavily armed with automatic weapons and SAM-7 missiles. Narcotics money keeps these separatist armies in business, and the junta itself is too weak, too illegitimate, and too corrupt to put them out of business.

The Chinese government supports the Burmese junta for geopolitical reasons: Burma provides a window to the Indian Ocean for China's military, and it is a useful counterbalance to potentially hostile ASEAN states on China's southern borders. ASEAN, despite its ambivalence about the junta and its concern with the drug trade, has embraced Burma's military leadership as a counterbalance to Chinese influence in Southeast Asia.

The United States, appalled by the junta's violent 1988 repression of Burma's indigenous democratic movement and its imprisonment of pro-democracy leader Aung San Suu Kyi, has kept the junta at arm's length. Yet the United States Drug Enforcement Administration (DEA) retains a 3-person liaison office in the Burmese capital of Rangoon. Officials in Washington face a wrenching dilemma: Which is worse, the brutal junta or the narcotrafficking separatist groups? Which is better, standing by the human rights champions of Burma's democracy movement, or suppressing the flow of heroin to American cities?

China remains central to Asia's narcotics problem, as it does to Asia's other transnational problems, such as illegal migration and environmental pollution, because of its sheer size and the turbulence of its transformation from "hard" to "soft" authoritarian politics.

The Communist authorities in Beijing have long feared the triads as potentially subversive organizations, a suspicion that goes back to 1927, when Chiang Kai-shek's Nationalist government used triad gangsters to slaughter Communists. Since it came to power in 1949, the Communist Party has taken a strong stand against narcotics, beginning with a nationwide suppression campaign that detoxed 20 million addicts between 1950 and 1952. Today the authorities in Beijing are deeply concerned about a recent heroin plague and mounting disorder in southern provinces such as Yunnan, Guangxi, and Guizhou. In 1992 the government sent People's Liberation Army (PLA) troops with armored vehicles and tanks to regain control of the border town of Pingyuan, which had been taken over by narcotraffickers.

However, China's economic growth since 1978 has been built on granting more authority to the country's regions, especially the southern coastal provinces. In the absence of the rule of law, and as the prestige and legitimacy of the Communist Party decline, "local corporatism"—interlocking interests between the local party apparatus, the local administrative bureaucracy, and the local state security organs—has become the de facto government in much of China. This creates an environment in which criminal enterprise and narcotrafficking flourish.

Beijing finds it difficult to suppress China's growing narcotics business with an iron fist. In addition to resistance from local corporatist interests, the fist itself may be unreliable. Corrupt elements of the Public Security Bureau and the PLA are widely involved in the drug trade. Beijing's official tolerance of PLA involvement in private business has tempted many officers with the quick profits to be made from narcotics production and distribution. As China's senior party leaders compete to solidify their personal networks of support among the PLA, cracking down on military complicity in the drug trade is not an attractive policy option.

As a result, although low-level criminals are periodically arrested and often executed as part of nationwide anticrime campaigns, these campaigns rarely do much harm to the narcotics trade or higher-level traffickers. A lack of faith in the integrity of Chinese law enforcement has made cooperation with foreign law enforcement difficult. This distrust is reciprocated; according to the United States State Department's 1997 narcotics report, Chinese authorities refused to allow the FBI and the DEA to establish offices in Beijing after an American court "ordered the release of alleged Chinese drug trafficker Wang Zongxiao, who had originally been escorted to the U.S. by Chinese police in 1989 to testify as a witness on the understanding that he would return to China."

The Wang case is a classic example of the pitfalls that hinder both bilateral and multilateral cooperation to solve transnational problems such as narcotics. The legal and institutional bases for cooperation in law enforcement are weak in Asia. For example, the United States lacks an extradition treaty with many countries in the region, such as Burma and Indonesia, and even where a treaty exists, as with Thailand, it requires enormous pressure to extradite an alleged trafficker for trial in the United States. Conversely, few American judges are eager to entrust an American citizen facing a drug charge to the tender mercies of Asian police.

... AND MULTILATERAL ROADBLOCKS

Bilateral attempts to deal with narcotics are inevitably infused with bilateral tensions, and narcotraffickers can easily elude bilateral crackdowns by slipping through third countries; therefore much faith has been placed in the efficacy of multilateral institutions to construct a common framework of policies to suppress demand and interdict smugglers. The UN has passed a series of conventions and protocols on narcotics, culminating in the UN International Drug Control Program in 1991, which consolidated a variety of efforts. In 1996 the UN also coordinated a memorandum on controlling the trade in narcotics precursor chemicals and on trafficking with Burma, Cambodia, China, Laos, Thailand, and Vietnam. Unfortunately, funding for the UN programs has been

sparse, and few would argue that they have made much of a dent in Asia's narcotics markets.

ASEAN has also dealt with narcotics, and the ASEAN ministers periodically issue statements deploring the problem. A special ASEAN forum was created to focus on the problem, but it has done little other than host regional seminars on treatment and law enforcement. Lack of funding is one problem, but a more serious roadblock is ASEAN's consensus decision-making style. With some high officials in Burma, Cambodia, and Thailand compromised by the narcotics trade, it is not difficult to see how ASEAN's progress on narcotics would be glacial.

APEC has a similar problem. Its larger umbrella covers not only Asia's drug-producing regions, but also the big markets—China, Japan, and the United States. Beijing has adamantly opposed expanding APEC's charter to deal with problems such as narcotics for fear that other, more sensitive political issues, such as Taiwan or the South China Sea islands dispute, might make their way onto the agenda.

Once narcotics become a multilateral agenda item, diplomats are not comfortable with the topic. Narcotrafficking can be fairly technical, and controlling it requires close cooperation between law enforcement agencies, which are rarely internationalist in any country. Nor does a diplomat want to be "typed" as a narcotics specialist.

Moreover, there are few organized domestic constituencies to applaud multilateral successes in narcotics control or to press governments to negotiate multilateral agreements. The nongovernmental organizations (NGOS) that have been vocal and frequently successful in lobbying for multilateral agreements on the environment or for labor standards have been conspicuously absent from the narcotics debate.

Many groups also oppose tough regulations to crack down on smuggling or money laundering, especially business firms whose shipping or financial interests would be complicated by such regulations. Suppressing the supply of narcotics in Asia requires more government and more regulation, not less; it requires movement against the current of liberalization and deregulation that has powerful advocates in the United States and Asia.

The apathy of officials, the silence of NGOS, and resistance from the business community in the Asian narcotics debate reflect the deep ambivalence toward drug policy that impedes solutions in Asia as well as in the United States. What combination of supply and demand suppression will be effective against the narcotics menace? Is it merely a fool's errand to spend money and political capital on interdiction efforts if the underlying demand for narcotics is so huge? Can demand suppression be dealt with independently of problems such as illegal migration, poverty, and poor health care in the United States and Asia?

Finally, are the Asian nations, authoritarian and liberal alike, prepared to pay the price of interfering with free trade and finance that effective interdiction will require, and—above all—declaring war on the criminal syndicates that have so deeply intertwined themselves with Asian politics?

Unit Selections

Key Points to Consider

❖ Are violent conflicts and warfare increasing or decreasing today? Explain your response.

❖ What changes have taken place in recent years in the types of conflicts that occur and in who participates?

❖ How is military doctrine changing to reflect new political realities?

❖ How is the role of the United States in global security likely to change? What about Russia and China?

❖ Are nuclear weapons more or less likely to proliferate in the post–cold war era? Why?

❖ What institutional structures can be developed to reduce the danger of nuclear war?

 **Links**   # www.dushkin.com/online/

These sites are annotated on pages 6 and 7.

Do you lock your door at night? Do you secure your personal property to avoid theft? These are basic questions that have to do with your sense of personal safety and security. Most people take steps to protect what they have, including their lives. The same is true for groups of people, including countries.

In the international arena, governments frequently pursue their national interest by entering into mutually agreeable "deals" with other governments. Social scientists call these types of arrangements "exchanges" (i.e., each side gives up something in order to gain something it values even more). In simple terms, it goes something like this: "I have the oil that you need. I will sell it to you if in turn you will sell me the agricultural products that I lack." Whether on a personal level ("If you help me with my homework, then I will drive you home this weekend") or on the governmental level, this is the process used by most individuals and groups to "secure" and protect what is of value. The exchange process, however, can break down. When threats and punishments replace mutual exchanges, conflict ensues. Neither side benefits, and there are costs to both. Each side may use threats and hope that the other will capitulate, but if efforts at intimidation and coercion fail, the conflict may escalate into violent confrontation.

With the end of the cold war, the issues of national security are changing for the world's major powers. Old alliances are changing, not only in Europe but in the Middle East as well. These changes have great policy implications not only for the major powers but also for participants in regional conflicts. Agreements between the leadership of the now-defunct Soviet Union and the United States led to the elimination of support for participants in low-intensity conflicts in Central America, Africa, and Southeast Asia. Fighting the cold war by proxy is now a thing of the past. Nevertheless, there is no shortage of conflicts in the world today.

The unit begins with a discussion of the post–cold war world and the emergence of new patterns of conflict. This is followed by a description of the types of conflicts that are likely to dominate and the challenges of keeping them from escalating into warfare. Then, specific case studies address ethnic violence, terrorism, China's and Russia's security problems, and the spread of nuclear weapons.

The unit concludes by examining one of the most important issues in history—the avoidance of nuclear war. Many experts initially predicted that the collapse of the Soviet Union would decrease the threat of nuclear war. However, many now believe that the threat has increased as control of nuclear weapons has become less centralized and the command structure less reliable. What these dramatically different circumstances mean for strategic weapons policy in the United States is also a topic of considerable debate. With this changing political context as the backdrop, the prospects for arms control and increased international cooperation are reviewed.

Like all the other global issues described in this anthology, international conflict is a dynamic problem. It is important to understand that it is not a random event, but there are patterns and trends. Forty-five years of cold war established a variety of patterns of international conflict as the superpowers contained each other with vast expenditures of money and technological know-how. The consequence of this stalemate was a shift to the developing world as the arena of conflict by superpower proxy. With the end of the cold war, these patterns are changing. Will there be more nuclear proliferation, or will there be less? Will the emphasis be shifted to low-intensity conflicts related to the interdiction of drugs or will some other issue determine the world's hot spots? Or will economic problems turn the industrial world inward and allow a new round of ethnically motivated conflicts to become brutally violent, as we have seen in Yugoslavia and its former republic, Bosnia-Herzegovina? The answers to these and related questions will determine the patterns of conflict in the post–cold war era.

The Post-Modern State and the World Order

Robert Cooper

ROBERT COOPER, A BRITISH DIPLOMAT BASED IN BONN, IS PERHAPS THE MOST INSIGHTFUL GEOPOLITICAL THINKER OF THE PRESENT MOMENT. THIS ARTICLE, THE FIRST PART OF WHICH APPEARED IN THE SUMMER 1997 ISSUE OF *NPQ*, HAS BEEN PUBLISHED IN PAMPHLET FORM BY DEMOS, A THINK TANK AND PUBLISHING HOUSE IN LONDON.

A COPY MAY BE OBTAINED BY CONTACTING DEMOS BY PHONE AT 011-44-171-353-4479 OR BY FAX AT 011-44-171-353-4481 OR E-MAIL @ DEMOS.CO.UK, WEBSITE: WWW.DEMOS.CO.UK.

THE OPINIONS EXPRESSED IN THIS ARTICLE ARE THE AUTHOR'S OWN AND SHOULD NOT BE TAKEN AS AN EXPRESSION OF OFFICIAL GOVERNMENT POLICY.

BONN—This is a new world, but there is neither a new world order—to use the phrase that was fashionable in the early 1990s; nor is there a new world disorder—to use the phrase that is more fashionable today. Instead there is a zone of safety in Europe, and outside it a zone of danger and a zone of chaos.

A world divided into three needs a threefold security policy and a threefold mindset. Neither is easy to achieve.

Before we can think about the security requirements for today and tomorrow, we have to forget the security rules of yesterday. The 20th century has been marked by absolutes. The war against Hitler and the struggle against communism had to be won. The only possible policy was absolute victory, unconditional surrender.

In the more complex and more ambiguous post–Cold War world we shall not face the same total threats or need to use the same total war against them. We have to forget therefore that the only purpose of the military is to win complete victories. In none of the three worlds that we live in will this be appropriate.

SECURITY AND THE POST-MODERN ZONE

There may be no new world order but there is a new European security order. Our task must be to preserve and extend it. Broadly speaking that is what European countries are doing. The task is to promote open democratic institutions, open market economies and open multilateral/transnational diplomacy with as many of our neighbors as possible. Among ourselves we have to maintain these habits and to improve them in the hope that the key transnational institutions—the EU and NATO—will eventually acquire some of the permanence and solidity that our national institutions enjoy. That means essentially acquiring more loyalty and more legitimacy.

> There is a zone of safety in Europe, and outside it a zone of danger and a zone of chaos.

The key question for European security, in the narrow sense, will be how Russia turns out. It must be our central interest to draw Russia into the post-modern European system. That means not just exporting democracy and markets but also bringing Russia into our system of multilateral diplomacy. This cannot be achieved overnight; for the moment, our goal should not be to close off any options. If the Russians decide to retreat to the old system of security by military power, that, regrettably, is their business. Our policy should be to do everything possible to make the alternative course of security by confidence and cooperation—that is to say post-modern security—possible and attractive to them.

 From *New Perspectives Quarterly*, Special Issue 1997, pp. 48-55. © 1998 by Blackwell Publishers. Reprinted by permission.

Advice for the post-modern state: Never forget that security can be achieved more by cooperation than by competition.

SECURITY AND THE MODERN WORLD

Dealing with the modern world, the world of ambitious states, requires a different approach. If eventually these states decide to join a post-modern system of open diplomacy, so much the better; but this will take time, and between now and then lie many dangers. The Gulf War provides an illustration both of the dangers and of how they should be dealt with. One ambitious state attacks another, threatening vital Western interests. In the case of the Gulf War, the interests in question were twofold: first, the maintenance of a plurality of states in an area of the world containing vital oil supplies (in global energy terms this is a policy similar to the traditional British requirement that there should be a plurality of powers on the European continent). The second interest was to ensure that a dangerous and ambitious state did not get its hands on weapons that could ultimately threaten the West itself. Had Saddam Hussein been allowed to retain Kuwait, he would have become the geopolitical master of the Gulf; and the wealth available to him would have financed whatever weapons program he desired.

> Never forget that security can be achieved more by cooperation than by competition.

The Western response was precisely as it should be: build the most powerful coalition possible, reverse the aggression, punish the aggressor, deal with the weapons programs. These limited goals required limited means. They did not imply that Iraq should be invaded or occupied or that Saddam Hussein should be removed from power (attractive is that idea undoubtedly is). The reference point for a war of this nature is the 18th or 19th century, not the 20th-century wars of absolutes. The Gulf War was a war of interests, not a clash of ideologies.

Note that the reasons for fighting this war were not that Iraq had violated the norms of international behavior. Unfortunately, the reality of the world is that if you invade a country which lies some way outside the vital interests of the powerful, you will probably get away with it. Very likely you will be condemned and your gains will not be recognized (if you choose to keep them); you will lose trust and reputation; you may suffer economic sanctions for a while. But you will not be attacked by the powerful. If India were to invade Nepal, for example, or Argentina Paraguay, it is unlikely that a Gulf War coalition would be put together to reverse the result.

The initial enthusiasm for the idea of a new world order that followed the Gulf War was based on the hope that the UN was going to function as originally intended: a world authority policing international law, that is to say a collective-security organization. In one sense that hope was not unreasonable. The end of the Cold War took us back to 1945. Institutions which had grown up because of or against the background of the Cold War, such as NATO or the EU, began to look in need of radical change. The UN was a pre–Cold War institution and, therefore, might become a workable post–Cold War institution. Up to a point this proved to be the case. The UN is more active today than it ever was during the Cold War (between 1946 and 1990 there were 683 Security Council Resolutions; in the period since then there have been more than 350; and, at the same time, there are some half a million UN troops in the field today).

> The reality of the world is that if you invade a country which lies some way outside the vital interests of the powerful, you will probably get away with it.

The UN is, however, active in peacekeeping and humanitarian work rather than as a collective-security organization.

A collective-security order is one in which the international community enforces international law on recalcitrant states. This would certainly be a new order in the sense that we have never seen anything of the kind in the history of international relations. Unfortunately we are never likely to see it either.

The complaint of many people about the UN's role in Yugoslavia is precisely that it is not enforcing international law. But then it is quite clear that no one is willing to do that. Perhaps that is just as well. War is a serious business. It is dangerous to get involved in wars for principles; one risks finding oneself in the position of the Americans in Vietnam, that "sometimes you have to kill people in order to save them." And in the end, because wars fought for other people are difficult to sustain in domestic opinion, one may end up not even saving them. War is, and should be, a last resort: The world would surely be a safer and more peaceful place if countries fought only when there are vital interests to defend. Some mistook the Gulf War as a war for principles or a collective-security action—and indeed the political rhetoric at the time fostered this impression. In fact, it was a collective defense of interests by the West. The Gulf War was fought to protect an old order, not to create a new one.

In a different sense though, a collective-security order would not really be new. Collective security is a combination of two old ideas: stability through balance and stability through hegemony. The *status quo* is maintained by a world body of overwhelming power (the hegemonic element), which throws its weight on the side of a state which is the victim of aggression—the balance of power, that is, with the world community as the balancing actor. This is the old world of state sovereignty in which others do not interfere, of coalitions, of security through military force. The UN-as-a-collective-security-organization, is there to defend the *status quo* and not to create a new order.

> The UN-as-a-collective-security-organization, is there to defend the status quo and not to create a new order.

For the post-modern state there is, therefore, a difficulty. We need to get used to the idea of double standards. Among ourselves we operate on the basis of laws and open cooperative security. But when dealing with more old-fashioned kinds of states we need to revert to the rougher methods of an earlier era—force, preemptive attack, deception, whatever is necessary for those who still live in the 19th-century world of every state for itself.

Advice for post-modern states: Those who have friendly, law-abiding neighbors should not forget that in other parts of the world the law of the jungle reigns. Among ourselves, we keep the law but when we are operating in the jungle, we also must use the laws of the jungle. In the coming period of peace in Europe there will be a temptation to neglect our defenses, both physical and psychological. This represents one of the great dangers for the post-modern state.

SECURITY AND THE PRE-MODERN WORLD

What of the pre-modern chaos? What should we do with that? On the basis of rational calculation of interest, the answer should be: as little as possible. Chaos does not represent a threat, at least not the kind that requires a conventional military response. One may need to bar one's door against its byproducts—drugs, disease, refugees—but these are not threats to vital interests that call for armed Western intervention. To become involved in a zone of chaos is risky—if the intervention is prolonged it may become unsustainable in public opinion; if the intervention is unsuccessful it may be damaging to the government that ordered it.

Besides, what form should intervention take? The most logical way to deal with chaos is by colonization, or hegemony. But this is unacceptable to post-modern states. So if the goal is not colonization, what should it be? Usually the answer will be that the goals will be ambiguous.

> The most logical way to deal with chaos is by colonization, or hegemony.

The risk of "mission creep" is therefore considerable. Those who become involved in the pre-modern world run the risk that ultimately they will be there because they are there. All the conventional wisdom and all realistic doctrines of international affairs counsel against involvement in the pre-modern world.

And yet such "realistic" doctrines, for all their intellectual coherence, are not realistic. The post–Cold War, post-modern environment is one where foreign policy will be driven by domestic politics; and these will be influenced by the media and by moral sentiment. We no longer live in the world of pure national interest. Human rights and humanitarian problems inevitably play an important part in our policy-making.

A new world order may not be a reality but it is an important aspiration, especially for those who live in a new European order. The wish to protect individuals, rather than to resolve the security problems of states, is a part of the post-modern ethos. In a world where many states suffer breakdowns there is wide scope for humanitarian intervention. Northern Iraq, Somalia, Yugoslavia and Rwanda are only the beginning of a trend. Operations in these areas are a halfway house between the calculation of interest which tells you not to get involved and the moral feeling which tells the public that something must be done. In different ways all these operations have been directed toward helping civilians—against the military, the government or the chaos. The results are not always impressive and the interventions are in some respects half-hearted. That is because they dwell in the ambiguous half-world where interest tells you to stay out and conscience tells you to go in—between Hobbes and Kant. Such interventions may not solve problems, but they may salve the conscience. And they are not necessarily the worse for that.

> *Advice to post-modern states: accept that intervention in the pre-modern is going to be a fact of life.*

Thus we must reconcile ourselves to the fact that we are going to get involved in situations where interest and calculation would tell us to stay out. In this case there are some rules to observe. The first is to moderate the objectives to the means available. The wars of ideology called for total victory; in the pre-modern world victory is not a relevant objective.

Victory in the pre-modern world would mean empire. The post-modern power that is there to save the lives of individual civilians wants to stop short of that. In consequence, goals must be even more carefully defined than in wars of interest. They will be goals of relatives and not of absolutes: more lives saved, lower levels of violence among the local populations; and these must be balanced by low casualties for the interveners. At the same time we must be prepared to accept, indeed we must expect, failure a good deal of the time. And then we must be prepared to cut our loses and leave. The operation in Somalia was not a success for anybody. And yet it was not unreasonable to try (though perhaps the trial might have been better organized). It gave those responsible in Somalia a breathing space, a chance to sort themselves out. That they failed to take that chance was not the fault of the intervention force. It follows also that when intervening in the pre-modern world, Clausewitz doctrine still applies: War is the pursuit of politics by other means. Military intervention should always be accompanied by political efforts. If these fail, or if the cost of the military operation becomes too great, then there is no alternative but to withdraw.

Advice to post-modern states: accept that intervention in the pre-modern is going to be a fact of life. To make it less dangerous and more sustainable in the long run, there are four requirements: clear, limited objectives; means also with clear limits attached to them; a political process to parallel the military operation; and a decision, taken in advance, to withdraw if objectives are not achieved in a given time.

THE NEW EUROPEAN ORDER
This essay is intended to say many things, but especially to say this one thing. That there is no new world order is a common conception. But it is less widely understood that there is a new European order, new in that it is historically unprecedented and also new because it is based on new concepts. Indeed the order has to a large extent preceded the concepts. One commentator who fails to understand this—though he understands most other things better than the rest of us and describes them with great elegance and clarity—is Henry Kissinger. In a recent speech he said the following: "In a world of players of operationally more or less equal strength, there are only two roads to stability. One is hegemony and the other is equilibrium." This was the choice in the past, but today it no longer works. Balance is too dangerous; hegemony is no longer acceptable in a liberal world that values human rights and self-determination.

> *Hegemony is no longer acceptable in a liberal world that values human rights and self-determination.*

Instead there is a third possibility. In fact there have been three sets of alternatives: first came the choice between chaos and empire, or instability or hegemony. Then it was a choice between empire and nationalism, or hegemony or balance. Finally, today we have a choice between nationalism and integration, or balance or openness. Chaos is tamed by empire; empires are broken up by nationalism; nationalism gives way, we hope, to internationalism. At the end of the process is the freedom of the individual, first protected by the state and later protected from the state.

The kind of world we have depends on the kind of states that compose it. For the pre-modern world success is empire and failure is disorder; in the modern system success is balance and failure means falling back into war or into empire. For the post-modern state success means openness and transnational co-operation. The open state system is the ultimate consequence of the open society. Failure, we shall come to in a moment.

This categorization is not intended to be exclusive—the future is full of surprises (and so indeed is the past). Nor is it intended to represent some inevitable Hegelian progression. Progress it certainly represents, but there is nothing inevitable about it. In particular there is nothing inevitable about the survival of the post-modern state in what remains basically a hostile environment.

> It may be that in Western Europe the era of the strong state–1648 to 1989– has now passed.

The post-modern order faces three dangers. First there is the danger from the pre-modern. The risk here is one of being sucked in for reasons of conscience and then being unwilling either to conquer or to get out. In the end the process may be debilitating for morale and dangerous for military preparedness.

In that case the coup de grace would be administered from the modern world. States reared on raison d'état and power politics make uncomfortable neighbors for the post-modern democratic conscience. Supposing the world develops (as Kissinger suggests it might) into an intercontinental struggle. Would Europe be equipped for that? That is the second danger—the danger from the modern.

The third danger comes from within. A post-modern economy can have the result that people live only for themselves, and not at all for the community—the decline of birth rates in the West is already evidence of this tendency. There is a risk too that the deconstruction of the state may spill over into the deconstruction of society. In political terms an excess of transparency and an over-diffusion of power could lead to a state and to an international order in which nothing can be done, because there is no central focus of power or responsibility. We may all drown in complexity.

It may be that in Western Europe the era of the strong state—1648 to 1989—has now passed, and we are moving toward a system of overlapping roles and responsibilities with governments, international institutions and the private sector all involved but none of them entirely in control. Can it be made to work? We must hope so, and we must try.

> "Because of the global upsurge in ethnic and sectarian conflict, policymakers have become more attuned to the role played by [light] arms in sparking and sustaining low-level warfare and have begun to consider new constraints on trade in these munitions. ... Although heavy weapons sometimes play a role, most of the day-to-day fighting is performed by irregular forces armed only with rifles, grenades, machine guns, light mortars, and other 'man-portable' munitions."

The New Arms Race: Light Weapons and International Security

MICHAEL T. KLARE

For most of the past 50 years, analysts and policymakers have largely ignored the role of small arms and other light weapons in international security affairs, considering them too insignificant to have an impact on the global balance of power or the outcome of major conflicts. Nuclear weapons, ballistic missiles, and major conventional weapons (tanks, heavy artillery, jet planes) are assumed to be all that matter when calculating the strength of potential belligerents. As a result, international efforts to reduce global weapons stockpiles and to curb the trade in arms have been focused almost exclusively on major weapons systems. At no point since World War II have international policymakers met to consider curbs on trade in light weapons, or to restrict their production.

Recently, world leaders have begun to take a fresh interest in small arms and light weapons. Because of the global upsurge in ethnic and sectarian conflict, policymakers have become more attuned to the role played by such arms in sparking and sustaining low-level warfare, and have begun to consider new constraints on trade in these munitions. "I wish to concentrate on what might be called 'micro-disarmament,'" United Nations Secretary General Boutros Boutros-Ghali declared in January 1995. By that, he explained, "I mean practical disarmament in the context of the conflicts the United

Nations *is actually dealing with,* and of the weapons, most of them light weapons, that are actually killing people in the hundreds of thousands" (emphasis added).

This focus on the conflicts the United Nations is "actually dealing with" represents a major shift in global priorities. During the cold war, most world leaders were understandably preoccupied with the potential threat of nuclear war or an East-West conflict in Europe. Today policymakers are more concerned about the immediate threat of ethnic and sectarian warfare. While such violence does not threaten world security in the same catastrophic manner as nuclear conflict or another major war in Europe, it could, if left unchecked, introduce severe instabilities into the international system.

This inevitably leads, as suggested by Boutros-Ghali, to a concern with small arms, land mines, and other light munitions; these are the weapons, he notes, that "are probably responsible for most of the deaths in current conflicts." This is true, for instance, of the conflicts in Afghanistan, Algeria, Angola, Bosnia, Burma, Burundi, Cambodia, Kashmir, Liberia, Rwanda, Somalia, Sri Lanka, Sudan, Tajikistan, and Zaire. Although heavy weapons sometimes play a role, most of the day-to-day fighting is performed by irregular forces armed only with rifles, grenades, machine guns, light mortars, and other "man-portable" munitions.

SMALL ARMS, GLOBAL PROBLEMS

The centrality of light weapons in contemporary warfare is especially evident in the conflicts in Liberia and Somalia. In Liberia, rival bands of guerrillas—armed, for the most part,

---

MICHAEL T. KLARE *is a professor of peace and world security studies at Hampshire College and director of the Five College Program in Peace and World Security Studies. He is the author of* Rogue States and Nuclear Outlaws: America's Search for a New Foreign Policy *(New York: Hill and Wang, 1995).*

Light Weapons in Worldwide Circulation

ASSAULT RIFLES:
- **Russian/Soviet AK-47 and its successors**
- **U.S. M-16**
- **German G3**
- **Belgian FAL**
- **Chinese Type 56 (a copy of the AK-47)**
- **Israeli Galil (also a copy of the AK-47)**

MACHINE GUNS:
- **U.S. M-2 and M-60**
- **Russian/Soviet RPK and DShK**
- **German MG3**
- **Belgian MAG**
- **Chinese Type 67**

LIGHT ANTITANK WEAPONS:
- **U.S. M-20 and M-72 rocket launchers**
- **U.S. Dragon and TOW antitank missiles**
- **Russian/Soviet RPG-2 and RPG-7 rocket-propelled grenades (and Chinese variants, Types 56 and 69)**
- **French-German MILAN antitank missiles**

LIGHT MORTARS:
- **Produced by many countries in a variety of calibers, including 60 mm, 81 mm, 107 mm, and 120 mm.**

ANTIPERSONNEL LAND MINES:
- **U.S. M-18A1 "Claymore"**
- **Russian/Soviet PMN/PMN-2 & POMZ-2**
- **Belgian PRB-409**
- **Italian VS-50 and VS-69**
- **Chinese Types 69 and 72**

SHOULDER-FIRED ANTI-AIRCRAFT MISSILES:
- **U.S. Stinger**
- **Russian/Soviet SAM-7**
- **British Blowpipe**
- **Swedish RBS-70**

with AK-47 assault rifles—have been fighting among themselves for control of the country, bringing commerce to a standstill and driving an estimated 2.3 million people from their homes and villages. In Somalia, lightly armed militias have been similarly engaged, ravaging the major cities, paralyzing rural agriculture, and at one point pushing millions to the brink of starvation. In both countries, UN-sponsored peacekeeping missions have proved unable to stop the fighting or disarm the major factions.

The widespread use of antipersonnel land mines (small explosive devices that detonate when stepped on or driven over) is a common feature of many of these conflicts. These munitions, which can cost as little as $10 apiece, are planted in roads, markets, pastures, and fields to hinder agriculture and otherwise disrupt normal life. An estimated 85 million to 110

million uncleared mines are thought to remain in the soil of some 60 nations, with the largest concentrations in Afghanistan, Angola, Cambodia, and the former Yugoslavia. Each year some 25,000 civilians are killed, wounded, or maimed by land mines, and many more are driven from their homes and fields.

There are many reasons why small arms, mines, and other light weapons figure so prominently in contemporary conflicts. The belligerents involved tend to be insurgents, ethnic separatists, brigands, and local warlords with modest resources and limited access to the international arms market. While usually able to obtain a variety of light weapons from black-market sources or through theft from government arsenals, they can rarely afford or gain access to major weapons systems. Furthermore, such forces are usually composed of ill-trained volunteers who can be equipped with simple infantry weapons but who lack the expertise to operate and maintain heavier and more sophisticated equipment.

Logistical considerations also mitigate against the acquisition of heavy weapons. Lacking access to major ports or airfields and operating largely in secrecy, these forces must rely on clandestine and often unreliable methods of supply that usually entail the use of small boats, pack animals, civilian vehicles, and light planes. These methods are suitable for delivering small arms and ammunition, but not heavy weapons. Tanks, planes, and other major weapons also require large quantities of fuel, which is not easily transported by such rudimentary methods.

The character of ethnic and sectarian warfare further reinforces the predominance of light weapons. The usual objective of armed combat between established states is the defeat and destruction of an adversary's military forces; the goal of ethnic warfare, however, is not so much victory on the battlefield as it is the slaughter or the intimidation of members of another group and their forced abandonment of homes and villages ("ethnic cleansing"). In many cases a key objective is to exact retribution from the other group for past crimes and atrocities, a task best achieved through close-up violence that typically calls for the use of handheld weapons: guns, grenades, and machetes.

While the weapons employed in these clashes are relatively light and unsophisticated, their use can result in human carnage of horrendous proportions. The 1994 upheaval in Rwanda resulted in the deaths of as many as 1 million people and forced millions more to flee their homeland. Similarly, the fighting in Bosnia is believed to have taken the lives of 200,000 people and has produced millions of refugees.

Although the availability of arms is not in itself a cause of war, the fact that likely belligerents in internal conflicts are able to procure significant supplies of light weapons has certainly contributed to the duration and intensity of these contests. Before the outbreak of violence in Rwanda, for example, the Hutu-dominated government spent millions of dollars on rifles, grenades, machine guns, and machetes that were distributed to the army and militia forces later implicated in the systematic slaughter of Tutsi civilians. In Afghanistan, the fact that the various factions were provided with so many weapons by the two superpowers during the cold war has meant that bloody internecine warfare could continue long after Moscow and Washington discontinued their supply operations. The ready availability of light weapons has also contributed to the persistence of violence in Angola, Kashmir, Liberia, Sri Lanka, and Sudan.

The widespread diffusion of light weapons in conflict areas has also posed a significant hazard to UN peacekeeping forces sent to police cease-fires or deliver humanitarian aid. Even when the leaders of major factions have agreed to the introduction of peacekeepers, local warlords and militia chieftains have continued to fight to control their territory. Fighting persisted in Somalia long after American and Pakistani UN peacekeepers arrived in 1992, leading to periodic clashes with UN forces and, following a particularly harrowing firefight in October 1993, to the withdrawal of American forces. Skirmishes like these were also a conspicuous feature of the combat environment in Bosnia before the signing of the Dayton peace accords, and remain a major worry for the NATO forces stationed there today.

Even when formal hostilities have ceased, the diffusion of light weapons poses a continuing threat to international security. In those war-torn areas where jobs are few and the economy is in ruins, many demobilized soldiers have turned to crime to survive, often using the weapons they acquired during wartime for criminal purposes or selling them to combatants in other countries. During the 1980s, South African authorities provided thousands of guns to antigovernment guerrillas in Angola and Mozambique; these same guns, which are no longer needed for insurgent operations, are now being smuggled back into South Africa by their former owners and sold to criminal gangs. Some of the guns provided by the United States to the Nicaraguan contras have reportedly been sold to drug syndicates in Colombia.

MAIMING PROGRESS

It is no longer possible to ignore the role of small arms and light weapons in sustaining international conflict. Although efforts to address this problem are at an early stage, policymakers have begun to consider the imposition of new international constraints on light weapons trafficking. The UN, for example, has established a special commission—the Panel of Governmental Experts on Small Arms—to look into the problem, while representatives of the major industrial powers have met under the auspices of the Wassenaar Arrangement (a group set up in 1996 to devise new international controls on the spread of dangerous military technologies) to consider similar efforts. Despite growing interest, movement toward the adoption of new controls is likely to proceed slowly because of the many obstacles that must be overcome. (Only in one area—the establishment of an international ban on the production and use of antipersonnel land mines—is rapid progress possible.)

One of the greatest obstacles to progress is the lack of detailed information on the international trade in small arms and light weapons. Although various organizations, including the

United States Arms Control and Disarmament Agency (ACDA) and the Stockholm International Peace Research Institute (SIPRI) have long compiled data on transfers of major weapons systems, no organization currently provides such information on light weapons. Those who want to study this topic must begin by producing new reservoirs of data on the basis of fragmentary and anecdotal evidence. Fortunately, this process is now well under way, and so it is possible to develop a rough portrait of the light weapons traffic.[1]

SUPPLY AND DEMAND

There is no precise definition of light weapons. In general, they can be characterized as conventional weapons that can be carried by an individual soldier or by a light vehicle operating on back-country roads. This category includes pistols and revolvers, rifles, hand grenades, machine guns, light mortars, shoulder-fired antitank and anti-aircraft missiles, and antipersonnel land mines. Anything heavier is excluded: tanks, heavy artillery, planes, ships, and large missiles, along with weapons of mass destruction.

Small arms and light weapons of the types shown (see box "Light Weapons in Worldwide Circulation") can be acquired in several ways. All the major industrial powers manufacture light weapons of various types, and tend to rely on domestic production for their basic military needs. Another group of countries, including some in the third world, has undertaken the licensed manufacture of weapons originally developed by the major arms-producing states. The Belgian FAL assault rifle has been manufactured in Argentina, Australia, Austria, Brazil, Canada, India, Israel, Mexico, South Africa, and Venezuela, while the Russian/Soviet AK-47 (and its variants) has been manufactured in China, the former East Germany, Egypt, Finland, Hungary, Iraq, North Korea, Poland, Romania, and Yugoslavia. All told, about 40 countries manufacture at least some light weapons in their own factories. All other nations, and those countries that cannot satisfy all of their military requirements through domestic production, must rely on the military aid programs of the major powers or the commercial arms market.

Historically, the military aid programs of the United States and the Soviet Union were an important source of light weapons for developing nations. In addition to the major weapons supplied by the superpowers to their favored allies, both Moscow and Washington also provided vast quantities of small arms, grenades, machine guns, and other light weapons. Today, direct giveaways of light weapons are relatively rare (although the United States still supplies some surplus arms to some allies), so most developing nations must supply their needs through direct purchases on the global arms market.

[1] Three basic sources constitute a provisional database on the topic: Jeffrey Boutwell, Michael T. Klare, and Laura W. Reed, eds., *Lethal Commerce: The Global Trade in Small Arms and Light Weapons* (Cambridge, Mass.: American Academy of Arts and Sciences, 1995); Michael Klare and David Andersen, *A Scourge of Guns: The Diffusion of Small Arms and Light Weapons in Latin America* (Washington, D.C.: Federation of American Scientists, 1996); and Jasjit Singh, ed., *Light Weapons and International Security* (New Delhi: Indian Pugwash Society and British-American Security Information Council, 1995).

Unfortunately, there are no published statistics on the annual trade in light weapons. However, the ACDA has estimated that approximately 13 percent of all international arms transfers (when measured in dollars) is comprised of small arms and ammunition. Applying this percentage to ACDA figures on the value of total world arms transfers in 1993 and 1994 would put global small arms exports at approximately $3.6 billion and $2.9 billion, respectively (in current dollars). Adding machine guns, light artillery, and antitank weapons to the small arms category would probably double these figures to some $6 billion per year, which is about one-fourth the total value of global arms transfers.

Further data on the sale of small arms and light weapons through commercial channels are simply not available. Most states do not disclose such information, and the UN Register of Conventional Arms (an annual listing of member states' arms imports and exports) covers major weapons only. However, some indication of the scope of this trade can be obtained from the information in *Jane's Infantry Weapons* on the military inventories of individual states. The FAL assault rifle is found in the inventories of 53 third world states; the Israeli Uzi submachine gun is found in 39 such states; the German G3 rifle in 43 states; and the Belgian MAG machine gun in 54 states.

For established nation-states (except those subject to UN arms embargoes), the commercial arms trade provides an ample and reliable source of small arms and light weapons. For nonstate actors, however, the global arms market is usually closed off. Most countries provide arms only to other governments, or to private agencies that employ or distribute arms with the recipient government's approval. (Such approval is sometimes given to private security firms that seek to import firearms for their own use, or to gun stores that sell imported weapons to individual citizens for hunting or self-defense.) All other groups, including insurgents, brigands, and ethnic militias, must rely on extralegal sources for their arms and ammunition.

THE OTHER ARMS MARKETS

Nonstate entities that want weapons for operations against the military forces of the state or against rival organizations can obtain arms in three ways: through theft from government stockpiles; through purchases on the international black market; and through ties to government agencies or expatriate communities in other countries.

Theft is an important source of arms for insurgents and ethnic militias in most countries, especially in the early stages of conflict. The fledgling armies of Croatia and Slovenia were largely equipped with weapons that had been "liberated" from Yugoslav government arsenals. Weapons seized from dead or captured soldiers also figure prominently in the arms inventories of many insurgent forces. Thus the mujahideen of Afghanistan relied largely on captured Soviet weapons until they began receiving arms in large quantities from outside sources. Many of the guerrilla groups in Latin America have long operated in a similar fashion.

For those insurgent and militia groups with access to hard currency or negotiable commodities (such as diamonds, drugs,

For those . . . with access to hard currency of negotiable commodities (such as diamonds, drugs, and ivory), a large variety of light weapons can be procured on the international black market.

and ivory), a large variety of light weapons can be procured on the international black market. This market is composed of private dealers who acquire weapons from corrupt military officials or surplus government stockpiles and ship them through circuitous routes—usually passing through a number of transit points known for their lax customs controls—to obscure ports or airstrips where they can be surreptitiously delivered to the insurgents' representatives. Transactions of this sort have become a prominent feature of the global arms traffic, supplying belligerents around the world. The various factions in Bosnia, for example, reportedly obtained billions of dollars in arms through such channels between 1993 and 1995. Many other groups, including the drug cartels in Colombia and the guerrilla groups in Liberia, have also obtained arms in this fashion.

Finally, insurgents and ethnic militias can turn to sympathetic government officials or expatriate communities in other countries for weapons (or for the funds to procure them from black-market suppliers). During the cold war, both the United States and the Soviet Union—usually operating through intelligence agencies like the CIA and the KGB—supplied weapons to insurgent groups in countries ruled by governments allied with the opposing superpower. At the onset of the 1975 war in Angola, for example, the CIA provided anticommunist insurgents with 20,900 rifles, 41,900 anti-tank rockets, and 622 mortars; later, during the Reagan administration, the United States supplied even larger quantities of arms to the contras in Nicaragua and the mujahideen in Afghanistan. The KGB also supplied insurgent groups with arms of these types, often routing them through friendly countries such as Cuba and Vietnam.

Superpower intervention has largely ceased with the end of the cold war, but other nations are thought to be engaged in similar activities. The Inter-Services Intelligence (ISI) agency of Pakistan is believed to be aiding in the covert delivery of arms to antigovernment insurgents in Kashmir. Likewise, the government of Iran has been accused of supplying arms to Kurdish separatists in Turkey, while Burkina Faso has been charged with aiding some of the guerrilla factions in Liberia. Expatriate groups have also been known to supply arms to associated groups in their country of origin. Americans of Irish descent have smuggled arms to the Irish Republican Army in Northern Ireland, while Tamil expatriates in Canada, Europe, and India are thought to be sending arms (or the funds to procure them) to the Tamil Tigers in Sri Lanka.

A DUAL STRATEGY FOR ARMS CONTROL

What are the implications of all this for the development of new international restraints on light weapons trafficking? We are dealing with two separate, if related, phenomena: the overt, legal transfer of arms to states and state-sanctioned agencies, and the largely covert, illicit transfer of arms to insurgents, ethnic militias, and other nonstate entities. While there is obviously some overlap between the two systems of trade, it is probably not feasible to deal with both through a single set of controls.

Any effort to control the light weapons trade between established states (or their constituent parts) will run into the problem that most government leaders believe the acquisition of such weaponry is essential to the preservation of their sovereignty and therefore sanctioned by the United Nations charter. Many states are also engaged in the sale of light weapons and would resist any new constraints on their commercial activities. It is unlikely, therefore, that the world community will adopt anything resembling an outright ban on light weapons exports or even a significant reduction in such transfers.

This does not mean that progress is impossible. It should be possible to insist on some degree of international transparency in this field. At present, governments are under no obligation to make available information on their imports and exports of light weapons. By contrast, most states have agreed to supply such data on major weapons systems, for release through the UN Register of Conventional Arms. Although compiling data on transfers of small arms and light weapons would undoubtedly prove more difficult than keeping track of heavy weapons (because small arms are normally transferred far more frequently, and with less government oversight, than heavy weapons), there is no technical reason why the UN register could not be extended over time to include a wider range of systems. Including light weapons in the register would enable the world community to detect any unusual or provocative activity in this area (for example, significant purchases of arms and ammunition by a government that is supposedly downsizing its military establishment in accordance with a UN-brokered peace agreement) and to respond appropriately.

The major arms suppliers could also be required to abide by certain specified human rights considerations when considering the transfer of small arms and light weapons to governments involved in violent internal conflicts. Such sales could be prohibited in the case of governments that have suspended the democratic process and employed brutal force against unarmed civilians. An obvious candidate for such action is Burma, whose military leadership has usurped national power, jailed pro-democracy activists, and fought an unrelenting military campaign against autonomy-seeking minority groups. Human rights considerations have already figured in a number of UN arms embargoes—such as that imposed on the apartheid regime in South Africa—and so it should be possible to develop comprehensive restrictions of this type.

Finally, the world community could adopt restrictions or a prohibition on the transfer of certain types of weapons that are deemed to be especially cruel or barbaric in their effects. The first target should be the trade in antipersonnel land mines.

President Bill Clinton called for a worldwide ban on the production, transfer, and use of such munitions in May 1996. Many other leaders have promised to support such a measure, but more effort is needed to persuade holdout states to agree. In addition to land mines, a ban could be imposed on bullets that tumble in flight or otherwise reproduce the effects of dumdum bullets (a type of soft-nosed projectile that expands on impact and produces severe damage to the human body). Bullets of this type were outlawed by the Hague Convention of 1899, but have reappeared in other forms.

STOPPING BLACK-MARKET TRAFFIC

An entirely different approach will be needed to control the black-market traffic in arms. Since such trafficking violates, by definition, national and international norms regarding arms transfers, there is no point in trying to persuade the suppliers and recipients involved to abide by new international restraints on the munitions trade. Instead, governments should be asked to tighten their own internal controls on arms trafficking and to cooperate with other states in identifying, monitoring, and suppressing illegal gun traffickers.

As a first step, all the nations in a particular region—such as Europe or the Western Hemisphere—should agree to uniform export restrictions and establish electronic connections between their respective customs agencies to permit the instantaneous exchange of data on suspect arms transactions. These measures should prohibit the export of arms to any agency or firm not subject to government oversight in the recipient nation, and the use of transshipment points in third countries that do not adhere to the uniform standards. At the same time, the law enforcement agencies of these countries should cooperate in tracking down and prosecuting dealers found to have engaged in illicit arms transfers. Eventually these measures could be extended on a worldwide basis, making it much more difficult for would-be traffickers to circumvent government controls.

It is unrealistic, of course, to assume that these measures will prevent all unwanted and illicit arms trafficking—there are simply too many channels for determined suppliers to employ. Nor should airtight control be the goal of international action. Rather, the goal should be to so constrict the flow of weapons that potential belligerents (including nonstate actors) are discouraged from achieving their objectives through force of arms and seek instead a negotiated settlement. Such controls should also be designed to reduce the death and displacement of civilians trapped in conflict areas, and to impede the activities of terrorist and criminal organizations.

Obviously, it will not be possible to make progress so long as policymakers view the trade in small arms and light weapons as a relatively insignificant problem. Educating world leaders about the dangerous consequences of this trade in an era of intensifying ethnic and sectarian conflict is a major arms control priority. Once these consequences are widely appreciated, it should be possible for the world community to devise the necessary controls and make substantial progress in curbing this trade.

ETHNIC CONFLICT

Ethnic conflict seems to have supplanted nuclear war as the most pressing issue on the minds of policymakers. But if yesterday's high priests of mutually assured destruction were guilty of hyper-rationality, today's prophets of anarchy suffer from a collective hysteria triggered by simplistic notions of ethnicity. Debates about intervention in Rwanda or stability in Bosnia demand a more sober perspective.

—by Yahya Sadowski

The Number of Ethnic Conflicts Rose Dramatically at the End of the Cold War

Nope. The idea that the number of ethnic conflicts has recently exploded, ushering us into a violent new era of ethnic "pandaemonium," is one of those optical illusions that round-the-clock and round-the-world television coverage has helped to create. Ethnic conflicts have consistently formed the vast majority of wars ever since the epoch of decolonization began to sweep the developing countries after 1945. Although the number of ethnic conflicts has continued to grow since the Cold War ended, it has done so at a slow and steady rate, remaining consistent with the overall trend of the last 50 years.

In 1990 and 1991, however, several new and highly visible ethnic conflicts erupted as a result of the dissolution of the Soviet Union and Yugoslavia. The clashes between the armies of Croatia, Serbia, and Slovenia, and the agonizing battle that pitted Bosnia's Croats, Muslims, and Serbs against each other, occurred on Europe's fringes, within easy reach of television cameras. The wars in Azerbaijan, Chechnya, Georgia, and Tajikistan, while more distant, were still impressive in the way that they humbled the remnants of the former Soviet colossus. Many observers mistook these wars for the start of a new trend. Some were so impressed that they began to reclassify conflicts in Angola, Nicaragua, Peru, and

Somalia—once seen as ideological or power struggles—as primarily ethnic conflicts.

The state-formation wars that accompanied the "Leninist extinction" now appear to have been a one-time event—a flash flood rather than a global deluge. Many of these battles have already been brought under control. Indeed, the most striking trend in warfare during the 1990s has been its decline: The Stockholm International Peace Research Institute documented just 27 major armed conflicts (only one of which, India and Pakistan's slow-motion struggle over Kashmir, was an interstate war) in 1996, down from 33 such struggles in 1989. Once the Cold War ended, a long list of seemingly perennial struggles came to a halt: the Lebanese civil war, the Moro insurrection in the Philippines, regional clashes in Chad, the Eritrean secession and related battles in Ethiopia, the Sahrawi independence struggle, fratricide in South Africa, and the guerrilla wars in El Salvador and Nicaragua.

The majority of the wars that survive today are ethnic conflicts—but they are mostly persistent battles that have been simmering for decades. They include the (now possibly defunct) IRA insurgency in the United Kingdom; the struggle for Kurdish autonomy in Iran, Iraq, and Turkey; the Israeli-Palestinian tragedy; the Sri Lankan civil war; and long-standing regional insurrections in Burma, India, and Indonesia.

Reprinted with permission from *Foreign Policy*, Summer 1998, pp. 12-23. © 1998 by the Carnegie Endowment for International Peace.

Most Ethnic Conflicts Are Rooted in Ancient Tribal or Religious Rivalries

No way. The claim that ethnic conflicts have deep roots has long been a standard argument for not getting involved. According to political journalist Elizabeth Drew's famous account, President Bill Clinton in 1993 had intended to intervene in Bosnia until he read Robert Kaplan's book *Balkan Ghosts*, which, as Drew said, conveyed the notion that "these people had been killing each other in tribal and religious wars for centuries." But the reality is that most ethnic conflicts are expressions of "modern hate" and largely products of the twentieth century.

The case of Rwanda is typical. When Europeans first stumbled across it, most of the country was already united under a central monarchy whose inhabitants spoke the same language, shared the same cuisine and culture, and practiced the same religion. They were, however, divided into several castes. The largest group, the Hutus, were farmers. The ruling aristocracy, who collected tribute from all other groups, was recruited from the Tutsis, the caste of cattle herders. All groups supplied troops for their common king, and intermarriage was not unusual. Social mobility among castes was quite possible: A rich Hutu who purchased enough cattle could climb into the ranks of the Tutsi; an impoverished Tutsi could fall into the ranks of the Hutu. Anthropologists considered all castes to be members of a single "tribe," the Banyarwanda.

Then came the Belgians. Upon occupying the country after World War I, they transformed the system. Like many colonial powers, the Belgians chose to rule through a local élite—the Tutsis were eager to collaborate in exchange for Belgian guarantees of their local power and for privileged access to modern education. Districts that had been under Hutu leadership were brought under Tutsi rule. Until 1929, about one-third of the chiefs in Rwanda had been Hutu, but then the Belgians decided to "streamline" the provincial administration by eliminating all non-Tutsi chiefs. In 1933, the Belgians issued mandatory identity cards to all Rwandans, eliminating fluid movement between castes and permanently fixing the identity of each individual, and his or her children, as either Hutu or Tutsi. As the colonial administration pene-

Ethnic Africa

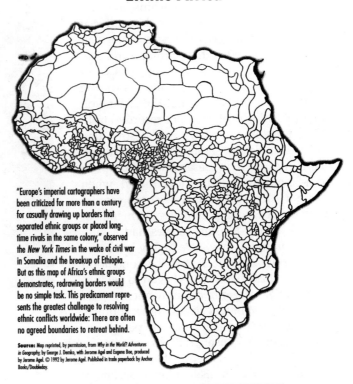

"Europe's imperial cartographers have been criticized for more than a century for casually drawing up borders that separated ethnic groups or placed long-time rivals in the same colony," observed the *New York Times* in the wake of civil war in Somalia and the breakup of Ethiopia. But as this map of Africa's ethnic groups demonstrates, redrawing borders would be no simple task. This predicament represents the greatest challenge to resolving ethnic conflicts worldwide: There are often no agreed boundaries to retreat behind.

Source: Map reprinted, by permission, from *Why in the World? Adventures in Geography*, by George J. Demko, with Jerome Agel and Eugene Boe, produced by Jerome Agel. © 1992 by Jerome Agel. Published in trade paperback by Anchor Books/Doubleday.

trated and grew more powerful, Belgian backing allowed the Tutsis to increase their exploitation of the Hutus to levels that would have been impossible in earlier times.

In the 1950s, the Belgians came under pressure from the United Nations to grant Rwanda independence. In preparation, Brussels began to accord the majority Hutus—the Tutsis constituted only 14 percent of the population—a share of political power and greater access to education. Although this policy alarmed the Tutsis, it did not come close to satisfying the Hutus: Both groups began to organize to defend their interests, and their confrontations became increasingly militant. Centrist groups that included both Hutus and Tutsis were gradually squeezed out by extremists on both sides. The era of modern communal violence began with the 1959 attack on a Hutu leader by Tutsi extremists; Hutus retaliated, and several hundred people were killed. This set in motion a cycle of violence that culminated in December 1963, when Hutus massacred 10,000 Tutsis and drove another 130,000–150,000 from the country. These tragedies laid the seeds for the genocide of 1994.

The late emergence of ethnic violence, such as in Rwanda, is the norm, not an exception. In Ceylon, riots that pitted Tamils against Sinhalese did not erupt until 1956. In Bosnia,

Serbs and Croats coexisted with one another, and both claimed Muslims as members of their communities, until World War II—and peaceful relations resumed even after the bloodshed of that conflict. Turks and Kurds shared a common identity as Ottomans and wore the same uniforms during World War I; in fact, the first Kurdish revolt against Turkish rule was not recorded until 1925. Muslims and Jews in Palestine had no special history of intercommunal hatred (certainly nothing resembling European anti-Semitism) until the riots of 1921, when nascent Arab nationalism began to conflict with the burgeoning Zionist movement. Although Hindu-Muslim clashes had a long history in India, they were highly localized; it was only after 1880 that the contention between these two groups began to gel into large-scale, organized movements. Of course, the agitators in all these conflicts tend to dream up fancy historic pedigrees for their disputes. Bosnian Serbs imagine that they are fighting to avenge their defeat by the Ottoman Turks in 1389; Hutus declare that Tutsis have "always" treated them as subhumans; and IRA bombers attack their victims in the name of a nationalist tradition they claim has burned since the Dark Ages. But these mythologies of hatred are themselves largely recent inventions.

Ethnic Conflict Was Powerful Enough to Rip Apart the USSR

Yeah, right. The idea that the Soviet Union was destroyed by an explosion of ethnic atavism has been put forth by a number of influential thinkers, most notably Senator Daniel Patrick Moynihan. But this theory is not only historically inaccurate, it has misleading policy implications. The collapse of states is more often the cause of ethnic conflicts rather than the result.

Prior to 1991, ethnic consciousness within the Soviet Union had only developed into mass nationalism in three regions: the Baltic states, Transcaucasia, and Russia itself. Russian nationalism posed no threat to Soviet rule: It had been so successfully grafted onto communism during World War II that even today Leninists and Russian ultranationalists tend to flock to the same parties. In Transcaucasia, the Armenians and Georgians had developed potent national identities but were much more interested in pursuing local feuds (especially with Muslims) than in dismantling

Major Genocides since World War II

COUNTRY	DATES	VICTIMS	NUMBER OF DEATHS (IN THOUSANDS)
USSR	1943–47	Repatriated nationals and ethnic minorities	500–1,100
China	1950–51	Landlords	800–3,000
Sudan	1955–72	Southern nationalists	100–500
Indonesia	1965–66	Communists and ethnic Chinese	80–1,000
China	1966–75	Cultural revolution victims	400–850
Uganda	1971–79	Opponents of Idi Amin	100–500
Pakistan	1971	Bengali nationalists	1,250–3,000
Cambodia	1975–79	Urbanites	800–3,000
Afghanistan	1978–89	Opponents of the regime	1,000
Sudan	1983–98	Southern nationalists	100–1,500
Iraq	1984–91	Kurds	100–282
Bosnia	1991–95	Bosnian Muslims and Croats	25–200
Burundi	1993–98	Hutu, Tutsi	150+
Rwanda	1994	Tutsi	500–1,000

Sources: Barbara Harff, "Victims of the State: Genocides, Politicides and Group Repression since 1945," *International Review of Victimology*, 1 (1989): 23-41; Conflict Resolution Program, *1995-1996 State of World Conflict Report* (Atlanta: Carter Center, 1997); *Los Angeles Times*; and the *Encyclopaedia Britannica*.

the Soviet Union. Only in the Baltic states, which had remained sovereign and independent until 1940, was powerful nationalist sentiment channeled directly against Moscow.

When the August 1991 coup paralyzed the Communist Party, the last threads holding the Soviet state together dissolved. Only then did rapid efforts to spread nationalism to other regions appear. In Belarus, Ukraine, and across Central Asia, the *nomenklatura*, searching for new instruments to legitimate their rule, began to embrace—and sometimes invent—nationalist mythologies. It was amidst this wave of post-Soviet nationalism that new or rekindled ethnic conflicts broke out in Chechnya, Moldova, Ukraine, and elsewhere. Yet even amid the chaos of state collapse, ethnonationalist movements remained weaker and less violent than many had expected. Despite the predictions of numerous pundits, revivalist Islamic movements only took root in a couple of places (Chechnya and Tajikistan). Relations between indigenous Turkic peoples and Russian immigrants across most of Central Asia remained civil.

Ethnic Conflicts Are More Savage and Genocidal Than Conventional Wars

Wrong. Although this assumption is inaccurate, the truth is not much more comforting. There appears to be no consistent difference between ethnic and nonethnic wars in terms of their lethality. In fact, the percentage of civilians in the share of total casualties is rising for all types of warfare. During World War I,

Tribal Wisdom

"For centuries, [Yugoslavia] marked a tense and often violent fault line between empires and religions. The end of the Cold War and the dissolution of that country . . . surfaced all those ancient tensions again. . . ."

—U.S. president Bill Clinton, addressing the U.S. Naval Academy in 1994

"We are confronted by contradictory phenomena in which both the factors of integration and cooperation and the tendencies of division and dispersal are both apparent. The technological and communications revolution is offset by the eruption of nationalist conflicts and ethnic hatreds."

—Egyptian foreign minister Amr Moussa, before the UN General Assembly in 1996

"In this Europe of ours, where no one would have thought a struggle between ethnic groups possible, tragically this has come about. It may serve to open people's eyes to the unspeakable possibilities in the future, even in unexpected places. Today we are threatened by the danger . . . of racial, religious, and tribal hatred."

—Italian president Oscar Luigi Scalfaro in 1997

"Yet even as the waves of globalization unfurl so powerfully across our planet, so does a deep and vigorous countertide. . . . What some have called a 'new tribalism' is shaping the world as profoundly on one level as the 'new globalism' is shaping it on another."

—His Highness the Aga Khan, at the Commonwealth Press Union Conference in Cape Town in 1996

" . . . all over the world, we see a kind of reversion to tribalism. . . . We see it in Russia, in Yugoslavia, in Canada, in the United States. . . . What is it about, all this globalization of communication that is making people return to more—to smaller units of identity?"

—Neil Postman, chair of the department of culture and communication at New York University, in 1995

civilian casualties constituted about 15 percent of all deaths. That number skyrocketed to 65 percent during World War II, which, by popularizing the use of strategic bombing, blockade-induced famine, and guerrilla warfare, constituted a real, albeit underappreciated, watershed in the history of human slaughter. Ever since, the number of civilian dead has constituted two-thirds or more of the total fatalities in most wars. Indeed, according to UNICEF, the share of civilian casualties has continued to grow since 1945—rising to almost 90 percent by the end of the 1980s and to more than 90 percent during this decade.

Furthermore, ethnic wars are less likely to be associated with genocide than "conventional" wars. The worst genocides of modern times have not been targeted along primarily ethnic lines. Rather, the genocides within Afghanistan, Cambodia, China, the Soviet Union, and even, to a great extent, Indonesia and Uganda, have focused on liquidating political dissidents: To employ the emerging vocabulary, they were politicides rather than ethnicides. Indeed, the largest genocides of this century were clearly ideologically driven politicides: the mass killings committed by the Maoist regime in China from 1949 to 1976, by the Leninist/Stalinist regime in the Soviet Union between 1917 and 1959, and by the Pol Pot regime in Cambodia between 1975 and 1979.

Finally, some pundits have claimed that ethnic conflicts are more likely to be savage because they are often fought by irregular, or guerrilla, troops. In fact, (a) ethnic wars are usually fought by regular armies, and (b) regular armies are quite capable of vicious massacres. Contrary to the stereotypes played out on television, the worst killing in Bosnia did not occur where combatants were members of irregular militias, reeling drunk on *slivovitz*. The core of the Serb separatist forces consisted of highly disciplined troops that were seconded from the Yugoslav army and led by a spit-and-polish officer corps. It was precisely these units that made the massacres at Srebrenica possible: It required real organizational skill to take between 6,000 and 10,000 Bosnian troops prisoner, disarm and transport them to central locations, and systematically murder them and distribute their bodies among a network of carefully concealed mass graves. Similarly, the wave of ethnic cleansing that followed the seizure of northern and eastern Bosnia by the Serbs in 1991 was not the spontaneous work of crazed irregulars. Transporting the male Bosnian population to concentration camps at Omarska and elsewhere required the talents of men who knew how to coordinate military attacks, read railroad schedules, guard and (under-) supply large prison populations, and organize bus transport for expelling women and children.

Globalization Makes Ethnic Conflict More Likely

Think again. The claim that globalization—the spread of consumer values, democratic institutions, and capitalist enterprise—aggravates ethnic and cultural violence is at the core of Samuel Huntington's "clash of civilizations" hypothesis, Robert Kaplan's vision of "the coming anarchy," and Benjamin Barber's warning that we face a future of "Jihad vs. McWorld." Although these suggestions deserve further study, the early indications are that globalization plays no real role in spreading ethnic conflict and may actually inhibit it.

Despite the fears of cultural critics that the broad appeal of "Baywatch" heralds a collapse of worldwide values, there is not much concrete evidence linking the outbreak of ethnic wars to the global spread of crude materialism via film, television, radio, and boombox. Denmark has just as many television sets as the former Yugoslavia but has not erupted into ethnic carnage or even mass immigrant bashing. Meanwhile, Burundi, sitting on the distant outskirts of the global village with only one television set for every 4,860 people, has witnessed some of the worst violence in this decade.

The spread of democratic values seems a slightly more plausible candidate as a trigger for ethnic violence: The recent progress of democracy in Albania, Armenia, Croatia, Georgia, Moldova, Russia, Serbia, and South Africa has been attended by ethnic feuding in each country. But this is an inconsistent trend. Some of the most savage internal conflicts of the post-Cold War period have occurred in societies that were growing less free, such as Egypt, India (which faced major secessionist challenges by Kashmiris, Sikhs, Tamils, etc.), Iran, and Peru. For that matter, many of the worst recent ethnic conflicts occurred in countries where the regime type was unstable and vacillated back and forth between more and less free forms, as in Azerbaijan, Bosnia, Lebanon, Liberia, Nigeria, and Tajikistan. Conversely, in numerous cases, such as the so-called third wave of democratization that swept Latin America and East Asia during the 1980s, political liberalization seems to have actually reduced most forms of political violence.

Investigating the impact of economic globalization leads to three surprises. First, the countries affected most by globalization—that is, those that have shown the greatest increase in international trade and benefited most significantly from foreign direct investment—are not the newly industrializing economies of East Asia and Latin America but the old industrial societies of Europe and North America. Second, ethnic conflicts are found, in some form or another, in every type of society: They are not concentrated among poor states, nor are they unusually common among countries experiencing economic globalization. Thus, the bad news is that ethnic conflicts do not disappear when societies "modernize."

The good news, however, lies in the third surprise: Ethnic conflicts are likely to be much less lethal in societies that are developed, economically open, and receptive to globalization. Ethnic battles in industrial and industrializing societies tend either to be argued civilly or at least limited to the political violence of marginal groups, such as the provisional IRA in the United Kingdom, Mohawk secessionists in Canada, or the Ku Klux Klan in the United States. The most gruesome ethnic wars are found in poorer societies—Afghanistan and Sudan, for example—where economic frustration reinforces political rage. It seems, therefore, that if economic globalization contributes to a country's prosperity, then it also dampens the level of ethnic violence there.

Fanaticism Makes Ethnic Conflicts Harder to Terminate

Not really. Vojislav Seselj, the commander of one of the most murderous Serb paramilitary groups in Bosnia, once warned that if U.S. forces were used there, "the war [would] be total. . . . We would have tens of thousands of volunteers, and we would score a glorious victory. The Americans would have to send thousands of body bags. It would be a new Vietnam." Of course, several years later, after Serb forces had been handily defeated by a combination of Croat ground forces and NATO airpower, the president of the Serb separatists, Radovan Karadzic, admitted their leadership had thought all along that "if the West put in 10,000 men to cut off our supply corridors, we Serbs would be finished." Militarily, ethnic conflicts are not intrinsically different from any other type of combat. They can take on the form of guerrilla wars or conventional battles; they can be fought by determined and disciplined cadres or by poorly motivated slobs. How much military force will be required to end the fighting varies widely from one ethnic conflict to the next.

However, achieving a military victory and building a durable peace are two very different matters. Sealing the peace in ethnic conflicts may prove harder for political—not military—reasons. Ethnic conflicts are fought among neighbors, among people who live intermingled with one other, forced to share the same resources and institutions. When two states end a war, they may need only to agree to stop shooting and respect a mutual border. But in ethnic conflicts there are often no established borders to retreat behind. Sometimes, ethnic disputes can be resolved by drawing new borders—creating new states (such as Bangladesh and "rump" Pakistan) that allow the quarreling groups to live apart. Other times, they can be terminated by convincing the combatants that they must share power peaceably and learn to coexist. This is the objective of the Dayton accord on Bosnia.

In either case, ending ethnic warfare often requires the expensive and delicate construction of new political institutions. Not only may this be more difficult than terminating a "normal" interstate war, it may also take much longer. Building truly effective states takes time. For this reason, ethnic wars whose participants are already organized into states or protostates (which was true of the combatants in Croatia and Bosnia) are probably easier to bring to a conclusion than battles in regions—Afghanistan, for example, not to speak of Somalia where real states have yet to congeal.

Want to Know More?

The classic introduction to the study of ethnic conflict is still Donald Horowitz, *Ethnic Groups in Conflict* (Berkeley: University of California Press, 1985). The Stockholm International Peace Research Institute (SIPRI) inventories changing patterns of warfare in the *SIPRI Yearbook* (Oxford: Oxford University Press, annual). For a specialist's tally of particular ethnic conflicts, see Ted Robert Gurr, *Minorities at Risk: A Global View of Ethnopolitical Conflicts* (Washington: U.S. Institute of Peace, 1993). An absorbing overview of the evolving relations between Tutsi and Hutu is Gérard Prunier, *The Rwanda Crisis: History of a Genocide* (New York: Columbia University Press, 1995). The Human Rights Watch report, *Slaughter among Neighbors: The Political Origins of Communal Violence* (New Haven: Yale University Press, 1995), provides a broader survey of modern hate. An excellent account of the diversity of forms that ethnicity and nationalism have taken in territories of the former Soviet Union is Ronald Grigor Suny's *The Revenge of the Past: Nationalism, Revolution and the Collapse of the Soviet Union* (Stanford: Stanford University Press, 1993). Neal Ascherson reflects upon issues of nationality and ethnicity in his book *Black Sea* (New York: Hill & Wang, 1995), which chronicles the expansive history of a region that has been a nexus of several Asian and European cultures. David Rohde's chilling *Endgame: The Betrayal and Fall of Srebrenica* (New York: Farrar Straus & Giroux, 1997) documents the careful organizational planning underlying the genocide in Bosnia. A recent work that dissects the question of whether, or how, the United States should intervene in ethnic conflicts is David Callahan's *Unwinnable Wars: American Power and Ethnic Conflict* (New York: Hill & Wang, 1998).

For links to relevant Web sites, as well as a comprehensive index of related articles, access **www.foreignpolicy.com**.

Nuclear brinkmanship in South Asia

James Hamill

The series of nuclear tests conducted by India and Pakistan in May 1998 ushered an era of more rapid nuclear proliferation not only in South Asia but also throughout the world. The Indian and Pakistani tests have caused a serious setback to international efforts to prevent the proliferation of nuclear capabilities in the light of their hostile relationship. The two countries were also trying to establish international self-confidence to boost their prestige in the global arena.

The campaign to prevent the spread or proliferation of nuclear weapons around the globe suffered a serious setback in May 1998. India and Pakistan between them carried out eleven nuclear tests thus confirming their long suspected potential in this area and bringing to seven the number of states with a declared nuclear weapons capability. The five Indian tests were carried out from 11–13 May, and the six Pakistani tests from 28–30 May. For almost 40 years membership of the nuclear club had been confined to the so-called 'Big Five'–the United States, Russia (formerly the Soviet Union), China, France and Britain–yet within the space of three weeks that club had increased in size by a third. These disturbing events drove a 'coach and horses' through the international non-proliferation regime which the United States has been seeking to construct and suggested that we may be about to enter an era of more rapid nuclear proliferation, a development which the big powers will deplore but may prove unable to prevent.

In most respects the Indian and Pakistani decisions were inevitable at some stage. Each had for some years been a so-called 'threshold' state, that is they possessed the technical expertise to 'go nuclear' at short notice but were choosing, for political reasons, to keep their options open. The two states were also locked into a bitter and acrimonious relationship dating back to the partition of India and the creation of Pakistan in 1947. Religious differences (India's population is predominantly Hindu, although with a significant Muslim component, whilst Pakistan is almost exclusively Muslim) and territorial disputes–particularly over Kashmir province–have added further layers of distrust. As the two sides have fought three separate wars against each other since partition–two over Kashmir and one over East Pakistan or what was to become Bangladesh–it is hardly surprising that they should define their national security interests in terms of military prowess with nuclear weapons being seen as the 'ultimate military insurance policy', to quote Fareed Zakaria (Newsweek, 8 June 1998). In effect, these were two nuclear weapons states waiting to happen and in May 1998, as Professor Brahma Chellaney stated, they 'gatecrashed the nuclear club' and lifted 'the veil of atomic ambiguity' which had persisted for almost two decades (International Herald Tribune, 14 May 1998).

The Immediate Catalysts

Each state has inevitably argued that its decision was forced upon it by the aggressive behaviour and provocations of the other. The dense fog of propaganda emanating from both New Delhi and Islamabad makes it difficult, if not impossible, to reach any definitive conclusions on that issue but three broad factors are worth mentioning by way of explanation. First, domestic political considerations were clearly a strong factor in shaping the calculations of each government. India's Hindu fundamentalist Bharatiya Janata Party (BJP), led by Prime Minister Atil Bihari Vajpayee, is currently the largest force in a highly unstable 14-party coalition government and it appears to have viewed the nuclear tests, quite cynically, as the ideal means with which to shore up its fragile political authority. The subsequent plaudits for the decision across the Indian political spectrum (the Communist Party excepted) and the nationalistic fervour it unleashed in the wider population–91 per cent support was recorded in immediate post-test opinion surveys–testifies to the success of the BJP's policy of 'nuclear machismo', although its durability may be in doubt when broader political and economic realities eventually resurface. The Indian tests made it essential for the Pakistan government of Nawaz Sharif to respond or else risk a serious erosion of its own political legitimacy, particularly in a country where the military has been such a dominant institution with a long track record of political interference. This always made it extremely unlikely that the Pakistani government would feel able to heed international, and specifically American, pleas for it to desist and to stake out the moral high ground on the issue. In fact, the eventual decision to conduct six tests–one more than India–was an assertion of Pakistani pride as well as an obvious attempt to play to a domestic constituency by upstaging its larger neighbour.

Second, each state was also seeking to establish its international self-confidence and to enhance its prestige on the global stage. Although still poor and underdeveloped, possession of nuclear weapons conveys the message that neither state should be considered technologically backward. Both countries may also see nuclear weapons as a basic requirement if a country is to sit at the international top table and the fact that the five nuclear powers are all permanent members of the United Nations Security Council, the organisation's 'nerve centre', will not have gone unnoticed in the Indian and Pakistani capitals. The message seems to be clear: nuclear weapons do bring geo-political influence and it is hardly surprising, therefore, that they have become something of a symbol of a state's international virility. Certainly there appeared to be a national consensus in India that the tests represented a further step along the country's road to full international maturity–a 'rite of passage' almost for any country aspiring to the ranks of the great powers. However, the US has been actively seeking to discourage the idea that there is any formal connection between the possession of nuclear weapons and great power status, preferring to stress economic and diplomatic weight–or 'soft power' to use the jargon of international relations scholarship–as the entry price for admission to the top table. Consequently, India may find that its ambition to secure a permanent seat on the Security Council is frustrated for the foreseeable future as the US seeks to ensure that New Delhi's nuclear tactics go unrewarded. India may not exactly become a pariah state–it is, after all, an established democracy in which the rule of law prevails–but it is likely to be pushed towards a 'semi-detached' position within the international system as opposed to the central role it obviously craves. India seems relatively relaxed about this, believing that the initial furore will fade and that the country's nuclear status will be one of the factors which helps deliver membership of a restructured Security Council, reform of which would be rendered absurd should it sanction the continuing exclusion of the world's largest democracy. Only time will tell which of these two views is to prevail.

Third, the Western nuclear powers have found themselves being embarrassed by their own rhetoric and behaviour in this area. India has taken every opportunity to expose what it sees as the blatant hypocrisy of the US in seeking to deny nuclear weapons to India whilst in the past it has discreetly encouraged the nuclear ambitions of Britain, France, and Israel to name but three. Some influential American voices have recognised the validity of this charge. For example, Zbigniew Brzezinski, the former National Security Adviser to President Carter and a veteran commentator on international affairs, has noted that 'non-proliferation is like pregnancy: you cannot be partially pregnant; you cannot pursue effectively a selective policy on nonproliferation' (International Herald Tribune, 19 May 1998). Moreover, India accuses the nuclear powers of paying no more than 'lip service' to the cause of nuclear disarmament which they fully committed themselves to during the 1995 negotiations to renew the 1970 Nuclear Non-Proliferation Treaty (NPT). The Russian parliament's failure to ratify the Strategic Arms Reduction Treaty (START) 2 and the failure of the US Congress to ratify the 1996 Comprehensive Test Ban Treaty (CTBT) are highlighted in this regard. Finally, India notes that the Western nations in particular have justified their possession of nuclear weapons on the grounds that they have helped to deter aggression and have thus played a vital role in maintaining peace. This orthodox realist thinking has struck a chord with aspiring nuclear powers such as India who now argue that the same logic can quite legitimately be applied to their own conflicts–a classic case of the West being hoist with its own petard. As Andrew Mack, of the University of Auckland, New Zealand, has written: 'Why, Indian analysts ask, are nuclear weapons supposedly security enhancing in the hands of Americans and the other declared nuclear weapons states and yet a threat to global peace and security in Indian hands? The nuclear powers have proffered no good answer' (International Herald Tribune, 18 May 1998).

Negative Consequences

It is not difficult to identify a host of negative consequences flowing from the Indian and Pakistani actions. First, nuclear weapons have now added a new and potentially lethal ingredient to an already volatile conflict. Some commentators have suggested that the India-Pakistan conflict is dangerous not only because the religious dimension supposedly makes it less receptive to compromise but also because the two sides lack the institutionalised procedures–or 'rules of the game'–for managing their nuclear relationship which the US and Soviet Union put in place following the 1962 Cuban missile crisis. The danger of war by miscalculation and a basic misreading of the other side's intentions has therefore been substantially increased. In a situation such as Kashmir where each side has only the most basic of intelligence systems and lacks the sophisticated technical infrastructure to know precisely what the other side is doing, the combatants will be forced to proceed on a 'worst case scenario' basis. In the words of The Economist, this will bring 'a new hair trigger instability to any future crisis' (16 May 1998).

Second, India's decision was at least partly motivated by a fear of China, its giant, nuclear armed, neighbour with whom it fought a war in 1962. Indeed, for India the Chinese and Pakistani threats are seen as intertwined given Beijing's strategic patronage of Pakistan, in particular its transfer of advanced missile technology to Islamabad and its role as a 'technical enabler', to quote The Washington Post, for that state's nuclear programme. The Indians, who have competed with the Chinese since the 1960s for a leadership role in the Third World, were now seeking to bring the military relationship with Beijing into balance or equilibrium. However, the decision has only succeeded in worsening relations between the two giants with China condemning India's actions as a threat to regional peace and security. This does not augur well for the future, particularly if it causes China to cement its de facto military alliance with Pakistan or, worse still in global terms, to resume testing itself.

Third, both states will now have to live with the economic repercussions of their actions. There is now a real danger that the escalation in regional tension will lead to an arms race at both the nuclear and conventional level thereby diverting precious re-

sources from the acute development needs of each country. As well as drawing stinging diplomatic rebukes from the US, the tests also triggered punitive American economic sanctions under the terms of the 1994 Nuclear Proliferation Prevention Act. Those sanctions can only retard economic development and further increase the hardship of millions of people already living in abject poverty. As the deputy Prime Minister of Malaysia, Anwar Ibrahim, has noted, India and Pakistan remain 'mired in poverty and destitution' and 'the contrast between the illusion of new found greatness and the reality of social and economic conditions is stark indeed' (International Herald Tribune, 2 June 1998). For the US, however, it is vitally important that the sanctions should bite hard not because they are likely to secure an Indian or Pakistani climbdown–this has now become a question of national pride in each country–but to dissuade other states from taking the same path. The Economist summed up US thinking in the aftermath of the Indian tests when writing: 'If the world's efforts to limit nuclear proliferation are to have any chance of success, India needs to pay a heavy price . . . unless India loses a lot more from its nuclear defiance than it gains, efforts to curb weapons of mass destruction–chemical and biological, not just nuclear–may be lost' (16 May 1998).

Japan also imposed its own measures immediately but the problem for the US here will be in persuading the Europeans–traditionally more sceptical of the value of sanctions–to come on board. Intense debate is now likely within the Bretton Woods institutions–the International Monetary Fund (IMF) and the World Bank–to determine the extent to which aid, loans, and credits to each state should now be scaled down or even suspended altogether. These are, of course, organisations in which the US is the major shareholder, a fact of international economic life with which India and Pakistan are about to become brutally reacquainted. Yet, Washington does need to be careful

not to push either state towards bankruptcy–more likely in the case of the tottering Pakistani economy than that of India–as this will risk leaving them with little to sell on the international market except their nuclear expertise. Sanctions would then become dangerously counter-productive. This need for sanctions which hurt but do not cripple will call for exceptionally fine tuning on the part of the US and will require a more subtle and nuanced policy approach than it has shown itself capable of to date.

Finally, the expansion of the general pool of nuclear expertise raises the possibility of that 'know-how' falling into the wrong hands, whether by accident or design. The US will be particularly concerned by descriptions of the Pakistani weapon as an 'Islamic bomb' (although the Pakistani government itself has discouraged such talk) and will be determined to ensure that nuclear technology and materials are not transferred to states which it has deemed to be international outcasts or 'rogues', such as Iran, Iraq, and Libya. If that should happen, then the Middle East region will become even more of a powder keg with Israel–a nuclear weapons state in all but name–perhaps feeling obliged to take pre-emptive action to protect its vital interests.

Searching for the Positives

Whilst it is more difficult to detect anything positive emerging from these events in the short term, there may be grounds for hope in three areas over the longer term. First, it is to be hoped that the introduction of this lethal new military ingredient may actually help to stabilise the India-Pakistan relationship by compelling each side to exercise maximum restraint and to initiate a comprehensive bilateral dialogue across all areas of their problematic relationship. The optimistic interpretation of these events suggests, therefore, that the presence of weapons of mass destruction (WMD) will serve to concentrate the minds of the elites on either side, will provide an obvious disincentive to 'adventurist' behaviour, and will ultimately open the way to peaceful co-existence or detente on the subcontinent. One early encouraging sign was each side's declaration of a moratorium on further testing. It remains doubtful, however, if that will lead directly to the signing of the 1996 CTBT as the West is demanding. India regards that treaty—already signed by 149 states—as highly discriminatory, noting that the established nuclear powers have conducted thousands of tests between them—over 1000 in the case of the US and over 700 in the case of Russia—and have little need, therefore, for further testing. Moreover, their state-of-the-art computer technology now allows them to simulate tests without having to carry out politically unpopular explosions, an option unavailable to the less technically advanced states. These factors make India reluctant to endorse the treaty's provisions and Pakistan will clearly not sign unless its neighbour does so.

Second, it is to be hoped that the major powers, principally the US, have now been shaken out of their complacent approach to the bitter nuclear politics of South Asia. In fact the entire episode has been something of a debacle for US foreign policy, first in failing to detect the preparations for the Indian tests—the latest in a series of post-Cold War blows to the credibility of the Central Intelligence Agency—and then in failing to persuade Pakistan not to respond in kind. This has all rather dented the image of the US as an effective manager of the post-Cold War international system. While it is absurd to speak of the US being paralysed, there can be little doubt that Washington's ability to fashion the post-Cold War world to its own specifications has been greatly exaggerated. As the nuclear tests demonstrate—following the effective collapse of the Middle East peace process, the Asian financial crisis and the Iraqi weapons dispute—the US may be 'first among equals' but it is not an outright hegemon of the type anticipated by many during the halcyon days at the end of the Gulf War in 1991. In fact, what becomes evident

from a sustained analysis of each of these issues is not so much American power but rather the inability of the US to control events or to impose its will.

Countering the proliferation of nuclear weapons will now require a more proactive, flexible and imaginative US policy approach embracing diplomatic measures, economic 'carrots' for co-operative states, and the use of 'sticks' such as isolation, sanctions, and even military measures against others. It may also require energetic mediation in various disputes to prevent states' security concerns worsening to the point where they feel the need to acquire such weaponry. In short, the US needs to accept the burdens of international leadership and to become much more deeply engaged in attempting to resolve global security problems. Unfortunately, post-Cold War US foreign policy has been characterised by spasmodic intervention in response either to those issues where American interests are very directly at stake or where the public's attention has been engaged by the media—the so-called 'CNN factor.' A policy of neglect, which is not an unreasonable description of the US approach to South Asia in recent years, will normally have serious long-term consequences as the current crisis is demonstrating. Indeed, allowing issues to fester whilst hoping, Micawber-like, for 'something to turn up' hardly amounts to a policy at all and is certainly not an approach remotely worthy of a superpower. The playing of the 'nuclear card' was really an implicit plea by India for greater respect and for the US to take it more seriously as a major player in international politics. Following several decades in which Washington has displayed a near obsessive interest in developing relations with China, as well as supporting Pakistan as a strategically important Cold War pawn, the Indian government was now reminding the US, in the most direct manner possible, of its status as both a regional power and the world's largest democracy. That sense of Indian isolation—and a genu-

ine resentment that, despite its size and democratic credentials, the West was according it a second-class status in world affairs—was instrumental in leading to the tests in the Rajasthan desert in May 1998 and it is a mindset for which Washington must accept its share of responsibility.

Finally, it is to be hoped that these events will give fresh momentum to the whole nuclear disarmament process. The established nuclear powers must now appreciate that it is no longer politically viable—or morally defensible—to hail the virtues of nuclear deterrence, and to retain their own vast arsenals, whilst advising others of the folly of pursuing the same course. This leaves them wide open to the charge of 'double standards', of seeking to preserve a 'nuclear apartheid', and even of 'racism', all of which have featured in the rhetoric of the Indian government. The time has now come for the nuclear powers to take their own verbal undertakings in this field more seriously even if—as seems likely—their actions fall short of complete nuclear disarmament. At the very least the Test Ban Treaty needs to be formally ratified by the US, Russia and China and the US-Russia START process needs to be re-invigorated if the two sides are to meet their commitment to reducing the number of strategic warheads to 2,000–2,500 each by the year 2007. The first sign of activity on this front came in July when Britain announced a 50 per cent cut in the number of warheads to be carried by its Trident nuclear missiles. This was presented as a further development of the 'ethical foreign policy' first unveiled by Foreign Secretary, Robin Cook, back in May 1997. However, it was also a clear indication that events on the Indian subcontinent had succeeded in convincing at least one of the major Western powers of the need for new thinking and for a more imaginative policy response in this whole vexed area.

James Hamill is a lecturer in the Politics Department, Leicester University.

> "[D]espite China's undoubted ambition to become a full-fledged great military power, . . . there is no evidence that Beijing has embarked on a crash course to correct all its well-known deficiencies . . . China's defense modernization strategy remains long-term and incremental."

Uncertainty, Insecurity, and China's Military Power

PAUL H. B. GODWIN

When Deng Xiaoping came to power in 1978, he inherited a defense establishment that was little more than a lumbering giant. In the 20 years following the Sino-Soviet split of 1959–1960 and Moscow's termination of military assistance, China's military power had eroded into obsolescence. The country's defense industrial base was incapable of producing anything more than copies of Soviet designs from the 1950s, and the defense research and development (R&D) infrastructure was equally backward. Even the nuclear weapons program, developed at great cost and to the neglect of conventional weaponry, had produced only crude strategic systems, including a single nuclear-powered ballistic missile submarine that had yet to launch a missile. Moreover, during this time the Chinese armed forces had become intensely involved in Mao Zedong's domestic political campaigns, especially the Cultural Revolution, and were no longer an effective combat force, a reality demonstrated by their poor performance in the 1979 incursion into Vietnam.

Deng Xiaoping's long-term objective for the military reforms he introduced in 1979 was to build a self-sustaining defense establishment so that China could not be intimidated by any military power, and Beijing's foreign policies would not be constrained by military weakness. Rebuilding military strength, however, was not given first priority in Deng's strategy for modernizing China. In the "four modernizations" that defined his program for transforming China into a nation capable of assuming a leading role in world politics, renovating

national defense came fourth, after the modernization of agriculture, industry, and science and technology.

Apprehension in Asia and the United States that China's military power was becoming potentially dangerous to the region did not emerge until the cold war's end. Four major developments in Beijing's defense policies intersected to create the image of potential peril. First, in 1985 Beijing transformed its national military strategy: China's armed forces were directed no longer to prepare for a major, possibly nuclear, war with the Soviet Union but for local, limited wars on China's borders. Second, annual double-digit percentage increases in Beijing's defense budgets began in 1989 (and continue), sustained by the dramatic growth in China's economy, which suggested a potential change in priorities. Third, the armament and military technology linkage established with the Soviet Union in 1990, and upheld by Russia after the Soviet Union's disintegration, was viewed as potentially revitalizing China's defense industrial base in addition to providing advanced weaponry. Finally, in the early 1990s, improvements in China's conventional forces were joined by the development of a new series of short-range, tactical battlefield ballistic missiles and land- and submarine-based strategic missiles.

These four elements converged as China's military security, in Beijing's own assessment, became more assured than at any time in the previous 150 years. Even as the threat to China's security diminished, Beijing demonstrated an assertive, if not aggressive, nationalism in its approach to territorial claims in the South and East China Seas. An assertive, nationalistic China, facing no major military threat but with growing military muscle bolstered by a rapidly expanding economy and increasing military expenditures, raised serious questions about Beijing's long-term international intentions. Beijing's belligerent use of military exercises to intimidate Taiwan in the summer of 1995 and the spring of 1996, leading to United States

PAUL H. B. GODWIN *is a professor of international affairs in the department of military strategy at the National War College in Washington, D.C., where he specializes in China's defense and security policies. The views expressed in this essay are those of the author.*

 Reprinted with permission from *Current History*, September 1997, pp. 252–257. © 1997 by Current History, Inc.

deployment of two aircraft carrier battle groups near Taiwan, served only to exacerbate these concerns.

CHINA'S MILITARY STRENGTH IN CONTEXT

Military power is relative, not absolute; any evaluation of a state's military strength must be comparative and placed in context. Despite widespread apprehension in Asia and the United States that Beijing's military modernization programs could overturn East Asia's balance of power early in the twenty-first century, China's military leadership has no such confidence. To the contrary, it looks forward to the twenty-first century with uncertainty and a sense of insecurity, knowing that the Chinese People's Liberation Army (PLA), as all four services and branches are collectively named, will enter the next century with armaments and equipment just beginning to incorporate technologies from the 1970s and 1980s. It is not that Beijing perceives an immediate military threat to China, but that in an uncertain future with military technology evolving quickly, the PLA's relative obsolescence is becoming increasingly difficult to overcome.

Even apart from America's overwhelming military strength, Beijing looks out on an Asia undergoing major military renovation that in many areas exceeds the PLA's current capabilities and will continue to outmatch China's programs for at least a decade. As Beijing examines Asia's defense modernization programs, its concerns can be fully understood. Notwithstanding Tokyo's long-standing security relationship with the United States, including the protection provided by American nuclear forces and ongoing discussions about joining the United States theater missile defense program, Japan's euphemistically named Self-Defense Forces (SDF) are technologically the most sophisticated in the region and supported by Asia's most advanced defense industrial base. Nor are these forces small. Japan's maritime Self-Defense Forces constitute the region's largest modern navy, with 63 major surface combatants and 17 submarines; many of these are armed with the most advanced military technology in the world. With the capability to operate up to 1,000 nautical miles from the home islands, Japan's navy is supported by a land-based air arm deploying cutting-edge antisubmarine and antiship weapons on 110 aircraft and 99 armed helicopters. Japan's air Self-Defense Forces are equally powerful, deploying 90 American F-4Es, 189 domestically produced copies of the United States F-15 (considered the world's finest interceptor), and 50 indigenous F-1 ground attack fighters, all supported by airborne warning and control system (AWACS) aircraft. Furthermore, Tokyo's current plans call for continued modernization of its air, ground, and naval forces with a defense budget, $46.8 billion, that is the third largest in the world.

Tokyo clearly intends to sustain Asia's most powerful navy and air force, even though the Soviet Union no longer exists to threaten Japan and its security ties with the United States are politically strong. Further heightening Beijing's insecurity is the fact that the PLA and Japan's SDF began their modernization programs at about the same time (Tokyo's National Defense Program Outline that guided the SDF to its current status was announced in 1976, and Deng Xiaoping's military reforms were initiated in 1979). In the two decades since China and Japan began modernizing their armed forces and defense industries, Tokyo has clearly made the most progress, and its edge will continue into the foreseeable future.

In addition to Japan, throughout East Asia most defense establishments have been rapidly modernizing their armed forces with advanced combat aircraft, ships, and submarines. Thailand is about to deploy the region's first aircraft carrier— the Spanish-built *Chakkrinareubet*. Displacing only about 11,500 tons, and intended for search-and-rescue and humanitarian operations, this carrier nevertheless can embark a small number of helicopters and aircraft, and thus represents East Asia's first sea-based airpower.

In Southeast Asia, naval forces are being acquired that, in combination with modernizing air forces deploying a variety of United States F-16 and F/A-18 combat aircraft and Russian MiG-29s, will be better able to defend territorial and maritime interests. Taiwan in particular continues programs to extensively upgrade its air and naval forces, including air defense capabilities highlighted by the deployment of Patriot surface-to-air missiles. Taiwan is also acquiring French and American combat aircraft, ships, and air defense systems that will be on line within the decade.

From Beijing's perspective, the renovation of China's armed forces is part of a pattern of Asian military modernization that began in the late 1970s and continues, with few exceptions, today. Furthermore, United States defense alliances and forward-deployed military forces provide an added complication to any net assessment Beijing would make of its regional capabilities. This is true not only of formal United States treaty relationships but also of America's less formal commitments. Beijing could not ignore the fact that the first of two United States aircraft carrier battle groups to arrive off Taiwan during the March 1996 crisis was based in Japan. Similarly, it is American technology and research that threaten to erode the credibility of China's small nuclear deterrent force and tactical battlefield missiles through the promise of theater missile defense systems and national missile defenses, both plausible in the next century. Once again, Japan's defense industrial and R&D capabilities are highlighted by United States pressure on Tokyo to join the theater missile defense research program and agree to future deployment.

RETHINKING NATIONAL MILITARY STRATEGY

When the Soviet Union was China's principal threat and Beijing's military strategy was based on defending continental China, most of the PLA's technological weaknesses could be overcome by a strategy of protraction, attrition, and the threat of nuclear retaliation—the so-called people's war under modern conditions. Continental defense, including the ability to conduct offensive operations short distances beyond China's borders, benefited from the sheer size of the 4 million-man PLA and the ultimate strategy of falling back into China's vast interior and simply exhausting an adversary through protracted war.

As the cold war ended, China began preparing for local, limited war on its periphery, including the defense of maritime borders and territorial claims in the East and South China Seas; this new orientation accentuated the obsolescence of the PLA's arms and equipment far more than had the requirements for continental defense. Beijing's new national military strategy required the PLA to prepare for early, offensive operations designed to defeat an adversary quickly and decisively, and potentially at some distance from the mainland. In modern warfare, these operations depend on the synergistic effect of ground, air, and naval forces operating together for common military objectives. China's armed forces had no experience with these complex operations, and therefore lacked the joint service command, staff, and logistic support to prepare them for the demands of the new military strategy.

Moreover, existing and emerging warfare technologies make defense against a sudden attack or a preemptive military operation far more difficult than in the past. Standoff weapons has become significantly more accurate and lethal, offers precision targeting at far greater ranges, and can be used at night and in other low-visibility conditions. Limited war involving high-technology weaponry and equipment raises the importance of the initial engagement far beyond what it was a decade ago. Equally important for military operations, the development of surveillance technology is making the battlefield increasingly transparent. The significance of contemporary military technologies was underlined by the devastatingly swift defeat of Iraqi forces by the United States—led coalition in 1991. While the PLA knows it is extremely unlikely it will face such capabilities in the near future, it recognizes that China's military environment is becoming more demanding with the spread of advanced weapons and equipment throughout East Asia. In a direct response to the Gulf War's demonstration of high-technology warfare, China's military leadership modified its definition of future military contingencies from "limited, local war" to "limited war under high-tech conditions."

THE PLA'S EMERGING CAPABILITIES

The PLA is undoubtedly seeking to overcome the deficiencies highlighted by the demands of China's revised national military strategy.[1] It is also the case that access to Russian military technology and weapons, and Israeli technological and design support, have hastened the day when China's defense industries and the PLA will be more competent and capable. The difficulty is determining when that day will arrive, and to what extent China's capabilities will exceed those of its neighbors—nearly all of whom are committed to continued modernization of their defense forces. The question for Asia,

---

[1]See the June 1996 issue of *The China Quarterly,* which is devoted to a thorough analytic survey of China's military affairs. Much of my assessment draws on this issue.

> *It will be many years before the PLA can be considered modern.*

---

however, is not whether the PLA will be better able to defend China in the improbable event of an attack on its mainland; apprehension within the region is instead based on China's potential force projection capabilities, especially as they apply to the future of Taiwan's and Beijing's territorial claims in the East and South China Seas. Thus, it is not the sheer size of China's armed forces and the vast amounts of largely obsolescent equipment it deploys, but the direction and intent of current modernization programs that are the source of anxiety.

Beijing has not sought to hide its recent focus on air and naval power. The PLA also has not tried to obscure its concentration on building "crack troops" capable of responding effectively to the kinds of military contingencies outlined in China's new national military strategy. For the past decade, but especially during the past five years, the PLA has focused on training and equipping selected ground units for quick-reaction and amphibious warfare roles. These are the "fist" (*quantou*) and "rapid response" (*kuaisu*) units, such as the 15th Group Army (Airborne) and the PLA navy's brigade-strength marine corps. Similarly, the PLA is attempting to establish command-and-control and logistic support systems that can effectively coordinate and sustain operations involving ground, air, and naval units. Training and exercises are explicitly concentrated on joint service operations. This training includes amphibious warfare exercises and naval maneuvers involving underway replenishment, as task forces train for surface combat and antisubmarine warfare.

Beijing's current weapons, equipment, and technology acquisition programs support the needs of its national military strategy. Air and naval forces answer the demand to defend far-flung maritime sovereignty claims, including Taiwan and those in the South China Sea. Strategic weapons are being replaced because of their age and the need to make new systems more survivable and accurate in the next century. Analyzing these acquisitions within the operational doctrine of today's PLA and Asia's military environment provides a measure of capability. There are, nonetheless, specific constraints that must be kept in mind as part of such an assessment.

Before Moscow began military technology transfers in 1990, the Western powers had placed stringent limits on what they would sell China. Following the Tiananmen tragedy of 1989, the West—with the exception of Israel—essentially embargoed all arms and military technology transfers to China. Because of these constraints, China's experience with advanced military technology is limited to, at most, the past five years, when the PLA began receiving Russian arms. Until China's defense industries place advanced weapons and equipment into series production, they cannot be considered an effective defense industrial base for China's armed forces.

Equally important, the small number of weapons purchased and the time it takes to train the first crews and maintenance personnel mean that it will be many years before the PLA can be considered modern.

ACQUIRING AND PROJECTING POWER

China has pursued programs designed to update obsolescent equipment with foreign technologies and develop new indigenous designs. The failure of these programs to meet the PLA's needs can be seen in acquisitions from Russia. The 1994 purchase of four Kilo-class diesel-electric-powered attack submarines from Russia indicates that China's own submarine programs were unsatisfactory. The submarine force is large, but 50 percent of the 50 or so deployed are based on outdated Soviet Romeo-types from the 1950s. China's newer designs are the 12 Romeo-derived Ming-class, and a single Song-class of more modern design currently undergoing operational evaluation. These ships are supplemented by 5 Han-class nuclear-powered submarines based on older technologies, and therefore undoubtedly very noisy and easily targeted by modern antisubmarine warfare systems. Similarly, the purchase in 1997 of 2 Russian Sovremenny-class destroyers is a strong indication that the new Luhu-class destroyer and Jiangwei-class frigate developed by China using primarily Western technologies are less than successful. Only 2 Luhus and 4 Jiangweis have been built in the past five years.

Long-standing efforts to improve the PLA air force and navy fleet air arm include the F-8, now operational but at beat representing early 1960s technologies, and the FB-7, originally developed for the navy but not yet in series production. The future of China's airpower is tied to the F10 that is being developed with Israeli assistance, and to the agreement for licensed production of Russia's Su-27 following the purchase of 72 completed aircraft. Over time these new aircraft will replace, but in much smaller numbers, China's obsolescent airpower composed primarily of about 4,400 fighter and ground attack aircraft derived from Soviet MiG-17, MiG-19, and MiG-21 designs. There is as yet no sign that the bomber force of some 420 aircraft derived from 1950s Soviet I1-28 and Tu-16 designs is to be replaced.

Forty-eight of the 72 Su-27s purchased from Russia have been delivered. Licensed production of these aircraft from complete kits supplied by Russia could begin in a year or so, but full Chinese-content Su-27s cannot be built for many years. It is unclear when the Israeli-assisted F-10 will enter production; even after years of development there is as yet no flying prototype. Two of the Kilo-class diesel-electric submarines have been delivered, and their first crews are completing Russian training programs. The two Sovremenny destroyers may be delivered by the end of this century and could be operational around 2004. Thus, from the PLA's point of view, true modernization of its weapons and the process of integrating them into operational and tactical doctrine have only just begun.

Military power projection requires the ability to sustain expeditionary forces in combat some distance from their home base. For the PLA, as with any other military, time and distance are critical variables in offensive operations. Should the PLA be called on to defend China's sovereignty claims in the South China Sea, military operations would require sustaining forces in combat as far as 600 miles (960 kilometers) from Hainan Island. If China sought to invade Taiwan, it would require an amphibious and/or air assault some 100 miles (160 km) from the mainland—essentially the distance covered by the allied invasion of France in 1944. At least for the next decade, China's armed forces will be incapable of successfully performing either operation against determined resistance.

With the exception of its ancient bomber fleet, combat operations in the South China Sea are beyond the effective range of China's airpower, which is entirely land-based and has no aerial refueling capability. Furthermore, Beijing's naval forces lack effective defenses against cruise missiles and air attack. Deployed naval air defenses consist of surface-to-air missiles (SAM) with a range of seven miles (11 km), providing an adversary the opportunity to launch antiship missiles beyond the range of the defending SAMs. Chinese warships have no defense against cruise missiles, since they do not mount radar-controlled close-in weapons systems designed for this purpose. Moreover, even with recent improvements, Chinese warships do not deploy antisubmarine warfare (ASW) systems capable of defeating modern, quiet submarines.

Should Beijing attempt combat air patrols over the South China Sea without aerial refueling, even its most modern fighter-bombers would have at most five minutes of loiter time. Without AWACS aircraft to detect and assign targets, the combat air patrols would be ineffective. Any of China's obsolescent long-range bombers deployed would be dangerously exposed to SAM defenses and modern interceptors firing medium-range air-to-air missiles. China can maintain a naval presence in the South China Sea, but it cannot conduct sustained combat operations like those rehearsed for three weeks this April in the region by Australia, Singapore, Malaysia, Brunei, and Britain (the British Commonwealth's Five-Power Defense Arrangement group). This exercise, dubbed "Flying Fish," involved the deployment of 160 aircraft and 36 ships, including a British aircraft carrier and nuclear-powered submarine.

An assault on Taiwan would be perhaps even more difficult for the PLA because of improvements in the island's defenses. Taipei is acquiring 60 French Mirage 2000 fighter-bombers, 150 United States F-16s, and 4 American E-2 AWACS aircraft, making it extremely difficult for the PLA to gain air superiority over the Taiwan Strait. Taipei's acquisition of 6 French La Fayette-class frigates, the construction of 6 improved United States Perry-class frigates, and the lease of 6 modernized United States Knox frigates (which augment 22 updated older American destroyers) provide Taiwan's navy with far more advanced ships than those currently deployed by the PLA. In particular, the Perry's SAM defenses have a range of at least 60 miles (97 km), and defense against cruise missiles is provided by close-in weapons systems. These ships also employ very effective ASW systems and surface-to-surface missiles. On a ship-to-ship basis, Taiwan's navy can outshoot China's. An amphibious assault across the 100 miles (160 km) of the Taiwan

Strait would require air superiority and sea control. Even with a large submarine force, it is doubtful the PLA could achieve such predominance except at great cost and over a considerable period of time.

Time is an extremely important consideration for Beijing. By deploying two carrier battle groups off Taiwan in response to China's aggressive military exercises, the United States clarified its commitment and added a clear complication to any PLA planning. Put simply, the PLA cannot plan military operations designed to subdue Taiwan without including the contingency of United States involvement. To the extent that Taiwan can prevent the PLA from rapidly achieving air superiority and sea control, American military support in the defense of Taiwan becomes more probable.

THE NUCLEAR DIMENSION

Beijing's strategy for nuclear deterrence is straightforward: China shall have the capability to respond to any nuclear attack with a second strike lethal enough to seriously harm the attacker. Beijing believes that this strategy can deter the kinds of nuclear threats made by the United States during the Korean War and the Taiwan Strait crises of the 1950s, and faced from the Soviet Union in the 1960s, 1970s, and 1980s.

China's small, aging, liquid-fueled intercontinental ballistic missile (ICBM) force of some 17 missiles was initially deployed in the mid-1970s and early 1980s. Deployment of its intermediate-range ballistic missile (IRBM) force of perhaps 70 weapons began in the late 1960s. To provide a survivable, quicker-reacting nuclear deterrent in an era when the United States and Russia continue to deploy thousands of strategic weapons and when missile defense is on the horizon, this force had to be modernized. Survivability is being sought through tactical mobility, with both the new solid-fueled 7,500-mile (12,000-km)-range DF-41 ICBM and the 5,000-mile (8,000-km)-range DF-31 designed to be road- and rail-mobile. The DF-41 is not anticipated to be operational before 2010, but the DF-31 will perhaps begin deployment in a year or two.

Solid fuels improve booster reliability and provide quicker response time, thereby reducing the missiles' vulnerability to a counterforce first strike. Solid propellants, however, have less boost power than liquid fuels, which means that the change to solid fuels required smaller warheads with greater yield-to-weight ratios. Smaller warheads have also been developed to prepare for the time when China masters multiple reentry vehicle technologies and missile defenses require penetration aids.

China's single nuclear-powered submarine (SSBN) entered service in 1983. This ship is not known to have test-launched a missile in a decade and may not be operational, if it ever was. Nonetheless, a new submarine-launched missile—the JL-2—has been derived from the DF-31, and it is assumed that a follow-on SSBN is under construction to take the weapon.

There are indications that some of Beijing's military strategists believe China's strategic forces are too small to be considered a credible deterrent. They would have China change from minimum deterrence, where a relatively small number of warheads capable of inflicting considerable damage in a second strike are considered sufficient, to a more robust strategy that calls for the deployment of a larger number of strategic forces. In an era when missile defenses are likely to be put in place, there will be continuing pressure on China to deploy more systems, with warheads equipped with multiple reentry vehicles, including penetration aids. Development of these technologies is almost certainly under way, but some years of testing will be required before they can be employed. This will provide sufficient lead time to determine that a major shift in nuclear strategy has occurred and that the number and capability of China's strategic systems is increasing.

A MIRROR-IMAGE FUTURE

Beijing's military planners face an increasingly difficult dilemma. Rapid advances in military technologies have created requirements that China's defense R&D infrastructure and industrial base cannot meet. Beijing's national military strategy and the proliferation of high-technology arms and equipment nonetheless accentuate the role of advanced technologies in operations conducted by China's conventional forces, especially offensive operations, and in maintaining a viable nuclear deterrent. Yet, despite China's undoubted ambition to become a full-fledged great military power and its quest for Russian assistance in achieving this objective, there is no evidence that Beijing has embarked on a crash course to correct all its well-known deficiencies. Rather, Beijing's limited purchase of advanced weapons and equipment, and its continued preference for technology over end-use items, demonstrate that China's defense modernization strategy remains long-term and incremental. Modernization of China's defense industrial base and R&D, as this term is understood in the United States, Europe, Russia, and Japan, remains at least two decades into the future—decades during which the rest of Asia will not be standing still, least of all Japan.

Need East Asia worry? Of course. Although China's capabilities are currently limited, Beijing's ambition to achieve the status of a major military power has never been hidden. Two or three decades from now, assuming China's economy can continue to support the long-term strategy of building a largely self-reliant defense establishment, Asia could have in its midst a new primary military power. How Beijing will choose to use this power is the critical uncertainty. Hence, the central question for East Asia's security analysts is how long the United States will continue to deploy the military forces that are such a crucial element in the region's military balance. Despite Washington's constant reiteration that significant United States forces will remain, much of the buildup in East Asia reflects uncertainty about the American commitment and the misgiving that in a decade or two the region will contain two giants, China and Japan, each potentially seeking dominance. Thus, in an ironic twist, the uncertainty and consequent insecurity marking the PLA's perception of the twenty-first century is mirror-imaged by the rest of the region.

Russian Foreign Policy in the Near Abroad and Beyond

KAREN DAWISHA

Boris Yeltsin's victory in the 1996 presidential election marked further progress in Russia's consolidation of democracy and movement toward a free-market economy. Yeltsin won, however, not least by shifting to the right in foreign policy and by advocating the pursuit of Russia's great power interests in the neighboring former Soviet republics—the so-called Near Abroad. In so doing he prevented the Communists from taking over the presidency, but his rightward shift was too late to prevent them or their allies from gaining control of the Duma, the Russian parliament, in the December 1995 elections. Thus, even with Boris Yeltsin as president, Russian foreign policy for the foreseeable future can be expected to be more assertive toward the West and more oriented toward reestablishing Russian primacy on the Eurasian continent.

Russia, however, currently lacks the capacity to reassert imperial control over the newly independent states of its former empire. The Russian military doctrine adopted in 1993 emphasizes war prevention and the maintenance of military sufficiency and eschews earlier doctrinal commitments to war fighting in forward areas and conventional superiority. The new doctrine sees two major roles for the Russian military: preventing local wars that might arise from secessionist claims (as in the fight for independence by the breakaway Chechen republic in southern Russia) and de-escalating conflicts in lands adjacent to Russian territory that could imperil Russian interests and spill over into Russia proper (as in the conflicts in the Georgian provinces of Abkhazia and South Ossetia). Moreover, in the five years since the break up of the Soviet Union, the Russian military has shrunk by more than half its peak level in the mid-1980s, and the call-up to go to war in Chechnya and other hot spots has produced widespread draft dodging.

Although Russia's ability to achieve imperial aims by force is currently limited, observers worry that the imperial idea may nevertheless be reborn, presaging a future round of expansion. While neither elite nor public opinion presently favors such a resurgence, there are minority currents in both that deserve examining.

THE DRIFT TO THE RIGHT

Beginning in 1993, the liberal, pro-Western orientation of Russian foreign policy, which had virtually ignored the Near Abroad in favor of reliance on ties with Europe and America, gave way. The 1993 and 1995 Duma elections and the two rounds of this summer's presidential election showcased right-wing leaders and parties that supported the expansion of Russian borders; these included the Liberal Democrats (led by Vladimir Zhirinovsky), the Communists (led by Gennadi Zyuganov), and the Congress of Russian Communities (led by retired General Aleksandr Lebed).

Under unrelenting pressure from the right, liberal and centrist politicians have increasingly had to concede that the Near Abroad should be a zone of Russian rights and interests. Even President Yeltsin's election platform stated that the two top priorities of Russian foreign policy were "the achievement of the utmost integration of the CIS [the Commonwealth of Independent States—the regional organization to which most of the former Soviet republics acceded after the Soviet Union collapsed] countries on a voluntary and mutually advantageous

KAREN DAWISHA *is a professor in the department of government and politics at the University of Maryland and director of its Center for the Study of Post-Communist Societies. Her most recent book is* Foreign Policy-Making in Russia and the New States of Eurasia *(Armonk, N.Y.: M. E. Sharpe, 1995). The author would like to thank Darya Pushkina for research assistance. A version of this paper was presented at the Aspen Institute's congressional program meeting in St. Petersburg, Russia, in August.*[1996]

basis and the active protection of the rights and interests of fellow-countrymen in the near and far abroad." In contrast, the improvement of Russian-American relations was not even mentioned among his priorities if elected, reflecting the political sensitivity of his prior commitment to that relationship.

After the first round of the presidential election, Yeltsin boosted his chances in the runoff by turning to the right and appointing General Lebed as his national security adviser. It had been Lebed's charisma and his reputation as an incorruptible supporter of law and order more than his hawkish stance on foreign policy that had won him over a sixth of the popular vote in the first round. Yet his new position undoubtedly assured his ability to shape future policy toward the Near Abroad.

The problem for Yeltsin in allying with Lebed and other rightist leaders is that many of them vehemently support the redrawing of borders by force and have only a lukewarm commitment to democracy and the rule of law. In 1991 and 1993, Communist and right-wing leaders attempted to take power by force, and they have remained active on the political stage. Even after being appointed national security adviser, Lebed labeled himself only a semidemocrat, and Yeltsin's own inner circle includes advisers who have favored both a get-tough policy toward Russia's neighbors and the use of extralegal means to ensure that Yeltsin stays in control. Given the connection between the antidemocratic and pro-imperial ideas of these groups, the further entrenchment of the latter could undermine democracy. Conversely, the further institutionalization of democracy should also weaken the force of imperial ideology.

Yet the institutionalization of democracy will not automatically or immediately decrease the influence of these groups since they do control the Duma. Although the Duma's powers are limited, it can and has passed any number of nonbinding resolutions that force a government response and shape the general political environment in which policy is made. Duma actions have included calls for military-basing agreements with all countries on Russia's borders; promotion of dual-citizenship agreements with Russia's neighbors; denunciation of preferences for the titular nationality in neighbors' citizenship laws; the elimination of Belarus's central bank as a precondition for accepting Belarus's request for economic union with Russia; a declaration of Russian sovereignty over Sevastopol, the Ukrainian port in the Crimea where the contested Black Sea Fleet is headquartered; and a resolution annulling the agreements that brought about the end of the Soviet Union.

The Duma's failure to deal with what are seen as more pressing domestic concerns has led to a decline in its reputation among the populace. Public opinion polls have consistently shown the people's low interest in foreign policy as compared to their concern with the rule of law, the fight against crime, and, above all, domestic economic recovery. In the December 1995 Duma elections, parties that were perceived as capable of dealing with foreign policy but less capable of addressing the country's economic ills (such as Lebed's Congress of Russian Communities) typically did not receive the 5 percent of the vote that would allow representation in the Duma.

Public opinion has also shown that while nostalgia for the Soviet era is widespread, the people are completely unwilling to use Russian troops to forcibly restore the Union. The revulsion at the loss of Russian life in the fight against the Chechens has shaped popular sentiment against imperial expansion abroad: polls repeatedly have shown that almost three-quarters of the population reject any form of reestablishment of the Union, and among those who support such an end, only 5 percent would sanction the use of force.

RUSSIA'S "NATIONAL SECURITY ZONE" DEFINED

While Russia is unlikely to seek the forcible reestablishment of empire, the country's leaders have moved clearly to mark out the Near Abroad as their "national security zone." As the largest and strongest country of the former Soviet Union, and the one that has benefited most from the institutional inheritance of the Soviet state, Russia has enormous comparative advantage. Thus, Russia has used its position as the least dependent economy in the former Soviet space to exert economic pressure, especially through the supply or withholding of energy or access to Russian-controlled pipelines. Because of the comparative weakness of most of the new states, Russia is able to exert enormous leverage with relatively little effort. The way Russia has been able to shift between the Armenians and the Azerbaijanis—supplying energy to one side and then the other—shows that it can punish and reward without suffering significant or proportionate losses.

That Russia has been willing to provide substantial energy and trade subsidies makes clear the extent to which it is concerned about not destabilizing the newly independent countries. According to IMF estimates, Russia provided $17 billion in goods at concessional and subsidized prices in 1993 alone—making it the single largest aid donor to the other newly independent states in that year. Furthermore, in February 1996 Russia and Belarus signed an agreement renouncing mutual debts, including the $600 million (plus the millions in penalties) Belarus owed to the Russian natural gas monopoly Gazprom.

Russian leaders encouraged all the former republics to join the Commonwealth of Independent States, which originally included a joint military command dominated by Russia. While currently incapable of mounting and maintaining a large-scale military operation beyond Russia's borders, the Russian military—via a network of formal basing agreements, contingents "temporarily" stationed abroad, a unified air defense system controlled by Moscow, and peacekeeping missions sanctioned by regional treaties—is the only force in the Eurasian space capable of sustained significant influence in the other states of the Near Abroad.

Russia's commitment of 25,000 troops to Tajikistan, its legal claims to Crimea, and its pledge to protect ethnic Russians living abroad are issues that spring from different situations and political motivations. But they reflect an overall consensus in Russia that the former Soviet area constitutes a natural russophone zone over which Moscow has "always" been able to exercise influence. Even President Yeltsin, whose initial foreign policy views emphasized international and Western links, has come to embrace the notion that "the sphere of Russia's economic, political, and humanitarian interests extends to the entire post-Soviet space."

One reason for this stance is that Russia lacks a regional alternative to cooperation with the other new states. While it is abundantly richer in natural resources than its neighbors, the psychological and organizational detritus of the Soviet era has created barriers to cooperation with new partners. Whereas in the 1960s Britain and France could simultaneously pursue decolonization in Africa and Asia and integration in Europe, Russia has little alternative but to pursue decolonization in Eurasia even as it seeks regional reintegration with countries in the region. Naturally, such a policy is fraught with the potential for misunderstanding.

Indeed it is difficult to read the official "Strategic Course of the Russian Federation" with the CIS countries without wondering whether the successful pursuit of this course could pave the way for a de facto imperial reassertion. The document is a clear statement of Russia's assertion of great power status over the other states. It asserts that Russia's main objective toward the CIS is the creation of "an economically and politically integrated association of states capable of claiming its proper place in the world community"; that Russia should be "the leading force in the formation of a new system of interstate political and economic relations"; and that when working with the UN and the Organization for Security and Cooperation in Europe on peacekeeping in the CIS, "it is necessary to seek their agreement that this region is primarily a zone of Russian interests."

CONTINUED COEXISTENCE

Many of Moscow's actions toward the Near Abroad since independence have met a stern rebuff. Indeed, it could be said that a central feature in the national identity of many of the new states is the imperative of resistance to any renewed Russian drive.

This resistance to Russian control is especially apparent in Latvia and Estonia, western Ukraine, western Moldova, Azerbaijan, and within Russia itself in the North Caucasus. It is less prevalent in Central Asia, Armenia, Georgia, eastern and southern Ukraine, eastern Moldova, Belarus, and Lithuania. In the first group there is a solid consensus among the elites and the population that independence means independence from Russia; the situation in the latter group is not so clear cut. Historic memories of Russia as a savior of local populations, common Slavic and Orthodox roots, an economic infrastructure still centered in Moscow, and russophone elites or large numbers of Russian nationals settled in and intermarried with the local population all lend themselves to Russia's continued coexistence with these countries.

This coexistence has under certain circumstances translated into significant Russian influence. In Georgia both the Abkhaz separatists and the Georgian state authorities called on Russia for military support to tip the balance in their favor and then to maintain the peace once the threat of separatism had subsided. In the process, the Georgian government acceded to Russian demands for military-basing rights in the country, bases that could be used both to support President Eduard Shevardnadze's embattled position and to promote Russia's interests in the Caucasus if needed.

In Armenia, the government has repeatedly enlisted Russian military support in its conflict with Azerbaijan over the Armenian-populated enclave of Nagorno-Karabakh in Azerbaijan. It received critical supplies of oil for its 1994 offensive into Azerbaijan and relies on those supplies for its continued occupation of western Azerbaijan. Both Armenia and Russia have sought to weaken Azerbaijan: Armenia wants to promote its own claims to Nagorno-Karabakh, and Russia wants to gain access to Azerbaijan's oil and weaken Baku's potential to reclaim its historic role as the beacon for the spread of pan-Turkic and Islamic appeals north and east from the Middle East.

Azerbaijan has been thrown onto the defensive in the face of this dual pressure. The Azerbaijani Popular Front and its leader, former President Abulfaz Elchibey, long an object of Russian concern, lost power to Gaidar Aliev, a former Soviet apparatchik. Since becoming president, Aliev has tried to protect the country from Armenia by acceding to virtually all Russian demands, including granting ever-larger percentages of stock in Azerbaijan's oil industry to Russian firms and guaranteeing that Azerbaijani [oil] would continue to be exported to the outside world through Russian pipelines. The Azerbaijanis have decided that the only way to buy security from Armenian attacks is to recognize Russian economic interests in the area.

None of the states in the Caucasus have become colonies of Russia; they have only accepted an increased Russian presence in return for the economic and security benefits it provides. In so doing, however, they have become more dependent on Russia and made it possible for Russia to exert pressure on the politics of the region at a lower cost than if Caucasian elites had not so easily accepted an increased Russian presence.

In Belarus the situation is different. While other states, including Kazakstan and Kyrgyzstan, have sought stronger ties with Russia, Belarus stands alone among the new states in actively favoring reunification. Opinion polls in Belarus have shown support from almost half the population for significantly closer relations with Russia—including support among a small minority for the complete restoration of the Soviet Union—and a popular referendum supported by the president called for union as well. (Indeed, President Alexander Lukashenko ran on a platform that promised complete union with Moscow.) Belarus has dismantled border posts along the frontier with Russia, restored Russian as the official language, promised to maintain its army's preparedness, agreed to continue paying pensions to the thousands of retired Soviet-era officers residing in Belarus, established a joint parliamentary assembly with the Russian Duma, and granted Russia leases for two bases.

Despite President Lukashenko's assurances that the two countries would soon become a single "unified state," a treaty creating only a "Community of Sovereign Republics" was signed in April 1996. Lawmakers in both countries expressed skepticism that Russia would undertake the economic burden of reincorporating Belarus and that authorities in Minsk would surrender the country's sovereignty completely.

In Central Asia, elites were clearly unprepared for independence and spent much of the first year trying to convince Russia to form a commonwealth. In contrast to elites in the Caucasus and the Baltics, most post-independence Central Asian leaders had not been involved in pre-independence national struggles, undergone any period of imprisonment, or formed or led popular fronts. The exception, of course, was Tajikistan; there, after a brief but bloody civil war, pro-Moscow elites gained the ascendancy and established a regime strongly in favor of a continued Russian presence.

In the region as a whole, elites have been unable or unwilling to act on their economic independence from Russia. Elites trained in central planning have continued to see Moscow as the center, and Russia has maintained its economic advantage; a treaty between Russia, Belarus, Kazakstan, and Kyrgyzstan signed in March 1996 called for the "deepening of integration" in the economic field.

However, in none of the Central Asian countries is there an indigenous trend favoring the surrender of political sovereignty. Most national elites (Tajikistan is the exception) have become more and not less committed to maintaining their countries' formal independence while continuing to rely on Moscow for economic and military support. Their reaction to Moscow's rhetoric that the Belarus-Russia treaty would be a model for future Russian relations with other CIS countries was almost uniformly negative.

Given the speed and circumstances of the Soviet collapse, the initial unpreparedness of so many elites and populations for independence is historically unique. With the passage of time their countries have come to value independence more, particularly since they have been able to enjoy its economic, security, psychological, and cultural benefits. Yet many of these new states, however hostile to Russia, are weaker and more fragile than Russia and will therefore remain dependent on it. Consequently, Russia is unlikely to recede as an economic or geopolitical presence in the area, and the temptation to empire will have to be contained by more than the varying will and ability of peoples in the bordering states.

RUSSIA AND THE WORLD

During the course of the twentieth century, the Russian empire was replaced by a Soviet empire; that empire has fallen, but talk of another has resurfaced and Western policymakers are considering whether an enlarged NATO will have to stand once again as a bastion against Russian expansion. In the weak and divided international community of the early 1920s, the Soviet Union succeeded in establishing itself and incorporating by force many of the territories of the former Russian empire. Would the international community allow a similar process to repeat itself today?

Several important factors make such a repetition unlikely. First, elites in neighboring countries have a greater awareness of the nature and potential of Russian power. For example, reabsorbing Kazakstan today, with its cities, educated elite, developed infrastructure, and communications links to the outside world would be a far more difficult task than it was in the 1920s, when the indigenous peoples were nomadic, illiterate, geographically isolated, and had no history of independent statehood. Moreover, if Russia attempted to forcibly re-integrate them, these states would undoubtedly seek and receive support from the international community for a renewed policy of containment. Regional security organizations of the kind developed during the early years of the cold war, such as NATO, SEATO, and CENTO, could be expanded to include not only new East-Central European members but also states of the former Soviet Union itself. Current restraints on forward basing of United States and Western European troops would also presumably be lifted under such circumstances.

Second, the post-1945 international system has largely come to accept the principles of state sovereignty, national self-determination, and the inadmissibility of the use of force to change boundaries of legitimate, popularly elected governments. At the close of the nineteenth century, the golden age of empires imposed a normative logic on the international system. A century later the defense of the nation-state (not the imperial state) and the promotion of decolonization, democracy, and human rights—and not the reestablishment of empire and authoritarian regimes—are the dominant norms upheld by the international community and from which international institutions derive their legitimacy. To the extent that force has been sanctioned by the international community through the United Nations, it has been to uphold these norms (as in Kuwait, Haiti, or Bosnia). It is virtually impossible to foresee a situation in which the clear use of Russian force against the wishes of a legitimately elected government would be formally sanctioned by the international community and its organizations.

Should there be a resurgence of imperial fervor, Russia's options will also be limited geopolitically. Eastern Europe and the West would undoubtedly move to expand NATO without taking Russian sensitivities into account, and any possibility of establishing joint committees from Russia and NATO states on foreign affairs or defense would vanish. While the Soviet Union could leapfrog over the American-sponsored regional security organizations that ringed it during the Cold War by establishing ties with leftist regimes in the third world, most of these regimes have now become integrated into the global economy. They would not gain by establishing relationships with a right-wing Russia that would threaten their connections with other trading partners.

Finally, the entrenchment of democracy in Russia and among its neighbors will decrease civil strife, diminish the influence of antidemocratic forces, increase the ability of the legislatures, courts, and media to oversee the "power ministries," and create growing incentives to respect international norms. Russia's size and wealth will ensure its continued preeminence in Eurasia, but it is its commitment to democracy and its new institutions, if sustained, that will ensure it a respected place in the international arena.

The Case for Nuclear Deterrence Today

by Robert G. Joseph and John F. Reichart

The morality and utility of nuclear weapons have been debated passionately since their creation. Trinity, the first atomic detonation in 1945, vividly demonstrated the awesome destructive power of this technological leap. The explosion, which Manhattan Project's chief scientist Robert Oppenheimer described in apocalyptic terms, had an instant impact on the bomb's creators, several of whom would later question the wisdom of developing the weapon even though it had been designed and employed to end a conventional war that claimed the lives of tens of millions. At the time, no one disputed that the destruction of Hiroshima and Nagasaki had had a decisive impact on the Japanese leadership's decision to end the war, thereby saving a million or more American and Japanese lives. But neither did anyone relish a future in which the use of nuclear weapons would become an accepted condition of warfare.

In a well-intentioned effort to control, if not disinvent, nuclear weapons, therefore, the United States launched an urgent initiative within the new United Nations organization. The Baruch Plan would fail, however, because neither the United States nor the Soviet Union believed it could risk the consequences of not possessing these weapons in a Cold War climate of secrecy and mistrust. Given the failure to achieve international control and the Soviet subjugation of Eastern Europe, a consensus soon emerged that nuclear weapons were an essential component of the security posture of the West. In the preceding fifty years, conventional deterrence had twice failed to prevent world war, and in any case neither the United States

Robert G. Joseph and John F. Reichart *are director and deputy director of the Center for Counterproliferation Research, National Defense University, and members of the National War College faculty. Ambassador Joseph is a former principal deputy assistance secretary of defense for international security policy. Dr. Reichart is a former member of the State Department policy planning staff. The opinions, conclusions, and recommendations expressed or implied in this article are solely those of the authors, and do not necessarily represent the views of the National Defense University, the Department of Defense, or any other government agency.*

nor the West Europeans had the will or means to match the Soviets' superior conventional forces. Hence, nuclear weapons seemed the only way to deter, even if based on a "balance of terror." Over the next four decades the names of deterrence doctrines would change with almost every administration, but the U.S. and NATO defense community consistently placed a reliance on nuclear weapons at the center of its strategy to deter Soviet bloc aggression.

Despite the sturdy public consensus in favor of nuclear weapons throughout the Cold War, some advocates continually called for abolition of these weapons. These political and religious groups ranged from ideological "peace" organizations cynically manipulated by Moscow, to dedicated pacifists, to mainline religious groups (epitomized by the work and guidance of both Catholic and Methodist bishops and others in the early and mid-1980's).[1] Despite their persistence, these movements had little influence on nuclear policy, force structure, or targeting largely because nuclear deterrence was seen by most observers, and almost all practitioners, as having worked to deter Soviet military forces from projecting force outward. The nuclear arsenal was thus a central ingredient in the broader strategy of containment and a critical tool of crisis stability during periodic bouts of brinkmanship.

While it is impossible to prove what would have happened had nuclear weapons not existed during the Cold War, the reality of what did *not* happen—World War III—would seem to vindicate those who advocated a strong nuclear deterrent. In the first half of the twentieth century tens of millions of combatants and civilians perished in war. In the second half of the century, millions more died in regional conflicts in which nuclear deterrence did not pertain. Yet, in Europe—arguably the most volatile Cold War battleground and potentially the deadliest because of the enormous concentration of armed forces there—war did not occur. The threat of escalation and nuclear annihilation made the prospect of war too horrific and reinforced caution in decision makers on both sides.

---

[1] See, for example, United States Catholic Conference, "The Challenge of Peace: God's Promise and Our Purpose," Washington, D.C., 1983.

From *ORBIS*, Winter 1998, pp. 7-19 © 1998 by JAI Press Inc. Reprinted by permission.

The Case of the "New Eliminationists"

Today, noted groups and individuals advocating the abolition of nuclear weapons have revived the debate, again calling into question the role of these weapons in the contemporary security environment. This renewed debate should be welcomed and encouraged. It is essential that the role of nuclear weapons be understood, and policies about their employment subject to broad public support. Failure to achieve this understanding will undercut the support that is necessary both inside and outside the government for fashioning and maintaining a sound nuclear policy and a credible nuclear deterrent posture. Without a sound policy foundation, Western states could again become victims of their own fancy, such as occurred in the interwar period when attention was focused on outlawing war rather than deterring aggression.

What is the nature of the new nuclear debate? In the forefront are the "new eliminationists"—those advocating either complete abolition of nuclear weapons or drastic reductions as a first step to a nuclear-free world. They include various high-profile commissions, self-appointed committees, and distinguished individuals, including several retired four-star officers who held the highest "nuclear commands" during and after the Cold War. Representative of the arguments of these "new eliminationists" are the Canberra Commission Report and the much publicized open letter from prominent generals and admirals concluding that nuclear weapons constitute "a peril to global peace and security," in light of which "the ultimate objective should be the complete and total elimination of nuclear weapons from all nations."[2]

Many, if not the majority of those who participated in the Canberra Commission and signed the open letter, as well as a large number of defense intellectuals who have since climbed on the bandwagon appear to support a two-step process. First, the major powers would quickly reduce their arsenals to a "few hundred" warheads. Secondly, they would pause for an assessment which, if conditions warrant, could then lead to total elimination. Often those taking this position explicitly disassociate themselves from the "abolition now" camp, and criticize those who take the abolitionists to task for creating a straw man. Nevertheless, both camps rely on a similar rationale for their positions and recommendations which, although differing on timing and conditions, share the same goal.

The conclusions and recommendations of the "new eliminationists" rest on four propositions:

(1) The use of nuclear weapons against nonnuclear states is morally and politically indefensible, and the threat of nuclear use to deter these states is incredible. States such as Iraq, Iran, North Korea and the other so-called rogues can be deterred (even if armed with chemical and biological weapons), and if necessary defeated by the West's vast technological superiority in conventional weaponry. The ability to hold at risk and destroy targets with nuclear weapons in these states provides no

benefit. The United States would never—for ethical and political reasons—exercise such options.

(2) The destructiveness of nuclear weapons is so great they have no military utility against another nuclear state except for deterrence. In this context, the justification for large deterrent stockpiles vanished with the demise of the Soviet Union. Russia, a new democracy struggling to reform, is now more a partner than competitor, and in any case cannot afford to maintain a modern nuclear arsenal.

(3) The indefinite deployment of nuclear weapons, especially in light of the erosion of Russian control over its nuclear forces, carries a high risk of use through accident or inadvertence. Moreover, the prospect of "leakage" of sensitive materials and expertise from the former Soviet Union makes it imperative to improve security measures which can be enhanced by the reduction in overall force levels, and especially the dismantling of warheads.

(4) The possession of nuclear weapons by some states stimulates others to acquire them, thereby reducing the security of all. The inherent double standard in the Non-Proliferation Treaty (NPT) regime must be overcome and its commitments to pursue complete nuclear disarmament must be fulfilled. Only in this manner will states such as India agree to become members. This strengthening of international norms will present further barriers to other states that clandestinely seek to acquire nuclear capabilities. The international community will thus come together to raise and enforce the barriers to acquisition of nuclear weapons.

Responding to the Call

A number of counter arguments have been made in response to the "new eliminationists." Perhaps the most direct is Sir Michael Quinlan's exposition of the dangers and fallacies of attempting to disinvent nuclear weapons.[3] Also, in well-argued testimony before Congress, Under Secretary of Defense Walter Slocombe has articulated the U.S. administration's case against abolishing nuclear weapons.[4] Neither, however, systematically addresses the core propositions of the new eliminationists which need to be examined one by one.

Morality and ethics. In terms of morality, the blanket charge that any use of nuclear weapons—and even reliance on the threat of nuclear retaliation for deterrence—would be immoral goes beyond past proclamations, such as those contained in the 1983 Catholic bishops' pastoral letter which, while calling for general disarmament and condemning the first use of nuclear weapons, left ambiguous the role of nuclear weapons for deterrence. If allowed to stand unchallenged, such a charge could carry substantial weight in the policy debate, especially in a democracy (and perhaps only in a democracy) built upon moral principles. But it does not take a trained ethicist to recognize that such blanket moral assertions are at best simplistic,

---

[2] "Statement on Nuclear Weapons," by International Generals and Admirals, Dec. 5, 1996, and George Lee Butler, "The General's Bombshell: Phasing Out the U.S. Nuclear Arsenal," *Washington Post*, Jan. 12, 1997. Both are reprinted in the *Washington Quarterly*, Summer 1997, pp. 125, 131.

[3] Sir Michael Quinlan, "The Future of Nuclear Weapons in World Affairs," *Bulletin* of the Atlantic Council of the United States, Nov. 20, 1996.
[4] Statement of the honorable Walter B. Slocombe, Under Secretary of Defense for Policy, before the Senate Governmental Affairs Subcommittee on International Security, Proliferation and Federal Services. Hearing on Nuclear Weapons and Deterrence, Feb. 12, 1997.

and perhaps—in light of what we know about human nature and history—dangerous in themselves.

The use, or even threat of use, of any weapon may contain elements of moral ambiguity. And like other weapons—whether a club in Rwanda or artillery surrounding Sarajevo—nuclear weapons could be used in ways that are clearly immoral. Moreover, the scale of destruction that could result from the employment of even a few nuclear weapons makes imperative the need to consider carefully the full range of moral issues associated with the possession of these weapons. Perhaps for this reason, well-intentioned people have for decades debated where ethical lines should be drawn regarding the possession and use of nuclear weapons.

> **Nuclear forces help deter chemical and biological weapons.**

Yet, within this realm of considerable ambiguity, policymakers during the Cold War were forced to decide where the greater risk lay and make decisions with real consequences. Given the awful consequences of failure, the choice was not simple. On the one hand, nuclear deterrence could fail. In the aftermath of such failure, it was possible (but by no means certain, insofar as a conscious choice for use would have to be made by political authorities) that nuclear weapons would be unleashed on civilian populations with truly catastrophic consequences. On the other hand, in the absence of a credible nuclear deterrent, conventional deterrence could fail, as it had so often in the past, twice globally, resulting in another devastating war with casualties perhaps even greater than those in World War II.

Looking back, one might even argue that those who condemned nuclear weapons as immoral were simply wrong. The Western alliance's nuclear weapons were in fact the moral weapon of choice. They worked precisely as intended by deterring an immoral totalitarian state from attacking Western Europe and undermining the peace, values, and freedom which the democracies cherished. Indeed, given the tens of millions of innocent noncombatants killed in two world wars, one can argue that the possession of nuclear weapons to deter yet another outbreak of mass slaughter by conventional weapons, either in Europe or Asia, was squarely in the just war tradition.

The argument that the external environment has changed so much with the end of the Cold War that no ethical or moral basis for nuclear arms remains is likewise unconvincing. American lives and interests remain threatened. In fact, the proliferation of chemical and biological weapons have made the likelihood of conflict and the prospect of the use of weapons of mass destruction even greater than in the past in several key regions. But just as before, sound public and defense policy will emerge only from a prudent calculation of risks and benefits, not from sweeping generalizations about the morality or immorality of possession or use of nuclear weapons.

The "new eliminationists" who wrap themselves in the cloak of moral superiority and certainty should be asked to address the consequences of disarming the great democracies in a world in which advanced conventional, chemical, and biological weapons (and in some cases nuclear capabilities) continue to spread among states explicitly hostile to democratic values.

Utility. The primary purpose of nuclear weapons is and will remain the deterrence of the use of nuclear weapons by others. But this is not, nor has it ever been, the only rationale for these weapons. As noted, nuclear weapons were a key in NATO's planning to deter a Soviet conventional attack on Western Europe. Today, nuclear forces also contribute to the deterrence of states that possess the full spectrum of weapons of mass destruction, including biological and chemical weapons, such as Iraq in the Gulf War. Use of nuclear weapons against such states is not inconceivable, given sufficient provocation and threat. Conventional weapons may not be able to induce the shock and potential decisiveness of a nuclear weapon. A plausible hypothetical makes the point: Given clear intelligence that an adversary was making immediate preparations to launch biological agents against U.S. forces or population centers from a remote, deeply buried site, would not the president be prudent to explore a nuclear option, inasmuch as immediate, complete, and certain destruction of the target would be beyond the ability of even the most advanced conventional weapons?

Accidents, unauthorized use, and the "hair trigger." It is a truism that there is and always has been some level of risk of accidental or inadvertent use of nuclear weapons. But, just as there is a risk of a major dam breaking or an accident at a nuclear power plant, the real issue is how to manage and mitigate these risks. Current programs that make our stockpile and that of the former Soviet Union more secure are essential. But reducing the numbers of warheads does not in itself guarantee a reduction in risk. In any event, the risk of accidents or unauthorized use, though real, must be judged low, and this risk must be measured against the national security benefits gained from retaining nuclear weapons.

One increasingly popularized variant of the concerns stemming from inadvertent use is the growing alarm over the so-called "hair trigger" posture of currently deployed nuclear forces, especially Russian forces. In a recent commentary, former Senator Sam Nunn and Bruce Blair note that as a consequence of the "budget crunch facing the Russian military," Russia has declared "its readiness to launch on warning."[5] This crunch, according to the authors, has strained the Russian posture "to the point that Russian generals can no longer be confident of reliable retaliation after absorbing a systematic U.S. first strike" and "threatens to undermine the entire Russian system of command and control over its nuclear arsenal." The best near-term solution, they argue, is "de-alerting," which consists of measures such as placing heavy objects on the lids of missile silos, facing Russian mobile intercontinental ballistic missiles south, removing the tires from their launchers, and placing submarine forces on a "modified" alert status. In the

---

[5] Sam Nunn and Bruce Blair, "From Nuclear Deterrence to Mutual Safety," *Washington Post,* June 22, 1997, sec. C, p. 1.

longer term, "as confidence builds," all nuclear warheads might be separated from their delivery vehicles.

While Nunn and Blair do appear to have made a conceptual leap forward by arguing that the United States and Russia should renounce the logic of "mutual assured destruction"—a position earlier articulated by Presidents Reagan and Bush—their recommendations fall far short of achieving their goal of "mutual assured safety." The measures they propose are neither "adequately verifiable" nor "equitable" as they are described. In fact, very much like the "de-targeting" actions which the authors note "can be reversed in a matter of seconds," most of the "de-alerting" measures are easily and quickly reversible with little if any real time warning. As a result, such steps could actually be counterproductive—leading to greater instability and mistrust.

Real solutions, not arms control gimmicks, are required to address the problems of the Russian nuclear posture. We know from experience that dialogue and agreements must be governed by greater transparency, effective verification, and realistic expectations. We also know from experience that we must hedge against failure, which is why a missile defense system would be the best insurance against a Russian accidental or unauthorized launch. At various times in the past, Nunn promoted such a light missile defense. Now that he has called for the end of Mutual Assured Destruction (MAD), the central foundation upon which the Antiballistic Missile (ABM) Treaty was based, there should no longer be any doctrinal impediments to his support in procuring this insurance policy.

Possession by one stimulates acquisition by others. The international nonproliferation community has long held as a self-evident truth the belief that further proliferation can best be stemmed by the United States and the other nuclear states drastically reducing or eliminating their own nuclear stockpiles. But little evidence exists to support this article of faith.

In the past decade, the United States and Russia have already made radical reductions in their strategic and tactical nuclear arsenals, but proliferant states have shown little sign of restraint. To argue that these states will give up their nuclear ambitions if only the United States and other declared weapon states would go to zero is wishful thinking. As evident in the examples of the five declared nuclear powers, as well as the unacknowledged nuclear weapon states, motives for acquisition of nuclear weapons are complex and varied, ranging from security to prestige. The new proliferants—the Iraqs, Irans, and North Koreas—seek weapons of mass destruction as instruments of coercion and aggression and are not going to be persuaded to forego these tools as a consequence of others disarming. In fact, radical nuclear disarmament by the United States might promote proliferation by emboldening these states to seek relative parity with the United States (especially in a regional context.)

Drastic reductions might also have a deleterious effect on the security calculations of U.S. allies who have long depended on the American nuclear umbrella. In an uncertain future, perhaps in the face of an aggressive China or resurgent Russia, the insecurities perceived by today's allies could compel them to develop their own nuclear deterrent capabilities or accommodate themselves to the threat in the absence of a credible American nuclear force.[6] The defection of even one major ally—Japan for instance—could have profoundly negative implications for global stability and U.S. security interests.

Continuing Rationale for Nuclear Deterrence

A principal rationale for maintaining a credible and effective nuclear weapon posture is based on the need to provide a hedge—an insurance policy—against a reversal in relations with Russia and China.[7] Over time, both of these nuclear states have demonstrated a tendency for radical shifts in their political orientation, as well as an enduring commitment to possess nuclear weapons both for the status they afford and as an essential part of their security strategy.

Neither Russia nor China would today seriously consider eliminating their nuclear arsenals, although they would both likely see real value in a unilaterally disarmed United States. Indeed, on the eve of the 1997 Helsinki Summit, while the United States was searching almost frantically to identify additional concessions to "broaden common ground" in the areas of a NATO-Russia charter and arms control, President Boris Yeltsin responded to a question involving a hypothesized NATO attack on Russia by emphasizing the importance of "nuclear means." This response was entirely consistent with an earlier remark by Russian defense minister Igor Rodionov, who stated: "We see the future of the Russian Armed Forces in using a rational composition of the Soviet Strategic Nuclear Forces to ensure guaranteed nuclear prevention of an all-out war and to prevent and localize armed conflicts in the vicinity of Russian borders."[8]

The contrast is stark. While Americans wring their hands over the pros and cons of dramatic reductions in U.S. nuclear forces, and even debate whether or not to go to zero nuclear weapons, the Russians and Chinese are modernizing their own nuclear forces. In the case of China, this entails building new missiles and warheads, recently tested. In the case of Russia, whose conventional forces are in desperate condition, nuclear modernization includes not only new missiles but elaborate and extraordinarily hardened command and control facilities. Russian doctrine today places more emphasis on nuclear weapons than did Soviet doctrine, as evidenced by Moscow's reversal of its long-standing no-first-use policy. The obvious point is that, given the inability to control or predict where these two states will be in five or ten years, it is essential to hedge against a reversal in relations. And the best hedge is to maintain a nuclear deterrent.

Turning to the contribution of nuclear weapons in a counterproliferation role, one can draw on the real world case of

---

[6] Germany and Japan are among the countries that are considered potential candidates for proliferation should the U.S. nuclear umbrella be removed. See Keith B. Payne, *Deterrence in the Second Nuclear Age* (Lexington, Ky.: University of Kentucky Press, 1996), pp. 21–22, for insights into Japanese views.
[7] This section is taken from Robert Joseph, "Nuclear Deterrence and Regional Proliferators," *Washington Quarterly,* Summer 1997
[8] "Russia and Its Armed Forces in Changing Europe," *Military News Bulletin,* December 1996.

Desert Storm. Iraqi leaders attribute their decision not to use chemical weapons—and we now know biological agents as well—to the coalition's nuclear capabilities and warning of catastrophic consequences if Iraq were to use such weapons. General Wafic Al Sammarai, former head of Iraqi military intelligence, has stated that Iraq did not arm its Scud missiles with chemical weapons "because the warning was quite severe, and quite effective. The allied troops were certain to use nuclear arms and the price will be too dear and too high."[9] In retrospect, it appears that Saddam Hussein simply could not count on the United States (or perhaps Israel) refraining from responding with nuclear weapons, especially given his view of the world and demonstrated absence of constraints in the use of force to achieve his personal objectives.

Other factors may have weighed in the Iraqi decision, for example, practical operational considerations such as the perceived preparedness of U.S. forces to protect themselves—perhaps even more effectively than Iraqi forces—from the effects of chemical weapons on the battlefield. Citing interviews with Iraqi POWs, some analysts credit American preparedness for chemical warfare as the rationale for their non-use of chemicals in the Gulf War.

Whatever the mix of reasons for why deterrence of Iraqi biological and chemical weapons worked in the Gulf, however, most of the policy-level participants in that conflict consider the implied threat of a nuclear response to have been crucial. To be sure, senior Bush administration officials have since testified that the United States would never have employed nuclear weapons, but they make this statement not to deny the deterrent value of nuclear weapons, but simply to emphasize that there appeared to be no operational role for these weapons given the stunningly rapid victory of the coalition's conventional forces.[10]

Yet, what was important for deterrence was what Saddam Hussein believed. In this context, Secretary of Defense Richard Cheney's position is perhaps the most thoughtful. He states that nuclear weapons use was never seriously considered but that, had chemical or biological weapons been used against the United States, a nuclear response may have come under consideration. This is clearly the right message to send if the objective is to strengthen deterrence.

Furthermore, as noted earlier, it has become popular to argue that radical reductions and even denuclearization might persuade regimes such as Iraq's to forego weapons of mass destruction entirely. This is simply astonishing. How can one believe that by drastically reducing or giving up its own nuclear weapons, one of the most important deterrent tools, the United States will strengthen deterrence? The opposite is surely the predictable outcome. For regimes such as those in

Iraq, Iran, Libya, and North Korea, weapons of mass destruction are their best counter to the West's *conventional* superiority. What is more, those governments say as much to the West and to their own people.

Why would these states grant the United States the overwhelming advantage of competing and conducting conflict on solely conventional terms? The answer is simple: they won't. As much as one would like to believe otherwise, all evidence is to the contrary. In the case of post-Desert Storm Iraq, Hussein has demonstrated his willingness to pay an enormous social and economic cost—estimated by some to approach $100 billion—to protect as much of his unconventional weapons infrastructure as possible.

Another argument of the nuclear abolitionists is that there are no "appropriate" targets for such weapons. Here, the premise of this argument is flawed. Deterrence suggests that the question of "appropriate targeting" resides, in large part, in the minds of the leaders one is seeking to deter—as was the case in Iraq. We also often hear that all relevant targets can be destroyed by advanced conventional weapons. Yet again, the evidence contradicts the assertion. In Desert Storm, the coalition was unsuccessful in its air strikes against underground targets which cannot in many cases be destroyed by conventional attack. The technology does not exist today—a fact recognized by states such as Libya which are placing their chemical and biological weapons facilities increasingly underground. In response to chemical attacks against American troops or biological attacks against U.S. population centers, the United States may want to destroy such targets promptly and with absolute certainty, rather than leave them operational even for a short time. It may also want to strike other military targets, perhaps even those that could be attacked with conventional forces, to cause shock and send a clear signal to all that any use of chemical and biological agents will be severely punished. What is essential is that the United States retain the option to respond and that this capability be known to potential adversaries. If one rules out these options, deterrence is undermined and the likelihood of conflict occurring increases, as well as the likelihood that chemical and biological weapons will be used against the United States and its allies.

Three Tests for a Sound Nuclear Policy

Policy decisions taken today regarding the U.S. nuclear stockpile will have real and long-standing consequences for peace and stability well into the next century. However one comes down on the core issues regarding nuclear weapons, policy recommendations derived from those convictions should be governed by three tests. First, the recommended policy prescriptions must be achievable in a real, not idealized, world. Secondly, understanding that unintended consequences can distort even the most well-intentioned policy, policy recommendations must be evaluated in light of all likely effects, with the risks and costs weighed carefully against the expected gains. Thirdly, the result of policy decisions must point us in

---

[9] Quoted in Payne, *Deterrence*, p. 84. An extensive discussion of deterrence in the Gulf War appears on pages 81–87.

[10] In the context of deterring the use of Iraqi chemical weapons, Secretary Baker writes: "I purposely left the impression that the use of chemical or biological agents by Iraq could invite tactical nuclear retaliation." James A. Baker, III, *The Politics of Diplomacy* (New York: G. P. Putnam's Sons, 1995), p. 359. See also, Colin Powell, *My American Journey* (New York: Random House, 1995). Powell looked at the operational utility of "small tactical nuclear weapons" only at the urging of Secretary Cheney and found them wanting.

the direction of a safer world and provide for greater security for the United States, its friends and allies.

Policy must be achievable. Even the "new eliminationists" argue that the move to abolish nuclear weapons, or even to go to very low numbers, should not be unilateral. But would all other nations with nuclear weapons or nuclear ambitions join the United States in this quest? Having led the world into the nuclear age, Americans in particular seem to possess a strong sense of responsibility to lead the world out of the nuclear age. While always quick to acknowledge that nuclear weapons can not be disinvented, the "new eliminationists" seek that very goal.

In fact, the optimism of these "new eliminationists"—some would say naiveté—appears to be almost uniquely American. Looking at actions rather than words, the currency of nuclear weapons may actually be increasing in other countries. In Europe, France has been actively playing the nuclear card in the continental political context. In South Asia, India and Pakistan continue on a potentially deadly collision course, one that could involve nuclear confrontation. In the Middle East, one sees little evidence that Israel would even consider giving up the nuclear option. There, the call to disarmament is perceived at best as academically interesting, but of little relevance to a state whose existence is threatened by proliferation in its immediate neighborhood. In Iran, Iraq, and other states aggressively pursuing nuclear weapons, one can only wonder about the amusement that the American debate must invoke.

The elimination or reduction of nuclear weapons to very low levels would in any case pose currently insurmountable technical challenges. Monitoring, verification, and enforcement of a worldwide "zero option" regime would require levels of certainty that have not been achieved in any arms control regime to date. At low levels these critical aspects—which have been characterized alternatively as either central concerns by arms control skeptics or relegated to the realm of minor technical details by supporters of arms control—would assume enormous, undeniable importance. It is certainly unclear that sufficient safeguards can be invented, let alone implemented, and the monetary costs associated with that effort would likely be staggering. Russian resistance to suggestions for greater transparency in the current process of warhead dismantlement has revealed the barriers, both technical and psychological, that would frustrate complete nuclear disarmament. There is no realistic basis for confidence that these barriers can be surmounted.

Policy must take into account possible unintended consequences. The strategic consequences of drastic reductions in the U.S. nuclear force structure appear not to have been thought through by the "new eliminationists." What would be the effect on crisis stability in the event of a reversal in our relations with Russia? What would be the effect on potential regional adversaries who might then see parity with the United States as desirable and achievable? What would be the effect on our allies who have long relied on the U.S. nuclear guarantee? In sum, would a move to abolish nuclear weapons have the unintended consequence of encouraging conventional war and proliferation.

> Elimination of nuclear weapons would pose insurmountable technical challenges.

Policy must point us to a safer world. Those who promote the movement toward a nuclear-free world often see nuclear weapons as an evil in and of themselves. Some even argue that the elimination of these weapons is a precondition for a peaceful international order. The enduring lessons from World War II—particularly the need to avoid simplistic policy approaches which contributed to the most deadly conflict in our history—have again become blurred. For the United States and its allies, deterrence rather than disarmament through denuclearization remains the basis for sound policy, as deterrence has worked in the past to save countless lives by making the prospect of war horrific.

The prescriptions of the "new eliminationists" fail to satisfy these three tests for a sound policy. This is most dramatically, if unintentionally, revealed in the words of those generals and admirals who signed the open letter calling for nuclear disarmament, which states: "The exact circumstances and conditions that will make it possible to proceed, finally, to abolition cannot now be seen or prescribed."[11] One could hardly agree more. The prerequisites established by these and other eliminationists (such as near perfect inspection, surveillance and control of nuclear weapons infrastructures, and agreed procedures for forcible international intervention), when taken together, suggest that in a perfect world there may be no need for nuclear weapons. Here again, one could hardly agree more. The problem is the large and dangerous gap between wish and reality. In reaching across this wide gap in search of a better world—especially in light of this past century that had, until the atomic age, managed to achieve unprecedented levels of death in conventional wars—one ought not abandon too soon even those imperfect tools which have helped achieve an imperfect but nonetheless unprecedented stability.

In thinking about the role of nuclear weapons today and in the future, one must remember that, even at the height of the Cold War, no one possessed an exact understanding of how deterrence worked. In the end, it may have been the very uncertainty that surrounded the nuclear enterprise—the how, the when, and the where of our response up to and including strategic nuclear strikes—that imbued it with the greatest deterrent value. An adversary who knew, or thought he knew, what our exact response to a given provocation would be could work actively to undermine that course of action. This may be the case with deterrence today. We may not have a precisely drawn nuclear response to the use of chemical and biological weapons against us. We may not be able to tell our adversary—or even ourselves—what targets would be put at risk to nuclear response if he unleashed these weapons against us. It is, however, this very uncertainty—coupled with the certainty that we will respond decisively—that should prey on the minds of adversaries and that ultimately provides the rationale for nuclear weapons.

---

[11] See international generals' "Statement on Nuclear Weapons."

Taking Nuclear Weapons off Hair-Trigger Alert

It is time to end the practice of keeping nuclear missiles constantly ready to fire. This change would greatly reduce the possibility of a mistaken launch

by Bruce G. Blair, Harold A. Feiveson and Frank N. von Hippel

On January 25, 1995, military technicians at a handful of radar stations across northern Russia saw a troubling blip suddenly appear on their screens. A rocket, launched from somewhere off the coast of Norway, was rising rapidly through the night sky. Well aware that a single missile from a U.S. submarine plying those waters could scatter eight nuclear bombs over Moscow within 15 minutes, the radar operators immediately alerted their superiors. The message passed swiftly from Russian military authorities to President Boris Yeltsin, who, holding the electronic case that could order the firing of nuclear missiles in response, hurriedly conferred by telephone with his top advisers. For the first time ever, that "nuclear briefcase" was activated for emergency use.

For a few tense minutes, the trajectory of the mysterious rocket remained unknown to the worried Russian officials. Anxiety mounted when the separation of multiple rocket stages created an impression of a possible attack by several missiles. But the radar crews continued to track their targets, and after about eight minutes (just a few minutes short of the procedural deadline to respond to an impending nuclear attack), senior military officers determined that the rocket was headed far out to sea and posed no threat to Russia. The unidentified rocket in this case turned out to be a U.S. scientific probe, sent up to investigate the northern lights. Weeks earlier the Norwegians had duly informed Russian authorities of the planned launch from the offshore island of Andoya, but somehow word of the high-altitude experiment had not reached the right ears.

That frightening incident (like some previous false alarms that activated U.S. strategic forces) aptly demonstrates the danger of maintaining nuclear arsenals in a state of hair-trigger alert. Doing so heightens the possibility that one day someone will mistakenly launch nuclear-tipped missiles, either because of a technical failure or a human error—a mistake made, perhaps, in the rush to respond to false indications of an attack.

Both the U.S. and Russian military have long instituted procedures to prevent such a calamity from happening. Designers of command systems in Russia have gone to extraordinary lengths to ensure strict central control over nuclear weapons. But their equipment is not foolproof, and Russia's early-warning and nuclear command systems are deteriorating. This past February the institute responsible for designing the sophisticated control systems for the Strategic Rocket Forces (the military unit that operates Russian intercontinental ballistic missiles) staged a one-day strike to protest pay arrears and the lack of resources to upgrade their equipment. Three days later Russia's defense minister, Igor Rodionov, asserted that "if the shortage of funds persists... Russia may soon approach a threshold beyond which its missiles and nuclear systems become uncontrollable."

Rodionov's warning may have been, in part, a maneuver to muster political support for greater defense spending. But recent reports by the U.S. Central Intelligence Agency confirm that Russia's Strategic Rocket Forces have indeed fallen on hard times. Local utility managers have repeatedly shut off the power to various nuclear weapons installations after the military authorities there failed to pay their electric bills. Worse yet, the equipment that controls nuclear weapons frequently malfunctions, and critical electronic devices and computers sometimes switch to a combat mode for no apparent reason. On seven occasions during the fall of 1996, operations at some nuclear weapons centers were severely disrupted when thieves tried to "mine" critical communications cables for their copper.

Many of the radars constructed by the former Soviet Union to detect a ballistic-missile attack no longer operate, so information provided by these installations is becoming increasingly unreliable. Even the nuclear suitcases that accompany the president, defense minister and chief of the General Staff are reportedly falling into disrepair. In short, the systems built to control Russian nuclear weapons are now crumbling.

In addition to these many technical difficulties, Russia's nuclear weapons establishment suffers from a host of human and organizational problems. Crews receive less training than they did formerly and are consequently less proficient in the safe handling of nuclear weapons. And despite President Yeltsin's promises to improve conditions, endemic housing and food shortages have led to demoralization and disaffection within the elite Strategic Rocket Forces, the strategic submarine fleet and the custodians of Russia's stockpiles of nuclear warheads. As a result, the likelihood increases that desperate low-level command-

ers might disregard safety rules or, worse still, that they might take unauthorized control of nuclear weapons—something a deteriorating central command might be unable to prevent or counter. Although most Russian launch crews would need to receive special codes held by the General Staff before they could fire their missiles, one recent CIA report warned that some submarine crews may be able to launch the ballistic missiles on board their vessels without having to obtain such information first.

Even at the top, control over nuclear weapons could splinter along various political fault lines. Relations between politicians and military leaders in Russia are strained, and physical control of the launch codes remains in the hands of the military. Thus, the authority to fire ballistic missiles could be usurped by military commanders during an internal crisis. In fact, during the August 1991 coup against President Mikhail S. Gorbachev, top-level allegiances suddenly shifted, and the normal chain of command for Russia's nuclear weapons was broken. For three days, the power to launch nuclear weapons rested in the hands

of Defense Minister Dmitri Yazov and the chief of the General Staff, Mikhail Moiseyev. Given the dire conditions in Russia, something similar could happen again.

The Nuclear Hair Trigger

Although international relations have changed drastically since the end of the cold war, both Russia and the U.S. continue to keep the bulk of their nuclear missiles on high-level alert. So within just a few minutes of receiving instructions to fire, a large fraction of the U.S. and Russian land-based rockets (which are armed with about 2,000 and 3,500 warheads, respectively) could begin their 25-minute flights over the North Pole to their wartime targets. Less than 15 minutes after receiving the order to attack, six U.S. Trident submarines at sea could loft roughly 1,000 warheads, and several Russian ballistic-missile submarines could dispatch between 300 and 400. In sum, the two nuclear superpowers remain ready to fire a total of more than 5,000 nuclear weapons at each other within half an hour.

Why do two countries at peace retain such aggressive postures, ones that perpetuate the danger of a mistaken or unauthorized launch? Because military planners on both sides remain fixated on the remote specter of a deliberate nuclear surprise attack from their former adversary. They assume that such a "first strike" would be aimed against their own strategic nuclear weapons and the command centers that direct them. To deter such an assault, each country strives to ensure that it could respond with a forceful counterattack against the full spectrum of military targets on its opponent's territory, including all nuclear weapons installations. This requirement saddles military planners with a task virtually identical in scope to mounting a first strike: they must be able to guarantee the rapid destruction of thousands of targets spread across a distant continent.

Submarine-Launched Missiles

To achieve START II limits, the U.S. plans to eliminate four of its 18 ballistic-missile submarines and to reduce the count of warheads on submarine-launched missiles from eight to five. Later, to meet the START III goals, the U.S. would most likely eliminate an additional four submarines and reduce the number of warheads on each missile to four. All these actions should be taken at once. Russia could then immediately remove the warheads from the submarines it plans to eliminate under the START agreements.

Without rather elaborate verification arrangements, neither country could determine the status of the other's submarines at sea. Both nations, however, should lower launch readiness. Approximately half the submarines that the U.S. has at sea today are traveling to their launch stations in a state of modified alert: the crew needs about 18 hours to perform the procedures, such as removing the flood plates from the launch tubes, that bring a submarine to full alert. Most U.S. submarines at sea could simply stay on modified alert. Their readiness could be reduced further by removing their missiles' guidance systems and storing them on board. Russian submarines lack this option; their missiles are not accessible from inside the vessel.

Russia should also pledge to keep its missiles on submarines in port off launch-ready alert. (The U.S. does not maintain submarines in port on alert.) The U.S. may be able to monitor the alert condition of these Russian submarines, but Russia should make their status obvious. —*B.G.B., H.A.F. and F.N. von H.*

Silo-Based Missiles

The START II ban on multiple-warhead, land-based missiles does not go into effect for a decade, but the U.S. and Russia could act earlier to take most of their silo-based warheads off alert. The easiest method would be to physically "pin" open the switches that allow the rocket engines to ignite. Maintenance crews would then have to enter each silo, manually remove the safety pins and close these switches before the missiles would be ready to fire remotely.

Negotiators at the Helsinki Summit envisioned actions that would take even longer to reverse. They agreed that Russia and the U.S. would have five extra years to dismantle the multiple-warhead missiles slated to be eliminated under START II, as long as these missiles are "deactivated by removing their nuclear warheads or taking other jointly agreed steps." The U.S. prefers that Russia deactivate missiles by removing warheads, an act that would take weeks to reverse. Such efforts would be apparent to surveillance satellites, and the absence of the warheads on the missiles could be checked during the inspections permitted under START.

Yet Russian experts argue that their country does not have adequate facilities to store a large number of warheads taken from missiles. They are now considering other options: immobilizing the massive silo lids so that heavy equipment would be required to open them, or removing the battery that operates the missile-guidance system during flight. A third possibility would be to replace the aerodynamic missile nose cones with flat-faced covers, which would shelter the warheads but not allow the missiles to fly.   —*B.G.B., H.A.F. and F.N. von H.*

RUSSIAN SILO LID would require a large crane to tilt upward if the device that generates high-pressure gas for its pneumatically operated hinge were purposefully removed.

thousands of warheads securely deployed at sea, the U.S. adheres to this quick-draw stance because of the vulnerability of its missile silos and command apparatus, including its political and military leadership in Washington, D.C.

Russian officials perceive an even greater need to launch their missiles on warning. The General Staff evidently fears that if its nuclear missiles are not launched immediately, then only tens of them would be able to respond after absorbing a systematic U.S. attack. Russian command posts and missile silos are as vulnerable as those of the U.S. to a massive assault.

Russia's current inability to deploy many of its most survivable forces—submarines at sea and mobile land-based rockets—amplifies this worry. A lack of resources and qualified personnel has forced the Russian navy to cut back operations considerably. At present, the Russian navy typically keeps only two of its 26 ballistic missile submarines at sea on combat patrol at any one time. Similar constraints prevent Russia from hiding more than one or two regiments of its truck-mounted mobile missiles by dispersing them in the field. The remaining 40 or so regiments, each controlling nine single-warhead missiles, keep their trucks parked in garages. These missiles are more exposed to attack than those housed in underground silos. Russia also has 36 10-warhead nuclear missiles carried on railway cars, which were designed to be hidden along Russia's vast rail network. But these railcars remain confined to fixed garrisons in keeping with a decision made by President Gorbachev in 1991.

These vulnerabilities have led Russia to ready some of its submarines in port and mobile missiles in garages to launch on warning, along with the missiles in silos. The time available for deciding to launch these weapons is shortened by the presence of American, British and French submarines cruising in the North Atlantic, only about 2,000

In order to meet this demand, both the U.S. and Russia rely on a launch-on-warning strategy—that is, each side is poised to release a massive retaliatory missile salvo after detecting an enemy missile attack but before the incoming warheads arrive (which might take just 15 minutes if they were fired from submarines nearby). Although it has

miles (3,200 kilometers) from Moscow. This proximity means that the nuclear-release procedures in Russia require a response time of less than 15 minutes: a few minutes for detecting an attack, another few minutes for top-level decision making and a few minutes for disseminating the launch order. Russian leaders and missile controllers are geared to work within this brief time frame and practice regularly with drills. U.S. nuclear forces operate with a similarly short fuse.

It is obvious that the rushed nature of this process, from warning to decision to action, risks causing a catastrophic mistake. The danger is compounded by the erosion of Russia's ability to distinguish reliably between natural phenomena or peaceful ventures into space and a true missile attack. Only one third of its modern early-warning radars are working at all, and at least two of the nine slots in its constellation of missile-warning satellites are empty.

The dangers stemming from this decline in Russia's technical capabilities are offset, to some extent, by the relaxation of tensions that has come with the end of the cold war. Given the milder political climate, decision makers on both sides should be more inclined to question the validity of any reports they receive of an impending missile attack. Nevertheless, the coupling of two arsenals geared for rapid response carries the inherent danger of producing a mistaken launch and an escalating volley of missiles in return. The possibility of such an apocalyptic accident cannot be ruled out even under normal conditions. And if the control of Russian nuclear weapons were to be stressed by an internal or international political crisis, the danger could suddenly become much more acute.

During the cold war, such risks were subordinated to the overriding requirement to deter an enemy believed to be willing to launch a nuclear attack. This rationalization is no longer defensible, if ever it was. Today, when both countries seek normal economic relations and cooperative security arrangements, perpetuating the readiness to launch nuclear weapons on the mere warning of an attack constitutes reckless behavior. Yet this thinking is so entrenched that it will yield only to steady pressure from the public on political leaders—especially presidents—to replace it with a safer policy.

"De-alerting" Missiles

The cuts in nuclear arms set by the Strategic Arms Reduction Treaties (START) should lessen the threat of an accidental nuclear exchange, but those changes will come only gradually. Under the START III framework, endorsed in Helsinki this past spring by President Yeltsin and President Bill Clinton, the U.S. and Russian strategic arsenals would shrink to about 2,000 warheads on each side by the year 2007. But if current practices are not revised, 10 years from now half of those nuclear weapons could still remain ready to launch on a few minutes' notice.

The chance of an accidental launch could be reduced much more rapidly by "de-alerting" the missiles—increasing the amount of time needed to prepare them for launch. The U.S. and Russia should move independently down this path to a safer world, preferably taking quick strides in parallel. Two prominent proponents of this approach are former senator Sam Nunn of Georgia and retired general George L. Butler, commander in chief of the U.S. Strategic Command from 1991 to 1994. This proposal is also gaining support in the community of nongovernmental organizations involved in nuclear security and from some members of the U.S. Congress. In Russia, the Ministry of Defense is seriously studying such an alteration.

President George Bush set a notable precedent for de-alerting nuclear weapons at the end of September 1991, when the Soviet Union began to split apart in the wake of the August coup attempt. On the advice of General Butler, President Bush ordered an immediate stand-down of the many U.S. strategic bombers that had remained ready for decades to take off with only a few minutes' warning. Soon afterward, air force personnel unloaded and stored the many nuclear weapons carried on these planes. In addition, President Bush ended the alert for the strategic missiles destined to be eliminated under START I, a set composed of 450 silo-based Minuteman II rockets, along with the missiles on 10 Poseidon submarines. These important actions took only a few days.

President Gorbachev reciprocated a week later by ordering the deactivation of more than 500 land-based rockets and six strategic submarines, by promising to keep his strategic bombers at a low level of readiness and by putting the rail-based missiles in garrison. In the subsequent months, both countries also withdrew many thousands of shorter-range tactical nuclear warheads that had been deployed with their armies and navies and placed these weapons in central storage depots.

Presidents Clinton and Yeltsin took a further step together in 1994, when they agreed to stop aiming strategic missiles at each other's country. This change, though a welcome gesture, has little military significance. Missile commanders can reload target coordinates into guidance computers within seconds. In fact, the 1994 pact does not even alleviate the concern about an accidental Russian launch, because an unprogrammed missile would automatically switch back to its primary wartime target, which might be a Minuteman silo in Montana or a command center in Washington, London, Paris or Beijing. And Russian missiles, like their American counterparts, cannot be ordered to self-destruct once they are launched.

Possessing the most robust forces and cohesive command system, the U.S. government should take the lead in a new round of voluntary actions by announcing that it will withdraw the U.S. warheads that most threaten Russia's nuclear deterrent (particularly those capable of hitting Russia's missile silos and underground command posts). The most menacing warheads are those deployed on the 50 MX silo-based missiles, which are armed with 10 warheads each, and the 400 high-yield W88 warheads fitted atop some of the missiles on Trident submarines. We also recommend immobilizing all of the land-based Minuteman IIIs (about 500 missiles), which are armed with three warheads each, halving the number of submarines deployed in peacetime and cutting the number of warheads on each submarine-borne missile from eight to four. The operation of ballistic-missile submarines should also be altered so that crews would require approximately one day to ready missiles for launching.

These measures would leave almost 600 U.S. warheads remaining invulnerable at sea, each capable of destroying the heart of a great city. With such a force, the U.S. would preserve ample capacity to deter any nuclear aggressor. Such a dramatic shift by the U.S. would fully establish its intention not to pose a first-strike threat to Russia. We believe this change in policy would persuade Russia to follow suit and take most of its missiles off hair-trigger alert. These changes would also help accelerate the implementation of agreements for disarmament already negotiated under START II and START III. We estimate that most of

the job could be completed within a year or two.

Capabilities already exist to confirm that nuclear weapons have been taken off alert. For instance, the number of ballistic-missile submarines in port can be monitored using satellites, and most other measures could be checked during the random on-site inspections permitted by START I. Over the longer term, additional technical means could be engineered to provide more frequent checks that nuclear missiles posed no immediate threat. For example, electronic "seals" could be used to ensure that a component removed from a missile had not been replaced. The integrity of such seals could be verified remotely through satellite relay using encrypted communications.

Global Zero Alert

This blueprint for taking U.S. and Russian nuclear forces off alert would substantially diminish the ability of either country to mount a first strike. Thus, it would eliminate both the capacity and rationale for keeping missiles ready to fire on warning. Leaders would have to wait out any alarm of an attack before deciding how to respond, drastically reducing the risk of a mistaken or unauthorized launch.

We recognize that military leaders in the U.S. and Russia might insist on maintaining small portions of their cur-

rent arsenals on high alert, perhaps hundreds of warheads each, until the other nuclear-weapon states—Britain, France and China—joined in adopting similar measures to reduce the readiness of their nuclear arsenals. But if the U.S. and Russia aspire to establish the highest possible standards of safety for their nuclear armaments, they should move as rapidly as possible to take all their missiles off alert and then follow with further steps to increase the time required to reactivate these weapons.

The ultimate goal would be to separate most, if not all, nuclear warheads from their missiles and then, eventually, to eliminate most of the stored warheads and missiles. To implement such an extensive program fully, the means for verification would have to be strengthened to ensure that every nuclear state would know whether another country was making nuclear missiles launch-ready.

Moving toward a global standdown of nuclear arms will undoubtedly encounter strong resistance from those whose dominant fear remains a secretly prepared surprise attack. The design of procedures to take nuclear missiles off constant alert needs to take into account this already remote possibility. But these plans must urgently go forward to remove the much more immediate hazard—the mistaken or unauthorized launch of nuclear missiles.

The Authors

BRUCE G. BLAIR, HAROLD A. FEIVESON and FRANK N. VON HIPPEL have studied nuclear arms policy intensively. Blair served for four years in the U.S. Air Force Strategic Air Command before earning a Ph.D. in operations research in 1984 from Yale University. He is currently a defense analyst at the Brookings Institution in Washington, D.C. Feiveson received a master's degree in theoretical physics in 1959 from the University of California, Los Angeles. He worked in the U.S. Arms Control and Disarmament Agency for four years before moving to Princeton University to study public and international affairs. Feiveson received his Ph.D. in 1972 and joined the Princeton faculty in 1974. Von Hippel, who received a doctorate in theoretical physics from the University of Oxford in 1962, served in the office of the president's science adviser in 1993 and 1994 as assistant director for national security. He is currently a professor of public and international affairs at Princeton.

Further Reading

THE LOGIC OF ACCIDENTAL NUCLEAR WAR. Bruce G. Blair. Brookings Institution, 1993.

GLOBAL ZERO ALERT FOR NUCLEAR FORCES. Bruce G. Blair. Brookings Institution, 1995.

CAGING THE NUCLEAR GENIE: AN AMERICAN CHALLENGE FOR GLOBAL SECURITY. Stansfield Turner. Westview Press, Boulder, Colo., 1997.

THE FUTURE OF U.S. NUCLEAR WEAPONS POLICY. National Academy of Sciences. National Academy Press, 1997.

Unit 6

Unit Selections

Key Points to Consider

❖ Itemize the products you own that were manufactured in another country.

❖ What recent contacts have you had with people from other countries? How was it possible for you to have these contacts?

❖ How can the conflict and rivalry between the United States and Russia be transformed into meaningful cooperation?

❖ What are the prospects for international governance? How would a trend in this direction enhance or threaten American values and constitutional rights?

 **Links** **www.dushkin.com/online/**

These sites are annotated on pages 6 and 7.

An individual at just about any location in the world can write a letter to another person just about anywhere else, and if it is properly addressed, the sender can be relatively certain that the letter will be delivered. This is true even though the sender pays for postage only in the country of origin and not in the country where it is delivered. A similar pattern of international cooperation is true when an individual boards an airplane in one country and never gives a second thought to the issues of potential language and technical barriers, even though the flight's destination is halfway around the world.

Many of the most basic activities of our lives are the result of international cooperation. International organizational structures to monitor public health on a global scale or to scientifically evaluate changing weather conditions are additional examples of governments recognizing that their self-interest directly benefits from cooperation (i.e., the creation of international governmental organizations, or IGOs).

Transnational activities, furthermore, are not limited to the governmental level. There are now literally tens of thousands of international nongovernmental organizations (INGOs). These organ- izations stage the Olympic Games or actively discourage the hunting of whales and seals, to illustrate just two of the diverse activities of INGOs. The number of these international organizations along with their influence has grown tremendously in the past 40 years.

In the same time period in which we have witnessed the growth in importance of IGOs and INGOs, there has been a parallel expansion of corporate activity across international borders. Most consumers are as familiar with products with a Japanese brand name as they are with products made in the United States, Germany, or elsewhere. The multinational corporation (MNC) is an important nonstate actor in the world today. The value of goods and services produced by the biggest MNCs is far greater than the gross domestic product (GDP) of many countries. The international structures that make it possible to buy a Swedish automobile in Sacramento or a Swiss watch in Singapore have been developed over many years. They are the result of governments negotiating treaties and creating IGOs to implement these agreements. The manufacturers engaged in these activities have created networks of sales, distribution, and service that grow more complex with each passing day.

These trends at a variety of levels indicate to many observers that the era of the nation-state as the dominant player in international politics is passing. Others have observed these trends and have concluded that the state system has a monopoly of power and that the diverse transnational organizations depend on the state system and in significant ways perpetuate it.

In many of the articles that appear elsewhere in this book, the authors have concluded by calling for greater international cooperation to solve our world's most pressing problems. The articles in this section show examples of successful cooperation. In the midst of a lot of bad news in the world, it is easy to overlook the fact that we are surrounded by international cooperation and that day-to-day activities in our lives often benefit from it.

The First Fifty Years

The Main Achievements

By Diogo Freitas do Amaral
President of the Fiftieth General Assembly

The League of Nations lasted a little more than 20 years; the United Nations has now lasted half a century. The League of Nations did not manage to achieve its principal objective: to avoid the Second World War; the United Nations has managed to achieve its principal goal: to avoid a third world war. The League of Nations concentrated all its peacemaking efforts on disarmament; the United Nations understood from the start that disarmament, while very important, was not the only way to prevent war, and strengthened its collective security system with a range of policies for economic, social and educational development.

Our "founding fathers" were endowed with foresight: the establishment in 1945 of the UN represented great hope for all people of good will throughout the world. It is true that these past 50 years have not been marked exclusively by successes and victories. The ex-

UN Photo 146677

The Palais des Nations in Geneva was originally the home of the League of Nations.

istence of the UN, like that of any organization, has been marked by many errors and defeats. But was that not inevitable, given the very nature of human beings, society and the world as it is?

In this connection, I should like to quote a remark about the UN which I consider apposite. It was made by a great President of the United States, John F. Kennedy, who said in 1962:

"Our instrument and our hope is the United Nations, and I see little merit in the impatience of those who

would abandon this imperfect world instrument because they dislike our imperfect world."

Today, after our Organization has been in existence for 50 years, should our assessment of its activities be positive or negative? We are all well aware of the Organization's failures, especially its most recent ones. And the critics have not ceased their criticism. So, in the interest of balance, it is only fair to enumerate the main achievements of the UN.

Avoiding a new world war

The first, of which I have already spoken, but to which I wish to return because of its exceptional importance and which can never be stressed too much, is the following: the UN succeeded in avoiding what many deemed inevitable—the outbreak of a third world war. Although this result cannot be ascribed solely to the UN, the Organization did play a primary role in the prevention of armed East-West conflict which would have been fatal for mankind.

Three very important elements demonstrate that the international community has rightfully valued the actions carried out by the UN over the last 50 years. First, five Nobel prizes were awarded to the Organization or to one of its elements. Secondly, the number of Member States has increased from 51 in 1945 to 185 in 1995. The fact that this number has more than tripled is because the great majority of countries of the world believe that the UN has more qualities and advantages than flaws and drawbacks. Thirdly, a decision was taken to hold in October a large meeting, with the participation of more than 150 Heads of State or Government from the entire world. And, indeed, it is obvious that if so many outstanding leaders have decided to come to New York to commemorate a mere anniversary, it is because this anniversary is unquestionably the occasion for celebrating a series of important events.

I have already spoken of that global peace which fortunately has been maintained successfully for some 50 years now despite numerous local or regional conflicts which it has been impossible to avoid. But here, even in that difficult area of war and peace, the UN can pride itself on having made a decisive contribution to noticeable progress in the fields of disarmament and nuclear non-proliferation, and on having conducted negotiations and concluded agreements within the framework of the peace process for which the outcome was positive as, for example, in Cambodia, El Salvador, Nicaragua, Eritrea, Mozambique and, we hope, also in Angola.

Secondly, the UN, more than any other institution, has contributed to establishing and attempting to guarantee in practice the primacy of international law, and it is well known that, without a state of law, a human being cannot know that peace, freedom or security, which allows him to lead a normal existence in a civilized society. We will never forget the nightmare of "man who is a wolf to man" described with insight in the "state of nature" of the *Leviathan* of Thomas Hobbes. And, in speaking of the contribution of the UN to the recognition of the primacy of international law, I wish to hail the outstanding action and lofty prestige achieved by one of its major bodies, the International Court of Justice, to which I wish to pay a very sincere tribute.

"The establishment in 1945 of the UN represented great hope for all people of good will throughout the world"

Thirdly, also to the credit of the UN, is the attention and importance which it attaches to human rights. It is the UN which has universalized them; it is the UN that has led States to accept, through the recognition of human rights, the fact that the State is at the service of man and not man at the service of the State. It is the UN which, not limiting itself to those classical human rights born of the American and the French revolutions, consecrated the fundamental rights of the second generation and, in particular, economic, social and cultural rights. And, once again, it is the UN which today is playing a leading role in the struggle for the respect of the fundamental rights of the third generation, in particular, rights dealing with the protection of nature and of the environment, an area in which, for the first time in the history of mankind, it is no longer exclusively a question of recognizing or establishing rights governing the relations of human beings among themselves or *vis-à-vis* the State, but also to attempt to establish and implement machinery which will lead to the recognition of the rights of animals and of nature in the face of acts of aggression perpetrated by the human being himself.

Conventions: Glorious landmarks

A major reason for pride and satisfaction is the fact that it has been possible, once again thanks to the UN, to draw up and implement international conventions which do honour mankind and which will form glorious landmarks in the history of the first 50 years of the Organization and will rank among its justified achievements. I am thinking, in particular, of the Convention on the Rights of the Child, the Convention on the Elimination of all Forms of Discrimination against Women, and the Convention against Torture and Other Cruel, Inhuman or Degrading Treatment or Punishment. What would mankind be without these basic texts? Would they ever have been produced without the intervention of the UN?

It is the UN to which we owe the contribution to universal awareness of the idea that our world is formed of equal beings all enjoying the same fundamental rights to human dignity. This ideal is already long-standing. Saint Paul affirmed that with the "new man" ..."there is neither Greek nor Jew, . . . barbarian, Scythian, bond nor free" (*The Holy Bible, Colossians* 3:10–11).

But while that ideal is indeed an ancient one, nevertheless 20 centuries were required to enshrine it in a legal declaration of universal scope and here the credit is due to the UN. That ideal must never be forgotten nor must we fail to mention it, whether or not we adhere to the religious tradition of which it was born.

Fourthly, the UN certainly has the right to claim the major credit linked with two other victories won by mankind in the twentieth century, namely, decolonization and the end of apartheid. The fact that the number of States Members of the Organization has increased from 51 to 185 is due basically to decolonization. And the fact is that if an end was put to the un-acceptable regime in South Africa, this is in great part due to the condemnations and criticisms levelled by the UN.

It is interesting to emphasize that the leaders who succeeded in bringing about decolonization, like those who put an end to apartheid, had the most wide-ranging political convictions, a fact which clearly demonstrates that the ideals enshrined in the Charter of the UN are neither partisan nor ideological, nor religious, but purely and simply humanitarian, and that it suffices to believe in the dignity of all human beings and to respect it in practice in order to be a law-abiding and consistent Member of the UN.

Consolidating internal democratization

Fifthly, the UN has contributed, especially since the end of the cold war, to consolidating and concretizing the process of internal democratization on which many countries have embarked, countries that have decided of their own will to move from a one-party regime to a multi-party system.

It is not for the UN to dictate to a Member State the form of government the latter must adopt in its political constitution. On the other hand, the UN can and must assist those who decide on their own to embark upon a process of democratization. This is what it has done to this very day in more than 45 countries, providing assistance not only in the electoral sphere, but in other fields as well. Those who are convinced, as I am, of the superiority of the pluralistic democratic model must stress this fact and welcome it.

Sixthly—and lastly—I should like to draw attention to one of the most relevant and positive aspects of the UN, one which in most cases the Organization's detractors, and even impartial observers, frequently overlook. Here, I am referring to the outstandingly commendable part played by a large number of autonomous UN agencies and bodies in promoting the economic, social and cultural development of the poorest and most disadvantaged of the world's peoples.

—Excerpted from his speech to the General Assembly on 19 September

A Watchful Eye
Monitoring the Conventional Arms Trade

BY JORDAN SINGER

ONE OF THE GREATEST LESSONS learned by the international community in the aftermath of the Persian Gulf War was that the unchecked proliferation of conventional armaments during the Cold War had left rogue nations in possession of significant destructive capabilities. Both the United States and the Soviet Union from the late 1940s onward exported conventional arms to satellite states in the developing world in hopes of influencing regional conflicts. However, the danger inherent in distributing conventional weapons to such states became manifestly apparent after the Iraqi invasion of Kuwait in August 1990. The Gulf War served as a testament to conventional weapons sales that had escalated largely without control during the Cold War. Indeed, so many arms had been sold to the regime of Saddam Hussein by so many Soviet bloc and Western nations that the members of the coalition that liberated Kuwait were unaware of the full array of weaponry that the Iraqi military held until after the war had concluded. An international debate emerged following the war as states sought to develop mutual strategies to curb the transfer of arms to unstable regimes. As the curtailment of the international arms trade itself would be both difficult to enforce and a violation of the right of nations to defend themselves, an alternative solution became necessary to prevent a repeat of the events that led to the build-up of the Iraqi military.

Jordan Singer is a Staff Writer for the Harvard International Review.

The concept of transparency in armaments is a compromise solution to this dilemma. Arms transparency monitors all arms transfers between states rather than regulating them. States are requested to make public information describing the type and number of arms that they export to, or import from, other states. The common goal of arms transparency is for states to increase international security by simultaneously sharing information on their own weapons acquisitions and gaining access to information on the weapons systems of other countries.

The primary mechanism for arms transparency measures in the 1990s has been the UN Register of Conventional Arms, established by the General Assembly on the recommendation of the First Committee on Disarmament and International Security in December 1991. The First Committee's recommendation was issued just months after the end of the Persian Gulf War. The draft resolution creating the Register, jointly sponsored by the European Community and Japan, drew heavily from a 1991 study that suggested the implementation of a non-discriminatory, universal register of conventional arms transfers. On November 15, 1991, the draft resolution passed the First Committee by a vote of 106–1–8. General Assembly Resolution 46/36 L, "Transparency in Armaments," was passed three weeks later by an overwhelming 150–0–2 vote. Under the resolution, the Secretary-General was invested with the responsibility of establishing the Register and convening a Panel of Government Experts (PGE) for the following year to evaluate its functioning.

Methods and Mechanisms

The UN Register of Conventional Arms requests transfer information for seven distinct categories of weapons: main battle tanks, armored combat vehicles, large-caliber artillery systems, combat aircraft, attack helicopters, warships, missiles, and missile launchers. States report transfers via a one-page form for imports and a similar form for exports. The forms are designed to be as simple to complete as possible in order to promote maximum possible participation in the registration process; they ask only for the state(s) of origin and destination of the weapons, the names of any intermediary transit states, and the number of items being transferred in each weapons category. Should participating states wish to divulge further information concerning the type or value of the weapons listed, a "Remarks" section on the form allows for more detailed description. The "Remarks" section may also be used to divulge information not specifically requested by the United Nations, including statistics on national arms holdings and armed forces. According to Dutch Ambassador to the United Nations Hendrik Wagenmakers, the driving force behind the creation and development of the Register, the sensitive nature of these latter statistics compels the Register form to include a disclaimer that "such information [as] might be affected by security or other relevant concerns... should be filled-in at the Member State's discretion."

States are asked to submit data for a given calendar year by April 30 of the following year. Thus, while the Register was

Reprinted with permission from *Harvard International Review,* Winter 1995/96, pp. 64–65, 83–84. © 1995 by the Harvard International Relations Council.

established in January 1992, it was not considered to hold pertinent data until May 1, 1993. While the April 30 date of each year is not a true deadline for submitting information (several states submitted 1992 information in late 1993 and even into 1994), efforts have been made to stress the importance of punctual submission. The calendar year format takes into account only arms that were physically imported or exported during any given calendar year, not weapons that were ordered or purchased in that given year but not yet delivered. After data are sent to the United Nations, experts cross-check the information to establish whether the data submitted by importing states matches that submitted by arms exporters. The information is then compiled into an annual report issued by the Secretary-General.

The Panel of Government Experts

In accordance with the directives of the First Committee, the Secretary-General has twice convened a Panel of Government Experts to make minor modifications to the Register and suggest more significant changes. The 1992 Panel concerned itself with two major tasks: revising the definitions of the weapons categories outlined in Resolution 46/36 L, and assessing the feasibility of expanding the Register to include data on additional military holdings.

Of these two agenda items, the former carried a greater sense of urgency, as the Panel needed to solidify definitions for arms categories before the reporting forms could be finalized. The Panel deliberated extensively over the final definitions. Although some members argued for the inclusion of small arms in one of the original categories as they are seen as a major source of destabilization in many regions, the Panel ultimately decided to retain the original seven weapons categories. The PGE did, however, make several modifications of widely varying significance. First, the definition of armored combat vehicles was broadened from the General Assembly's resolution to include all vehicles with an armament caliber of 12.5 millimeters or greater. The standard had previously been 20 millimeters. Second, the original anti-tank missile launcher category was expanded to include all types of missile launchers. Third, the scope of combat aircraft and attack helicopters was broadened to encompass armed reconnaissance aircraft, but fell short of including unarmed vehicles that performed the same mission. The most major changes in definitions, however, were focused on the remaining two weapons categories: warships and missiles. The tonnage threshold of warships was lowered from 800 tons to 750 tons, although many countries involved in the Panel favored either lowering the threshold even further or eliminating it

altogether. The missiles category was expanded to cover unguided rockets as well as remotely piloted vehicles, but ground-to-air missiles were eliminated on the basis that they were designed to serve purely defensive purposes. The Panel also made other significant changes in the interpretation of existing definitions and terminology for the Register. For example, certain types of leases, grants, and longterm loans were for the first time construed as being arms transfers. Ironically, although these changes were intended to clarify definitions and ease reporting, it was later speculated that the existence of two sets of formal definitions (one from the General Assembly resolution and one from the Panel of Experts) made several states more reluctant to report the arms transfers in which they had participated.

As part of its mission, the 1992 Panel also sought to evaluate expansion of the arms register to include other types of armaments. To this effect, the members of the Panel posed a series of questions for their successors in 1994. Chiefly, these questions involved the issue of whether data on military holdings arising from domestic arms production should be requested. The main rationale motivating this action was one of fairness. Under current conditions, states that assemble their arsenals almost exclusively through arms imports effectively divulge their entire arms capacity to neighboring states by participating in the Register; by contrast, net arms-producing states, due to domestic production for domestic military use, are regularly able to avoid reporting the full extent of their national armed forces. The 1992 Panel felt that this inequality should be rectified by requesting information on domestic arms production for domestic use as well as the total number and type of armaments in the possession of a nation's military forces.

Non-Compliance and Discrepancies

Formally titled the Group of Government Experts (GGE), the 1994 Panel engaged in a comprehensive study of the Register's functionality, evaluated the formal suggestions of the 1992 panel, and reviewed the first two years of data submitted to the Register. After many months of research and evaluation, the GGE submitted its own recommendations to the Secretary-General in the fall of 1994. These recommendations fell into three major categories: participation and reporting, further development of the Register, and regional considerations. First, the GGE noted that it was encouraged by the fact that participation in the Arms Register during 1993 and 1994 was extremely high when compared to similar international reporting instruments. The GGE also asserted that most major arms exporters had submit-

ted data to the Register; as a result, the majority of international arms transfers could be accounted for from at least the exporter's side.

At the same time, however, the GGE concluded that there still existed much work to be done in terms of increasing the level of state participation. By August 1, 1993, only 71 members of the United Nations—or 40 percent of member states—had submitted reports to the register for calendar year 1992. By August 1, 1994, the number of participants for 1993 had reached 77 states—or 42 percent of the total UN membership. Based upon these experiences, the GGE was guardedly optimistic that the slow growth of the number of participants in the UN Register of Conventional Arms would continue in the future. Principally, the GGE noted that once a nation has submitted to the Register once, it is politically more difficult to justify to the international community a termination of submissions than to justify never having participated at all. Therefore, the GGE argued that it seemed likely that the 28 states that filed reports in 1992 but not in 1993 would resume submitting reports soon under targeted international pressure.

Even more disturbing to the GGE than non-submission of arms data was the fact that much of the arms data submitted by exporters and importers did not match. For the calendar year 1993, for example, exporters reported the transfer of 2,921 battle tanks and 2,060 armored combat vehicles, but importers reported less than half of these totals in the same categories. Similarly, exporters showed transfers of almost 68,000 missiles and missile launchers for calendar year 1992, but importers showed less than 9,000 for the same year. In only 22 percent of cases did the reported items match. Nine percent of transfers were reported by both exporter and importer, but with inconsistent amounts of weaponry. Thirty-three percent of arms transfers were only reported by one party because the other party did not participate in the Register. In the remaining 36 percent of cases, transfers were reported by only one party even though the other party completed a report.

Such discrepancies in reporting are clearly troubling. First, there is the question of what figures, if any, are accurate. Currently, only in the relatively few cases in which both parties reported a transfer with corresponding figures can the information be considered truly correct. Second, if one party's figures are accurate, there remains the question of why the other party refused to provide correct figures.

Attempts at Reform

The 1994 GGE also attempted to address each of the terminology questions left unanswered by its predecessor. The GGE claimed that there existed "three dimensions to be considered: adjustments to the existing definitions for the seven categories of equipment; the addition of new categories for conventional weapons; and the early expansion of the scope of the Register as called for in General Assembly Resolution 46/36 L." In terms of the first dimension, the Group discussed possible adjustments to current weapons definitions, but decided not to alter them for the time being. The Group did reserve the right to review the definitions at a later date, however.

Several proposals were submitted regarding the addition of new weapons categories, including small arms and anti-personnel land mines. As in 1992, the various proposals to include small arms were eventually rejected; this occurred largely due to concern from small arms importing states that if small arms were added to the Register, no part of the composition of their arsenals would be shielded from becoming a part of the public domain. The inclusion of land mines under the UN Arms Register standards was debated at length, but also ultimately rejected. In the final analysis, the Secretary-General reported that "The Group's view was that the issue of anti-personnel land mines is largely one of international legal regulation."

Finally, the Group considered the directive of Resolution 46/36 L with regards to expanding the scope of the Register to include all military holdings and domestic arms production. The Group maintained that early expansion of the Register remained a valuable goal, but could not agree on the best way to include such information on the same basis as arms transfers. The final conclusion was that more consideration of the issue was necessary. Likewise, the related question of whether to expand the Register to include weapons of mass destruction or to establish separate registers for this purpose was debated but left unsettled pending further consideration.

In the final part of the GGE's evaluation, it noted that some regions participated in the Register of Conventional Arms with much greater frequency than other regions. The GGE concluded that this pattern of participation was a result of the varying security concerns present in each region. Participation in two regions was particularly dismal: three months after the deadline for 1992 reports, only 12 percent of African nations had submitted data, as had only 32 percent of Asian states. For the following year, these numbers had modestly increased to 17 percent and 40 percent, respectively. Although participation was high in Europe and North America, the percentage of submissions in these areas declined from 1993 to 1994. To combat this decline, the Group reaffirmed the need for regional and sub-regional registers that "should complement and not detract from the operation of the universal and global United Nations Register of Conventional Arms." Efforts to create regional registers have already begun under the jurisdiction of the Organization of American States (OAS) and the Organization for Security and Cooperation in Europe (OSCE).

The failure of the GGE to arrive at a plan of action to remedy inconsistencies in current reporting practices represents an important and disturbing development in international arms transparency efforts. Complete and accurate reporting lies at the heart of transparency theory; if states do not report information in a thorough and timely manner, international confidence in the validity of transparency measures such as the Register plummets, and thus overall security declines. In order to promote consistent and valuable reporting, concerted efforts must be made to diminish the "security excuse" of small arms-importing states for not reporting data. Under the UN Register of Conventional Arms, states need not report information that they feel jeopardizes their national or international security. For many states, especially arms importers, however, divulging any information may be considered a security threat primarily because there is no guarantee that its neighbors and adversaries will similarly comply with requests to submit information.

While there are admittedly no easy steps to resolving this conundrum, some measures can be taken almost immediately to improve international confidence. The first of these is to specifically request domestic arms production information from states. Requesting this information places net exporting states and net importing states alike on level ground. The General Assembly might also seek to coordinate its efforts with outside organizations that independently collect similar information. For example, SIPRI, a Swedish research institute, currently publishes an annual yearbook detailing international arms transfers. Coordinating UN and SIPRI data (after the standardization of definitions, timetables, and weapons categories has taken place) offers the United Nations an independent source of verification for its Register of Conventional Arms. Yet, given all of the technical and security challenges that have surfaced since the initiation of the United Nations Register of Conventional Arms in 1992, the current functioning of the system stands in part as a tribute to the resolve of the international community to avoid a repetition of the situation that coalition forces encountered in the Persian Gulf War against Iraq. Deliberate attempts to bring about full participation and consistent reporting will render the Register more than a useful tool for enhancing arms transparency. A fully functioning Arms Register would likely build trust between neighboring states. First, however, further efforts by the international community are necessary to bring the present Arms Register closer to its intended form.

Justice Goes Global
(International Criminal Court Is Created)

More than 160 nations voted to establish the International Criminal Court, which will be located in The Hague, Netherlands. The U.S. refused to sign the treaty to create the global tribunal to judge war crimes because of reservations about sovereignty and jurisdiction.

Despite U.S. dissent the world community finally creates a new court to judge the crimes of war.

The spectre of the century's slaughtered millions haunted Rome as the world's nations struggled for five weeks to create the first permanent international body dedicated to punishing the crimes of war. "Victims of past crimes and potential victims are watching us," said U.N. Secretary-General Kofi Annan. "They will not forgive us if we fail."

They did not fail. Cheers and applause echoed as representatives of some 160 nations, assisted by more than 200 non-governmental organizations, gathered last week in the plush maze of the U.N. Food and Agriculture Organization's building, voted overwhelmingly to create the International Criminal Court (I.C.C.). But success came only after frantic last-minute negotiations to bridge philosophical divides that left the U.S. in opposition to the treaty and at odds with most of its major allies. Just how viable the court will be if the world's superpower carries out its threat to "actively oppose" the new institution remains to be seen, but 18 judges will gather in The Hague within the next few years, ready to try cases of genocide, war crimes and crimes against humanity.

The duality of mankind's urges to both wage war and curb its own bellicosity is virtually as old as warfare itself. But it was only in the 19th century that refinements in the technology of battle concentrated minds on serious attempts to find judicial ways to combat their brutality. The laws and customs of war were codified at Conventions in The Hague in 1899 and 1907, and efforts continued between the two World Wars. But those laudable agreements were impotent in face of the unprecedented carnage of the 20th century's first half, when an estimated 58 million died in Europe alone. After World War II, international tribunals at Nuremburg and Tokyo tried and convicted the conflict's instigators for war crimes, crimes against peace and against humanity itself. But these judgments were carried out within a temporary judicial framework imposed by the victors.

The Geneva Conventions of 1949 continued to build a body of international law governing the conduct of war, but the problem of applying the provisions remained. The newly formed U.N. had commissioned a study in 1948 to look into establishing a permanent tribunal, but the cold war prevented any real progress. The topic surfaced again only in 1989, when the International Law Commission began preparing a draft statute for an International Criminal Cowl. But what really galvanized the international community was the chaotic disintegration of Yugoslavia and the atrocities that accompanied it.

The U.N. eventually moved to create an ad hoc criminal tribunal on the crimes committed during the Bosnian war in 1993, followed a year later by another one-off body for Rwanda. The distinguished South African jurist Richard Goldstone, the original chief prosecutor for both tribunals, says that those courts represented "the first real international attempt to enforce international humanitarian law." But establishing those bodies took up to two years of preparatory work and negotiation. "The thing is to avoid having to spend six months looking for a prosecutor," notes Theodor Meron, professor of international law at New York University Law School, "and a year looking for a building."

Even though Bosnia's most notorious accused war criminals have not yet been brought before The Hague tribunal, it has indicted some 60 people, holds 27 men in custody and has handed down two judgments. This month the court launched the first genocide prosecution in Europe. Deputy Prosecutor Graham Blewitt says that "We have been a model for the creation of the new court."

International law has always involved an inherent tension between national sovereignty and accountability. But the continuing carnage since 1945—another 18 million dead and the likes of Idi Amin, Pol Pot and Saddam Hussein reigning in terror—reinforced the U.N.'s determination to act. As it did so, Washington began to fret. Michael Scharf, currently professor of law at New England Law School, was the State Department's point man on the court under President George Bush. "One of my jobs, which I did not enjoy," recalls Scharf, "was to find ways to stall it forever." President Clinton has been far more supportive, but his administration, too, developed serious qualms. Recalling the invasions of Grenada and Panama, and the bombing of Libya, the U.S. worried that similar actions in the future could involve officials all the way up the chain of command being hauled before the I.C.C.

As the conference convened in Rome on June 15, it was beset by disagreement. The most divisive questions revolved around the precise definition of the crimes to be within the court's jurisdiction, the breadth of that jurisdiction and just who would determine which cases should be brought. The U.S. went in with goals that allied it uncomfortably with China, Russia and India, as well as Libya and Algeria, but put it at odds with most of its usual friends who gathered among the so-called Like-Minded Nations seeking a strong and independent Court. "We are not here," said Washington's U.N. ambassador, Bill Richardson, "to create a court that sits in judgment on national systems." The U.S. is concerned that its many soldiers serving overseas could become involved in confrontations that would make them vulnerable to what an Administration official called "frivolous claims by politically motivated governments."

The Washington negotiators—who rejected universal jurisdiction, subjecting any state, signatory or not, to the court's remit—agreed that the court should have automatic jurisdiction in the case of genocide, giving it the ability to prosecute individuals of any country that had signed the treaty. But they sought a clause allowing countries to opt out of the court's jurisdiction on war crimes and crimes against humanity for 10 years. The agreed statute allows states to opt out of the court's jurisdictions only on war crimes and only for seven years. It also includes the crime of "aggression" within the court's jurisdiction, subject to a precise definition of aggression. Washington had also wanted to give only the Security Council and states party to the agreement the right to bring cases to the court. The statute, however, also empowers the prosecutor to initiate cases. The U.S. did manage to get a compromise, promoted by Singapore, allowing the Security Council to call a 12-month renewable halt to investigations and prosecutions included in the text. "If states can simply opt in or out when they want, the court will be unworkable," said a senior official in the German delegation. Without an independent prosecutor, he added, "crimes will be passed over for political reasons."

Although conference chairman Philippe Kirsch of Canada had already successfully chaired at least eight international conferences—brokering agreements on issues such as terrorism and the protection of war victims—all his undoubted mediation skills failed to resolve the disputes. As Washington became increasingly isolated, a copy of U.S. "talking points" circulated among the delegations, suggesting that if the court did not meet U.S. requirements Washington might retaliate by withdrawing its troops overseas, including those in Europe. Although few believed in that possibility and the Administration downplayed it, State Department spokesman Jamie Rubin explained that "The U.S. has a special responsibility that other governments do not have."

After all the wrangling, what emerged was a court to be located in The Hague—where the International Court of Justice already deals with cases brought on a civil basis by states against other states. It is to contain four elements: a Presidency with three judges; a section encompassing an appeals division, trial and pre-trial divisions; a Prosecutor's office; and a Registry to handle administration. The court, which will act only when national courts are "unwilling or unable genuinely" to proceed, will confine its maximum penalty to life imprisonment.

How the court will fare without the support of the U.S. is unclear. Washington has provided vital political backing for the Yugoslav and Rwanda tribunals and continues to be their leading financier. "We have shown that the only way to get war criminals to trial is for the U.S. to take a prominent role," said one Administration official last week. "If the U.S. is not a lead player in the creation of this court, it doesn't happen."

Nevertheless, the fact that a court with teeth has actually been created was an unprecedented move by the world community to make the rule of law finally prevail over brute force—a step towards fulfilling Secretary-General Annan's pledge that "At long last we aim to prove we mean it when we say 'Never Again.'"

Peace Prize Goes to Land-Mine Opponents

By CAREY GOLDBERG

PUTNEY, Vt., Oct. 10—The Nobel Peace Prize was bestowed today on the International Campaign to Ban Landmines and on Jody Williams, an American who coordinates it—and the newly minted laureate immediately wielded the award to step up political pressure on recalcitrant countries, including the United States.

Barefoot in her rustic yard here, and bare-knuckled as ever in her approach, Ms. Williams taunted President Clinton today, saying he would be branded a coward if the United States continued to refuse to sign the international treaty banning land mines.

"If President Clinton wants the legacy of his administration to be that he did not have the courage to be the Commander in Chief of his military, that is his legacy, and I feel sorry for him," she said. "I think it's tragic that President Clinton does not want to be on the side of humanity."

Just hours after the award was announced, President Boris N. Yeltsin unexpectedly declared that Russia had decided to sign the accord.

But the United States and China remain the big holdouts, and the White House spokesman said today that President Clinton's refusal to sign the treaty, based on his insistence that it contain exceptions for the Korean peninsula, still stands.

In awarding the prize to the group and to Ms. Williams, the Nobel committee said it was openly trying to influence the treaty process. "This could be interpreted as a message to the great powers that we hope they also will eventually choose to sign the treaty," Francis Sejersted, the committee chairman, said in Oslo.

He and others also praised the anti-land-mine campaign as an exciting new form of post-cold-war political action in which a broad, grassroots coalition of citizens' groups and smaller nations, working on their own outside the bounds of major institutions like the United Nations, led to world change.

The agreement would outlaw land mines, which are estimated to kill or maim 26,000 people a year, and require countries to clean up those already on their soil. Nearly 100 governments approved a draft of the treaty last month, and world figures ranging from Diana, Princess of Wales, to President Nelson Mandela of South Africa have supported the campaign.

The treaty, to be signed in Ottawa in December, is to go into effect after 40 nations have ratified it.

The International Campaign to Ban Landmines is a coalition of more than 1,000 organizations in more than 60 countries, and argues that with more than 100 million buried mines around the world taking such a high human toll, they must be banned.

Ms. Williams, 47, first became politically active protesting the Vietnam War, and later focused her efforts on influencing American policy in Central America and providing aid there. She joined the Vietnam Veterans of America Foundation, which began the land mines campaign, at the end of 1991.

The campaign is a descendant of the anti-war movement. It was the idea of Robert Muller, a Marine veteran who lost the use of his legs during the Vietnam War and started organizing to improve conditions at the veterans' hospitals where he was treated. He then moved into anti-war activism, and also fought for compensation for veterans who had been exposed to Agent Orange.

During the 1980's he returned to Vietnam and set up projects to provide wounded Vietnamese veterans with prosthetics. When he went to Cambodia to do similar work in 1991, Mr. Muller found that the victims were largely civilians and that their injuries were more recent—from land mines still embedded in the countryside.

He realized, he said, "that there is more we got to do—just putting on legs don't cut it." And the campaign to ban land mines was born.

Men and Women of Peace, 1971–1997

By The Associated Press

1997—The International Campaign to Ban Landmines.

1996—Filipe Ximenes Belo and José Ramos-Horta of East Timor.

1995—Joseph Rotblat and the Pugwash Conference on Science and World Affairs, Britain.

1994—Yasir Arafat of the Palestine Liberation Organization and Yitzhak Rabin and Shimon Peres of Israel.

1993—Nelson Mandela and F. W. de Klerk, South Africa.

1992—Rigoberta Menchu, Guatemala.

1991—Aung San Suu Kyi, Burma.

1990—Mikhail S. Gorbachev, Soviet Union.

1989—The Dalai Lama, Tibet.

1988—The United Nations peacekeeping operations.

1987—Oscar Arias Sanchez, Costa Rica.

1986—Elie Wiesel, United States.

1985—International Physicians for the Prevention of Nuclear War.

1984—Bishop Desmond Tutu, South Africa.

1983—Lech Walesa, Poland.

1982—Alva Myrdal, Sweden, and Alfonso Garcia Robles, Mexico.

1981—The United Nations High Commission for Refugees.

1980—Adolfo Pérez Esquivel, Argentina.

1979—Mother Teresa, Calcutta.

1978—Anwar el-Sadat, Egypt, and Menachem Begin, Israel.

1977—Amnesty International, London.

1976—Betty Williams and Mairead Corrigan, Northern Ireland.

1975—Andrei Sakharov, Soviet Union.

1974—Sean MacBride, Ireland, and Eisaku Sato, Japan.

1973—Henry A. Kissinger, United States, and Le Duc Tho, North Vietnam.

1972—No prize awarded.

1971—Willy Brandt, Germany.

It started with Mr. Muller and the Vietnam Veterans of America Foundation and a German group. "That way, we could call ourselves international," Mr. Muller said. Soon the movement was growing quickly enough to hire a coordinator, Ms. Williams.

While efforts in the United Nations stagnated, the anti-land-mine campaign found support from such figures as Lloyd Axworthy, the Canadian Foreign Minister; Senator Patrick J. Leahy, Democrat of Vermont, and Gen. Norman Schwarzkopf. The International Committee of the Red Cross also helped, with a worldwide publicity campaign beginning in 1995.

The campaign and Ms. Williams are to share the $1 million Nobel monetary award equally.

Today Ms. Williams was praised by Susannah Sirkin, deputy director of Physicians for Human Rights, a campaign member, as "an extraordinarily determined individual."

"She is fearless," Ms. Sirkin said. "She has never been reluctant to stand in front of a general or world leader with a conviction that she was right on this issue, and tell them what needs to be done."

But at her Vermont home, set near a beaver pond among trees glowing ruby and gold in the autumn sunlight, Ms. Williams adamantly refused to take the prize as a personal tribute, focusing her remarks instead on the campaign's progress and the work it has yet to do.

The group plans to focus its pressure on hold-out countries, she said, and hopes to have all countries on board by 2000. She has not decided what issue she will work on next, she said, but assumes something will evolve.

The overall message of the campaign against land mines, she said, was not only the damage the mines cause but also the concept that in this post-cold-war world, "the military cannot operate with impunity."

"I hope to educate the world that while war may not go away in our lifetime, that there are rules about how you conduct yourself in war," she said, "that if the military think they have to fight with each other, they should point the guns at each other; they should not involve all of civil society."

And entire countries should not become battlefields, she said, citing Cambodia and Angola. Cambodia is believed to harbor more than 10 million land mines, Angola 9 million.

For all her serious arguments, however, and for all her solemn appreciation of the honor inherent in joining the ranks of Nobel recipients, Ms. Williams retains a streak of irrepressible irreverence, particularly in regard to the President of the United States, whom she referred to as "Billy" and "a weenie."

When, by midafternoon, he still had not called to congratulate her, she complained comically, "He has time to call the winners of the Super Bowl, but the winner of the Nobel Peace Prize he can't call?"

Of course, she added, he probably had not called because, "If he calls me, he knows I'm going to say, 'What's your problem?' "

Child Labour: Rights, risks, and realities

by Carol Bellamy

"Dust from the chemical powders and strong vapours in both the storeroom and the boiler room were obvious . . . We found 250 children, mostly below 10 years of age, working in a long hall, filling in a slotted frame with sticks. Row upon row of children, some barely five years old, were involved in the work."

The description could come from an observer appalled at the working conditions endured by children in the 19th century in British mills and factories.

But the quote is from a report on the matchstick-making industry of modern day Sivakasi, in India.

Similar descriptions of children at work in hazardous conditions can be gathered from countries across the world. In Malaysia, children may work up to 17-hour days on rubber plantations, exposed to insect- and snakebites. In the United Republic of Tanzania, they pick coffee beans, inhaling pesticides. In Portugal, children as young as 12 are subject to heavy labour and the myriad dangers of the construction industry. In Morocco, they hunch at looms for long hours and little pay, knotting the strands of luxury carpets for export. In the United States, children are exploited in garment-industry sweatshops. In the Philippines, young boys dive in dangerous conditions to help set nets for deep-sea fishing. Statistical data on child labour is scarce, but our most reliable estimates indicate about 250 million child labourers (ages 10–14) in developing countries alone.

The world should, indeed, have outgrown the many forms of abuse that labouring children endure. But it hasn't, although not for lack of effort. Child labour was one of the first and most important issues addressed by the international community, resulting in the 1919 Minimum Age Convention of the International Labour Organization.

Early efforts were hobbled, in part, because campaigners struggling to end child labour appealed to morality and ethics, values easily sidelined by the drive for profit and hard realities of commercial life.

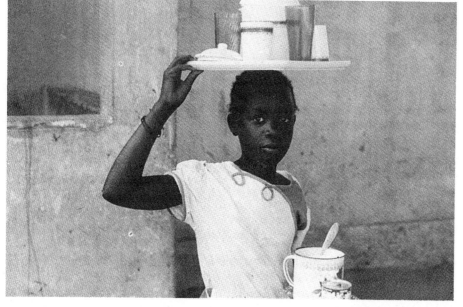

A domestic servant in Mauritania

C-88 UNICEF/L. GOODSMITH

From *The Rotarian*, September 1997, pp. 26-29. Adapted from *The State of the World's Children* by Carol Bellamy. © 1997 by Oxford University Press. Reprinted by permission.

86-147 UNICEF/YANN GAMBLIN

Herding cattle in Kenya

Child labourers were objects of charity and humanitarian concern, but they had no rights.

Today's world is somewhat different. Children have rights established in international laws, not least in the Convention on the Rights of the Child, which has now been ratified by 191 countries—all but the U.S. and Somalia—making it the most universally embraced human rights instrument in history. One provision—Article 32—obligates governments to protect children "from economic exploitation and from performing any work that is likely to be hazardous or to interfere with the child's education, and/or to be harmful to the child's health or physical, mental, spiritual, moral, or social development."

Children's exploitation in work also contravenes many more of the rights enshrined in the Convention, among them children's rights to parental care, to compulsory and free primary education, to the highest attainable standard of health, to social security, and to provisions for rest and recreation.

Looking at children's work through the lens of the Convention on the Rights of the Child offers not only new ways of understanding the problem of child labour, but also provides new impetus and direction to the movement against it.

Child labour is often a complex issue. Powerful forces sustain it, including many employers, vested interest groups, economists proposing that the market must be free at all costs, and traditionalists who believe that the low caste or class of certain children denudes them of rights.

The overriding consideration must always be the best interests of the child. It can never be in the best interests of a child to be exploited or to perform heavy and dangerous forms of work. No child should labour under hazardous and exploitative conditions, just as no child should die of causes that are preventable.

Work that endangers children's physical, mental, spiritual, moral, or social development must end. Hazardous child labour is a betrayal of every child's rights as a human being and is an offence against civilization.

Most children who work do not have the power of free choice. They do not choose between career options with varying advantages, drawbacks, and levels of pay. A fortunate minority have sufficient material means behind them to be pulled toward work as an attractive option offering them even more economic advantages.

But the vast majority are pushed into work that is often damaging to their development for three reasons: the exploitation of poverty, the absence of education, and the restrictions of tradition.

The exploitation of poverty

The most powerful force driving children into hazardous, debilitating labour is the exploitation of poverty. Where society is characterized by poverty and inequity, the incidence of child labour is likely to increase, as does the risk that it is exploitative.

187

For poor families, the small contribution of a child's income or assistance at home that allows the parents to work can make the difference between hunger and a bare sufficiency. Survey after survey makes this clear. A high proportion of child employees give all their wages to their parents. Children's work is considered essential to maintaining the economic level of the household.

If employers were not prepared to exploit children, there would be no child labour. The parents of child labourers are often unemployed or underemployed, desperate for secure employment and income. Yet it is not they but their children who are offered the jobs. Why? Because children can be paid less, of course. (In Latin America, for example, children ages 13 to 17 earn on average half the pay of a wage-earning adult with seven years of education.) Because children are more malleable, they will do what they are told without questioning authority. Because children are largely powerless before adults, they are less likely to organize against oppression and can be physically abused without striking back.

Put simply, children are employed because they are easier to exploit.

Exploitation of the poor and the powerless not only means that adults are denied jobs that could better have sustained their families. It not only means that children are required to work in arduous, dangerous conditions. It also means a life of unskilled work and ignorance not only for the child, but often for the children of generations to come. Any small, short-term financial gain for the family is at the cost of an incalculable long-term loss. Poverty begets child labour begets lack of education begets poverty.

A serious attack on poverty will reduce the number of children vulnerable to exploitation at work. Social safety nets are essential for the poor, as are access to credit and income-generating schemes, technology, education, and basic health services. Budgetary priorities need to be re-examined in this light.

Tackling the exploitation itself does not have to wait until some future day when world poverty has been brought to an end. Hazardous child labour provides the most pow-erful of arguments for equality and social justice. It can and must be abolished here and now.

The lack of relevant education

Cuts in social spending worldwide have hit education—the most important single factor in ending child labour—particularly hard.

In all regions, spending per student for higher education fell during the 1980s, and in Africa and Latin America, spending per pupil also fell for primary education.

A pilot survey, sponsored by the United Nations Educational, Scientific, and Cultural Organization (UNESCO) and the United Nations Children's Fund (UNICEF) and carried out in 1994 in 14 of the world's least-developed countries, reinforced concerns about the actual conditions of primary schools. In half of these countries, classrooms for the equivalent of first grade have sitting places for only four in 10 pupils. Half the pupils have no textbooks and half the classrooms have no chalkboards. Teachers commonly have to attempt to handle huge classes—an average

88-002 UNICEF/ASLAK AARBUS

Picking cotton in El Salvador

of 67 pupils per teacher in Bangladesh and nearly 90 per teacher in Equatorial Guinea. In 10 of the 14 countries, most children are taught in a language not spoken at home. And most homes, of course, have no books or magazines in any language.

Education everywhere is clearly underfunded, but the school system as it stands in most developing countries of the world is blighted by more than just a lack of resources. It is often too rigid and uninspiring in approach, promoting a curriculum that is irrelevant to and remote from children's lives.

Education has become part of the problem. It has to be reborn as part of the solution.

Traditional expectations

The economic forces that propel children into hazardous work may be the most powerful of all. But traditions and entrenched social patterns play a part, too.

In industrialized countries, it is now almost universally accepted that if children are to develop normally and healthily, they must not perform disabling work. In theory at least, education, play and leisure, friends, good health, and proper rest must all have an important place in their lives. This idea emerged only relatively recently. In the early decades of industrialization, work was thought to be the most effective way of teaching children about life and

the world. Some residue of this notion remains in the widespread expectation that teenage children should take on casual jobs alongside school, both to gain an understanding of the way the world functions and to earn spending money of their own.

There is a darker side to the expectations about children's work. The harder and more hazardous the jobs become, the more they are likely to be considered traditionally the province of the poor and disadvantaged, the lower classes, and ethnic minorities. In India, for example, the view has been that some people are born to rule and to work with their minds while others, the vast majority, are born to work with their bodies. Many traditionalists have been unperturbed about lower-caste children failing to enroll in or dropping out of school. And if those children end up doing hazardous labour, it is likely to be seen as their lot in life.

Understanding all the various cultural factors that lead children into work is essential. But deference to tradition is often cited as a reason for not acting against intolerable forms of child labour. Children have an absolute, unnegotiable right to freedom from hazardous labour—a right now established in international law and accepted by every country that has ratified the Convention on the Rights of the Child. Respect for diverse cultures should not deflect us from using all the means at our disposal to make every

society, every economy, every corporation, regard the exploitation of children as unthinkable.

Mobilizing society

Nongovernmental organizations, such as Rotary International, have a vital role to play both in raising levels of public concern and in protecting children. You can monitor the conditions in which children work and help launch the long, indispensable process of changing public attitudes.

R.I. President Glen W. Kinross has asked Rotarians this year to "strike out at the root causes of child abuse and abandonment and child labour. Children are our most precious treasure and the future belongs to them." And we know that today many Rotary clubs are working to improve the lives of children by striving to fight poverty and hunger, provide education, and prevent child abuse and exploitation. On behalf of the world's children, thank you, Rotarians, for your concern and actions.

As we step into the next millennium, hazardous child labour must be left behind, consigned to history as completely as those other forms of slavery that it so closely resembles.

• *Carol Bellamy is Executive Director of the United Nations Children's Fund (UNICEF).*

Unit Selections

Key Points to Consider

❖ Comment on the idea that it is naive to speak of international politics and economics in terms of ethics. What role can governments, international organizations, and the individual play in making the world a more ethical place?

❖ How easily are the values of democracy transferred to new settings such as Russia?

❖ What are the characteristics of leadership?

❖ In addition to the ideas presented here, what other new ideas are being expressed, and how likely are they to be widely accepted?

❖ How do the contemporary arts reflect changes in the way humanity views itself?

❖ How will the world be different in the year 2030? What factors will contribute to these changes? What does your analysis reveal about your own value system?

 **Links**   # www.dushkin.com/online/

These sites are annotated on pages 6 and 7.

The final unit of this book considers how humanity's view of itself is changing. Values, like all other elements discussed in this anthology, are dynamic. Visionary people with new ideas can have a profound impact on how a society deals with problems and adapts to changing circumstances. Therefore, to understand the forces at work in the world today, values, visions, and new ideas must be examined.

Novelist Herman Wouk, in his book *War and Remembrance*, observed that many institutions have been so embedded in the social fabric of their time that people assumed that they were part of human nature. Slavery and human sacrifice are two examples. However, forward-thinking people opposed these institutions. Many knew that they would never see the abolition of these social systems within their own lifetimes, but they pressed on in the hope that someday these institutions would be eliminated.

Wouk believes the same is true for warfare. He states, "Either we are finished with war or war will finish us." Aspects of society such as warfare, slavery, racism, and the secondary status of women are creations of the human mind; history suggests that they can be changed by the human spirit.

The articles of this unit have been selected with the previous six units in mind. Each explores some aspect of world affairs from the perspective of values and alternative visions of the future.

New ideas are critical to meeting these challenges. The examination of well-known issues from new perspectives can yield new insights into old problems. It was feminist Susan B. Anthony who once remarked that "social change is never made by the masses, only by educated minorities." The redefinition of human values (which, by necessity, will accompany the successful confrontation of other global issues) is a task that few people take on willingly. Nevertheless, in order to deal with the dangers of nuclear war, overpopulation, and environmental degradation, educated people must take a broad view of history. This is going to require considerable effort and much personal sacrifice.

When people first begin to consider the challenges of contemporary global problems, they often become disheartened and depressed. They might ask: What can I do? What does it matter? Who cares? There are no easy answers to these questions, but people need only look around to see good news as well as bad. How individuals react to the world in which they live is not a function of that world but a reflection of themselves. Different people react differently to the same world. The study of global issues, therefore, is the study of people, and the study of people is the study of values. Ideally, people's reactions to these issues will help provide them with some insight into themselves as well as the world at large.

Values and Visions

UNIVERSAL HUMAN VALUES

Finding an Ethical Common Ground

Rushworth M. Kidder

Rushworth M. Kidder, former senior columnist for The Christian Science Monitor, *is president of the Institute for Global Ethics, Box 563, Camden, Maine 04843. Telephone 207/236-6658. He has spoken at several World Future Society conferences and at "Toward the New Millennium: Living, Learning, and Working," July 24–26, 1994, in Cambridge, Massachusetts.*

In the remote New Zealand village of Panguru, tucked into the mountains at the end of a winding gravel road, a Maori woman nearly a century old pauses for a moment as she talks about the moral values of her people. "This is God's country!" says Dame Whina Cooper with great feeling, gesturing toward the flowers blooming among the bird songs outside her modest frame house. "Only, we the people running it must be doing something wrong."

Halfway around the world, in a United Nations office perched under the eaves of a fifteenth-century building in Florence, a leading journalist from Sri Lanka is asked what will happen if the world enters the twenty-first century with the ethics of the twentieth. "I feel it will be disastrous," Varindra Tarzie Vittachi replies simply.

Midway between, in his well-appointed residence in San Jose, Costa Rica, former president Oscar Arias explains that our global survival "will become more complicated and precarious than ever before, and the ethics required of us must be correspondingly sophisticated."

Turn where you will in the world and the refrain is the same. The ethical barometer is falling, and the consequences appear to be grave. That, at least, is one of the impressions to be drawn from the two dozen individuals from 16 nations interviewed over the past few years by the Institute for Global Ethics.

These interviews did not seek to discover the ethical failings of various nations, but rather to find the moral glue that will bind us together in the twenty-first century. These voices speak powerfully of an underlying moral presence shared by all humanity—a set of precepts so fundamental that they dissolve borders, transcend races, and outlast cultural traditions.

There is a pressing need for shared values in our age of global interdependence without consensus. But there is one very real question unanswered: Is there in fact a single set of values that wise, ethical people around the world might agree on? Can there be a global code of ethics? If there is a common core of values "out there" in the world, it ought to be identifiable through examination of contemporary modes of thought in various cultures around the world. Can it be found?

On that topic, the two dozen "men and women of conscience" interviewed had a clear point of view. "Yes," they said, "there is such a code, and it can be clearly articulated." These interviewees were chosen not because they necessarily know more about ethics than their peers—although some do, having made it a lifelong study. Nor were they chosen because they are the single most exemplary person of their nation or community—though some could easily be nominated for that honor. They are, however, ethical thought-leaders within their different cultures, each viewed by his or her peers as a kind of ethical standard-bearer, a keeper of the conscience of the community, a center of moral gravity.

Each of the interviews began with a common question: If you could help create a global code of ethics, what would be on it? What moral values, in other words, would you bring to the table from your own culture and background?

In an ideal world, one would have assembled all the interviewees around a table, had each talk for an hour, had each listen intently to all the others, and finally had them arrive at a consensus. If they could have done so, here's the core of moral values upon which they probably would have agreed:

LOVE

Despite the concern of foundation executive James A. Joseph in Washington that "the L-word, Love," is falling sadly into disuse, it figured prominently in these interviews. "Love, yes," said children's author Astrid Lindgren in Stockholm. "This is the main word for what we need—love on all stages and with all people."

"The base of moral behavior is first of all solidarity, love, and mutual assistance," said former first lady Graça Machel of Mozambique. Buddhist monk Shojun Bando in Tokyo agreed, detailing three different kinds of love and insisting that "it shouldn't be that *others* should tell you to love others: It should just come of its own will, spontaneously." Or, as author Nien Cheng from China put it, "You cannot guide without love."

For tribal chief Reuben Snake of Nebraska, the central word is *compassion*. "We have to be compassionate with one another and help one another, to hold each other up, support one another down the road of life," he recalled his grandfather telling him. Thinking back on her dealings with a global spectrum of cultures at the United Nations, former ambassador Jeane Kirkpatrick in Washington noted that, no matter

how severe the political differences, "there was a kind of assumption, on the part of almost everyone, that people would help one another at the personal level."

TRUTHFULNESS

Of the four theses that form Harvard University ex-president Derek Bok's code of ethics, two center on truth. "You should not obtain your ends through lying and deceitful practices," he said, and you have a "responsibility to keep [your] promises." Astrid Lindgren put it with equal clarity when she spoke of the need to "be honest, not lying, not afraid to say your opinion."

Looking through the lens of science, the late economist Kenneth Boulding of Colorado also put "a very high value on veracity—telling the truth. The thing that gets you run out of the scientific community is being caught out telling a lie." Fortunately, said Bangladeshi banker Muhammad Yunus, the spread of technology makes it increasingly difficult for the truth to be hidden. In the future, "people will be forced to reveal themselves," he said. "Nothing can be kept hidden or secret—not in computers, not in the halls of government, nothing. People will feel much more comfortable when they're dealing in truth. You converge around and in truth."

Here, however, as with many of these global values, there was also a residue of concern—a fear that trust, which is central to honesty and truthfulness, seems to be falling into abeyance. "The idea that you ought to be able to trust somebody is out of fashion," worried Katharine Whitehorn, columnist for *The Observer* of London. That's a point seconded by corporate executive James K. Baker of Indiana. "Little by little," he said, "if we let that trust go out of our personal dealings with one another, then I think the system really begins to have trouble."

24 MEN AND WOMEN OF CONSCIENCE

Dame Whina Cooper: founding president of Maori Women's Welfare League in New Zealand; presented with the Order of Dame Commander of the British Empire by Queen Elizabeth.

"God wants us to be one people."

Varindra Tarzie Vittachi: Sri Lankan journalist and author; assistant secretary-general of the United Nations.

"One man in the twentieth century . . . led us back into morality as a practical thing and not as a cloud-cuckoo-land idea, and that was Mohandas Gandhi."

Oscar Arias: former president of Costa Rica; 1987 winner of the Nobel Peace Prize.

"The effect of one upright individual is incalculable."

James A. Joseph: former undersecretary of the U.S. Department of the Interior.

"I relate fairness to treating other people as I would want to be treated."

FAIRNESS

Elevating the concept of justice to the top of his list, philosopher and author John W. Gardner of Stanford University said, "I consider that probably the number-one candidate for your common ground." By *justice*, he meant "fair play, or some word for even-handedness."

"Here, one could get caught up in the very complicated theories of social justice," warned James A. Joseph. "Or one could simply look at the Golden Rule. I relate fairness to treating other people as I would want to be treated. I think that [rule] serves humanity well. It ought to be a part of any ethic for the future."

For many, the concern for fairness goes hand in hand with the concept of equality. "The pursuit of equality is basic," said columnist and editor Sergio Muñoz of Mexico City and Los Angeles. "The people who come from Mexico and El Salvador have the same values, in my point of view, as the person who comes from Minnesota or from Alabama or from California—those basic principles that are common to all civilizations."

Astrid Lindgren: Swedish author of *Pippi Longstocking*.

"Love, yes. This is the main word for what we need—love on all stages and with all people."

Graça Machel: former first lady of Mozambique.

"The base of moral behavior is first of all solidarity, love, and mutual assistance."

Shojun Bando: Japanese Buddhist monk, studied under Zen scholar D. T. Suzuki.

"[Parents'] actions speak more than words. Their everyday doings teach the kids how to behave."

Nien Cheng: author of *Life and Death in Shanghai*; suffered over six years of solitary confinement and torture at the hands of Chinese Communists.

"You cannot guide without love."

Reuben Snake: former chairman of the American Indian Movement.

"The spirit that makes you stand up and walk and talk and see and hear and think is the same spirit that exists in me."

For some, like Joseph, the concept of fairness and equality focuses strongly on racial issues. Others, like author Jill Ker Conway from Australia, see the need for "greater equity between the sexes." Still others, like UNESCO Director-General Federico Mayor of Spain, see the problem as one of international relations: Despite the groundswell of interest in democracy arising within the former East Bloc nations, Westerners "have not reacted as humans, but only as economic individuals. . . . Even equity—the most important value in all the world—has collapsed."

FREEDOM

Very early in human history, said John Gardner, "the concept of degrees of freedom of my action—as against excessive constraints on my action by a tyrant or by military conquerors—emerged." Even the earliest peoples "knew when they were subjugated"—and didn't like it. That desire for liberty, he said, persists to the present as one of the defining values of humanity.

But liberty requires a sense of individuality and the right of that individual to express ideas freely, many of the interviewees said. "Without the principle of individual conscience, every attempt to institutionalize ethics must necessarily collapse" said Oscar Arias. "The effect of one upright individual is incalculable. World leaders may see their effect in headlines, but the ultimate course of the globe will be determined by the efforts of innumerable individuals acting on their consciences."

Such action, for many of these thinkers, is synonymous with democracy. "I think democracy is a must for all over the world," said Salim El Hoss, former prime minister of Lebanon. He defined the ingredients of democracy as "freedom of expression plus accountability plus equal opportunity." While he worried that the latter two are lacking in many countries, he noted that the first condition, freedom of expression, is increasingly becoming available to "all peoples."

UNITY

As a counterbalance to the needs of individual conscience, however, stands the value that embraces the individual's role in a larger collective. Of the multitude of similar terms used for that concept in these interviews (*fraternity, solidarity, cooperation, community, group allegiance, oneness*) unity seems the most encompassing and the least open to misconstruction. For some, it is a simple *cri de coeur* in a world that seems close to coming undone. "I want unity," said Dame Whina Cooper of New Zealand, adding that "God wants us to be one people." For Tarzie Vittachi of Sri Lanka, the idea of unity embraces a global vision capable of moving humanity from "unbridled competition" to cooperation. "That is what is demanded of us now: putting our community first, meaning the earth first, and all living things."

The problem arises when the common good is interpreted "by seeing the relation between the individual and the common in individualistic terms," said Father Bernard Przewozny of Rome. Carried to the extreme, individualism is "destructive of social life, destructive of communal sharing, destructive of participation," he said, adding that "the earth and its natural goods are the inheritance of all peoples."

TOLERANCE

"If you're serious about values," said John Gardner, "then you have to add tolerance very early—*very* early. Because you have to have constraints. The more you say, 'Values are important,' the more you have to say, 'There are limits to which you can impose your values on me.'"

"It is a question of respect for the dignity of each of us," said Graça Machel. "If you have a different idea from mine, it's not because you're worse than me. You have the right to think differently." Agreeing, Derek Bok defined tolerance as "a decent respect for the right of other people to have ideas, an obligation or at least a strong desirability of listening to different points of view and attempting to understand why they are held."

"You have your own job, you eat your own food," said Vietnamese writer and activist Le Ly Hayslip.

"How you make that food is up to you, and how I live my life is up to me."

Reuben Snake traced the idea of tolerance back to a religious basis. "The spirit that makes you stand up and walk and talk and see and hear

---

Jeane Kirkpatrick: former U.S. ambassador to the United Nations.

"I don't think life is the supreme good. It's very nearly the supreme good, but quality of life matters a lot, too. And freedom matters a lot—prosperity, a decent standard of living, possibilities for self-development."

Derek Bok: president of Harvard University, 1971–1991.

"A decent respect for the right of other people to have ideas."

Kenneth Boulding: author of over 30 books; professor at the University of Colorado.

"[I put] a very high value on veracity—telling the truth."

Muhammad Yunus: managing director of the Grameen Bank, Dhaka, Bangladesh.

"The oneness of human beings is the basic ethical thread that holds us together."

Katharine Whitehorn: senior columnist for the London Sunday newspaper *The Observer.*

"I don't think that people habitually do anything unless they are programmed so that they are appalled with themselves when they don't."

---

and think is the same spirit that exists in me—there's no difference," he said. "So when you look at me, you're looking at yourself—and I'm seeing me in you."

Abstracting from the idea of tolerance the core principle of respect for variety, Kenneth Boulding linked it to the environmentalist's urgency

over the depletion of species. "If the blue whale is endangered, we feel worried about this, because we love the variety of the world," he explained. "In some sense I feel about the Catholic Church the way I feel about the blue whale: I don't think I'll be one, but I would feel diminished if it became extinct."

RESPONSIBILITY

Oxford don A. H. Halsey placed the sense of responsibility high on his list of values because of its impact on our common future. "We are responsible for our grandchildren," he explained, "and we will make [it] easier or more difficult for our grandchildren to be good people by what we do right here and now." This was a point made in a different way by Katharine Whitehorn, who noted that, while as a youth "it's fun to break away," it's very much harder to "grow up and have to put it together again."

For Nien Cheng, the spotlight falls not so much on the actions of the future as on the sense of self-respect in the present. "This is Confucius' teaching," she said. "You must take care of yourself. To rely on others is a great shame."

Responsibility also demands caring for others, Hayslip said. But, under the complex interactions of medicine, insurance, and law that exists in the West, "If you come into my house and see me lying here very sick, you don't dare move me, because you're not a doctor," she pointed out. "So where is your human obligation? Where is your human instinct to try to save me? You don't have it. You lost it, because there are too many rules."

Yet, paradoxically, "responsibility is not often mentioned in discussions of world politics or ethics," said Oscar Arias. "There, the talk is all of rights, demands, and desires." Human rights are "an unquestionable and critical priority for political societies and an indispensable lever for genuine development," he said. "But the important thing is not just

to assert rights, but to ensure that they be protected. Achieving this protection rests wholly on the principle of responsibility."

Chicago attorney Newton Minow agreed. "I believe the basic reason we got off the track was that

---

James K. Baker: former president of U.S. Chamber of Commerce.

"There's only one 'ethics.' . . . Let's not think you've got to adhere to one standard at home and another standard at work."

John W. Gardner: philosopher; founder of Common Cause; author; Stanford University professor.

"[Even the earliest peoples] knew when they were subjugated."

Sergio Muñoz: executive editor, *La Opinion,* the largest Spanish-language daily newspaper in the United States.

"The pursuit of equality is basic."

Jill Ker Conway: Australian author of *The Road from Coorain;* feminist historian and former president of Smith College.

"Greater equality between the sexes."

Federico Mayor: director-general of UNESCO.

"There are a lot of fundamental values that are reflected in the Universal Declaration of Human Rights that nobody opposes."

---

rights became more important than responsibilities, that individuals became more important than community interests. We've gotten to the point where everybody's got a right and nobody's got a responsibility."

At its ultimate, this sense of responsibility extends to the concept of the right use of force. "You shouldn't perpetrate violence," said Derek Bok simply, finding agreement with Jeane Kirkpatrick's insistence that "war is always undesirable" and that "any resort to force should be a very late option, never a first option."

RESPECT FOR LIFE

Growing out of this idea of the responsible use of force, but separate from and extending beyond it, is a value known most widely in the West from the Ten Commandments: Thou shalt not kill. For Shojun Bando, it is an inflexible principle: Even if ordered in wartime to defend his homeland by killing, he said, "I would refuse. I would say, 'I cannot do this.' "

Such an idea, expressed in today's peaceable Japan, may seem almost naive when examined through the lens of such war-riddled areas as the Middle East. Yet, Salim El Hoss took much the same view. "I was a prime minister [of Lebanon] for seven and a half years. I can't imagine myself signing a death penalty for anybody in the world. I think that is completely illegitimate, and I think that is the kind of thing a code of ethics should deal with."

Reuben Snake, noting that the North American Indians have a warlike reputation, said, "Probably the most serious shortcoming of tribal governments is their inability to effectively resolve conflict within the tribe and externally." He described earlier Indian traditions, however, in which great efforts were made by the tribal elders to prevent killing. That's a point with which Tarzie Vittachi—himself from the much-bloodied nation of Sri Lanka—felt perfectly at home. The first element of the Buddhist "daily prayer" under which he was raised, he recalled, is "I shall not kill." It is also central to the Ten Commandments of the Jewish decalogue under which Newton Minow was raised and which he said he still feels form the basis for the world's code of ethics.

Salim El Hoss: former head of state of Lebanon.

"I can't imagine myself signing a death penalty for anybody in the world."

Bernard Przewozny: professor of Christology at the Pontifical Theological Faculty of St. Bonaventure in Rome.

"The earth and its natural goods are the inheritance of all peoples."

Le Ly Hayslip: survivor of Vietnam War; author; founder of the East Meets West Foundation.

"What are we here for? We're here so that we can help each other to grow."

A. H. Halsey: professor of social and administrative studies at Oxford University.

"We will make [it] easier or more difficult for our grandchildren to be good people by what we do right here and now."

Newton Minow: chairman of the Federal Communications Commission; chairman of the board of the Carnegie Corporation.

"We've gotten to the point where everybody's got a right and nobody's got a responsibility."

OTHER SHARED VALUES

There were, of course, other significant values that surfaced in these interviews. Nien Cheng, for instance, pointed to *courage*. "One should basically know what is right and what is wrong," she said, "and, when you know that, be courageous enough to stand for what is right."

Figuring strongly in Shojun Bando's pantheon was *wisdom*, which he defined as "attaining detachment, getting away from being too attached to things."

Whina Cooper put *hospitality* high on her list, recalling that her father said, "If you see any strangers going past, you call them—*Kia Ora*—that means to call them to come here."

Astrid Lindgren put an emphasis on *obedience*—a quality that runs throughout the life of her most famous character, Pippi Longstocking, though usually in reverse.

Kenneth Boulding pointed to *peace*, which he defined simply as "well-managed conflict." Thinking of peace brought Salim El Hoss to the concept of *stability*. "Peace is equivalent to stability," he said, adding that "stability means a long-term perspective of no problems." These and other values, while they don't find broad support, had firm proponents among those we interviewed and deserve serious attention.

Other values mentioned included the burning public concerns for racial harmony, respect for women's place, and the protection of the environment. Many of the interviewees touched on them, and some elevated them to high priority. Speaking of the need for racial harmony, James Joseph put at the top of his list a sense of "respect for the cultures of other communities, respect for the need to begin to integrate into our collective memory appreciation of the contributions and traditions of those who are different." Jill Conway topped her list with a warning about the "increasing exploitation of women" around the world. And of the many human rights identified by Father Bernard Przewozny, the one to which he has dedicated his life is the "right to a healthy environment."

So what good is this code of values? It gives us a foundation for building goals, plans, and tactics, where things really happen and the world really changes. It unifies us, giving us a home territory of consensus and agreement. And it gives us a way—not *the* way, but *a* way—to reply when we're asked, "Whose values will you teach?" Answering this last question, as we tumble into the twenty-first century with the twentieth's sense of ethics, may be one of the most valuable mental activities of our time.

A group of "Latin intellectuals and left-leaning politicians" is determined to put Latin America on a new course to prosperity and equality. "The group's goal of rolling back the Washington Consensus and ushering in a model based on productive investment and a democratized economy sounds like a pipe dream. But time and trouble may be on its side."

A Fourth Way?
The Latin American
Alternative to Neoliberalism

LUCY CONGER

Latin America weathered fairly well the initial financial shock from the Asian turbulence that began last fall, primarily because Brazil spent $8 billion to defend its currency and thereby kept the region's largest economy on course. In subsequent months, Latin America suffered a trade shock as the Asian tsunami lapped at its shores, gouging prices of key Latin commodity exports such as oil and copper and creating stiffer competition for Latin products in markets like the United States.

Hopes that the region could withstand the buffeting from Asia were dashed when Russia devalued the ruble and defaulted on its debt this August. In the last hellish week of that month, Latin American stock markets sank as much as 10 percent on investor concerns about Russia, and some of the region's leading economies suffered attacks on their currencies. Still licking their wounds, the large Latin nations were hammered again on September 3 when Moody's, the international credit-rating agency, downgraded the ratings of Brazilian and Venezuelan debt and placed Mexico and Argentina on a "watch" for a possible debt downgrade.

Financial markets voted no confidence in Latin America despite the sweeping reforms most of the region's countries had implemented in an attempt to meet the demands of international investors. In the past decade, most Latin governments have adopted what is called the "Washington Consensus": reforms backed by the IMF and the United States Treasury Department that include lifting restrictions on trade and foreign investment, privatizing state enterprises, stabilizing local currencies, and clamping down on government spending to achieve balanced budgets.

The reforms have created a dramatic turnaround in Latin American economies, ending the state-dominated populist and protectionist regimes. Yet implementing the policy package that Latins call "neoliberalism" has been costly: millions have lost jobs because of privatization, public services including health care and education have been sharply reduced, and in many countries the number of people living below the poverty line has increased. Benefits have accrued to the reformed countries as trade and foreign investment have increased and sound finances have spurred growth. But, as the August rout proves, Latin America remains subject to recurrent crises.

LUCY CONGER *is a writer based in Mexico City covering Latin American finance and economy. She is a correspondent for* Institutional Investor *magazine and writes for* U.S. News and World Report *and other publications. Some of the material in this article was originally reported for* Institutional Investor *and is included with permission.*

POINTING TO AN ALTERNATIVE

Well before the weakness in Asia drove home the vulnerability of Latin American economies, a group of Latin intellectuals and left-leaning politicians had begun to debate an alternative program that would promise development for their countries. By November 1997, after 18 months of meetings, they had forged a consensus and launched a platform called the "Latin American Alternative" (Alternative Latinoamericana). The group is spearheaded by Jorge Castañeda, a Mexican political scientist (and *Current History* contributing editor), and Roberto Mangabeira Unger, a Brazilian and professor at Harvard Law School. They have been joined in the debate by some two dozen Latin politicians, including two presidential candidates from Brazil and presidential hopefuls from Argentina, Chile, and Mexico, as well as former finance ministers, senators, governors, and mayors from throughout the region.

The alternative model endorsed by this group accepts the market economy, global economic integration, free trade, and privatization of state companies—all central tenets of the Washington Consensus. But the model proposes radical new policy directions to achieve sustained economic growth, link the poor to national and global economies, and encourage greater democratic political participation. "We can reform the market economy to tighten the link between savings and production and make money more complicit in the real economy," says Unger, who complains that the "financial casino" of stock markets and currency trading dissipates savings worldwide, and especially in emerging market countries.

A guiding principle of the alternative model is to combat the social and economic dualism that pervades life in Latin America. The region can claim the most inequitable income distribution in the world and rigid barriers to social mobility. The model would raise taxes to increase government funding for social services and education, which would improve the productive capacity of the workforce. Locally based credit institutions would be promoted to fund the upgrading and expansion of undercapitalized small businesses, which employ the majority of Latin Americans. Incentives for savings would be established to reduce the dependence of the region's emerging markets on volatile foreign capital inflows. Referendums and recall elections would be used to circumvent political impasses that blocked passage of reforms.

This effort to create a program for leftist politicians and generate an alternative to the neoliberal model is ambitious. Winning a hearing for the Latin group's vision and implementing its program will be uphill battles. "The basic objective is to establish in Latin America a movement of ideas, a current of opinion to get at economic orthodoxy and economic populism," says Unger.

Most of the politicians in the group predictably take a more optimistic and pragmatic view, believing they can win office and govern better with some of these ideas. They are also motivated by the need to build center-left political alliances strong enough to defeat the center-right elected regimes that predominate and then enact an alternative economic program. "The center-left is in a boom period" in Latin America, says Senator Carlos Ominami of Chile, a former economy minister. Others in the group advocate the alternative model with all of its ideas, including some that may seem unrealistic. "If you ask me do we have to put forward maximum utopias, I say yes," says Graciela Fernández Meijide, a former human rights activist and now the likely presidential candidate for Argentina's center-left alliance. "You have to propose a lot to get what you get."

The group's goal of rolling back the Washington Consensus and ushering in a model based on productive investment and a democratized economy sounds like a pipe dream. But time and trouble may be on its side. "The present world financial crisis has strengthened the need for such a debate and ultimately strengthened the readiness to hear this message," argues Unger. Certainly, the Asian crisis puts the IMF's credibility to the test and may overturn the conventional wisdom favoring unrestricted movements of capital. For market watchers willing to open their minds to other doubts, here are the ideas that these Latin Americans propose.

BUILDING THE MODEL

Supporters of the Latin American Alternative aim to correct the errors of both neoliberalism and populism. Neoliberalism has failed in Latin America, they argue, because it has not achieved sustained economic growth and it condemns large parts of the population to social and economic misery. The social programs of neoliberalism are inadequately funded and cannot reduce inequities because they are combined with orthodox economic structures that reinforce the highly unequal distribution of income that typifies Latin economies. Populism, meanwhile, is "merely distributive" and has failed to spawn deep reforms of the productive structure, says Unger.

"Alternative Latinoamericana" promises a democratized market economy that would bridge the gap between technologically advanced industries and undercapitalized, inefficient small and microbusinesses; it also promises a strong federal government with increased revenues that would support social and educational services to narrow the chasm separating the rich from the poor (who make up 40 percent of the population in many Latin countries).

A basic underpinning of the model is an increase in taxes and tax collection so that state revenues top 30 percent of gross domestic product. "In no country in the world has it been possible to generate solid social equilibrium with [government] spending levels below 30 percent of GDP," according to Alternative Latinoamericana. This poses an enormous challenge in Latin America, where tax collection averages about 12 percent of GDP and tax evasion is a national pastime. The increase in revenues would come from raising taxes on consumption, known as a value-added tax. At the outset, an increase in income taxes is not foreseen. The tax hike to all consumers, rich and poor alike, would be compensated for by social spending that would redistribute income and opportunities. In addition, the proceeds from the privatization of state companies would be used to pay off domestic public debt and reduce domestic

> *The group argues that speculative short-term capital flows threaten the sovereignty of states.*

interest rates to levels competitive with those in the industrialized nations.

To combat social inequities, state spending would guarantee equal access to quality education for all citizens and would provide meals and medical care to all children. Workers' salaries would be increased so that they made up a greater percentage of national income.

The model would attempt to reduce the predominance of what Unger dubs the "financial casino." The group proposes to adopt controls on short-term capital flows by imposing taxes or requiring reserve deposits. The controls would help stimulate domestic savings and create incentives to channel investment to productive uses. "Financial logic tends to impose itself over productive logic," the group's proposal notes. The group argues that speculative short-term capital flows threaten the sovereignty of states because international financial markets pressure governments to lift regulations and throw open their borders to stateless private capital. They have gained some powerful allies on their point recently. In late September, IMF officials indicated that the fund may encourage the use of controls on short-term volatile capital flows.

Alternativa Latinoamericana also proposes that savings be increased to exceed 30 percent of the national economy; this would be accomplished principally by creating private pension funds. To encourage the use of these savings for productive purposes, special investment funds would be set up, and incentives would be created for investing in undercapitalized small and medium-sized firms. The investment funds are meant to offer an alternative to conventional stock market and banking investments that fuel the financial sector but fail to create employment or goods and services for unskilled and poor workers. A key would be to make financial services, especially credit, available to all citizens. The traditional financial system should expand its coverage through the formation of credit unions, savings and loans, microcredit lending groups, and other locally based finance agencies scattered throughout the countryside.

The model must attempt to overcome the separation between the productive niches Unger calls the "vanguard" and the "rear guard." The vanguard includes innovative, technologically sophisticated, internationally competitive industries; in most emerging markets they capture a huge share of profits but represent a small slice of employment and the production of goods and services consumed by the poor domestically. The rear guard includes the legions of unproductive, undercapitalized small and medium-sized firms and cottage industries that work with obsolete technology and are not linked to the global economy. In Latin America, most employment is generated by firms in the rear guard, and typically the jobs lack social benefits for the workers.

Bridging the gulf between the vanguard and the rear guard would require a new type of linkage between government and private industry to allow flexible and decentralized coordination with small and medium-scale firms at a local level. The alternative model proposes to group small firms together in networks to gain access to investment funds, public and private bank credits, and assistance programs. These relationships would create channels to transmit vanguard practices, especially permanent innovation, reduction of the layers of hierarchy among personnel, and the mixing of cooperation and competition, to the rear guard.

The model would make big business play by the rules of market competition instead of reaping benefits from government support and protection. Policy reform to level the playing field in Latin market economies would include reorienting government support programs toward small and medium-sized companies, advancing stiff antimonopoly laws, ensuring protection for minority shareholders, and eliminating nonvoting shares in companies. The principle of "free trade without dogma" would include adopting selective temporary tariffs to encourage long-term, high-risk investment and reduce the favoritism often shown to big business.

The left also argues that political institutions must be modified so that frequent change is easier. The model proposes giving presidents and congresses the power to call a new election for both executive and legislative branches when reform is blocked. Presidents would be granted "fast-track" procedures to speed decisions on strategic issues.

DEMOCRACY: A KEY INGREDIENT

Deepening democracy in Latin America is a pillar of the model to bridge the region's social and economic divide. Honest elections and constant civic mobilization are but the first steps to this goal. Unger takes a dim view of recent constitutional changes in several Latin countries that allow for the reelection of the president. The reforms have given a second term to Carlos Menem in Argentina and Alberto Fujimori in Peru and returned Brazil's Fernando Henrique Cardoso to power in elections in October. "The development of the reelection system threatens to return Latin America to the era of civilian caudillos," or strongmen, says Unger.

Additional proposals aim to reduce the influence of money in politics through public financing of campaigns, disclosure of private contributions, and the expansion of free access to television for political parties and social movements. To hold governments accountable for their acts, instruments must be created that allow citizens and legislators to call bureaucrats to task. These instruments would include popularly initiated recall votes, referendums, congressional oversight of government agencies, independent accounting offices to combat corruption, and citizen selection and supervision of public works projects.

Democratization of information is also required in the vision of a strengthened society and a transparent government. Practical means must be found to inform constituents of their rights as citizens, as men and women, and as members of ethnic groups, and to encourage them to defend their rights. Private monopolies that control the policy and content of mass media, especially television, must be broken up by limiting the concentration of concessions or frequencies. Television cries out most urgently for this reform because across Latin America it is the leading source of news for most people. In Brazil, for example, 80 percent of adults never read newspapers. The power of Latin media magnates and the ongoing wave of privatizations of media-related industries such as telecommunications companies combine to create strong allegiances between the information industry and government, says Unger.

PUTTING THE PLAN TO THE POLITICAL TEST

While some elements of this model may seem far-fetched, more than a few are gaining currency among economists and government and development officials. "What seemed fringe ideas two to three years ago are becoming more mainstream," Castañeda observes. In particular, creating controls to regulate flows of short-term capital seems like an idea whose time has come. To reduce the volatility that afflicts emerging markets, controls on short-term capital have been endorsed since the Asian crisis by prominent figures including billionaire hedge fund investor George Soros, World Bank chief economist Joseph Stiglitz, and Goldman Sachs managing director E. Gerald Corrigan. Stiglitz condemns free movement of capital, citing economic research that shows there is no relationship between unrestricted capital flows and economic growth.

Long a taboo in Latin America, tax reform designed to increase government revenues by raising taxes and broadening the tax base is being put before legislatures across the region. Latin governments, the World Bank, and regional development banks such as the Inter-American Development Bank are now taking a closer look at poverty. There is a growing consensus that attacking poverty requires broad social programs beyond the transfer payments and slim subsidies widespread today. Finally, Castañeda points out, the dangers of maintaining an overvalued currency and monetary instability are widely accepted in financial circles.

PROMISING RESULTS

The politicians in the group have led innovative programs with successful results that show how the model could work. In Brazil, Workers' Party leader Tarso Genro is a case in point. While serving as mayor of the southern city of Porto Alegre, he established a partnership between the municipal government and the private sector to finance a fund to make small loans to small-scale businesses. He created participatory budgeting

by dividing the city into 16 districts, each with an elected council that set priorities on public works projects such as schools, community health clinics, and roads. Citizen groups managed the budget and supervised the construction of projects in their neighborhoods. The result: money was spent carefully and about one-third more projects than usual were completed. Genro also raised municipal revenues by 25 percent by taxing undeveloped urban land being held for speculation and placing a levy on urban services. At the end of his four-year term in 1997, he boasted a 75 percent approval rating.

Vicente Fox, the governor of Guanajuato state in central Mexico and presidential hopeful from the conservative National Action Party, is promoting microlending. He used $5 million from state funds and raised an equal amount from the private sector to create the initial capital for the nonprofit Banco Santa Fé de Guanajuato. Modeled after the Grameen Bank of Bangladesh, the bank grants microcredits of as little as $100 to tiny enterprises such as pig-raising in a backyard stable and sidewalk food-stands. The bank has made many loans to working women who often are the mainstay of the family, since Guanajuato sends many migrant workers to the United States.

Also in Mexico, a recent referendum on national economic issues has strengthened the opposition mandate to hold the government accountable for federal spending. Opposition politicians have seized on a government bank bailout scheme—which would have cost taxpayers $65 billion in public debt—to mobilize citizen demands for greater control over the budget. Andrés Manuel López Obrador, president of the left-wing Democratic Revolution Party (PRD), led the referendum, which drew more than 3 million votes nationwide on August 31. The PRD referendum marked the first time since the economic reforms began that the citizenry has been consulted on economic policy. More than 95 percent of those voting opposed the government's proposal to assume bad bank loans as public debt.

The referendum provided overwhelming support for PRD proposals to audit large corporate loans, which make up about half the bad debt; provide aid to small debtors; and restrict foreign investment in banks. Although government and banking officials discredited the referendum, saying it was skewed to favor PRD positions, it nevertheless strengthened the opposition mandate to demand that banks shoulder more of the burden of the bailout.

The mechanisms for combating neoliberalism and the possibilities of forming center-left alliances will vary with each country. But there is agreement that the Alternativa group provides a prized function as a forum for exchanging ideas and practical experiences to improve Latin American societies. "It can contribute to the formation of a bloc that is political, democratic, anti-neoliberal, and is occupying spaces in Latin America," Brazil's Genro said in a recent interview. This group is preparing to influence regional issues, in particular to set an agenda for labor and social issues in the negotiations of the Free Trade Area of the Americas, the hemisphere-wide free trade area that is to be set up in the next seven years. The debate over center-left alliances has been maturing with the group's deliberations. "Our countries require great transformations [that] cannot be made without wide citizen backing and that require alliances, and that requires pluralism," said Gabriel Gaspar, a research fellow at Flacso, a research institution in Santiago, Chile.

It was not possible to build such an alliance for the October 4 presidential race in Brazil, the first of a wave of elections in Latin America between now and mid-2000. "That was not due to the impotence of the group, it was due to objective conditions of the Brazilian political process," says Genro. Brazil's Workers' Party backed its two-time presidential candidate, Luis Inácio "Lula" da Silva, because the traditional left within his party resisted an alliance with centrist Ciro Gomes and hoped to win congressional seats on Lula's coattails.

In other countries, however, the chances for center-left alliances are strong and the coalitions might defeat neoliberal regimes in coming elections. In El Salvador, the guerrilla force turned political party, the Farabundo Martí National Liberation Front, is seen as the front-runner in the March 1999 presidential race it will run in an alliance with a range of civic organizations. In Argentina, the Alianza, a political grouping made up of the Frepaso and Unión Cívica Radical parties, is a strong contender in the 1999 presidential race. In Chile, the ruling center-left coalition is expected to keep the presidency in December 1999 elections with front-runner candidate Ricardo Lagos, a moderate socialist, backed by the Christian Democrats. The Mexican election in July 2000 is too far off to call, but the Alternative's meetings have provided a setting for dialogue between the two most likely opposition candidates, Mexico City mayor Cuauhtémoc Cárdenas and Vicente Fox.

The model has yet to be adopted by Latin America's conventional leftist parties. However, it is gaining ground as left-wing and center politicians search for a program to offer constituents in the postcommunist era. For some leftist parties in Latin America, the model fuels splits that were already brewing by providing ideas for those who have accepted the inevitability of globalization. The aim of Alternativa Latinoamericana is to stimulate a process of gradual economic, political, and societal change to combat a destiny that the continent does not deserve.

By Robert W. Fisher

The Future of Energy

Changing our fuel sources requires changing our values, but it's happened before and may already be happening again.

Since the first Earth Day in 1970, we have made important moves to clean up energy production and use: Drilling for oil and gas and mining coal are now done less harmfully, power plants burn coal more cleanly, and vehicles get better gas mileage and emit far fewer pollutants. But these changes do not get at the root of the problem—our use of "dirty" fossil fuels.

The numbers tell the story: In 1971, the world consumed 4,722 million tons of oil equivalent (MTOE). Twenty years later, consumption was up to 7,074 MTOE, and it still was almost all fossil fuels—97% in 1971 and 90% in 1991. The 7% drop was captured by nuclear power. By 2010, consumption is projected to rise to 11,500 MTOE, with fossil fuels still accounting for 90% of that demand. Our energy choices simply do not reflect our concerns about the environment and sustainability of our supply.

Concerns about Fossil Fuel Supply

Many people are worried that we are going to run out of fossil fuels, especially oil and natural gas. Running out of oil has been a worry ever since people first began to use it in large quantities. In 1908, the U.S. Geological Survey (USGS) predicted that total future supply of U.S. oil would not exceed 23 billion barrels. In 1914, the U.S. Bureau of Mines was even more pessimistic, putting the limit at 5.7 billion barrels. In 1920, the USGS proclaimed the peak in U.S. oil production was almost reached. In 1939, the Department of Interior declared that there was only 13 years of production remaining. In 1977, President Jimmy Carter said,

"We are now running out of oil." Despite these gloomy projections, the United States has produced over 200 billion barrels of oil since the early 1900s.

Belying the forecasts, the oil industry keeps on finding new producing regions, developing more effective methods of finding oil fields, reducing costs, and coming up with innovative technology that lets them produce oil in places they could not even look before, such as very deep water.

The future for oil supplies looks promising as well. [Editor's note: For another viewpoint, see "Get Ready for Another Oil Shock!" by L. F. Ivanhoe in the January-February 1997 issue of THE FUTURIST.] Saudi Arabia has just begun to explore in older, deeper rocks that produce oil in surrounding countries. Iraq has the potential to surpass Saudi Arabia in oil reserves once exploration and development work is restarted there. Khazakstan and Eastern Siberia are relatively unexplored potential oil-producing giants. Deep water technology is opening up large areas of the Gulf of Mexico for exploration

From *The Futurist,* September/October 1997, pp. 43–46. © 1997 by The World Future Society, Bethesda, MD. http://www.wfs.org/wfs. Reprinted by permission.

and production. And some recent testing suggests there are oil deposits in the abyssal depths of the Atlantic Ocean. Then we have immense tar sand deposits in Canada and very heavy oil in the Orinoco Belt of Venezuela, both of which contain hundreds of billions of barrels of oil.

The industry is also improving the recovery rates from established fields. On average, producers get only 35% of the oil out of a reservoir before they abandon it. The remaining oil is either too difficult or too expensive to recover. But one producer in the North Sea now claims to be able to recover 40% and expects to recover up to 60% in a few years.

Natural gas resources have also been subjected to pessimistic forecasts, partly because, in the United States, government-controlled prices were so low that few companies were willing to explore for gas fields. Today, the conservative estimate is that there is at least a 100-year supply of standard gas resources in North America. In addition, there are large deposits of gas hydrates that the industry doesn't yet know how to use economically.

Internationally, the natural gas supply is even larger. Europe hasn't used much natural gas because it had an infrastructure in place to mine, transport, and burn coal and did not see any advantage to going to the expense of building a gas pipeline system. Southeast Asia has only recently begun to tap and use its gas resources.

Coal will last much longer than either oil or natural gas. Known deposits of coal are huge, and there is a massive infrastructure in place to mine, deliver, and burn it. And it is the cheapest of fossil fuels.

So sustainability of supply is not an issue today. Does that mean we will continue to rely on fossil fuels

for the next 30 years or longer? Unless we change our values, the answer is yes.

Changing Values and Changing Energy Sources

Before discussing that needed change in values, I want to make a historic connection between changes in value systems and shifts in energy use. The underlying motivation for technological development has primarily been to gain wealth and power—that is not to disparage the thrill of discovery or of innovation for its own sake, but to acknowledge its secondary importance.

Wood was the primary source of energy for humans up to 1880, when coal gained first place. Wind, water, and solar power were also used. What happened to trigger the switch from wood to coal to oil as our main source of energy? And why did wind and water power, which for centuries had ranked right behind wood as major sources of energy, fall so far behind?

> "The prime motivation behind energy choice has been to increase wealth and power."

The transition from wood to coal to oil began because of shifts in the economy and two shifts in thinking that occurred in late Medieval Europe: First, people who were engaged in manufacturing, trade, and creating innovative technology were

given a higher human value than those who could fight. Second, it became acceptable for the elite to become involved in devising practical applications from scientific knowledge.

The elite of the age were heavily focused on wealth and power. But people at all levels began to look with less favor on fighting, raiding, and plundering as the primary means of acquiring and enhancing wealth and power. Grain-grinding water mills became important profit centers as innovations enabled them to saw logs, make paper and gunpowder, full woolens, and perform other manufacturing tasks. People who could make machines, run mills, and engage in expanded trading were bringing in more profits than the lords could gain from maintaining a retinue of knights. The other values change that occurred about the same time was that highly educated philosophers and scientists began to get involved in developing practical mechanical devices. Up to that time, such activity was considered beneath their dignity.

Change began in earnest following these economic and value shifts. Better manufacturing processes required better machines, which needed more efficient fuels. Coke made from coal was a more efficient fuel for smelting iron than was charcoal made from wood, but the surface outcrops of coal soon became exhausted. Mines had to go deeper, and that made flooding a problem. Steam engines, which also burned coal, were developed to pump water out of mines.

The improved steam engines suggested steam-powered locomotives on iron rails as a solution to roads that were being constantly torn up from transporting coal. Railroading was born, pushing coal demand higher still, and by 1880, coal became the most used energy source. Water power and wind power for mills gave way to coal-fired steam engines that were more efficient, provided for greater flexibility of use, and produced greater profits.

B.J. NIXON/DEEPSEA VENTURES, INC.

FRENCH TECHNOLOGY PRESS OFFICE/COURTESY OF VERGNET

NATIONAL COAL ASSOCIATION

MODULAR SOLAR ELECTRIC POWER GENERATOR

From petroleum to wind, from coal to solar. Whether or not there is enough fossil fuel to keep us going, we should switch to renewables for the sake of the environment, says author Fish er.

Sailing ships yielded to coal-fired steam ships for the same reasons.

Steam-powered road carriages using external combustion engines were in use even before railroading began, but they required a separate furnace and boiler, making them too heavy and bulky for practical road use. Internal combustion was seen as the solution. Gunpowder, hydrogen explosions, and benzene made from coal tar were tried without much success, but gasoline distilled from oil made internal combustion a commercial success. This stimulated the development of the automobile industry, a major consumer of oil.

Better cars required better engines, which needed higher performance fuels. The performance

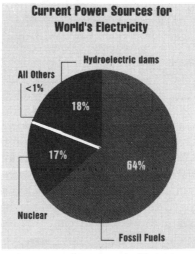

Current Power Sources for World's Electricity

All Others <1%

Hydroelectric dams

18%

17%

64%

Nuclear

Fossil Fuels

Source: International Energy Agency

spiral went up until it was possible to build a gasoline engine powerful enough but still light and small

enough to power an airplane. Air travel was born, and by 1950 oil passed coal as the most used energy source in the world.

Energy Choices Reflect Our Values

The prime motivation behind energy choice has been to increase wealth and power. We continue to rely on fossil fuels today because they are cheap, efficient, and bring the most profit to their developers. Today, 64% of the world's electricity is generated by burning fossil fuels, mostly coal; 18% comes from hydroelectric dams, 17% from nuclear power plants, and less than 1% from all other sources, including geothermal, biomass, wind, and solar. For the next couple of decades, the outlook of the International Energy Agency is for most expansion of electrical generating capacity to be met by fossil fuels. Nuclear power use is projected to decline and to be replaced by fossil fuel plants. Hydropower and the other renewable sources are projected to increase only slightly.

Wind turbines, photovoltaic arrays on Earth and in space, solar thermal plants, ocean thermal generators, biomass, and tidal power are renewable sources of energy that we know will work. But we use these renewable sources only in special situations, because fossil fuels are cheaper when environmental and health costs are ignored.

It will take a major shift in thinking today to move us away from fossil fuels and into renewable resources. It will be a shift away from placing our highest human value on becoming rich and powerful to giving our highest esteem to those who improve how we relate to each other. That shift has begun and needs nurturing.

Signs of Change

The numerous human rights movements indicate that we are beginning to value people more highly than we have in the past. As these movements gain momentum, people as people will move higher on the priority list, while the personal accumulation of wealth and power will decline.

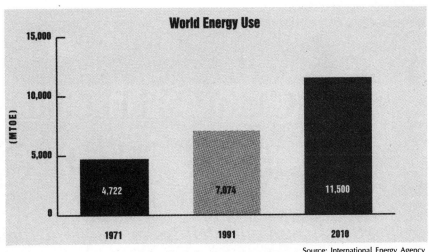

Source: International Energy Agency

Another promising development is the rise of ISO 14000, a set of internationally accepted standards for environmental management systems being promoted by the International Organization for Standardization in Geneva. The drive to adopt ISO 14000 standards comes from consumers, not from government command-and-control regulations. Retailers are beginning to tell their suppliers, who are in turn telling their suppliers, that they will buy only from those who manufacture or produce in an environmentally sound manner. ISO 14000 certification assures all customers that the company not only is operating cleanly, but is committed to continual improvement of its environmental performance. The shift in thinking here is that we are beginning to accept responsibility for our part in the environmental impact of a product through its entire life cycle.

With these changes in our value system, our choices of energy sources will no longer be based solely on their ability to produce immediate profits for someone, but rather on how well they fit into the overall quality of life for everyone—employees, customers, and neighbors. But until we make such changes, the world will continue to rely most heavily on fossil fuels for its future energy needs.

About the Author

Robert W. Fisher, an energy analyst, is president of The Consortium International, Apartado Postal #1, Marfil, Guanajuato C.P. 36251, Mexico. E-mail consintl@redes.int.com.mx.

The International Energy Agency is located at 9, rue de la Federation, 75739 Paris Cedex 15, France. Telephone 33-1 4057 6554; fax 33-1 4057 6559; e-mail info@iea.org.

Telecommunications for the 21st Century

Systems based on satellites and high-altitude platforms will merge with optical-fiber and terrestrial wireless networks to provide global, high data-rate, mobile communications

by Joseph N. Pelton

Space-based telecommunications systems will change our lives over the next two decades, providing rapid access to information of all types, from handheld or briefcase-size terminals anywhere on the planet. Mass virtual-reality entertainment, videos on demand and expanded tele-health and tele-education services are just some of the developments we can expect to arrive with this torrent of data—along with mounting information overload and the 168-hour workweek.

In five years' time there will very likely be 1,000 commercial communications satellites in service, up from about 220 today. Many of these switching stations in the sky will zoom in low earth orbit (LEO) only a few hundred kilometers overhead. But satellites in the more traditional geosynchronous earth orbit (GEO), which turn with the earth 36,000 kilometers (22,300 miles) up, will remain very much in the picture.

The proximity of LEO satellites offers some important advantages over today's orbiters. Signals will zip back and forth to low orbits in hundredths of a second, a decisive advantage over the quarter of a second that data take to travel to and from GEO. On the pro side of the ledger, this faster performance will make interactive global access to networks and video teleconferencing practical and appealing. On the con side, LEO systems require 20 times more satellites than a GEO system to cover the globe and five times more than a medium-earth-orbit (MEO) network.

Satellites will soon not be the only type of space-based telecommunications system. By the year 2000 we could see High Altitude Long Endurance (HALE) platforms hovering over cities and beaming down thousands of data-rich signals. These innovative pilotless, electronically powered craft will fly or float for days at a time in "proto-space" at an altitude of more than 20,000 meters, safely above commercial air traffic.

By far the most significant change in coming decades is that space-based systems will increasingly deliver information directly to the consumer, rather than to a commercial data hub. This shift means that aerospace corporations will, early in the next century, find themselves competing directly with AT&T, MCI, British Telecom (BT) and other carriers.

Only a few years ago cumbersome dish antennas were needed to obtain a satellite connection faster than simple telephone service. Moreover, such links were in short supply, and service at sea cost as much as $10 per minute. Those limitations are disappearing. The coming torrent of high-speed data from space should be a colossal boon for individuals and corporations around the world. It will be especially important in developing countries such as Brazil, India and China, which do not have extensive fiber-optic networks.

The key innovation for handling the burgeoning demand is the phased-array antenna. This sophisticated electronic device, used until now mainly for military communications, consists of multiple transmitting elements arranged in a fixed geometric array. Arrays can be programmed to send a grid of electronically formed radio beams to track moving targets or, alternatively, to receive signals from only certain directions.

In concept, these antennas are something like miniature versions of the Very Large Array, the cluster of radio telescopes in Socorro, N.M., used for studying astrophysical phenomena. Phased arrays achieve directional selectivity by electronically imposing minute delays on the signals moving from (or to) different parts of the array. Beams focused in this way reduce interference, an important advantage in view of the growing demand for radio spectrum. The pressure on spectrum will intensify, because high data-rate signals need much more bandwidth—a far bigger slice of spectrum—than do low data rates.

Mounted on satellites, phased arrays can steer beams as little as half a degree across toward their intended recipients. Moreover, they are fully "adaptive": under the control of onboard supercomputers the size of a shoebox that are now being built (a spin-off from "Star Wars" research), they will be continually reprogrammed. This flexibility began a decade ago with modified parabolic antennas, and the trend will continue. Satellites of the 21st century will thus be able to "reuse" the same slice of spectrum many times over. Reuse will soon reach 100-fold on some satellites and should in time reach 1,000-fold.

We can expect phased arrays to become familiar on terra firma as well, because they can direct beams to satellites moving in known orbits overhead. In addition, these arrays can be constructed to conform to almost any desired shape, which makes them particularly attractive for aircraft and cars. Within the next five years we should even see miniature versions in handheld transceivers.

Competition from the Ground

The biggest economic hurdle for satellites in industrial countries will be competing with optical-fiber systems to provide high data-rate, or broadband, services directly to the home or office. A satellite system cannot match the transmission speed of a simple span of fiber-optic cable. In reality, however, most consumers rely on a mile or so of much slower paired copper telephone wires or coaxial cable to bring voice and data from a local distribution center.

This "last-mile problem," as it is known, is a major bottleneck for wired networks. Telephone companies have developed a way to increase data rates carried by cable and wires from tens of thousands of bits per second to a few million. Yet despite improvements in the price and performance of this technology, known as xDSL, it is still expensive and is unlikely to meet demand for broadband data.

Many home users of the World Wide Web, for example, are frustrated by delays fetching graphics. A broadband Internet connection transports data 50 times faster than a typical 28.8-kilobit-per-second dial-up telephone connection; high-definition television swallows bits at rates 20 to 30 times faster still. Many users will want multimegabits of data per second by halfway through the next decade. Consequently, satellites have perhaps a 10-year window of opportunity in the multimedia marketplace.

The coming renaissance of satellite systems was not always obvious. In 1993 Nicholas Negroponte of the Massachusetts Institute of Technology suggested that the future of telecommunications would be a huge flip-flop. Narrowband services, telephone and paging services that are now often carried long-distance by glass fiber would migrate to wireless transmission. At the same time, cost and the limited amount of available radio spectrum would force broadband services to migrate in the opposite direction, from radio waves and satellites to fiber optic and coaxial cable. This became known as the Negroponte Flip.

In a dissenting article in *Telecommunications* magazine, I argued that Negroponte was wrong. The future would feature a "rich but confused" digital mixture of fiber, coaxial cable, terrestrial wireless and satellite services carrying everything from voice to broadband multimedia and video services. In this scenario, users would demand access from mobile terminals to broadband services as well as to less demanding narrowband ones. Glass fiber, satellites and terrestrial wireless networks would, I suggested, each be important in the mix, and protocols for seamless interconnection between these would become the technical crunch point.

Telecommunications dubbed this view the Pelton Merge. If correct, it meant that engineers would face the challenge of developing broadband satellite-based services that could be interconnected with glass fiber and coaxial cable-based systems. It followed that the next generation of communications satellites would have to be 1,000 times faster than even those of the early 1990s. And there would be an urgent need for new data-conversion protocols and "open systems" standards, specifications that manufacturers could use to build compatible new devices.

Breakthroughs in satellite technology are making the merge model increasingly credible. During the past five years, wireless services and satellites have been experiencing record growth. Today they can provide a telephone-line transmission at a cost below 0.1 cent a minute. Moreover, the most rapidly growing type of telecommunications service is direct broadcast satellite (DBS) television, which uses geosynchronous orbiters to beam signals to more than 20 million subscribers worldwide. Market studies have projected the total could triple by 2005. Yet according to the Negroponte Flip, television should be carried by cable.

Exploiting a Finite Resource

Satellites still face significant technical obstacles. A crucial one is the extremely high cost of launching a payload and insuring it. There is an urgent need for innovative ways to put equipment into orbit reliably and at much lower expense. New launch concepts are being investigated, including reusable rockets and jets. So far, though, none has proved itself.

Other challenges stem from the need to make the most efficient use of the finite radio spectrum. All modern systems transmit information in digital form. One important approach is to compress data digitally. DBS, for example, benefits from a new Motion Picture Experts Group standard, MPEG2, which allows transmission of high-quality video images to home TV screens using only six megabits per second. This now enables a one-gigabit-per-second DBS satellite such as DirecTV to transmit over 150 television channels plus many CD-quality audio channels. Some mobile systems compress voice data for the same reason.

Because high frequencies can carry more data than low ones, the bands used for wireless have steadily increased in frequency from tens of megahertz midcentury to almost 100 gigahertz in today's most ambitious schemes. But transmitting and processing thousands of signals takes considerable power—a scarce resource on satellites. It is a particular challenge for GEO satellites, which must cope with very large numbers of beams and transmit them 40,000 kilometers.

Power is also a challenge for satellites offering mobile services, because the small antennas now used in portable transceivers intercept only a tiny fraction of a satellite's signal. That increases the power and sensitivity required of the satellite. As a result, the typical solar array on a geosynchronous satellite has increased in power from around two kilowatts to more than 10 kilowatts over the past five years. This trend has been achieved partly through the use of larger solar arrays and partly by higher efficiency. Solar cells made of new materials, such as the combination of gallium arsenide and germanium, have reached efficiencies of about 23 percent, twice the figure for amorphous silicon.

Solar concentrators that reflect light so as to expose cells to more radiation, together with multijunction devices that capture infrared and ultraviolet as well as visible light, could push efficiencies above 30 percent in the next five years. Flexible solar arrays capable of generating 60 kilowatts or more are a distinct possibility for the future, and improved fuel cells and high-performance batteries will also help.

High data rates necessitate large antennas, especially for GEO systems. Parabolic satellite antennas 10 meters in diameter can now be built, and it should be possible to extend that to 20 or 30 meters. So far the most ambitious phased-array satellite antenna is on the Japanese Gigabit Satellite. The antenna this satellite will use to receive signals is some three meters in diameter and will be made up of 2,700 cells or individual antenna elements. Larger antennas with tens of thousands of cells may become feasible as designers gain experience and manufacturers learn how to mass-produce the devices at low cost.

To win mass-market acceptance, however, service providers will need to bring the cost of ground terminals to the lowest possible levels. Better designs and the adoption of large-scale manufacturing techniques should help achieve this end. Some DBS terminals are now only 30 centimeters in diameter, and their price is falling to below $200. In the future, gallium arsenide–based

phased arrays are likely to help reduce antenna costs in space and on the ground.

Location, Location—GEO versus LEO

Most communications satellites today are in GEO. Starting with the International Telecommunications Satellite Organization (Intelsat) in 1965, most of them have communicated with fixed ground stations. Over a decade ago, the International Maritime Satellite Organization (Inmarsat) pioneered mobile telephony and data links for ships, and within the last year, American Mobile Satellite Corporation and Telesat Mobile in Canada have introduced similar services in North America for land-based mobile users. By building satellites with bigger antennas, these companies have reduced costs, but their services have suffered because of transmission difficulties (and poor marketing).

The engineering challenges of geosynchronous satellites account for the surge of interest in recent years in systems using satellites in LEO, or at an altitude of less than 1,600 kilometers, or MEO, at 10,000 to 16,000 kilometers. (The intervening zone is avoided because the Van Allen radiation belts threaten the operation of satellites there.)

LEO systems, beside being faster than GEO systems, can be used with smaller terminals, because the satellite is typically 40 times nearer the earth. Three new LEO and MEO global land-mobile systems—Iridium, ICO (ICO Global Communications) and Globalstar—are scheduled to start offering telephony and global paging within a year or two, with Iridium first off the blocks.

The disadvantage of LEO and MEO systems is that satellites close to the earth move across the sky in an hour or two, rather than seeming to remain at a fixed point. For good reception, users must always be able to see at least one satellite that is well clear of the horizon, because a steep "look angle" minimizes losses caused by buildings and trees. This requirement explains why MEO and LEO systems have to employ so many satellites in order to provide continuous global coverage—around 60 for LEO networks. Launching and building the multiple satellites costs billions of dollars, and stringent precautions will be needed to ensure that abandoned satellites and orbiting launch debris do not become a danger.

To offer affordable broadband services—such as interactive multimedia applications—via desktop antennas, satellite systems will have to employ the very highest frequencies, over 20 gigahertz. Even with the extensive reuse of frequencies made possible by phased-array antennas, these systems will need large slices of spectrum. Several broadband LEO and MEO systems are now in development, notably Bill Gates and Craig McCaw's Teledesic, Alcatel's Skybridge and Motorola's Celestri (LEO-GEO hybrid). Various consortia have proposed at least a dozen other broadband multimedia networks, most of them GEO systems. These networks would employ massive power systems to blast their signals down to microterminals, although not all of them will be built.

Tomorrow's Technologies

The high cost of broadband multisatellite systems accounts for the growing enthusiasm for HALE platforms. These craft can be launched at moderate cost, and they can be called back for servicing. Studies indicate that such platforms could support phased-array antennas with some 3,500 beams, making feasible not only mobile two-way communications but also video distribution in an area 500 kilometers across. These systems will have to reuse frequencies 100-fold, and they will talk to satellites to make global connections.

Four basic types of HALE platforms are being discussed: helium-filled, robotically piloted dirigibles stabilized by ion engines; units powered by solar or fuel cells; piston-driven platforms; and jet engine–driven platforms. These approaches face contrasting limitations: fuel- and solar-cell-powered platforms will be hard-pressed to muster enough power, but piston- and jet-powered types will stay aloft only a few days.

Another way to provide broadband services is to move to frequencies so high that less reuse is needed. Unfortunately, there is an obstacle: rainy weather. The highest-frequency satellite systems now contemplated utilize wavelengths comparable to the size of raindrops. The droplets consequently act as lenses, bending the waves and distorting the signals. This effect can be miti-gated by error-correction techniques, by using more power when necessary and by employing more ground terminals (so data can follow diverse paths). These measures, however, come at a price.

Moving to wavelengths below a millimeter presents even more obstacles. Infrared and optical beams—the logical next step—are easily absorbed in the atmosphere, so in the near future they will probably be restricted to use within buildings. But experiments carried out with the Japanese Engineering Test Satellite VI in the mid-1990s have revived hopes that communicating with satellites via laser beams might one day be feasible. A laser-based network would most likely carry only very heavy streams of traffic and would rely on multiple ground stations to minimize losses incurred by bad weather.

What is clear is that wireless systems will become more dominant over the next 20 years and that they will be based on a mixture of technologies. Universities, government and industry all have roles bringing these schemes to fruition. Unfortunately, there are very few courses of study in the U.S. or in other industrial countries to train students to tackle the emerging issues.

One possibility that deserves serious consideration is to establish a global institute that would foster the requisite expertise. I and several others are now investigating the feasibility of such a plan. But even if such an institute is established, a shortage of suitable scientific and engineering skills may still be an important barrier to progress. More solutions are needed, because the benefits of better communication and education are immense for all nations.

The Author

JOSEPH N. PELTON is professor of telecommunications at the University of Colorado at Boulder and has an appointment at the International Space University in Strasbourg, France. He is currently chair of a panel undertaking a review of satellite systems for the National Science Foundation and the National Aeronautics and Space Administration. Pelton is the author of 16 books on wireless and satellite communications, including the recent *Cyberspace Chronicles*. He will shortly move to Washington, D.C., to the Institute for Applied Space Research at George Washington University.

Further Reading

PRINCIPLES OF COMMUNICATIONS SATELLITES. G. D. Gordon and W. L. Morgan. Wiley-Interscience, 1993.

A EUROPEAN STRATEGY FOR FUTURE SATELLITE COMMUNICATIONS SYSTEMS. E. W. Ashford in *Space Communications*, Vol. 14, No.3, pages 151–154; 1996.

OVERVIEW OF SATELLITE COMMUNICATIONS. J. N. Pelton in *Encyclopedia of Telecommunications*, Vol. 14., Marcel Dekker, 1997.

GLOBAL SATELLITE COMMUNICATIONS TECHNOLOGY AND SYSTEMS. Joseph N. Pelton et al. WTEC, Baltimore (in press).

Women in Power: From Tokenism to Critical Mass

by Jane S. Jaquette

Never before have so many women held so much power. The growing participation and representation of woman in politics is one of the most remarkable developments of the late twentieth century. For the first time, women in all countries and social classes are becoming politically active, achieving dramatic gains in the number and kind of offices they hold. Why is political power, off limits for so long, suddenly becoming accessible to women? And what are the implications of this trend for domestic and foreign policy?

Women have been gaining the right to vote and run for office since New Zealand became the first country to authorize women's suffrage in 1893. By 1920, the year the United States amended the Constitution to allow women to vote, 10 countries had already granted women the franchise. Yet many European countries did not allow women to vote until after World War II, including France, Greece, Italy, and Switzerland. In Latin America, Ecuador was the first to recognize women's political rights, in 1929; but women could not vote in Mexico until 1953. In Asia, women voted first in Mongolia, in 1923; then, with the U.S. occupation after 1945, women secured the right to vote in Japan and South Korea. The former European colonies in Af-rica and Asia enfranchised women when they gained independence, from the late 1940s into the 1970s.

Historically, women began to demand the right to vote by claiming their equality: If all men are created equal, why not women? The American and British suffrage movements inspired "women's emancipation" efforts among educated female (and sometimes male) elites worldwide, and most contemporary feminist movements trace their roots to these stirrings at the turn of the century. The nineteenth-century European movements had a strong influence on the thinking of Friedrich Engels, who made gender equality a central tenet of socialist doctrine. A similar movement among the Russian intelligentsia ensured that the equality of women in political and economic life would be an important goal of the Soviet state—and subsequently of its Central and Eastern European satellites.

Historically, a country's level of economic development has not been a reliable indicator of women's representation.

But if the logic existed to support women's claims to political equality, the facts on the ground did not. As educated women mobilized to demand the right to vote, men in all

JANE S. JAQUETTE *is chair of the department of diplomacy and world affairs and B. H. Orr professor of liberal arts at Occidental College. Her latest book* Trying Democracy: Women in Post–Authoritarian Politics in Latin America and Central and Eastern Europe *will be published by The Johns Hopkins University Press in 1998.*

Reprinted with permission from *Foreign Policy,* Fall 1997, pp. 23-27. © 1997 by the Carnegie Endowment for International Peace.

countries largely resisted, with the result that most of the world's women gained this basic right of citizenship only in the last 50 years. Before women could vote, they organized to influence legislation, from the marriage and property rights acts of the mid-nineteenth century to the early twentieth century wave of Progressive legislation in the United States and Western Europe's generous maternal and protective labor laws.

However, the vote itself did not bring women into politics. On the contrary, some countries gave women the right to vote but not to run for office. In virtually every nation, women who tried to enter politics were subject to popular ridicule. Political parties routinely excluded women from decision-making positions, resisted nominating them as candidates, and denied their female candidates adequate campaign support.

Cultural factors partially explain the varying degrees of women's representation from region to region and country to country. Predictably, women in the Nordic and northern European countries, with long traditions of gender equality, have been the most successful in breaking through traditional resistance and increasing their representation. In contrast, those in Arab countries, with curbs against women in public life and contemporary pressures to abandon secular laws for religious rules, have consistently registered the lowest levels of female participation (and the lowest levels of democratization).

But "culture" does not fully explain why women in the United States and Great Britain, which rank high on various measures of gender equality, accounted for less than 7 percent of all parliamentarians as late as 1987. Nor have women been excluded from politics in all Islamic nations. The legislatures of Syria

and Indonesia, while decidedly undemocratic, are composed of 10 to 12 percent women. Former prime ministers Benazir Bhutto of Pakistan and Khaleda Zia of Bangladesh have wielded major power in Muslim societies.

Historically, a country's level of development has not been a reliable indicator of women's representation. Of the 32 most developed countries that reported electoral data in 1975, 19 had fewer than 10 percent female legislators and 11 had fewer than 5 percent. In France, Greece, and Japan—all developed, industrialized countries—female members accounted for 2 percent or less of their legislatures.

Although more women than ever are working for wages, even an increase in female participation in the work force does not necessarily translate into greater political clout for women. In recent years, for example, much of the growth in participation has been in low-wage labor. And although women's managerial participation has increased dramatically in many countries, from New Zealand to Peru, women are still rarely found at the highest levels of corporate management and ownership. Their underrepresentation in top management limits the number of private sector women invited to enter government as high-level appointees; women's lower salaries, in turn, restrict an important source of financial support for female candidates.

One can, however, discern significant worldwide increases in female representation beginning in 1975, the year in which the United Nations held its first international women's conference. From 1975 to 1995, the number of women legislators doubled in the developed West; the global average rose from 7.4 percent to nearly 11 percent.

Between 1987 and 1995 in particular, women's representation registered a dramatic increase

Percent of Women in National Legislatures, by region, 1975–97

	1975	1987	1997*
Arab States	3.5	2.8	3.3
Asia	8.4	9.7	13.4
(Asia excluding China, Mongolia, N. Korea, Vietnam)†	(3.8)	(6.2)	(6.3)
Central and Eastern Europe and Former Soviet Union	23.3	23.1	11.5
Developed countries (excluding East Asia)	5.1	9.6	14.7
Latin America and the Caribbean	6.0	6.9	10.5
Nordic Countries	16.1	28.8	36.4

* 1997 statistics for lower houses and single house systems. (Mongolia excluded.)
† women's representation under party control

Sources: *Democracy Still in the Making: A World Comparative Study* (Geneva: Inter-Parliamentary Union, 1997) and *The World's Women, 1970–1990: Trends and Statistics* (New York: United Nations, 1991).

in the developed countries, Africa, and Latin America. Of the 32 women who have served as presidents or prime ministers during the twentieth century, 24 were in power in the 1990s. In the United States, women now make up 11.2 percent of Congress, about one-third the proportion in Nordic countries, but substantially higher than the 5 percent in 1987. And although only 23 women won seats in the Diet in Japan's 1996 elections, an unprecedented 153 women ran for office. In 1997, the Inter-Parliamentary Union reported only nine countries with no women in their legislatures. From 1987 to 1995, the number of countries without any women ministers dropped from 93 to 47, and 10 countries reported that women held more than 20 percent of all ministerial-level positions, although generally in "female" portfolios like health, education, and environment rather than the "power ministries" like finance and defense.

The only exception to the global acceleration in women's representation during the past decade is in the New Independent States of the former Soviet Union and the former members of the Eastern bloc. Here, representation has dropped from earlier highs under communist rule of 25 to 35 percent women (although they exercised little real power) to around 8 to 15 percent today, and numbers are lower in the largely Muslim states of Central Asia. Where women's representation is still under Communist Party control, as in China, North Korea, and Vietnam, women still account for about 20 percent of the national legislators.

THE GLOBALIZATION OF THE WOMEN'S MOVEMENT

Why the surge in women officeholders in the last 10 years?

Three interconnected reasons seem to stand out: First, the rise of women's movements worldwide has heightened women's awareness of their political potential and developed new issues for which women are ready to mobilize. Second, a new willingness by political parties and states to ease the constraints on women's access to politics, from increasing their recruitment pools to modifying electoral systems and adopting quotas. And third, as social issues supplant security concerns in the post–Cold War political environment, opportunities have opened for new styles of leadership and have reordered political priorities.

The recent wave of female mobilization is a response to a series of political and economic crises—and opportunities—over the last two decades. On the political front, women's groups like the Madres de la Plaza de Mayo (Argentine mothers who demonstrated on behalf of their "disappeared" husbands and children) helped to inspire the defense of human rights in Latin America and beyond. Women were also recognized as valued participants in the opposition to authoritarian rule in the former Soviet bloc, where they took up the cause of human rights when their husbands and sons were arrested—dissident Andrei Sakharov's wife, Yelena Bonner, is just one example. In Africa and Asia, women are increasingly regarded as important opposition figures. In South Africa, for example, women were among prominent anti-apartheid leaders and have helped to lead the new government-sponsored effort to develop a women's charter for the post–apartheid period. In Iran, women have played an impor-

Women on Women

"A man, who during the course of his life has never been elected anywhere, and who is named prime minister (it was the case with George Pompidou and Raymond Barre, who had never been elected to any position)—everyone found that absolutely normal. A woman who has been elected for 10 years at the National Assembly . . . at the regional level, who is the mayor of a city, it is as if she were coming out of nowhere."
—**Edith Cresson, former prime minister of France**

"I really do think that women are more cautious in adopting . . . decisions [to go to war]. . . . But I don't think that the woman will ever sacrifice the interests of the nation or the interest of the state due to . . . weakness."
—**Kazimiera Prunskiene,
former prime minister of Lithuania**

"The traditional issues we were steered into—child care, health care, and education—have now become the sexy issues of the decade."
—**Nancy K. Kopp, former speaker pro tem.
of the Maryland House of Delegates**

"Women cannot lead without men, but men have to this day considered themselves capable of leading without women. Women would always take men into consideration. That's the difference."
—**Vigdis Finnbogadóttir,
former president of Iceland**

"Do I have an option?"
—**Patricia Schroeder, former U.S. representative,
when asked by the press if she
was "running as a woman."**

Sources: Laura Liswood, *Women World Leaders* (London: HarperCollins, 1994); Linda Witt, Karen M. Paget, & Glenna Matthews, *Running as a Woman: Gender and Power in American Politics* (New York: Free Press, 1994).

tant role in defining electoral outcomes, despite the conventional wisdom that they are powerless.

On the economic front, the widespread adoption of market-oriented reforms, often accompanied by austerity programs, has had a severe impact on many women, who in turn have organized against price rises and the loss of health care and other public services. Women created communal kitchens in Chile and Peru to help feed their communities. Other small-scale, self-help programs like the Grameen Bank in Bangladesh and the Self-Employed Women's Association in India were

---

The Old Girls Network

Historically, one of the greatest barriers to elected office for women has been inadequate financial support. Often lacking incumbent status or access to financial networks, they have had to build their own fund-raising networks from scratch.

One of the most successful such groups has been EMILY's List (EMILY stands for Early Money is Like Yeast), the first partisan organization set up to fund women candidates in the United States. Ironically for an organization that is now America's largest political action committee (PAC), its roots lie in a political defeat. In 1982, Harriet Woods won the Democratic primary for a Senate seat in Missouri but then received only token financial backing from her party. She called on Washington, D.C., philanthropist Ellen Malcolm for help. But the money proved to be too little and too late to counter her male opponent's negative advertising campaign. Stung by this defeat, Malcolm went on to found EMILY's List in 1985 to raise money for Democratic women candidates who support abortion rights (a.k.a., "pro-choice").

EMILY's List received a major boost in 1992, when the all-male Senate Judiciary Committee confirmed Clarence Thomas to the U.S. Supreme Court despite law professor Anita Hill's accusations of sexual harassment. A torrent of female outrage turned into a record flood of financial support for female candidates in that year's elections. EMILY's List grew from 3,000 to 23,000 members and raised $6 million. It also inspired several state-level imitators, including May's List in Washington State and the Minnesota $$ Million. And EMILY's List now has a number of Republican competitors, including WISH (Women in the Senate and House), which supports pro-choice female candidates, and the Women's Leadership Fund.

According to Rutgers University's Center for the American Woman and Politics, 11 national and 47 state or local PACs and donor networks now either give money predominantly to women or receive most of their contributions from women. Organizations to fund women candidates have been established in several other nations as well. In 1993, Britain's Labour Party launched EMILY's List U.K. In 1995, the Australian Labor Party decided to form its own version of EMILY's List to meet its target of a 35 percent female Parliament by 2002.

---

developed to meet women's needs for credit. The war in Bosnia put an international spotlight on rape as a weapon of war and led to the demand that "women's rights" be considered "human rights" rather than some different or lesser category of concern.

These efforts were reinforced by international connections, many of which were created by the U.N. Decade for Women (1976–85). Three times during the decade (in 1975, 1980, and 1985) and again in 1995, the United Nations convened official delegations from member countries to report on the status of women and to commit governments to remedy women's lack of access to political, economic, and educational resources. Not only did these conferences encourage a flurry of local and national organizing, but they produced parallel meetings of nongovernmental organizations (NGOs), including the nearly 30,000 women who participated in the NGO conference in Beijing in 1995.

The Decade for Women originally meant that women's issues were geared to the U.N. agenda, which in the 1970s focused on the creation of a "new international economic order", and a more equitable sharing of resources between North and South. By the mid-1980s, however, attention had shifted from integrating women into world development efforts to enhancing roles for women in the promotion of market economics and democracy. The turn toward democracy made it easier for women to seek explicitly political goals, and the footdragging by the U.N. and its member countries on implementing their international pledges helped to stimulate women's interest in increasing their political power.

BREAKING THE POLITICAL CLASS CEILING

Since some of the public policies holding women back from greater political power—particularly women's access to education—have been easing rapidly, attention has turned to other barriers. Chief among them have been the constraints on the pool of women available to run for office. Although women constitute a growing proportion of the rank and file in political parties, unions, and civil services, they still account for only a small proportion of the higher echelons that provide a springboard to higher political office.

Although women participate more actively in local government than they do at the national level, many more men make the jump from local to national leadership. One problem has been a lack of campaign funds. In the United States, women began to address that obstacle in the 1980s through innovative fundraising strategies. In other countries, women have organized voting blocs to support female candidates. Yet there is only one women's political party, in Iceland, that has succeeded over time in electing women to office. By the mid-1990s, the European-based Inter-Parliamentary Union was holding meetings twice a year for female parliamentarians aimed at improving their electoral skills as well as their abilities to perform more effectively in office. In another innovative effort, a group called Women of Russia organized to stem the decline in women's representation under the new democratic electoral rules. Women of Russia surprised everyone by gathering over 100,000 signatures and winning 8 percent of the vote in the 1993 Duma elections, but in the 1995 elections they failed to maintain the minimum level of support necessary under Russian electoral rules. As a result of Women in Russia's initial success, however, other Russian parties are nominating more women.

Research has shown that different kinds of voting systems can dramatically affect women's chances of election. The widely accepted explanation for the relatively low numbers of female legislators in the United States and Britain is their "single-member district" electoral systems. When each district elects only one candidate, minority votes are lost. Significantly more women are elected in countries with electoral systems based on proportional representation (in which candidates are elected from party lists according to the percentage of total votes the party receives) or on at-large districts ("multi-member constituencies"). Several countries have experimented with different electoral systems, including mixed single-member and multi-member district systems, to improve the participation of underrepresented groups, particularly women.

The surest way to achieve an increased number of women in national legislatures is to adopt a quota system that requires a certain percentage of women to be nominated or elected. Although the issue of quotas is scarcely open to debate in the United States—where Lani Guinier's nomination for U.S. attorney general in 1993 was torpedoed by detractors' interpretations of essays she had written in support of "group" representation—many political parties (especially on the Left) and national legislatures around the world are experimenting with gender quotas. Quotas account for the high levels of female representation in the Nordic countries and for the recent doubling (to 18 percent) of the number of women in the House of Commons in Britain when the Labour Party swept the election. A quota law in Argentina increased the women in its house of representatives from 4 percent in 1991 to over 16 percent in 1993 and 28 percent in 1995. In Brazil, when quotas were used in the 1997 congressional elections, the number of women legislators increased by nearly 40 percent since the last elections.

Quotas are used in Taiwan, by some of the political parties in Chile, and are under active discussion in Costa Rica, Ecuador, Paraguay, South Korea, and several other countries. The Indian constitution now mandates that one-third of the seats in local government bodies be "reserved" for women, and Pakistan is debating a similar measure. In Mexico, the Institutional Revolutionary Party (PRI) and its leftist opposition have adopted quotas, while the right-of-center party accepts the goal but maintains that it can promote women as effectively without them. Japan has adopted measures to ensure that more women are appointed to ministerial posts, and Bangladesh, among other countries, is experimenting with quotas for top civil service jobs.

It is obvious that quotas increase the number of women officeholders, but why are they being adopted now? Even where quotas are not seen to violate fundamental notions of democracy, as they appear to be in the United States, there are powerful arguments against them. Some insist that they will ghettoize women legislators and their issues. Others object that quotas lead to "proxy" representation, where women legislators run as "fronts" for their husbands or other male interests. In India, for example, there are many anecdotal cases of this phenomenon, and in Argentina there are complaints that many of the women nominated by the majority Peronist Party (which pushed through the quota law) have been chosen because of their unquestioning loyalty to President Carlos Saul Menem rather than because of their qualifications as candidates—as if only women could be considered party hacks.

Despite the controversy quotas raise, they have become popular not only because women

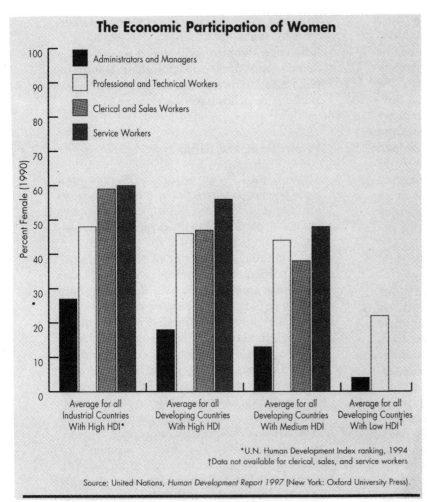

The Economic Participation of Women

Percent Female (1990)

- ■ Administrators and Managers
- □ Professional and Technical Workers
- ▨ Clerical and Sales Workers
- ■ Service Workers

Average for all Industrial Countries With High HDI*

Average for all Developing Countries With High HDI

Average for all Developing Countries With Medium HDI

Average for all Developing Countries With Low HDI†

*U.N. Human Development Index ranking, 1994
†Data not available for clerical, sales, and service workers

Source: United Nations, *Human Development Report 1997* (New York: Oxford University Press).

jection of "unbridled capitalism" and the desire to retain social welfare policies explain the victories of the Labour Party in Britain, the socialists in France, and the electoral loss of the PRI in Mexico last July. Rightly or wrongly, many voters also associate market reforms with a rise in corruption. Despite accusations of corruption against leaders such as Pakistan's Bhutto and Tansu Ciller in Turkey, women's perceived "purity" and their status as outsiders, once considered political weaknesses, are now seen as strengths. In the last 10 years, it is not so much the case that women have come to politics; rather, politics has come to women.

If the trend continues, quotas will soon produce a quantum leap in women's political power. For the first time, women will form a "critical mass" of legislators in many countries, able to set new agendas and perhaps create new styles of leadership. How will women use their growing political influence?

One way to predict the direction of change is to look at how the political attitudes of women differ from those of men. Surveys show that one of the most persistent gender differences regards attitudes toward peace and war: Women are more pacifistic than men, less likely to favor defense spending, or to support aggressive policies abroad. Recent interviews of women heads of state show that most believe that they are more committed to peace than their male counterparts. Historically and today, women and women leaders are more interested in the so-called "soft" issues, including the environment and social welfare. On some measures, women are more conservative than men: They are less likely to vote for the parties on the Left, and rather than pursue their own self-interests, they more often mobilize for defensive reasons—namely to protect the interests of the family. As a result, these tendencies will probably place more focus on policies to support the family and to strengthen local communities.

But women are far from conservative in one important sense: Women are more likely than men to support state regulation of business to protect the consumer and the environment and to assure that the needs of society's

have organized to push for them, but—importantly—because more men have become convinced that quotas serve useful political goals in a more democratic environment. A sea change in attitudes about women in public office is occurring at a time when the number of countries under some form of democratic governance is expanding rapidly, giving new salience to the question of whether national legislatures are truly representative of pluralistic societies. Adequate representation of all groups could strengthen the consolidation of democracies that are open and responsive— and thus make them more durable.

WHAT DO WOMEN WANT?

The post–Cold War shift in national priorities from defense and security concerns to social and environmental issues also plays to women's strong suits. So do the negative impacts of economic globalization and structural adjustment policies, which have put the need for effective social safety nets high on domestic agendas. Many observers argue that the re-

weakest members are addressed. Because women are often more skeptical than men about the effectiveness of market reforms, the election of more women may signal a softening of some of reform's harsher aspects. The market's continued dominance in global politics will reinforce women s efforts to improve their access to the resources that count, from education and credit to the ownership of land and housing.

Women who find themselves experiencing real power for the first time may decide to try out blanket initiatives in areas that they believe male leaders have traditionally neglected: declarations banning war and legislation on children's rights and social or political morality.

However, radical change is unlikely. Predictions that women will act as a bloc have never been borne out in the past. Like their male counterparts, female officeholders come from all parts of the ideological spectrum and depend on the support of diverse and often divided constituencies. Women leaders are not necessarily pacificists or environmentally oriented. While former prime minister Gro Harlem Brundtland of Norway or Ireland's president Mary Robinson may support the "soft" issues, Indira Gandhi or Margaret Thatcher is capable of using force to achieve her ends.

Further, few of the initiatives on those social issues mobilizing women today directly confront male power. Global support for efforts to stem violence against women is an important exception. Antidiscrimination legislation has been developed at the international level through the U.N. Convention on the Elimination of All Forms of Discrimination Against Women—which has been ratified by 160 countries, but not the United States. The implementation of the instrument by signatories, however, lags far behind. And women leaders themselves disagree on many of the issues affecting women most, from reproductive rights and family law to genital mutilation.

Today, women are recruited aggressively into politics not to right past inequities or to recognize their equal citizenship—but to bring a different, explicitly female perspective to the political arena and to appeal to the women's vote. Whether the rationale for increasing female representation is equality or difference, women will have an unprecedented opportunity to put their stamp on politics and to increase the range of alternatives available to policymakers across the globe.

WANT TO KNOW MORE?

Merilee Karl's compendium *Women and Empowerment: Participation and Decision-Making* (London: Zed Books, 1995) discusses women's participation in a range of institutional settings from an activist perspective. A rich and thoughtful treatment of women's political participation covering a variety of cases is *Women and Politics Worldwide,* Barbara Nelson & Najma Chowdhury, eds. (New Haven: Yale University Press, 1994). Laura Liswood interviews 15 female politicians in *Women World Leaders* (London: Pandora, 1994). For information on the impact of electoral systems, consult Wilma Rule & Joseph F. Zimmerman's *Electoral Systems in Comparative Perspective: Their Impact on Women and Minorities* (Westport, Connecticut: Greenwood Press, 1994). The story of women's ascent into U.S. politics is found in Linda Witt, Karen M. Paget, & Clenna Matthews' *Running as a Woman: Gender and Power in American Politics* (New York: The Free Press, 1994). Nancy Adler & Dafna Izraeli, on the other hand, present notable research on women in the private sector in *Competitive Frontiers: Women Managers in a Global Economy* (Cambridge: Blackwell, 1994).

A key source for data on women in power is the United Nations' *Human Development Report 1995* (New York: Oxford University Press, 1995), which is dedicated to gender comparisons. For some historical statistics, see *The World's Women, 1970–1990: Trends and Statistics* (New York: United Nations, 1991). Updates and special studies on women's political participation are available through the Inter-Parliamentary Union's Web page. Access this site and others on women in political and economic power through **www.foreign-policy.com.**

Absolute poverty: The condition of people whose incomes are insufficient to keep them at a subsistence level.

Adjudication: The legal process of deciding an issue through the courts.

African, Caribbean, and Pacific Countries (ACP): Fifty-eight countries associated with the European Community.

African National Congress (ANC): South African organization founded in 1912 in response to the taking of land from Africans and the restrictions on their employment and movement. Following attempts at peaceful resistance, its leaders were tried for treason and imprisoned. In 1990, ANC de facto leader Nelson Mandela was released from prison, and a continued resistance against the apartheid state grew. The ANC was legalized in 1991.

Airborne Warning and Control System (AWACS): Flying radar stations that instantaneously identify all devices in the air within a radius of 240 miles and detect movement of land vehicles.

Air-launched cruise missile (ALCM): A cruise missile carried by and launched from an aircraft.

Antiballistic missile (ABM): A missile that seeks out and destroys an incoming enemy missile in flight before the latter reaches its target. It is not effective against MIRVs.

Apartheid: A system of laws in the Republic of South Africa that segregates and politically and economically discriminates against non-European groups.

Appropriate technology: Also known as intermediate technology. It aims at using existing resources by making their usage more efficient or productive but adaptable to the local population.

Arms control: Any measure limiting or reducing forces, regulating armaments, and/or restricting the deployment of troops or weapons.

Arms race: The competitive or cumulative improvement of weapons stocks (qualitatively or quantitatively), or the buildup of armed forces based on the conviction of two or more actors that only by trying to stay ahead in military power can they avoid falling behind.

Association of Southeast Asian Nations (ASEAN): A regional regrouping made up of Indonesia, the Philippines, Singapore, and Thailand.

Atomic bomb: A weapon based on the rapid splitting of fissionable materials, thereby inducing an explosion with three deadly results: blast, heat, and radiation.

Autarky: Establishing economic independence.

Balance of payments: A figure that represents the net flow of money into and out of a country due to trade, tourist expenditures, sale of services (such as consulting), foreign aid, profits, and so forth.

Balance of trade: The relationship between imports and exports.

Ballistic missile: A payload propelled by a rocket, which assumes a free-fall trajectory when thrust is terminated. Ballistic missiles could be of short range (SRBM), intermediate range (IRBM), medium range (MRBM), and intercontinental (ICBM).

Bantustans: Ten designated geographical areas or "homelands" for each African ethnic group created under the apartheid government of South Africa. Beginning in the late 1970s, South Africa instituted a policy offering "independence" to the tribal leaders of these homelands. The leaders of four homeland governments accepted independent status, but no outside actors recognized these artificial entities as independent nation-states. Under the terms of the new constitution, all homeland citizens are now considered to be citizens of South Africa.

Barrel: A standard measure for petroleum, equivalent to 42 gallons or 158.86 liters.

Basic human needs: Adequate food intake (in terms of calories, proteins, and vitamins), drinking water free of disease-carrying organisms and toxins, minimum clothing and shelter, literacy, sanitation, health care, employment, and dignity.

Bilateral diplomacy: Negotiations between two countries.

Bilateral (foreign) aid: Foreign aid given by one country directly to another.

Binary (chemical) munitions/weapons: Nerve gas canisters composed of two separate chambers containing chemicals that become lethal when mixed. The mixing is done when the canister is fired. Binary gas is preferred for its relative safety in storage and transportation.

Biosphere: The environment of life and living processes at or near Earth's surface, extending from the ocean floors to about 75 kilometers into the atmosphere. It is being endangered by consequences of human activities such as air and water pollution, acid rain, radioactive fallout, desertification, toxic and nuclear wastes, and the depletion of nonrenewable resources.

Bipolar system: A world political system in which power is primarily held by two international actors.

Buffer stocks: Reserves of commodities that are either increased or decreased whenever necessary to maintain relative stability of supply and prices.

Camp David Agreements/Accords: Agreements signed on September 17, 1978, at Camp David—a mountain retreat for the U.S. president in Maryland—by President Anwar al-Sadat of Egypt and Prime Minister Menachem Begin of Israel, and witnessed by President Jimmy Carter.

Capitalism: An economic system based on the private ownership of real property and commercial enterprise, competition for profits, and limited government interference in the marketplace.

Cartel: An international agreement among producers of a commodity that attempts to control the production and pricing of that commodity.

CBN weapons: Chemical, biological, and nuclear weapons.

Chemical Weapons Convention Treaty: Signed in 1993, the treaty requires its 130 signatories to eliminate all chemical weapons by the year 2005 and to submit to rigorous inspection.

Cold war: A condition of hostility that existed between the U.S. and the Soviet Union in their struggle to dominate the world scene following World War II. It ended with the collapse of the Soviet Union in 1991.

Collective security: The original theory behind UN peacekeeping. It holds that aggression against one state is aggression against all and should be defeated by the collective action of all.

Commodity: The unprocessed products of mining and agriculture.

Common Heritage of Mankind: A 1970 UN declaration that states that the "seabed and ocean floor, and the subsoil thereof, beyond the limits of national jurisdiction . . . , as well as the resources of the area, are the common heritage of mankind."

Common Market: A customs union that eliminates trade barriers within a group and establishes a common external tariff on imports from nonmember countries.

Commonwealth of Independent States (CIS): In December 1991 the Soviet Union was dissolved and fifteen independent countries were formed: Armenia, Azerbaijan, Byelorussia (Belarus), Estonia, Georgia, Kazakhstan, Kirghizia (Kyrgyzstan), Latvia, Lithuania, Moldavia (Moldova), Russia, Tadzhikistan (Tajikistan), Turkmenistan, Ukraine, and Uzbekistan. Some of the republics have since changed their names. CIS represents a collective term for the group of republics.

Compensatory Financing Facility: An IMF program established in 1963 to finance temporary export shortfalls, as in coffee, sugar, or other cyclically prone export items.

Concessional loans: Loans given to LLDCs by MBDs that can be repaid in soft (nonconvertible) currencies and with nominal or no interest over a long period of time.

Conditionality: A series of measures that must be taken by a country before it could qualify for loans from the International Monetary Fund.

Conference on International Economic Cooperation (CIEC): A conference of 8 industrial nations, 7 oil-producing nations, and 12 developing countries held in several sessions between December 1975 and June 1977. It is composed of four separate commissions (energy, raw materials, development, and financing). It is the forum of the North-South dialogue between rich and poor countries.

Conference on Security and Cooperation in Europe (CSCE): Series of conferences among 51 NATO, former Soviet bloc, and neutral European countries (52 counting Serbia or rump Yugoslavia). Established by 1976 Helsinki Accords. There are plans to establish a small, permanent CSCE headquarters and staff.

Consensus: In conference diplomacy, a way of reaching agreements by negotiations and without a formal vote.

Counterforce: The use of strategic nuclear weapons for strikes on selected military capabilities of an enemy force.

Countervalue: The use of strategic nuclear weapons for strikes on an enemy's population centers.

Cruise missile: A small, highly maneuverable, low-flying, pilotless aircraft equipped with accurate guidance systems that periodically readjusts its trajectory. It can carry conventional or nuclear warheads, can be short-range or long-range, and can be launched from the air (ALLUM), the ground (GLCM), or the sea (SLCM).

Cultural imperialism: The attempt to impose your own value systems on others, including judging others by how closely they conform to your norms.

Current dollars: The value of the dollar in the year for which it is being reported. Sometimes called inflated dollars. Any currency can be expressed in current value. *See* **Real dollars.**

Decision making: The process by which humans choose which policy to pursue and which actions to take in support of policy goals. The study of decision making seeks to identify patterns in the way that humans make decisions. This includes gathering information, analyzing information, and making choices. Decision making is a complex process that relates to personality and other human traits, to the sociopolitical setting in which decision makers function, and to the organizational structures involved.

Declaration of Talloires: A statement issued in 1981 by Western journalists who opposed the UNESCO-sponsored New World Information and Communication Order, at a meeting in Talloires, France.

Delivery systems or vehicles or launchers: Land-based missiles (ICBMs), submarine-launched missiles (SLBMs), and long-range bombers capable of delivering nuclear weapons.

Dependencia model: The belief that the industrialized North has created a neocolonial relationship with the South in which the LDCs are dependent on and disadvantaged by their economic relations with the capitalist industrial countries.

Deployment: The actual positioning of weapons systems in a combat-ready status.

Détente: A relaxation of tensions or a decrease in the level of hostility between opponents on the world scene.

Deterrence: Persuading an opponent not to attack by having enough forces to disable the attack and/or launch a punishing counterattack.

Developed countries (DCs): Countries with relatively high per capita GNP, education, levels of industrial development and production, health and welfare, and agricultural productivity.

Developing countries (also called less developed countries): These countries are mainly raw materials producers for export with high growth rates and inadequate infrastructures in transportation, educational systems, and the like. There is, however, a wide variation in living standards, GNPs, and per capita incomes among LCDs.

Development: The process through which a society becomes increasingly able to meet basic human needs and ensure the physical quality of life of its people.

Direct investment: Buying stock, real estate, and other assets in another country with the aim of gaining a controlling interest in foreign economic enterprises. Different from portfolio investment, which involves investment solely to gain capital appreciation through market fluctuations.

Disinformation: The spreading of false propaganda and forged documents to confuse counterintelligence or to create political confusion, unrest, and scandal.

Dumping: A special case of price discrimination, selling to foreign buyers at a lower price than that charged to buyers in the home market.

Duty: Special tax applied to imported goods, based on tariff rates and schedules.

East (as in the East–West struggle): A shorthand, nongeographic term that included nonmarket, centrally planned (communist) countries.

East–West axis: The cold war conflict between the former Soviet Union and its allies and the United States and its allies.

Economic Cooperation among Developing Countries (ECDC): Also referred to as intra-South, or South-South cooperation, it is a way for LCDs to help each other with appropriate technology.

Economic statecraft: The practice of states utilizing economic instruments, such as sanctions, to gain their political ends. Economic statecraft is closely related to "mercantilism," or the use of political power to advance a country's economic fortunes.

Economically developing countries (EDCs): The relatively wealthy and industrialized countries that lie mainly in the Northern Hemisphere (the North).

Escalation: Increasing the level of fighting.

Essential equivalence: Comparing military capabilities of two would-be belligerents, not in terms of identical mix of forces, but in terms of how well two dissimilarly organized forces could achieve a strategic stalemate.

Euro: The single European currency among the majority of European Union members.

Eurodollars: U.S. dollar holdings of European banks; a liability for the U.S. Treasury.

Euromissiles: Shorthand for long-range theatre nuclear forces stationed in Europe or aimed at targets in Europe.

Europe 1992: A term that represents the European Community's decision to eliminate by the end of 1992 all internal barriers (between member countries) to the movement of trade, financial resources, workers, and services (banking, insurance, etc.).

European Community (EC): The Western European regional organization established in 1967 that includes the European Coal and Steel Community (ECSC), the European Economic Community (EEC), and the European Atomic Energy Community (EURATOM).

European Currency Unit (ECU): The former common unit of valuation among the eight members of the European Monetary System (EMS); was replaced by the euro in January 1999.

European Economic Community (EEC). See **European Union.**

European Free Trade Association (EFTA): Austria, Finland, Iceland, Liechtenstein, Norway, Portugal, Sweden, and Switzerland. Each member keeps its own external tariff schedule, but free trade prevails among the members.

European Monetary System (EMS): Established in 1979 as a preliminary stage toward an economic and monetary union in the European Community. Fluctuations in the exchange rate value of the currencies of the participating countries are kept with a 2¼ percent limit of divergence from the strongest currency among them. The system collapsed in 1993, thus slowing progress toward monetary integration in Europe.

European Union: Known as the European Economic Community, and also the Common Market, until 1994, the European Union has 12 full members: Belgium, Denmark, France, Germany, Greece, Ireland, Italy, Luxembourg, Netherlands, Portugal, Spain, and the United Kingdom. (Austria, Finland, Norway, and Sweden are expected to enter the Union in 1995.) Originally established by the Treaty of Rome in 1958, the Union nations work toward establishing common defense and foreign policies and a common market.

Exchange rate: The values of two currencies relative to each other—for example, how many yen equal a dollar or how many lira equal a pound.

Export subsidies: Special incentives, including direct payments to exporters, to encourage increased foreign sales.

Exports: Products shipped to foreign countries.

Finlandization: A condition of nominal neutrality, but one of actual subservience to the former Soviet Union in foreign and security policies, as is the case with Finland.

First strike: The first offensive move of a general nuclear war. It implies an intention to knock out the opponent's ability to retaliate.

Fissionable or nuclear materials: Isotopes of certain elements, such as plutonium, thorium, and uranium, that emit neutrons in such large numbers that a sufficient concentration will be self-sustaining until it explodes.

Foreign policy: The sum of a country's goals and actions on the world stage. The study of foreign policy is synonymous with state-level analysis and examines how countries define their interests, establish goals, decide on specific policies, and attempt to implement those policies.

Forward-based system (FBS or FoBS): A military installation, maintained on foreign soil or in international waters, and conveniently located near a theatre of war.

Fourth World: An expression arising from the world economic crisis that began in 1973–74 with the quadrupling in price of petroleum. It encompasses the least developed countries (LLDCs) and the most seriously affected countries (MSAs).

Free trade: The international movement of goods unrestricted by tariffs or nontariff barriers.

Functionalism: International cooperation in specific areas such as communications, trade, travel, health, or environmental protection activity. Often symbolized by the specialized agencies, such as the World Health Organization, associated with the United Nations.

General Agreement on Tariffs and Trade (GATT): Created in 1947, this organizaiton is the major global forum for negotiations of tariff reductions and other measures to expand world trade. Its members account for four-fifths of the world's trade.

General Assembly: The main representative body of the United Nations, composed of all member states.

Generalized System of Preferences (GSP): A system approved by GATT in 1971, which authorizes DCs to give preferential tariff treatment to LCDs.

Global: Pertaining to the world as a whole; worldwide.

Global commons: The Antarctic, the ocean floor under international waters, and celestial bodies within reach of planet Earth. All of these areas and bodies are considered the common heritage of mankind.

Global negotiations: A new round of international economic negotiations started in 1980 over raw materials, energy, trade, development, money, and finance.

Golan Heights: Syrian territory adjacent to Israel, which has occupied it since the 1967 war and that annexed it unilaterally in 1981.

Gross domestic product (GDP): A measure of income within a country that excludes foreign earnings.

Gross national product (GNP): A measure of the sum of all goods and services produced by a country's nationals, whether they are in the country or abroad.

Group of Seven (G-7): The seven economically largest free market countries: Canada, France, Great Britain, Italy, Japan, the United States, and Germany.

Group of 77: Group of 77 Third World countries that cosponsored the Joint Declaration of Developing Countries in 1963 calling for greater equity in North–South trade. This group has come to include more than 120 members and represents the interests of the less developed countries of the South.

Hegemonism: Any attempt by a larger power to interfere, threaten, intervene against, and dominate a smaller power or a region of the world.

Hegemony: Domination by a major power over smaller, subordinate ones within its sphere of influence.

Helsinki Agreement. See **Conference on Security and Cooperation In Europe.**

Horn of Africa: The northeast corner of Africa that includes Ethiopia, Djibouti, and Somalia. It is separated from the Arabian peninsula by the Gulf of Aden and the Red Sea. It is plagued with tribal conflicts between Ethiopia and Eritrea, and between Ethiopia and Somalia over the Ogaden desert. These conflicts generated a large number of refugees who faced mass starvation.

Human rights: Rights inherent to human beings, including but not limited to the right of dignity; the integrity of the person; the inviolability of the person's body and mind; civil and political rights (freedom of religion, speech, press, assembly, association, the right to privacy, habeas corpus, due process of law, the right to vote or not to vote, the right to run for election, and the right to be protected from reprisals for acts of peaceful dissent); social, economic, and cultural rights. The most glaring violations of human rights are torture, disappearance, and the general phenomenon of state terrorism.

Imports: Products brought into a country from abroad.

Inkatha Freedom Party (IFP): A Zulu-based political and cultural movement led by Mangosuthu Buthelezi. It is a main rival of the African National Congress in South Africa.

Innocent passage: In a nation's territorial sea, passage by a foreign ship is innocent so long as it is not prejudicial to the peace, good order, or security of the coastal state. Submarines must surface and show their flag.

Intercontinental ballistic missile (ICBM): A land-based, rocket-propelled vehicle capable of delivering a warhead to targets at 6,000 or more nautical miles.

Interdependence (economic): The close interrelationship and mutual dependence of two or more domestic economies on each other.

Intergovernmental organizations (IGOs): International/transnational actors comprised of member countries.

Intermediate-range ballistic missile (IRBM): A missile with a range from 1,500 to 4,000 nautical miles.

Intermediate-range nuclear forces: Nuclear arms that are based in Europe with a deployment range that easily encompasses the former USSR.

Intermediate-range Nuclear Forces (INF) Treaty: The treaty between the former USSR and the United States that limits the dispersion of nuclear warheads in Europe.

International: Between or among sovereign states.

International Atomic Energy Agency (IAEA): An agency created in 1946 by the UN to limit the use of nuclear technology to peaceful purposes.

International Court of Justice (ICJ): The World Court, which sits in The Hague with 15 judges and which is associated with the United Nations.

International Development Association (IDA): An affiliate of the World Bank that provides interest-free, long-term loans to developing countries.

International Energy Agency (IEA): An arm of OECD that attempts to coordinate member countries' oil imports and reallocate stocks among members in case of disruptions in the world's oil supply.

International Finance Corporation: Created in 1956 to finance overseas investments by private companies without necessarily requiring government guarantees. The IFC borrows from the World Bank, provides loans, and invests directly in private industry in the development of capital projects.

International Monetary Fund (IMF): The world's primary organization devoted to maintaining monetary stability by helping countries fund balance-of-payments deficits. Established in 1947, it now has 170 members.

International political economy (IPE): A term that encapsulates the totality of international economic interdependence and exchange in the political setting of the international system. Trade, investment, monetary relations, transnational business activities, aid, loans, and other aspects of international economic interchange (and the reciprocal impacts between these activities and politics) are all part of the study of IPE.

Interstate: International, intergovernmental.

Intifada (literally, resurgence): A series of minor clashes between Palestinian youths and Israeli security forces that escalated into a full-scale revolt in December 1987.

Intra-South. *See* **Economic Cooperation among Developing Countries.**

Islamic fundamentalism: Early nineteenth-century movements of fundamentalism sought to revitalize Islam through internal reform, thus enabling Islamic societies to resist foreign control. Some of these movements sought peaceful change, while other were more militant. The common ground of twentieth-century reform movements and groups is their fundamental opposition to the onslaught of materialistic Western culture and their desire to reassert a distinct Islamic identity for the societies they claim to represent.

Kampuchea: The new name for Cambodia since April 1975.

KGB: Security police and intelligence apparatus in the former Soviet Union, engaged in espionage, counterespionage, antisubversion, and control of political dissidents.

Khmer Rouge: Literally "Red Cambodians," the communist organization ruling Kampuchea between April 1975 and January 1979 under Pol Pot and Leng Saray.

Kiloton: A thousand tons of explosive force. A measure of the yield of a nuclear weapon equivalent to 1,000 tons of TNT (trinitrotoluene). The bomb detonated at Hiroshima in World War II had an approximate yield of 14 kilotons.

Launcher. *See* **Delivery systems.**

League of Nations: The first true general international organization. It existed between the end of World War I and the beginning of World War II and was the immediate predecessor of the United Nations.

Least developed countries: Those countries in the poorest of economic circumstances. Frequently it includes those countries with a per capita GNP of less than $400 in 1985 dollars.

Less developed countries (LDCs): Countries, located mainly in Africa, Asia, and Latin America, with economies that rely heavily on the production of agriculture and raw material and whose per capita GNP and standard of living are substantially below Western standards.

Linkage diplomacy: The practice of considering another country's general international behavior as well as the specifics of the question when deciding whether or not to reach an agreement on an issue.

Lisbon Protocol: Signed in 1992, it is an agreement between ex-Soviet republics Kazakhstan and Belarus to eliminate nuclear weapons from their territories.

Lome Convention: An agreement concluded between the European Community and 58 African, Caribbean, and Pacific countries (ACP), allowing the latter preferential trade relations and greater economic and technical assistance.

Long-range theatre nuclear forces (LRTNF): Nuclear weapon systems with a range greater than 1,000 kilometers (or 600 miles), such as the U.S. Pershing II missile or the Soviet SS-20.

Maastricht Treaty: Signed by the European Community's 12 member-countries in December 1991, the Maastricht Treaty outlines steps toward further political/economic integration. At this time, following several narrow ratification votes and monetary crises, it is too early to foretell the future evolution of EC political integration.

Medium-range ballistic missile (MRBM): A missile with a range from 500 to 1,500 nautical miles.

Megaton: The yield of a nuclear weapon equivalent to 1 million tons of TNT (approximately equivalent to 79 Hiroshima bombs).

Microstates: Very small countries, usually with a population of less than one million.

Missile experimental (MX): A mobile, land-based missile that is shuttled among different launching sites, making it more difficult to locate and destroy.

Most favored nation (MFN): In international trade agreements, a country grants most-favored-nation status to another country in regard to tariffs and other trade regulations.

Multilateral: Involving many nations.

Multinational: Doing business in many nations.

Multinational corporations (MNCs): Private enterprises doing business in more than one country.

Multiple independently targetable reentry vehicle (MIRV): Two or more warheads carried by a single missile and capable of being guided to separate targets on reentry.

Munich syndrome: A lesson that was drawn by post-World War II leaders that one should not compromise with aggression.

Mutual and Balanced Force Reductions (MBFR): The 19-nation Conference on Mutual Reduction of Forces and Armaments and Associated Measures in Central Europe that has been held intermittently from 1973 to the end of the 1980s.

Mutual Assured Destruction (MAD): The basic ingredient of the doctrine of strategic deterrence that no country can escape destruction in a nuclear exchange even if it engages in a preemptive strike.

Namibia: African name for South-West Africa.

National Intelligence Estimate (NIE): The final assessment of global problems and capabilities by the intelligence community for use by the National Security Council and the president in making foreign and military decisions.

Nation-state: A political unit that is sovereign and has a population that supports and identifies with it politically.

Nautical mile: 1,853 meters.

Neocolonialism: A perjorative term describing the economic exploitation of Third World countries by the industrialized countries, in particular through the activities of multinational corporations.

Neutron bomb: Enhanced radiation bomb giving out lower blast and heat but concentrated radiation, thus killing people and living things while reducing damage to physical structures.

New International Economic Order (NIEO): The statement of development policies and objectives adopted at the Sixth Special Session of the UN General Assembly in 1974. NIEO calls for equal participation of LDCs in the international economic policy-making process, better known as the North-South dialogue.

New world order: A term that refers to the structure and operation of the post-cold war world. Following the Persian Gulf War, President George Bush referred to a world order based on nonaggression and on international law and organization.

Nonaligned movement (NAM): A group of Third World countries interested in promoting economic cooperation and development.

Nongovernmental organizations (NGOs or IN-GOs): Transnational (international) organizations made up of private organizations and individuals instead of member states.

Nonproliferation of Nuclear Weapons Treaty (NPT): Nuclear weapon states, party to the NPT, who pledge not to transfer nuclear explosive devices to any recipient and not to assist any nonnuclear weapon state in the manufacture of nuclear explosive devices.

Nontariff barriers (NTB): Subtle, informal impediments to free trade designed for the purpose of making importation of foreign goods into a country very difficult on such grounds as health and safety regulations.

Normalization of relations: The reestablishment of full diplomatic relations, including de jure recognition and the exchange of ambassadors between two countries that either did not have diplomatic relations or had broken them.

North (as in North–South dialogue): (a) A shorthand, nongeographic term for the industrialized countries of high income, both East and West; (b) Often means only the industrialized, high-income countries of the West.

North Atlantic Cooperation Council (NACC): Consists of 37 members, including all members of NATO, the former Warsaw Pact members, and former Soviet republics (Russia, Ukraine, Belarus, Georgia, Moldova, Armenia, Azerbaijan, Kazakhstan, Uzbekistan, Kyrgyzstan, Turkmentistan, and Tajikstan), the Czech Republic, Slovakia, Poland, Hungary, Romania, Bulgaria, Estonia, Latvia, Lithuania, and Albania.

North Atlantic Treaty Organization (NATO): Also known as the Atlantic Alliance, NATO was formed in 1949 to provide collective defense against the perceived Soviet threat to Western Europe. It consists of the United States, Canada, 13 Western European countries, and Turkey.

North-South axis: A growing tension that is developing between the North (economically developed countries) and the South (economically deprived countries). The South is insisting that the North share part of its wealth and terminate economic and political domination.

Nuclear proliferation: The process by which one country after another comes into possession of some form of nuclear weaponry, and with it develops the potential of launching a nuclear attack on other countries.

Nuclear reprocessing: The separation of radioactive waste (spent fuel) from a nuclear-powered plant into its fissile constituent materials. One such material is plutonium, which can then be used in the production of atomic bombs.

Nuclear terrorism: The use (or threatened use) of nuclear weapons or radioactive materials as a means of coercion.

Nuclear Utilization Theory (NUT): Advocates of this nuclear strategy position want to destroy enemy weapons before the weapons explode on one's own territory and forces. The best way to do this, according to this theory, is to destroy an enemy's weapons before they are launched.

Nuclear-free zone: A stretch of territory from which all nuclear weapons are banned.

Official Development Aid (ODA): Government contributions to projects and programs aimed at developing the productivity of poorer countries. This is to be distinguished from private, voluntary assistance, humanitarian assistance for disasters, and, most importantly, from military assistance.

Ogaden: A piece of Ethiopian desert populated by ethnic Somalis. It was a bone of contention between Ethiopia and Somalia that continued until 1988 when a peace agreement was reached.

Organization of Arab Petroleum Exporting Countries (OAPEC): A component of OPEC, with Saudi Arabia, Kuwait, the United Arab Emirates, Qatar, Iraq, Algeria, and Libya as members.

Organization of Economic Cooperation and Development (OECD): An organization of 24 members that serves to promote economic coordination among the Western industrialized countries.

Organization of Petroleum Exporting Countries (OPEC): A producers' cartel setting price floors and production ceilings of crude petroleum. It consists of Venezuela and others such as Ecuador, Gabon, Nigeria, and Indonesia, as well as the Arab oil-producing countries.

Palestine: "Palestine" does not exist today as an entity. It refers to the historical and geographical entity administered by the British under the League of Nations mandate from 1918 to 1947. It also refers to a future entity in the aspirations of Palestinians who, as was the case of the Jews before the founding of the State of Israel, are stateless nationalists. Whether Palestinians will have an autonomous or independent homeland is an ongoing issue.

Palestine Liberation Organization (PLO): A coalition of Palestinian groups united by the goal of a Palestinian state.

Partnership for Peace Program: A U.S.–backed policy initiative for NATO formulated by the Clinton administration in 1994. The proposal was designed to rejuvenate the Atlantic Alliance and contribute to the stability of recent independent countries in Eastern Europe and the former Soviet Union. No NATO security guarantees or eventual membership in the alliance are specifically mentioned.

Payload: Warheads attached to delivery vehicles.

Peacekeeping: Occurs when an international organization such as the United Nations uses military means to prevent hostilities, usually by serving as a buffer between combatants. This international force will remain neutral between the opposing forces and must be invited by at least one of the combatants. *See* **Collective security.**

People's Republic of China (PRC): Communist or mainland China.

Petrodollars: U.S. dollar holdings of capital-surplus OPEC countries; a liability for the U.S. Treasury.

Physical Quality of Life Index (PQLI): Developed by the Overseas Development Council, the PQLI is presented as a more significant measurement of the well-being of inhabitants of a geographic entity than the solely monetary measurement of per capita income. It consists of the following measurements: life expectancy, infant mortality, and literacy figures that are each rated on an index of 1–100, within which each country is ranked according to its performance. A composite index is obtained by averaging these three measures, giving the PQLI.

Polisario: The liberation front of Western Sahara (formerly Spanish Sahara). After years of bitter fighting over Western Sahara, Polisario guerrillas signed a cease-fire agreement with Morocco in 1990. The UN has yet to conduct a referendum in Western Sahara on whether the territory should become independent or remain part of Morocco.

Postindustrial: Characteristic of a society where a large portion of the workforce is directed to nonagricultural and nonmanufacturing tasks such as servicing and processing.

Precision-guided munitions (PGM): Popularly known as "smart bombs." Electronically programmed and controlled weapons that can accurately hit a moving or stationary target.

Proliferation: Quick spread, as in the case of nuclear weapons.

Protectionism: Using tariffs and nontariff barriers to control or restrict the flow of imports into a country.

Protocol: A preliminary memorandum often signed by diplomatic negotiators as a basis for a final convention or treaty.

Quota: Quantitative limits, usually imposed on imports or immigrants.

Rapprochement: The coming together of two countries that had been hostile to each other.

Real dollars (uninflated dollars): The report of currency in terms of what it would have been worth in a stated year.

Regionalism: A concept of cooperation among geographically adjacent states to foster region-wide political, military, and economic interests.

Reprocessing of nuclear waste: A process of recovery of fissionable materials among which is weapons-grade plutonium.

Resolution: Formal decisions of UN bodies; they may simply register an opinion or may recommend action to be taken by a UN body or agency.

Resolution 242: Passed by the UN Security Council on November 22, 1967, calling for the withdrawal of Israeli troops from territories they captured from Egypt (Sinai), Jordan (West Bank and East Jerusalem), and Syria (Golan Heights) in the 1967 war, and for the right of all nations in the Middle East to live in peace in secure and recognized borders.

Resolution 435: Passed by the UN Security Council in 1978, it called for a cease-fire between belligerents in the Namibian conflict (namely SWAPO, Angola and other front-line states on the one side, and South Africa on the other) and an internationally supervised transition process to independence and free elections.

Resolution 678: Passed by the UN in November 1990 demanding that Iraq withdraw from Kuwait. It authorized the use of all necessary force to restore Kuwait's sovereignty after January 15,1991.

SALT I: The Strategic Arms Limitation Treaty that was signed in 1972 between the U.S. and the former Soviet Union on the limitation of strategic armaments.

SALT II: The Strategic Arms Limitation Treaty signed in 1979. SALT II was to limit the number and types of former Soviet Union and U.S. strategic weapons. It never went into effect, as it was not ratified by the U.S. Senate.

Second strike: A nuclear attack in response to an adversary's first strike. A second-strike capability is the ability to absorb the full force of a first strike and still inflict heavy damage in retaliation.

Secretariat: (a) The administrative organ of the United Nations, headed by the secretary-general; (b) An administrative element of any IGO; this is headed by a secretary-general.

Short-range ballistic missiles (SRBM): A missile with a range up to 500 nautical miles.

Solidarity: Independent self-governing trade union movement started in Poland in 1980. It was terminated in December 1981 after radical members of its Presidium passed a resolution calling for a national referendum to determine if the communist government of Poland should continue to govern.

South (as in North-South axis): A shorthand, nongeographic term that includes economically less developed countries, often represented by the Group of 77.

Sovereignty: The ability to carry out laws and policies within national borders without interference from outside.

Special Drawing Rights (SDRs): Also known as paper gold. A new form of international liquid reserves to be used in the settlement of international payments among member governments of the International Monetary Fund.

State: Regarding international relations, it means a country having territory, population, government, and sovereignty, e.g., the United States is a state, while California is not a state in this sense.

State terrorism: The use of state power, including the police, the armed forces, and the secret police to throw fear among the population against any act of dissent or protest against a political regime.

"Stealth": A code name for a proposed "invisible" aircraft, supposedly not detectable by hostile forces, that would be the main U.S. strategic fighter-bomber of the 1990s.

Strategic Arms Limitation Talks. *See* **SALT I** and **SALT II.**

Strategic Defense Initiative (SDI): A space-based defense system designed to destroy incoming missiles. It is highly criticized because the technological possibility of such a system is questionable, not to mention the enormous cost.

Strategic minerals: Minerals needed in the fabrication of advanced military and industrial equipment. Examples are uranium, platinum, titanium, vanadium, tungsten, nickel, chromium, etc.

Strategic nuclear weapons: Long-range weapons carried on either intercontinental ballistic missiles (ICBMs) or submarine-launched ballistic missiles (SLBMs) or long-range bombers.

Strategic stockpile: Reserves of certain commodities established to ensure that in time of national emergency such commodities are readily available.

Structural Adjustment Program. *See* **Conditionality.**

Submarine-launched ballistic missile (SLBM): A ballistic missile carried in and launched from a submarine.

Superpowers: Countries so powerful militarily (the United States and Russia), demographically (Pacific Rim countries), or economically (Japan) as to be in a class by themselves.

Supranational: Above nation-states.

Tactical nuclear weapons: Kiloton-range weapons for theatre use. The bomb dropped on Hiroshima would be in this category today.

Tariff: A tax levied on imports.

Technetronic: Shorthand for technological-electronic.

Territorial sea: The territorial sea, air space above, seabed, and subsoil are part of sovereign territory of a coastal state, except that ships (not aircraft) enjoy right of innocent passage. As proposed, a coastal state's sovereignty would extend 12 nautical miles beyond its land territory.

Terrorism: The systematic use of terror as a means of coercion.

Theatre: In nuclear strategy, it refers to a localized combat area such as Europe, as opposed to global warfare that would have involved the United States and the former Soviet Union in a nuclear exchange.

Theatre nuclear forces (TNF): Nuclear weapons systems for operations in a region such as Europe, including artillery, cruise missiles, SRBMs, IRBMs, and MRBMs.

Third World: Often used interchangeably with the terms less developed countries, developing countries, or the South, its two main institutions are the nonaligned movement (which acts primarily as the political caucus of the Third World) and the Group of 77 (which functions as the economic voice of the Third World).

Tokyo Round: The sixth round of GATT trade negotiations, begun in 1973 and ended in 1979. About 100 nations, including nonmembers of the GATT, participated.

Torture: The deliberate inflicting of pain, whether physical or psychological, to degrade, intimidate, and induce submission of its victims to the will of the torturer. It is a heinous practice used frequently in most dictatorial regimes in the world, irrespective of their ideological leanings.

Transnational: An adjective indicating that a nongovernmental movement, organization, or ideology transcends national borders and is operative in dissimilar political, economic, and social systems.

Transnational enterprise (TNE) or corporation (TNC). *See* **Multinational corporations.**

Triad (nuclear): The three-pronged U.S. strategic weapons arsenal, composed of land-based ICBMs, underwater SLBMs, and long-range manned bombers.

Trilateral: Between three countries or groups of countries, e.g., United States, Western Europe, and Japan; United States, Russia, and China.

Unilateral: One-sided, as opposed to bilateral or multilateral.

United Nations Conference on Trade and Development (UNCTAD): A coalition of disadvantaged countries that met in 1964 in response to their effort to bridge the standard-of-living gap between themselves and developed countries.

Verification: The process of determining that the other side is complying with an agreement.

Vietnam syndrome: An aversion to foreign armed intervention, especially in Third World conflicts involving guerrillas. This is an attitude that is especially common among those who opposed U.S. participation in the Vietnam War.

Visegrad Group: Term used to refer to Poland, Hungary, Slovakia, and the Czech Republic. These countries were subject to the same conditions and status in their recent application to participate in NATO's Partnership for Peace initiative.

Walesa, Lech: Leader of the independent trade union movement known as *Solidarity*, which came into existence in August 1980 and was dissolved in December 1981 by martial law decree. He was elected president of Poland in December 1990.

Warhead: That part of a missile, projectile, or torpedo that contains the explosive intended to inflict damage.

Warsaw Pact or Warsaw Treaty Organization: Established in 1955 by the Soviet Union to promote mutual defense. It was dissolved in July 1991. Member countries at time of dissolution were: the Soviet Union, Bulgaria, Czechoslovakia, Hungary, Poland, and Romania.

West (as in the East–West conflict): Basically the market-economy, industrialized, and high-income countries that are committed to a political system of representative democracy. The three main anchors of the West today are North America, Western Europe, and Japan, also known as the Trilateral countries. Australia and New Zealand are also parts of the West.

"Window of vulnerability": An expression often used, but not consistently defined, by President Ronald Reagan and his administration during the 1980s. Military specialists used the word to refer to a period of time in the late 1980s when it was predicted that the United States' silo-based ICBMs could be accurately hit by Soviet missiles while the mobile MX system (now scrapped) would not yet be operational, and when the aging B-52 bombers would no longer be serviceable while the Stealth aircraft would not yet be operational. President Reagan planned to close this "window" by MIRVing the silo-based ICBMs, by hardening their concrete covers, by building B-1 bombers, and by the "Star Wars" initiative.

World Bank (International Bank for Reconstruction and Development [IBRD]): Makes loans, either directly to governments or with governments as the guarantors, and through its affiliates, the International Finance Corporation and the International Development Association.

Xenophobia: A dislike, fear, or suspicion of other nationalities.

Yield: The explosive force, in terms of TNT equivalence, of a warhead.

Zimbabwe: Formerly Rhodesia.

Zionism: An international movement for the establishment of a Jewish nation or religious community in Palestine and later for the support of modern Israel.

SOURCES

International Politics on the World Stage, Seventh Edition, 1997, Dushkin/McGraw-Hill.

Global Studies: Africa, Seventh Edition, 1997, Dushkin/McGraw-Hill.

Global Studies: Russia, The Eurasian Republics, and Central/Eastern Europe, Seventh Edition, 1998, Dushkin/McGraw-Hill.

Global Studies: The Middle East, Seventh Edition, 1998, Dushkin/McGraw-Hill.

Ghoitom, Fikad, 123–124
Global Biodiversity Assessment, 78
global ethics, code of, 192–196
global warming, 12–13, 65, 66,
  67, 68–75, 82
globalization, 88–92, 93–97, 98–102
Goldstone, Richard, 182
Goree Island, 126
Great Britain, 82, 99–100, 101, 112
Great Depression, 42, 82
Great Salinity Anomaly, 72
Greece, 57, 211
Green Revolution, 11
greenhouse gases, 65
Group of Government Experts (GGE),
  42, 48, 180–181
Gulf War, 135, 136

H

Hage-Ali, Sarah Galloway, 125–126
Haiti, 28, 30, 162
Haptemariam, Olga, 121, 123
heat waves, 84
High Altitude Long Endurance (HALE)
  platform, 206, 209
Hindu civilization, 18
Hinduism, 30
Hong Kong, 20, 24
hospitality, as global ethic, 196
Huguenots, 50
human behavior, income inequality
  and, 21–22
human rights, child labor and, 186–189
"hundred-year storms," 12–13
Hungary, 57, 141
Hutus, 145
hydropower, 203, 204–205

I

Ibrahim, Anwar, 152
India, 24, 29, 30, 47, 83, 119–
  120, 141, 142, 150–153, 213
Indonesia, 25, 77, 95, 96, 102,
  103, 105, 106, 211
industrial revolution, 41–48
inequality, developing countries and,
  19–26
infanticide, female, 47
International Criminal Court (ICC),
  182–183
International Monetary Fund (IMF),
  22, 94, 100, 103, 104, 105,
  107, 115, 152
Iran, 28, 80, 82, 166, 167
Iraq, 28, 141, 166, 179
Ireland, 57, 142
Islamic civilization, 18, 30
ISO 14000, 205
Israel, 141, 167
Italy, 82

J

Japan, 27, 82–85, 100–101, 102,
  104, 106, 108–110, 152, 155,
  156, 211, 212
Jonah, Sam, 125

K

Kaplan, Robert, 145
Karadzic, Radovan, 148
Karl, Thomas, 12–13
Kashmir, 28, 139, 141, 150
Kazakhstan, 79, 80, 161
Kiriyenko, Sergei, 114, 115
Kirsch, Philippe, 183
Kissinger, Henry, 112, 137
Konaré, Alpha Oumar, 124
Koné, Awa, 125
Kurds, 146
Kuwait, 162

L

laissez-faire economics, poverty and, 24
language, 16
Laos, 128
"last mile problem," telecommunica-
  tions and, 207
Latin American Alternative, 197–201
Latin American civilization, 18
Latvia, 161
Law of the Sea Treaty, 65
League of Nations, 176
Lebed, Aleksandr, 117
Liberal Democratic Party, of Russia, 116
Liberia, 27, 28, 29, 139, 141,
  142, 226
Libya, 28, 57, 167
light weapons, 139–143
López Obrador, Andrés Manuel, 200
love, as global ethnic, 193
Luzhkov, Yuri, 117

M

Maastricht Treaty, 20
Mack, Andrew, 151
Magna Carta, 16
Mahathir, Mohammed, 103
Malaysia, 20, 95, 103, 105, 106
Mali, 121, 122, 124–125
Malthusian theory of population limita-
  tions, 42
Manhica, Felfiel, 122
Marshall Plan, 42, 100
Marx, Karl, 19, 25
Marxist Mozambique Liberation Front
  (Frelimo), 122
Medellín cartel, 130
methane, 12, 65
Mexico, 20, 24, 93, 94, 95, 141,
  200, 201
middle class, 25

mines, land, 140
"mission creep," 136
modernity, West and, 17
Moment on the Earth, A (Easter-
  brook), 14
Morocco, 186
Mozambique, 121, 122–123, 141, 177
Mubarak, Hosni, 35
Mucavele, Francisco, 121, 122
mutton, demand for, 81

N

National Action Party, of Mexico, 200
natural gas, 203
Negroponte, Nicholas, 207
Nemtsov, Boris, 114
Netherlands, 24, 55
"new eliminationists," 163–168
Nicaragua, 142, 177
Nigeria, 24, 95
nitrogen, 12
nitrous oxide, 65
Niyazov, Saparmurat, 79
Nkrumah, Kwame, 125
nongovernmental organizations
  (NGOs), 189, 213
non-refoulement, principle of, 53
North Atlantic Current, climate
  change and, 68–75
North Atlantic Oscillation (NAO), 73
North Atlantic Treaty Organization
  (NATO), 27, 31, 141, 162, 163
North Korea, 27, 28, 141, 166, 167
Nuclear Non-Proliferation Treaty
  (NPT), 151, 164
nuclear power plants, 204–205
Nuclear Proliferation Prevention Act, 152
nuclear waste, 67
nuclear weapons, 163–168, 169–
  173; in South Asia, 150–153
nuclear-powered submarines (SSBN), 158
Nuno-Amarteifio, Nat Nii Amar, 125

O

obedience, as global ethic, 196
ocean thermal generators, 205
oceans: climate change and, 68–75;
  pollution of, 65
oil: in Caspian Sea, 79–80; prices,
  45–46; use of, in developing countries, 204
Ominami, Carlos, 198
Orthodox civilization, 18
ozone depletion, 67

P

Pakistan, 29, 34–35, 36–37, 141,
  150–153, 211
"palaver tree" approach, 124
Panel of Government Experts (PGE), 180
paper, demand for, 81
peace, 98, 102; as global ethic, 196
peacekeeping, UN, 141

AE Article Review Form

We encourage you to photocopy and use this page as a tool to assess how the articles in **Annual Editions** expand on the information in your textbook. By reflecting on the articles you will gain enhanced text information. You can also access this useful form on a product's book support Web site at **http://www.dushkin.com/online/.**

NAME: DATE:

TITLE AND NUMBER OF ARTICLE:

BRIEFLY STATE THE MAIN IDEA OF THIS ARTICLE:

LIST THREE IMPORTANT FACTS THAT THE AUTHOR USES TO SUPPORT THE MAIN IDEA:

WHAT INFORMATION OR IDEAS DISCUSSED IN THIS ARTICLE ARE ALSO DISCUSSED IN YOUR TEXTBOOK OR OTHER READINGS THAT YOU HAVE DONE? LIST THE TEXTBOOK CHAPTERS AND PAGE NUMBERS:

LIST ANY EXAMPLES OF BIAS OR FAULTY REASONING THAT YOU FOUND IN THE ARTICLE:

LIST ANY NEW TERMS/CONCEPTS THAT WERE DISCUSSED IN THE ARTICLE, AND WRITE A SHORT DEFINITION:

ANNUAL EDITIONS revisions depend on two major opinion sources: one is our Advisory Board, listed in the front of this volume, which works with us in scanning the thousands of articles published in the public press each year; the other is you—the person actually using the book. Please help us and the users of the next edition by completing the prepaid article rating form on this page and returning it to us. Thank you for your help!

ANNUAL EDITIONS: Global Issues 99/00

ARTICLE RATING FORM

Here is an opportunity for you to have direct input into the next revision of this volume. We would like you to rate each of the 42 articles listed below, using the following scale:

1. **Excellent: should definitely be retained**
2. **Above average: should probably be retained**
3. **Below average: should probably be deleted**
4. **Poor: should definitely be deleted**

Your ratings will play a vital part in the next revision. So please mail this prepaid form to us just as soon as you complete it. Thanks for your help!

RATING

ARTICLE

1. A Special Moment in History
2. The Many Faces of the Future
3. Life Is Unfair: Inequality in the World
4. Redefining Security: The New Global Schisms
5. Before the Next Doubling
6. Worldwide Development or Population Explosion: Our Choice
7. Refugees: The Rising Tide
8. How Much Food Will We Need in the 21st Century?
9. Angling for 'Aquaculture'
10. The Global Challenge
11. The Great Climate Flip-Flop
12. Stumped by Trees
13. The Rush for Caspian Oil
14. We Can Build a Sustainable Economy
15. The Complexities and Contradictions of Globalization
16. Prosper or Perish? Development in the Age of Global Capital
17. An Illusion for Our Time
18. The End of a "Miracle": Speculation, Foreign Capital Dependence, and the Collapse of the Southeast Asian Economies
19. Fallen Idol
20. America and the Euro Gamble
21. Russia's Summer of Discontent

RATING

ARTICLE

22. A New Tiger
23. Africa Rising
24. Asia's Drug Menace and the Poverty of Diplomacy
25. The Post-Modern State and the World Order
26. The New Arms Race: Light Weapons and International Security
27. Ethnic Conflict: Think Again
28. Nuclear Brinkmanship in South Asia
29. Uncertainty, Insecurity, and China's Military Power
30. Russian Foreign Policy in the Near Abroad and Beyond
31. The Case for Nuclear Deterrence Today
32. Taking Nuclear Weapons Off Hair-Trigger Alert
33. The First Fifty Years: The Main Achievements
34. A Watchful Eye: Monitoring the Conventional Arms Trade
35. Justice Goes Global
36. Peace Prize Goes to Land-Mine Opponents
37. Child Labour: Rights, Risks, and Realities
38. Universal Human Values: Finding an Ethical Common Ground
39. A Fourth Way? The Latin American Alternative to Neoliberalism
40. The Future of Energy
41. Telecommunications for the 21st Century
42. Women in Power: From Tokenism to Critical Mass

(Continued on next page)

NO POSTAGE
NECESSARY
IF MAILED
IN THE
UNITED STATES

BUSINESS REPLY MAIL
FIRST-CLASS MAIL PERMIT NO. 84 GUILFORD CT

POSTAGE WILL BE PAID BY ADDRESSEE

Dushkin/McGraw-Hill
Sluice Dock
Guilford, CT 06437-9989

IIl....IIl...I...IuIIl..IIl..I.I..I.I..I.I..I.I..Ll.I

ABOUT YOU

Name   Date

Are you a teacher? ☐   A student? ☐
Your school's name

Department

Address   City   State   Zip

School telephone #

YOUR COMMENTS ARE IMPORTANT TO US !

Please fill in the following information:
For which course did you use this book?

Did you use a text with this *ANNUAL EDITION*? ☐ yes ☐ no
What was the title of the text?

What are your general reactions to the *Annual Editions* concept?

Have you read any particular articles recently that you think should be included in the next edition?

Are there any articles you feel should be replaced in the next edition? Why?

Are there any World Wide Web sites you feel should be included in the next edition? Please annotate.

May we contact you for editorial input? ☐ yes ☐ no
May we quote your comments? ☐ yes ☐ no